Naturalizing Epistemology

⎤⎦ BRADFORD BOOKS
Selected List

Daniel C. Dennett. BRAINSTORMS. 1979.
Fred I. Dretske. KNOWLEDGE AND THE FLOW OF INFORMATION. 1981.
Jerry A. Fodor. REPRESENTATIONS. 1981.
Hubert L. Dreyfus, Editor, in collaboration with Harrison Hall. HUSSERL,
    INTENTIONALITY AND COGNITIVE SCIENCE. 1981.
Jerry A. Fodor. THE MODULARITY OF MIND. 1983.
George D. Romanos. QUINE AND ANALYTIC PHILOSOPHY. 1983.
Stephen P. Stich. FROM FOLK PSYCHOLOGY TO COGNITIVE SCIENCE. 1983.
Robert Cummins. THE NATURE OF PSYCHOLOGICAL EXPLANATION. 1983.
Paul M. Churchland. MATTER AND CONSCIOUSNESS. 1984.
Owen J. Flanagan, Jr. THE SCIENCE OF THE MIND. 1984.
Ruth Garrett Millikan. LANGUAGE, THOUGHT, AND OTHER BIOLOGICAL
    CATEGORIES. 1984.
Myles Brand. INTENDING AND ACTING. 1984.
Robert C. Stalnaker. INQUIRY. 1985.
William G. Lycan. LOGICAL FORM AND NATURAL LANGUAGE. 1985.
Hilary Kornblith. NATURALIZING EPISTEMOLOGY. 1985.

Naturalizing Epistemology

Edited by Hilary Kornblith

A Bradford Book
The MIT Press
Cambridge, Massachusetts
London, England

Third printing, 1988

This book was set in Apollo by Asco Trade Typesetting Ltd., Hong Kong, and
printed and bound by The Murray Printing Co. in the United States of America.

Library of Congress Cataloging in Publication Data

Main entry under title:

Naturalizing epistemology.

   "A Bradford book."
   Bibliography: p.
   Includes index.
   1. Knowledge, Theory of—Addresses, essays, lectures.
I. Kornblith, Hilary.
BD161.N29   1985   121   84-27228
ISBN 0-262-11099-7 (hard)
        0-262-61051-5 (paper)

Contents

Acknowledgments   vii

Introduction: What Is Naturalistic Epistemology?
Hilary Kornblith   1

1. Epistemology Naturalized
   W. V. O. Quine   15

2. Natural Kinds
   W. V. O. Quine   31

3. Pattern Matching as an Essential in Distal Knowing
   Donald T. Campbell   49

4. The Significance of Naturalized Epistemology
   Barry Stroud   71

5. What Is Justified Belief?
   Alvin I. Goldman   91

6. Beyond Foundationalism and the Coherence Theory
   Hilary Kornblith   115

7. A Priori Knowledge
   Philip Kitcher   129

8. Truth and Confirmation
   Michael Friedman   147

9. Précis of *Knowledge and the Flow of Information*
   Fred I. Dretske   169

10. Judgmental Heuristics and Knowledge Structures
    Richard Nisbett and Lee Ross   189

11. Epistemics: The Regulative Theory of Cognition
    Alvin I. Goldman   217

12. Positive versus Negative Undermining in Belief Revision
     Gilbert Harman   231

13. Could Man Be an Irrational Animal? Some Notes on the
     Epistemology of Rationality
     Stephen P. Stich   249

     Bibliography
     Frederick F. Schmitt   269

     Index   301

Acknowledgments

Almost a year ago Fred Schmitt wrote to me suggesting that I put together an anthology of papers on naturalistic epistemology. I wrote back immediately and told him that although I thought it was a terrific idea, I was not willing to put the work into it. Within a week I had changed my mind. Since that time I have received many thoughtful suggestions not only from Schmitt but from Christopher Cherniak, John Heil, Alvin Goldman, Philip Kitcher, George Sher, and especially Louis Loeb. Jodi Beccue and Leslie Weiger provided expert assistance in preparing the manuscript under extreme time pressures. Work on this anthology was in part supported by a grant from the University of Vermont.

Naturalizing Epistemology

Introduction: What is Naturalistic Epistemology?

Hilary Kornblith

In recent years the naturalistic approach to epistemology has been gaining currency. The goal of this introduction is to answer my title question and at the same time to place the essays that follow in appropriate perspective.

Three Questions

Consider the following three questions.

1. How ought we to arrive at our beliefs?

2. How do we arrive at our beliefs?

3. Are the processes by which we do arrive at our beliefs the ones by which we ought to arrive at our beliefs?

Different theorists will answer these questions differently. The topic I wish to deal with here has to do with the relations among these three questions. If we wish to answer all of these questions, which should we deal with first? Can any of these questions be answered independently of the others, or will the answers to each constrain the range of answers we might give to those remaining? Just as different theorists disagree about answers to questions 1, 2, and 3, there are disagreements about the relations among these questions. What I want to suggest here is that what is distinctive about the naturalistic approach to epistemology is its view about the relations among these three questions.

The Traditional View

One view, which I will label the *traditional view*, suggests a strategy of divide and conquer. Question 1 is to be assigned to philosophers, question 2 to psychologists. Each of these groups is to conduct its research independently of the other. When both groups have completed their work, they must get together to answer question 3. It is permissible, of course, for philosophers and psychologists to meet prior to each group's completion of its assigned task. Such meetings will allow them to check progress on question 3. These meetings will not, however, have any effect on work on questions 1 or 2. Question 1 is in the bailiwick of philosophers; question 2 in the bailiwick of psychologists; and the answer to question 3 is produced by comparing the answers to questions 1 and 2.

Most research in philosophy as well as psychology seems to be guided by the traditional view. On the philosophical side consider one kind of answer that has been offered to question 1: the coherence theory of justification. Coherence theorists hold, roughly, that in deciding whether to accept or reject any statement, one ought to consider how well it fits in with or coheres with one's other beliefs; one ought to adopt beliefs cohering with beliefs one already has. Whatever the merits of this view, it seems to have nothing to do with any possible answer to question 2. Suppose that psychologists were to discover that people actually arrive at their beliefs by some kind of nonconscious mechanism that measures the coherence of candidate beliefs with the body of beliefs already held; candidates that cohere are adopted and those that do not are rejected. What bearing would this psychological theory have on the merits of the coherence theory of justification as an answer to question 1? None, it seems. How we actually arrive at our beliefs need have nothing to do with how we ought to arrive at them. By the same token if we are evaluating the merits of some psychological account of belief acquisition, a purported account of how people actually arrive at their beliefs in some situation, theories about how we ought to arrive at our beliefs seem to be irrelevant.

An analogy with ethics seems apt here. Consider the following three questions about human action:

A. How ought people to act?

B. How do people act?

C. Do people act the way they ought?

These questions bear the same relations to each other as questions 1, 2, and 3. Moreover it seems clear that it is the job of ethical theorists to answer question A and psychologists concerned with human motivation to answer question B. Only by comparing the results of these two independent investigations will the answer to C emerge. Note how absurd it would be for a philosopher to object to a psychological account of how people act on the grounds that action of that sort is immoral. It would be equally absurd it a psychologist were to object to a philosophical account of how we ought to act on the grounds that people do not act that way. There is a straightforward explanation of the absurdity of these challenges. The normative questions that philosophers ask are completely independent of the descriptive questions psychologists ask. This seems to be true not only in the case of questions A and B but also in the case of questions 1 and 2.

I do not mean to endorse the arguments of this section for the traditional view, nor do I mean to suggest that no other arguments for it are available. Instead I hope only to have presented enough of the traditional view and its motivation so that it may clearly be distinguished from a naturalistic approach to questions 1, 2, and 3.

The Replacement Thesis

I take the naturalistic approach to epistemology to consist in this: question 1 cannot be answered independently of question 2. Questions about how we actually arrive at our beliefs are thus relevant to questions about how we ought to arrive at our beliefs. Descriptive questions about belief acquisition have an important bearing on normative questions about belief acquisition.

There are, of course, different camps within the naturalistic approach; naturalistic epistemologists differ on how direct a bearing psychology has on epistemology. The most radical view here is due to Quine:

Epistemology still goes on, though in a new setting and a clarified status. Epistemology, or something like it, simply falls into place as a chapter of psychology and hence of natural science. It studies a natural phenomenon, viz., a physical human subject. This human subject is accorded a certain experimentally controlled input—certain patterns of irradiation in assorted frequencies, for instance—and in the fullness of time the subject delivers as output a description of the three dimensional external world and its history. The relation between the meager input and the torrential output is a relation that we are prompted to study for somewhat the same reasons that always prompted epistemology; namely, in order to see how evidence relates to theory, and in what ways one's theory of nature transcends any available evidence.[1]

I will speak of the view that epistemological questions may be replaced by psychological questions as the *replacement thesis*.

Quine's argument for the replacement thesis in chapter 1 is this: the history of epistemology is largely the history of the foundationalist program. Foundationalists tried to show that there is a class of beliefs—typically beliefs about our own sense experience—about which it is impossible to be wrong. These beliefs were held to be sufficient to justify the rest of our beliefs; thus, in addition to identifying those beliefs that would serve as the foundation of knowledge, foundationalists sought to show how foundational beliefs provide us with good reason for adopting the remainder of our beliefs. The history of epistemology shows that the foundationalist program has faced one failure after another. The lesson to be learned from these failures, according to Quine, is not just that foundationalists had mistakenly answered question 1 in claiming that the appropriate way to arrive at one's beliefs is to begin with beliefs about which one cannot be wrong and build upon that foundation. Rather, according to Quine, foundationalists were asking the wrong questions. Once we see the sterility of the foundationalist program, we see that the only genuine questions there are to ask about the relation between theory and evidence and about the acquisition of belief are psychological questions. In this view question 2 is relevant to question 1 because it holds all the content that is left in question 1. The relation between these two questions is much like the relation atheists believe to hold between questions about God's act of creation and questions about the details of, for example, the big bang; the latter questions exhaust all the content there is in the former questions.

One illustration of the way in which traditional epistemological questions have become transformed through our newly gained understanding forms the heart of chapter 2. Philosophers have long asked, how is knowledge possible? This question has been understood for centuries as a request for a response to the skeptic, and the result has been the various attempts to work out the details of the foundationalist program. What we are now in a position to understand is precisely how foundationalists misinterpreted this important question. If the question about the possibility of knowledge is interpreted as a request to respond to the skeptic on his or her own terms, then any attempt to answer the question is doomed to failure. Quine argues, however, that this interpretation mislocates the very worries that gave rise to the question in the first place. It is through the rise of science that we were first led to question the limits and possibility of knowledge. As science made clear the falsity of our former beliefs and our susceptibility to illusion, the question naturally arose as to whether the beliefs we arrive at, even under the best of conditions, are likely to be true. In short the question arose as to whether knowledge is possible. Insofar as this question arises from within science, we may call on the resources of science to answer it. Far from making epistemology a necessary prerequisite to doing science, this makes epistemology continuous with the scientific enterprise.

Fortunately, when we turn to science to answer our question, we are not disappointed. As Quine suggests, "There is some encouragement in Darwin." Creatures whose belief generating mechanisms do not afford them cognitive contact with the world "have a pathetic but praiseworthy tendency to die before reproducing their kind." Since believing truths has survival value, the survival of the fittest guarantees that our innate intellectual endowment gives us a predisposition for believing truths. Knowledge is thus not only possible but a necessary by-product of natural selection. (This reconstruction of the skeptical challenge and the possibility of responding to it is examined by Barry Stroud in chapter 4.)

This Darwinian argument may be thought to provide a motivation for the replacement thesis quite different from that offered by Quine in chapter 1. If the Darwinian argument can be worked out in detail, it may provide a way of tackling the original three questions by taking on question 3 first. If nature has so constructed us that our belief-generating processes are inevitably biased in favor of true beliefs, then it must be that the processes by which we arrive at beliefs just are those by which we ought to arrive at them. Question 3 is thus answered with an emphatic affirmative, and we may move on to the remaining two questions. If we know in advance, however, that we arrive at beliefs in just the way we ought, one way to approach question 1 is just by doing psychology. In discovering the processes by which we actually arrive at beliefs, we are thereby discovering the processes by which we ought to arrive at beliefs. The epistemological enterprise may be replaced by empirical psychology.

Notice that the attempt to defend the replacement thesis by way of the Darwinian argument requires that the conclusion of that argument be given a very strong reading. Someone who concludes on the basis of natural selection that the processes by which we acquire beliefs must be roughly like the processes by which we ought will not be in a position to defend the replacement thesis. If psychological investigation is to be able to replace epistemological theorizing, there must be a perfect match between the processes by which we do and those by which we ought to acquire beliefs. Without such a perfect match, the results of psychological theorizing will only give an approximate answer to question 1, and epistemology will be called on to make up the slack. Psychology would thus be strongly relevant to epistemology, and this version of the Darwinian argument would thus motivate a version of naturalistic epistemology, but the resulting view would be far weaker than the replacement thesis.[2]

Still a third argument for the replacement thesis is to be found in such writers as Davidson,[3] Dennett,[4] Harman,[5] and, once again, Quine.[6] In Harman's version, the argument is as follows:

We normally assume that there are basic principles of rationality that apply to all normal human beings. . . . We come to understand someone else by coming

to appreciate that person's reasons for his or her beliefs and actions, or by
seeing how that person made a mistake. Someone who reasoned in a fundamentally different way from the way in which we reason would really and
truly be unintelligible to us. . . . In assuming, as we normally do, that we can
make sense of other people, given sufficient information about them, we
presuppose that everyone else operates in accordance with the same basic
principles as we do.[7]

As Harman makes clear, he does not mean to be arguing only for the conclusion
that we all arrive at our beliefs in the same way but rather that rational belief
acquisition consists of arriving at beliefs in the way we all do. In Harman's
view since individuals who reason in a way different than we do would be
unintelligible to us, we would not count them as rational; the only rational
individuals are thus ones who reason as we do. Once again this allows us to
approach the original three questions by answering question 3 first, and in
answering it in the affirmative, the way is paved for the replacement of
epistemology by psychology. It should also be noted that the conclusion of
Harman's argument must be interpreted in quite a strong way if it is to serve as
an argument for the replacement thesis. When Harman argues that someone
who reasons in a fundamentally different way would be unintelligible to us, he
cannot simply mean that large differences in the way individuals reason would
result in mutual uninterpretability, for this view is compatible with the claim
that individuals differ from one another in minor respects in the way they
reason. Psychology could then describe the different ways in which individuals reason but it would be impotent to pick out which of these ways (if any)
were rational. Harman must therefore be arguing for the conclusion that any
difference whatsoever in the ways individuals reason would result in mutual
uninterpretability. Weaker conclusions than this will not support the replacement thesis.

We are now in a position to distinguish between a strong and a weak version
of the replacement thesis. The strong version of the replacement thesis is
argued for by Quine in chapter 1. Quine argues not only that epistemological
questions may be replaced by psychological questions but also that this
replacement must take place; psychological questions hold all the content
there is in epistemological questions. On this view psychology replaces epistemology in much the same way that chemistry has replaced alchemy. This
approach is further elaborated on in chapter 3 by Donald Campbell. The other
two arguments examined for the replacement thesis, however—the Darwinian argument and the argument from mutual interpretability—suggest a
weak version of the replacement thesis. In this view psychology and epistemology provide two different avenues for arriving at the same place. Psychology may replace epistemology because the processes psychologists identify

as the ones by which we do arrive at our beliefs will inevitably turn out to be the very processes epistemologists would identify as the ones by which we ought to arrive at our beliefs. Thus even if all epistemologists were to give up their trade and turn to auto mechanics, the questions they tried to answer would nevertheless be addressed, in a different guise, by psychologists. This view is carefully scrutinized in chapter 13 by Stephen Stich, "Could Man Be an Irrational Animal?"

The Autonomy of Epistemology

There is a world of difference between the strong and the weak version of the replacement thesis. The question at issue is the autonomy of epistemology. Are there legitimate epistemological questions that are distinct in content from the questions of descriptive psychology? Advocates of the strong version of the replacement thesis answer this question in the negative, advocates of the weak version answer it in the affirmative. The consequences of the strong version of the replacement thesis for the study of epistemology are clear: epistemology must go the way of alchemy and be absorbed into another science. In this section I examine some of the consequences of the weak replacement thesis for epistemological theorizing. If epistemology is an autonomous discipline but subject nevertheless to the constraints of the weak replacement thesis, what will epistemology look like? What kind of relationship does this dictate between psychology and epistemology?

If the weak replacement thesis is true, epistemologists need not fear that they will be replaced by descriptive psychologists. The weak replacement thesis is a two-way street. If psychologists and epistemologists inevitably will receive the same answers to the different questions they ask, psychologists are just as subject to replacement by epistemologists as epistemologists are by psychologists. We may leave the unemployment issue aside, however, for if the weak replacement thesis is true, no kind of replacement is likely to go on. Either discipline could replace the other, but there are extremely good pragmatic reasons why they should not.

If the thesis under discussion is true, the psychology of belief acquisition and epistemology are two different fields, which ask different but equally legitimate questions and have different methodologies. In spite of these differences a complete (and true) psychology of belief acquisition will describe the same processes that a complete (and true) epistemology will prescribe. That these two fields will, when complete, single out the same processes of belief acquisition does not, however, suggest that at stages short of completion, the processes singled out by philosophers and those singled out by psychologists will match perfectly. Indeed it is clear that if pursued independently of one another, anything short of a complete psychology would look very different from anything short of a complete epistemology, in spite of their ultimate convergence. Because the two fields deal with different questions and because these questions are approached with different methodologies, processes that are easily identified by psychologists as ones that occur in us may not easily be identified by philosophers as ones that ought to be used; by the same token processes easily identified by philosophers as ones we ought to use need not be easily identified by psychologists as processes we actually make use of. The upshot is that even if the weak replacement thesis is true, no actual replacement can occur until each field has completed its work. Moreover, in order to hasten progress, philosophers and psychologists ought to be eagerly examining each other's work. If philosophers correctly identify some process as one by which we ought to arrive at our beliefs, psychologists will thereby know, even if they have not independently discovered it, that it occurs in us. Similarly if psychologists identify some process as one that occurs in us, epistemologists can be confident that this is a process by which we ought to arrive at our beliefs, even if they have not yet reached that conclusion independently. Thus if the weak replacement thesis is true, we can look forward to rapid progress in both psychology and epistemology as a result of their interaction, rather than either field being co-opted by the other.

Psychologism

Psychologism is the view that the processes by which we ought to arrive at our beliefs are the processes by which we do arrive at our beliefs; in short it is the view that the answer to question 3 is "yes." If the weak replacement thesis is true, then so is psychologism. Nevertheless it may be that psychologism is true and yet the weak replacement thesis is false. In this section I explain how that might be so.

Consider Alvin Goldman's answer to question 1 in chapter 11. Goldman suggests that we ought to arrive at our beliefs by processes that are reliable, that is, by whatever processes tend to produce true beliefs. Let us assume that Goldman is correct, and let us also assume, as Goldman does not, that psychologism is true. It thus follows that the processes by which we actually arrive at our beliefs are reliable. Even though, as we are assuming, a complete psychology of belief acquisition would describe the same processes Goldman's theory prescribes, a completed psychology would look nothing like a completed Goldman-style epistemology. It would not do for a psychologist to say merely that the processes by which we arrive at our beliefs are reliable and leave it at that. Obviously a complete psychological theory must be far more detailed and specific. The added specificity of the psychological account is not merely unnecessary, however, to answering the epistemological question, if anything like Goldman's theory is correct; the psychological theory is simply spelled out in terms at the wrong level of generality to do epistemological work. Imagine that we have a complete list of all the belief acquisition processes that take place in human beings. This list, it seems, will not answer our epistemological question (even assuming psychologism to be true), for we wish to know what all these processes have in common in virtue of which we ought to acquire beliefs by way of them. Our psychological theory will not answer this question. By the same token our philosophical theory, even if given in full detail, will not answer all our psychological questions.

I have used Goldman's theory only by way of illustration; what I say about Goldman's account is doubtless true of many rival accounts as well. If a proper epistemological theory must be cashed out at a different level of generality than psychological theories, then even if psychologism is true, the weak replacement thesis is false; no replacement could ever occur, even in completed theories, if they are not couched in terms of the same generality. Psychologism is thus still weaker that the weak replacement thesis.

What implications does psychologism have for the relation between philosophy and psychology? If psychologism is true and the weak replacement thesis false, we will not be able to read our epistemology directly from our psychology nor psychology directly from epistemology. In spite of this there will be significant constraints cast on each theory by the other. If our epistemological theory tells us that we ought adopt only beliefs arrived at by processes that have a certain property, then we know that our psychological theory must attribute to believers only belief acquisition processes with that property. If our psychological theory isolates a number of different processes of belief acquisition, then an epistemologist would do well to consider what these processes have in common. This mutual readjustment will allow each discipline to advance at a more rapid rate than it would were it to proceed independently of the other. We may thus look forward to a long and fruitful relationship between philosophy and psychology.

Antiskepticism and Ballpark Psychologism

Many philosophers who reject psychologism nevertheless believe that the processes by which we arrive at beliefs are at least roughly like the processes by which we ought to arrive at our beliefs; the one set of processes is in the same ballpark as the other. I will speak of this view as *ballpark psychologism*. It will be difficult to give a precise statement of this view; it is, for example, compatible with the suggestion that some of the processes by which we arrive at our beliefs are nothing like processes by which we ought to arrive at our beliefs. It is also compatible with the view that different people arrive at their beliefs in different ways. In spite of this vagueness it will be clear that this view has important implications for the relation between philosophy and psychology.

Anyone who rejects skepticism should embrace ballpark psychologism. To know something, it seems, is to arrive at a true belief in the way one ought, or, at the very least, in a way very much like the way one ought. If most people know a great many things, then many of their beliefs are arrived at by processes at least roughly like the processes by which they ought to arrive at their beliefs. In short antiskepticism implies ballpark psychologism.

If ballpark psychologism is true, there may be a fruitful interaction between epistemology and psychology, although the connection between the two will be weaker than that just outlined for psychologism. To the extent that psychologists are successful in describing some of the processes by which paradigm cases of knowledge are produced and to the extent that epistemologists are successful in describing certain general features of some belief acquisition processes, useful interaction between the disciplines will be likely.

Some are bound to object to this conclusion. I anticipate the following sort of objection:

You insist that once we reject skepticism we are committed to the mutual relevance of psychology and epistemology. Suppose epistemological questions can be answered *a priori*; that is, suppose it is possible to figure out, independent of any experience, which the processes are by which we should arrive at our beliefs. In this case, there would be no reason for epistemologists to consult with psychologists, for psychological work is unnecessary to reaching epistemological conclusions. There may be some sense in which psychology is relevant to epistemology, but there is no sense in which epistemologists must consult with psychologists in order to answer the questions they wish to have answered.

I want to deal with this objection. Most naturalistic epistemologists will reject the suggestion that anything is knowable a priori.[8] I do not wish to enter that debate here. Rather I will argue that the issue of a priority is a red herring. Whether the answers to epistemological questions can be known a priori in principle, epistemologists would do well to consult psychologists in practice.

It will be useful to begin by considering an example from the theory of probability.[9] Suppose I decide to start an insurance company and after lengthy actuarial calculations determine the rates to charge for various policies. I determine the rates in the following way. First, I write out the part of the probability calculus relevant to my problem. Then I gather information about mortality rates. By combining the abstract statements of the probability calculus with the data about mortality rates, I can determine how much I need to charge for policies to make a profit. With this information in hand, I go about the business of selling policies.

After many years I find that my company is losing large sums of money. It may be that I am simply unlucky. It may also be that I have made mistakes in my attempt to gather information about mortality rates. There is, however, a third possibility: I may have mistakenly formulated the theory of probability. It would be foolish for me to ignore this third possibility.

Now the theory of probability is a priori knowable if anything is.[10] I may be led, however, to revise my formulation of the probability theory by empirical tests. Although it may be true that in the absence of this or any other experience, a priori reasoning alone could have straightened out my errors, the fact remains that a posteriori testing may contribute to locating my errors. Indeed empirical test may be the most efficient means of discovering errors.

What is important here is not whether the theory of probability is a priori knowable but how obvious it is. A priority and obviousness do not go hand in hand. Once we recognize that in the light of the difficulty of determining some of the statements of the probability theory we are liable to err in arriving at them, we may subject out theory to test by conjoining it with obviously empirical bits of information to yield a prediction. If the prediction is falsified, it may well have been that our attempt to formulate the a priori theory was mistaken.

What is true of probability theory is also true in the theory of knowledge. Even granting for the sake of argument that in principle it is possible to answer epistemological questions a priori, epistemological truths are anything but obvious. It would thus be foolhardy not to subject epistemological theories to empirical tests. If skepticism is to be rejected, then epistemology and psychology impose significant constraints on each other. The best way to develop epistemological theories is thus to employ these constraints in a way that allows us to prod the theory along by confronting it with empirical tests.

An epistemological example is in order here. Consider again Goldman's suggestion that justified beliefs are beliefs that are reliably produced. It does not matter whether one regards this suggestion as arrived at by a priori means; in any case we may subject it to empirical test. Let us consider a paradigm case of justified belief: beliefs obtained by induction. It surely seems that everyone has a great deal of inductive knowledge. If Goldman's account is correct and we are not skeptics about induction, we should expect that when psychologists investigate human induction, they will find that inductive beliefs are reliably produced. Chapter 10 by Richard Nisbett and Lee Ross discusses some of the processes by which inductive beliefs are formed. The processes described do not seem to be reliable. In the light of this result, we have three choices: (1) to give up our antiskepticism and simply say that beliefs formed in the way Nisbett and Ross describe are not justified, (2) to deny that Nisbett and Ross accurately describe the way in which inductive beliefs are acquired, or (3) to revise or reject reliabilism.

It would be unreasonable to refuse even to consider option 3 on the grounds that epistemological truths are a priori knowable. In the end we may have good reason for maintaining reliabilism but we must seriously entertain the possibility that we have erred. Even if we want to insist that revisions in our epistemological theories are always the product of a priori recognition of previous errors even when prompted by empirical results, it would be foolhardy to ignore this additional check on our a priori reasoning.

Goldman's theory is used only as an example. The kinds of test I have described may apply to any other epistemological theory. In particular the Nisbett and Ross results provide an interesting test for any epistemological theory.

Exactly how epistemology will look if we allow it to be shaped by psychology remains to be seen. Fred Dretske suggests in chapter 9 that we will receive important illumination if we draw on work in the mathematical theory of communication. Chapter 6, which I wrote, attempts to resolve the dispute between foundationalists and coherence theorists. More general arguments for the relevance of empirical work for epistemology are presented in chapter 8 by Michael Friedman and chapter 11 by Goldman. Chapter 12 by Gilbert Harman is part of a larger project: a defense of psychologism. Whatever the upshot of this interaction may be, it clearly deserves further examination.

Conclusion

If the arguments of the last section are sound, any epistemologist who rejects skepticism ought to be influenced in his or her philosophical work by descriptive work in psychology. The chapters in this book are a product of this influence, even when it does not appear on the surface. My hope is that this book will encourage a careful evaluation of the prospects and problems of naturalizing epistemology.[11]

Notes

1. See below, Quine 1969a.

2. This weaker view, which I call ballpark psychologism, is discussed below.

3. See, e.g., Davidson 1973.

4. Dennett 1978, pp. 3–22.

5. Harman 1982.

6. E.g., Quine 1960, chapter 2.

7. Harman 1982, pp. 570–571.

8. For a naturalistic reconstruction of the concept of a priori knowledge, see chapter 7.

9. For a historical discussion of probability theory in which the interaction between putatively a priori reasoning and a posteriori reasoning is beautifully illustrated, see Hacking 1975.

10. I do not mean to suggest that the theory of probability is a priori knowable.

11. I have received helpful suggestions from John Heil, Philip Kitcher, Linda Polson, Fred Schmitt, George Sher, and especially Louis Loeb.

1   Epistemology Naturalized

W. V. O. Quine

Epistemology is concerned with the foundations of science. Conceived thus broadly, epistemology includes the study of the foundations of mathematics as one of its departments. Specialists at the turn of the century thought that their efforts in this particular department were achieving notable success: mathematics seemed to reduce altogether to logic. In a more recent perspective this reduction is seen to be better describable as a reduction to logic and set theory. This correction is a disappointment epistemologically, since the firmness and obviousness that we associate with logic cannot be claimed for set theory. But still the success achieved in the foundations of mathematics remains exemplary by comparative standards, and we can illuminate the rest of epistemology somewhat by drawing parallels to this department.

Studies in the foundations of mathematics divide symmetrically into two sorts, conceptual and doctrinal. The conceptual studies are concerned with meaning, the doctrinal with truth. The conceptual studies are concerned with clarifying concepts by defining them, some in terms of others. The doctrinal studies are concerned with establishing laws by proving them, some on the basis of others. Ideally the obscurer concepts would be defined in terms of the clearer ones so as to maximize clarity, and the less obvious laws would be proved from the more obvious ones so as to maximize certainty. Ideally the definitions would generate all the concepts from clear and distinct ideas, and the proofs would generate all the theorems from self-evident truths.

The two ideals are linked. For, if you define all the concepts by use of some favored subset of them, you thereby show how to translate all theorems into these favored terms. The clearer these terms are, the likelier it is that the truths couched in them will be obviously true, or derivable from obvious truths. If in

Reprinted from *Ontological Relativity and Other Essays*, by W. V. O. Quine (New York: Columbia University Press, 1969), pp. 69–90, by permission of the publisher. Copyright © 1969, Columbia University Press.

particular the concepts of mathematics were all reducible to the clear terms of logic, then all the truths of mathematics would go over into truths of logic; and surely the truths of logic are all obvious or at least potentially obvious, i.e., derivable from obvious truths by individually obvious steps.

This particular outcome is in fact denied us, however, since mathematics reduces only to set theory and not to logic proper. Such reduction still enhances clarity, but only because of the interrelations that emerge and not because the end terms of the analysis are clearer than others. As for the end truths, the axioms of set theory, these have less obviousness and certainty to recommend them than do most of the mathematical theorems that we would derive from them. Moreover, we know from Gödel's work that no consistent axiom system can cover mathematics even when we renounce self-evidence. Reduction in the foundations of mathematics remains mathematically and philosophically fascinating, but it does not do what the epistemologist would like of it: it does not reveal the ground of mathematical knowledge, it does not show how mathematical certainty is possible.

Still there remains a helpful thought, regarding epistemology generally, in that duality of structure which was especially conspicuous in the foundations of mathematics. I refer to the bifurcation into a theory of concepts, or meaning, and a theory of doctrine, or truth; for this applies to the epistemology of natural knowledge no less than to the foundations of mathematics. The parallel is as follows. Just as mathematics is to be reduced to logic, or logic and set theory, so natural knowledge is to be based somehow on sense experience. This means explaining the notion of body in sensory terms; here is the conceptual side. And it means justifying our knowledge of truths of nature in sensory terms; here is the doctrinal side of the bifurcation.

Hume pondered the epistemology of natural knowledge on both sides of the bifurcation, the conceptual and the doctrinal. His handling of the conceptual side of the problem, the explanation of body in sensory terms, was bold and simple: he identified bodies outright with the sense impressions. If common sense distinguishes between the material apple and our sense impressions of it on the ground that the apple is one and enduring while the impressions are many and fleeting, then, Hume held, so much the worse for common sense; the notion of its being the same apple on one occasion and another is a vulgar confusion.

Nearly a century after Hume's *Treatise*, the same view of bodies was espoused by the early American philosopher Alexander Bryan Johnson.[1] "The word iron names an associated sight and feel," Johnson wrote.

What then of the doctrinal side, the justification of our knowledge of truths about nature? Here, Hume despaired. By his identification of bodies with impressions he did succeed in construing some singular statements about bodies as indubitable truths, yes; as truths about impressions, directly known. But general statements, also singular statements about the future, gained no increment of certainty by being construed as about impressions.

On the doctrinal side, I do not see that we are farther along today than where Hume left us. The Humean predicament is the human predicament. But on the conceptual side there has been progress. There the crucial step forward was made already before Alexander Bryan Johnson's day, although Johnson did not emulate it. It was made by Bentham in his theory of fictions. Bentham's step was the recognition of contextual definition, or what he called paraphrasis. He recognized that to explain a term we do not need to specify an object for it to refer to, nor even specify a synonymous word or phrase; we need only show, by whatever means, how to translate all the whole sentences in which the term is to be used. Hume's and Johnson's desperate measure of identifying bodies with impressions ceased to be the only conceivable way of making sense of talk of bodies, even granted that impressions were the only reality. One could undertake to explain talk of bodies in terms of talk of impressions by translating one's whole sentences about bodies into whole sentences about impressions, without equating the bodies themselves to anything at all.

This idea of contextual definition, or recognition of the sentence as the primary vehicle of meaning, was indispensable to the ensuing developments in the foundations of mathematics. It was explicit in Frege, and it attained its full flower in Russell's doctrine of singular descriptions as incomplete symbols.

Contextual definition was one of two resorts that could be expected to have a liberating effect upon the conceptual side of the epistemology of natural knowledge. The other is resort to the resources of set theory as auxiliary concepts. The epistemologist who is willing to eke out his auster ontology of sense impressions with these set-theoretic auxiliaries is suddenly rich: he has not just his impressions to play with, but sets of them, and sets of sets, and so on up. Constructions in the foundations of mathematics have shown that such set-theoretic aids are a powerful addition; after all, the entire glossary of concepts of classical mathematics is constructible from them. Thus equipped, our epistemologist may not need either to identify bodies with impressions or to settle for contextual definition; he may hope to find in some subtle construction of sets upon sets of sense impressions a category of objects enjoying just the formula properties that he wants for bodies.

The two resorts are very unequal in epistemological status. Contextual definition is unassailable. Sentences that have been given meaning as wholes are undeniably meaningful, and the use they make of their component terms is therefore meaningful, regardless of whether any translations are offered for those terms in isolation. Surely Hume and A. B. Johnson would have used contextual definition with pleasure if they had thought of it. Recourse to sets, on the other hand, is a drastic ontological move, a retreat from the austere ontology of impressions. There are philosophers who would rather settle for bodies outright than accept all these sets, which amount, after all, to the whole abstract ontology of mathematics.

This issue has not always been clear, however, owing to deceptive hints of continuity between elementary logic and set theory. This is why mathematics was once believed to reduce to logic, that is, to an innocent and unquestionable logic, and to inherit these qualities. And this is probably why Russell was content to resort to sets as well as to contextual definition when in *Our Knowledge of the External World* and elsewhere he addressed himself to the epistemology of natural knowledge, on its conceptual side.

To account for the external world as a logical construct of sense data—such, in Russell's terms, was the program. It was Carnap, in his *Der logische Aufbau der Welt* of 1928, who came nearest to executing it.

This was the conceptual side of epistemology; what of the doctrinal? There the Humean predicament remained unaltered. Carnap's constructions, if carried successfully to completion, would have enable us to translate all sentences about the world into terms of sense data, or observation, plus logic and set theory. But the mere fact that a sentence is *couched* in terms of observation, logic, and set theory does not mean that it can be *proved* from observation sentences by logic and set theory. The most modest of generalizations about observable traits will cover more cases than its utterer can have had occasion actually to observe. The hopelessness of grounding natural science upon immediate experience in a firmly logical way was acknowledged. The Cartesian quest for certainty had been the remote motivation of epistemology, both on its conceptual and its doctrinal side; but that quest was seen as a lost cause. To endow the truths of nature with the full authority of immediate experience was as forlorn a hope as hoping to endow the truths of mathematics with the potential obviousness of elementary logic.

What then could have motivated Carnap's heroic efforts on the conceptual side of epistemology, when hope of certainty on the doctrinal side was abandoned? There were two good reasons still. One was that such constructions could be expected to elicit and clarify the sensory evidence for science, even if the inferential steps between sensory evidence and scientific doctrine must fall short of certainty. The other reason was that such constructions would deepen our understanding of our discourse about the world, even apart from questions of evidence; it would make all cognitive discourse as clear as observation terms and logic and, I must regretfully add, set theory.

It was sad for epistemologists, Hume and others, to have to acquiesce in the impossibility of strictly deriving the science of the external world from sensory evidence. Two cardinal tenets of empiricism remained unassailable, however, and so remain to this day. One is that whatever evidence there *is* for science *is* sensory evidence. The other, to which I shall recur, is that all inculcation of meanings of words must rest ultimately on sensory evidence. Hence the continuing attractiveness of the idea of a *logischer Aufbau* in which the sensory content of discourse would stand forth explicitly.

If Carnap had successfully carried such a construction through, how could he have told whether it was the right one? The question would have had no point. He was seeking what he called a *rational reconstruction*. Any construction of physicalistic discourse in terms of sense experience, logic, and set theory would have been seen as satisfactory if it made the physicalistic discourse come out right. If there is one way there are many, but any would be a great achievement.

But why all this creative reconstruction, all this make-believe? The stimulation of his sensory receptors is all the evidence anybody has had to go on, ultimately, in arriving at his picture of the world. Why not just see how this construction really proceeds? Why not settle for psychology? Such a surrender of the epistemological burden to psychology is a move that was disallowed in earlier times as circular reasoning. If the epistemologist's goal is validation of the grounds of empirical science, he defeats his purpose by using psychology or other empirical science in the validation. However, such scruples agains circularity have little point once we have stopped dreaming of deducing science from observations. If we are out simply to understand the link between observation and science, we are well advised to use any available information, including that provided by the very science whose link with observation we are seeking to understand.

But there remains a different reason, unconnected with fears of circularity, for still favoring creative reconstruction. We should like to be able to *translate* science into logic and observation terms and set theory. This would be a great epistemological achievement, for it would show all the rest of the concepts of science to be theoretically superfluous. It would legitimize them—to whatever degree the concepts of set theory, logic, and observation are themselves legitimate—by showing that everything done with the one apparatus could in principle be done with the other. If psychology itself could deliver a truly translational reduction of this kind, we should welcome it; but certainly it cannot, for certainly we did not grow up learning definitions of physicalistic language in terms of a prior language of set theory, logic, and observation. Here, then, would be good reason for persisting in a rational reconstruction:

we want to establish the essential innocence of physical concepts, by showing them to be theoretically dispensable.

The fact is, though, that the construction which Carnap outlined in *Der logische Aufbau Der Welt* does not give translational reduction either. It would not even if the outline were filled in. The crucial point comes where Carnap is explaining how to assign sense qualities to positions in physical space and time. These assignments are to be made in such a way as to fulfill, as well as possible, certain desiderata which he states, and with growth of experience the assignments are to be revised to suit. This plan, however illuminating, does not offer any key to *translating* the sentences of science into terms of observation, logic, and set theory.

We must despair of any such reduction. Carnap had despaired of it by 1936, when, in "Testability and meaning," [2] he introduced so-called *reduction forms* of a type weaker than definition. Definitions had shown always how to translate sentences into equivalent sentences. Contextual definition of a term showed how to translate sentences containing the term into equivalent sentences lacking the term. Reduction forms of Carnap's liberalized kind, on the other hand, do not in general give equivalences; they give implications. They explain a new term, if only partially, by specifying some sentences which are implied by sentences containing the term, and other sentences which imply sentences containing the term.

It is tempting to suppose that the countenancing of reduction forms in this liberal sense is just one further step of liberalization comparable to the earlier one, taken by Bentham, of countenancing contextual definition. The former and sterner kind of rational reconstruction might have been represented as a fictitious history in which we imagined our ancestors introducing the terms of physicalistic discourse on a phenomenalistic and set-theoretic basis by a succession of contextual definitions. The new and more liberal kind of rational reconstruction is a fictitious history in which we imagine our ancestors introducing those terms by a succession rather of reduction forms of the weaker sort.

This, however, is a wrong comparison. The fact is rather that the former and sterner kind of rational reconstruction, where definition reigned, embodied no fictitious history at all. It was nothing more nor less than a set of directions— or would have been, if successful—for accomplishing everything in terms of phenomena and set theory that we now accomplish in terms of bodies. It would have been a true reduction by translation, a legitimation by elimination. *Definire est eliminare*. Rational reconstruction by Carnap's later and looser reduction forms does none of this.

To relax the demand for definition, and settle for a kind of reduction that does not eliminate, is to renounce the last remaining advantage that we supposed rational reconstruction to have over straight psychology; namely, the advantage of translational reduction. If all we hope for is a reconstruction that links science to experience in explicit ways short of translation, then it would seem more sensible to settle for psychology. Better to discover how science is in fact developed and learned than to fabricate a fictitious structure to a similar effect.

The empiricist made one major concession when he despaired of deducing the truths of nature from sensory evidence. In despairing now even of translating those truths into terms of observation and logico-mathematical auxiliaries, he makes another major concession. For suppose we hold, with the old empiricist Peirce, that the very meaning of a statement consists in the difference its truth would make to possible experience. Might we not formulate, in a chapter-length sentence in observational language, all the difference that the truth of a given statement might make to experience, and might we not then take all this as the translation? Even if the difference that the truth of the statement would make to experience ramifies indefinitely, we might still hope to embrace it all in the logical implications of our chapter-length formulation, just as we can axiomatize an infinity of theorems. In giving up hope of such translation, then, the empiricist is conceding that the empirical meanings of typical statements about the external world are inaccessible and ineffable.

How is this inaccessibility to be explained? Simply on the ground that the experiential implications of a typical statement about bodies are too complex for finite axiomatization, however lengthy? No; I have a different explanation. It is that the typical statement about bodies has no fund of experiential implications it can call its own. A substantial mass of theory, taken together, will commonly have experiential implications; this is how we make verifiable predictions. We may not be able to explain why we arrive at theories which make successful predictions, but we do arrive at such theories.

Sometimes also an experience implied by a theory fails to come off; and then, ideally, we declare the theory false. But the failure falsifies only a block of theory as a whole, a conjunction of many statements. The failure shows that one or more of those statements is false, but it does not show which. The predicted experiences, true and false, are not implied by any one of the component statements of the theory rather than another. The component statements simply do not have empirical meanings, by Peirce's standard; but a sufficiently inclusive portion of theory does. If we can aspire to a sort of *logischer Aufbau der Welt* at all, it must be to one in which the texts slated for translation into observational and logico-mathematical terms are mostly broad theories taken as wholes, rather than just terms or short sentences. The translation of a theory would be a ponderous axiomatization of all the experiential difference that the truth of the theory would make. It would be a queer translation, for it would translate the whole but none of the parts. We might better speak in such a case not of translation but simply of observational evidence for theories; and we may, following Peirce, still fairly call this the empirical meaning of the theories.

These considerations raise a philosophical question even about ordinary unphilosophical translation, such as from English into Arunta or Chinese. For, if the English sentences of a theory have their meaning only together as a body, then we can justify their translation into Arunta only together as a body. There will be no justification for pairing off the component English sentences with component Arunta sentences, except as these correlations make the translation of the theory as a whole come out right. Any translations of the English sentences into Arunta sentences will be as correct as any other, so long as the net empirical implications of the theory as a whole are preserved in translation. But it is to be expected that many different ways of translating the component sentences, essentially different individually, would deliver the same empirical implications for the theory as a whole; deviations in the translation of one component sentence could be compensated for in the translation of another component sentence. Insofar, there can be no ground for saying which of two glaringly unlike translations of individual sentences is right.[3]

For an uncritical mentalist, no such indeterminacy threatens. Every term and every sentence is a label attached to an idea, simple or complex, which is stored in the mind. When on the other hand we take a verification theory of meaning seriously, the indeterminacy would appear to be inescapable. The Vienna Circle espoused a verification theory of meaning but did not take it seriously enough. If we recognize with Peirce that the meaning of a sentence turns purely on what would count as evidence for its truth, and if we recognize with Duhem that theoretical sentences have their evidence not as single sentences but only as larger blocks of theory, then the indeterminacy of translation of theoretical sentences is the natural conclusion. And most sentences, apart from observation sentences, are theoretical. This conclusion, conversely, once it is embraced, seals the fate of any general notion of propositional meaning or, for that matter, state of affairs.

Should the unwelcomeness of the conclusion persuade us to abandon the verification theory of meaning? Certainly not. The sort of meaning that is basic to translation, and to the learning of one's own language, is necessarily empirical meaning and nothing more. A child learns his first words and sentences by hearing and using them in the presence of appropriate stimuli.

These must be external stimuli, for they must act both on the child and on the speaker from whom he is learning.[4] Language is socially inculcated and controlled; the inculcation and control turn strictly on the keying of sentences to shared stimulation. Internal factors may vary *ad libitum* without prejudice to communication as long as the keying of language to external stimuli is undisturbed. Surely one has no choice but to be an empiricist so far as one's theory of linguistic meaning is concerned.

What I have said of infant learning applies equally to the linguist's learning of a new language in the field. If the linguist does not lean on related languages for which there are previously accepted translation practices, then obviously he has no data but the concomitances of native utterance and observable stimulus situation. No wonder there is indeterminacy of translation—for of course only a small fraction of our utterances report concurrent external stimulation. Granted, the linguist will end up with unequivocal translations of everything; but only by making many arbitrary choices—arbitrary even though unconscious—along the way. Arbitrary? By this I mean that different choices could still have made everything come out right that is susceptible in principle to any kind of check.

Let me link up, in a different order, some of the points I have made. The crucial consideration behind my argument for the indeterminacy of translation was that a statement about the world does not always or usually have a separable fund of empirical consequences that it can call its own. That consideration served also to account for the impossibility of an epistemological reduction of the sort where every sentence is equated to a sentence in observational and logico-mathematical terms. And the impossibility of that sort of epistemological reduction dissipated the last advantage that rational reconstruction seemed to have over psychology.

Philosophers have rightly despaired of translating everything into observational and logico-mathematical terms. They have despaired of this even when they have not recognized, as the reason for this irreducibility, that the statements largely do not have their private bundles of empirical consequences. And some philosophers have seen in this irreducibility the bankruptcy of epistemology. Carnap and the other logical positivists of the Vienna Circle had already pressed the term "metaphysics" into pejorative use, as connoting meaninglessness; and the term "epistemology" was next. Wittgenstein and his followers, mainly at Oxford, found a residual philosophical vocation in therapy: in curing philosophers of the delusion that there were epistemological problems.

But I think that at this point it may be more useful to say rather that epistemology still goes on, though in a new setting and a clarified status.

Epistemology, or something like it, simply falls into place as a chapter of psychology and hence of natural science. It studies a natural phenomenon, viz., a physical human subject. This human subject is accorded a certain experimentally controlled input—certain patterns of irradiation in assorted frequencies, for instance—and in the fullness of time the subject delivers as output a description of the three-dimensional external world and its history. The relation between the meager input and the torrential output is a relation that we are prompted to study for somewhat the same reasons that always prompted epistemology; namely, in order to see how evidence relates to theory, and in what ways one's theory of nature transcends any available evidence.

Such a study could still include, even, something like the old rational reconstruction, to whatever degree such reconstruction is practicable; for imaginative constructions can afford hints of actual psychological processes, in much the way that mechanical simulations can. But a conspicuous difference between old epistemology and the epistemological enterprise in this new psychological setting is that we can now make free use of empirical psychology.

The old epistemology aspired to contain, in a sense, natural science; it would construct it somehow from sense data. Epistemology in its new setting, conversely, is contained in natural science, as a chapter of psychology. But the old containment remains valid too, in its way. We are studying how the human subject of our study posits bodies and projects his physics from his data, and we appreciate that our position in the world is just like his. Our very epistemological enterprise, therefore, and the psychology wherein it is a component chapter, and the whole of natural science wherein psychology is a component book—all this is our own construction or projection from stimulations like those we were meting out to our epistemological subject. There is thus reciprocal containment, though containment in different senses: epistemology in natural science and natural science in epistemology.

This interplay is reminiscent again of the old threat of circularity, but it is all right now that we have stopped dreaming of deducing science from sense data. We are after an understanding of science as an institution or process in the world, and we do not intend that understanding to be any better than the science which is its object. This attitude is indeed one that Neurath was already urging in Vienna Circle days, with his parable of the mariner who has to rebuild his boat while staying afloat in it.

One effect of seeing epistemology in a psychological setting is that it resolves a stubborn old enigma of epistemological priority. Our retinas are irradiated in two dimensions, yet we see things as three-dimensional without conscious inference. Which is to count as observation—the unconscious two-dimensional reception or the conscious three-dimensional apprehension. In the old epistemological context the conscious form had priority, for we were out to justify our knowledge of the external world by rational reconstruction, and that demands awareness. Awareness ceased to be demanded when we gave up trying to justify our knowledge of the external world by rational reconstruction. What to count as observation now can be settled in terms of the stimulation of sensory receptors, let consciousness fall where it may.

The Gestalt psychologists' challenge to sensory atomism, which seemed so relevant to epistemology forty years ago, is likewise deactivated. Regardless of whether sensory atoms or Gestalten are what favor the forefront of our consciousness, it is simply the stimulations of our sensory receptors that are best looked upon as the input to our cognitive mechanism. Old paradoxes about unconscious data and inference, old problems about chains of inference that would have to be completed too quickly—these no longer matter.

In the old anti-psychologistic days the question of epistemological priority was moot. What is epistemologically prior to what? Are Gestalten prior to sensory atoms because they are noticed, or should we favor sensory atoms on some more subtle ground? Now that we are permitted to appeal to physical stimulation, the problem dissolves; A is epistemologically prior to B if A is causally nearer than B to the sensory receptors. Or, what is in some ways better, just talk explicitly in terms of causal proximity to sensory receptors and drop the talk of epistemological priority.

Around 1932 there was debate in the Vienna Circle over what to count as observation sentences, or *Protokollsätze*.[5] One position was that they had the form of reports of sense impressions. Another was that they were statements of an elementary sort about the external world, e.g., "A red cube is standing on the table." Another, Neurath's, was that they had the form of reports of relations between percipients and external things: "Otto now sees a red cube on the table." The worst of it was that there seemed to be no objective way of settling the matter: no way of making real sense of the question.

Let us now try to view the matter unreservedly in the context of the external world. Vaguely speaking, what we want of observation sentences is that they be the ones in closest causal proximity to the sensory receptors. But how is such proximity to be gauged? The idea may be rephrased this way: observation sentences are sentences which, as we learn language, are most strongly conditioned to concurrent sensory stimulation rather than to stored collateral information. Thus let us imagine a sentence queried for our verdict as to whether it is true or false; queried for our assent or dissent. Then the sentence is an observation sentence if our verdict depends only on the sensory stimulation present at the time.

But a verdict cannot depend on present stimulation to the exclusion of stored information. The very fact of our having learned the language evinces much storing of information, and of information without which we should be in no position to give verdicts on sentences however observational. Evidently then we must relax our definition of observation sentence to read thus: a sentence is an observation sentence if all verdicts on it depend on present sensory stimulation and on no stored information beyond what goes into understanding the sentence.

This formulation raises another problem: how are we to distinguish between information that goes into understanding a sentence and information that goes beyond? This is the problem of distinguishing between analytic truth, which issues from the mere meanings of words, and synthetic truth, which depends on more than meanings. Now I have long maintained that this distinction is illusory. There is one step toward such a distinction, however, which does make sense: a sentence that is true by mere meanings of words should be expected, at least if it is simple, to be subscribed to by all fluent speakers in the community. Perhaps the controversial notion of analyticity can be dispensed with, in our definition of observation sentence, in favor of this straightforward attribute of community-wide acceptance.

This attribute is of course no explication of analyticity. The community would agree that there have been black dogs, yet none who talk of analyticity would call this analytic. My rejection of the analyticity notion just means drawing no line between what goes into the mere understanding of the sentences of a language and what else the community sees eye-to-eye on. I doubt that an objective distinction can be made between meaning and such collateral information as is community-wide.

Turning back then to our task of defining observation sentences, we get this: an observation sentence is one on which all speakers of the language give the same verdict when given the same concurrent stimulation. To put the point negatively, an observation sentence is one that is not sensitive to differences in past experience within the speech community.

This formulation accords perfectly with the traditional role of the observation sentence as the court of appeal of scientific theories. For by our definition the observation sentences are the sentences on which all members of the community will agree under uniform stimulation. And what is the criterion of membership in the same community? Simply general fluency of dialogue. This criterion admits of degrees, and indeed we may usefully take the community more narrowly for some studies than for others. What count as observation sentences for a community of specialists would not always so count for a larger community.

There is generally no subjectivity in the phrasing of observation sentences, as we are now conceiving them; they will usually be about bodies. Since the distinguishing trait of an observation sentence is intersubjective agreement under agreeing stimulation, a corporeal subject matter is likelier than not.

The old tendency to associate observation sentences with a subjective sensory subject matter is rather an irony when we reflect that observation sentences are also meant to be the intersubjective tribunal of scientific hypotheses. The old tendency was due to the drive to base science on something firmer and prior in the subject's experience; but we dropped that project.

The dislodging of epistemology from its old status of first philosophy loosed a wave, we saw, of epistemological nihilism. This mood is reflected somewhat in the tendency of Polányi, Kuhn, and the late Russell Hanson to belittle the role of evidence and to accentuate cultural relativism. Hanson ventured even to discredit the idea of observation, arguing that so-called observations vary from observer to observer with the amount of knowledge that the observers bring with them. The veteran physicist looks at some apparatus and sees an x-ray tube. The neophyte, looking at the same place, observes rather "a glass metal instrument replete with wires, reflectors, screws, lamps, and pushbuttons." [6] One man's observation is another man's closed book or flight of fancy. The notion of observation as the impartial and objective source of evidence for science is bankrupt. Now my answer to the x-ray example was already hinted a little while back: what counts as an observation sentence varies with the width of community considered. But we can also always get an absolute standard by taking in all speakers of the language, or most. [7] It is ironical that philosophers, finding the old epistemology untenable as a whole, should react by repudiating a part which has only now moved into clear focus.

Clarification of the notion of observation sentence is a good thing, for the notion is fundamental in two connections. These two correspond to the duality that I remarked upon early in this lecture: the duality between concept and doctrine, between knowing what a sentence means and knowing whether it is true. The observation sentence is basic to both enterprises. Its relation to doctrine, to our knowledge of what is true, is very much the traditional one: observation sentences are the repository of evidence for scientific hypotheses. Its relation to meaning is fundamental too, since observation sentences are the ones we are in a position to learn to understand first, both as children and as field linguists. For observation sentences are precisely the ones that we can correlate with observable circumstances of the occasion of utterance or assent, independently of variations in the past histories of individual informants. They afford the only entry to a language.

The observation sentence is the cornerstone of semantics. For it is, as we just saw, fundamental to the learning of meaning. Also, it is where meaning is firmest. Sentences higher up in theories have no empirical consequences they can call their own; they confront the tribunal of sensory evidence only in more or less inclusive aggregates. The observation sentence, situated at the sensory periphery of the body scientific, is the minimal verifiable aggregate; it has an empirical content all its own and wears it on its sleeve.

The predicament of the indeterminacy of translation has little bearing on observation sentences. The equating of an observation sentence of our language to an observation sentence of another language is mostly a matter of empirical generalization; it is a matter of identity between the range of stimulations that would prompt assent to the one sentence and the range of stimulations that would prompt assent to the other.[8]

It is no shock to the preconceptions of old Vienna to say that epistemology now becomes semantics. For epistemology remains centered as always on evidence, and meaning remains centered as always on verification; and evidence is verification. What is likelier to shock preconceptions is that meaning, once we get beyond observation sentences, ceases in general to have any clear applicability to single sentences; also that epistemology merges with psychology, as well as with linguistics.

This rubbing out of boundaries could contribute to progress, it seems to me, in philosophically interesting inquiries of a scientific nature. One possible area is perceptual norms. Consider, to begin with, the linguistic phenomenon of phonemes. We form the habit, in hearing the myriad variations of spoken sounds, of treating each as an approximation to one or another of a limited number of norms—around thirty altogether—constituting so to speak a spoken alphabet. All speech in our language can be treated in practice as sequences of just those thirty elements, thus rectifying small deviations. Now outside the realm of language also there is probably only a rather limited alphabet of perceptual norms altogether, toward which we tend unconsciously to rectify all perceptions. These, if experimentally identified, could be taken as epistemological building blocks, the working elements of experience. They might prove in part to be culturally variable, as phonemes are, and in part universal.

Again there is the area that the psychologist Donald T. Campbell calls evolutionary epistemology.[9] In this area there is work by Hüseyin Yilmaz, who shows how some structural traits of color perception could have been predicted from survival value.[10] And a more emphatically epistemological topic

that evolution helps to clarify is induction, now that we are allowing epistemology the resources of natural science.[11]

Notes

1. Johnson 1947.

2. Carnap 1936.

3. See Quine 1969, pp. 2 ff.

4. See Quine 1969, p. 28.

5. Carnap 1932; Neurath 1932.

6. N. R. Hanson 1966.

7. This qualification allows for occasional deviants such as the insane or the blind.
Alternatively, such cases might be excluded by adjusting the level of fluency of
dialogue whereby we define sameness of language. (For prompting this note and
influencing the devlopment of this paper also in more substantial ways I am indebted to
Burton Dreben.)

8. Cf. Quine 1960, pp. 31–46, 68.

9. D. T. Campbell 1959.

10. Huseyin Yilmaz 1962, 1967.

11. See Quine 1969b.

2

Natural Kinds

W. V. O. Quine

What tends to confirm an induction? This question has been aggravated on the one hand by Hempel's puzzle of the non-black non-ravens,[1] and exacerbated on the other by Goodman's puzzle of the grue emeralds.[2] I shall begin my remarks by relating the one puzzle to the other, and the other to an innate flair that we have for natural kinds. Then I shall devote the rest of the paper to reflections on the nature of this notion of natural kinds and its relation to science.

Hempel's puzzle is that just as each black raven tends to confirm the law that all ravens are black, so each green leaf, being a non-black non-raven, should tend to confirm the law that all non-black things are non-ravens, that is, again, that all ravens are black. What is paradoxical is that a green leaf should count toward the law that all ravens are black.

Goodman propounds his puzzle by requiring us to imagine that emeralds, having been identified by some criterion other than color, are now being examined one after another and all up to now are found to be green. Then he proposes to call anything *grue* that is examined today or earlier and found to be green or is not examined before tomorrow and is blue. Should we expect the first one examined tomorrow to be green, because all examined up to now were green? But all examined up to now were also grue; so why not expect the first one tomorrow to be grue, and therefore blue?

The predicate "green," Goodman says,[3] is *projectible*; "grue" is not. He says this by way of putting a name to the problem. His step toward solution is his doctrine of what he calls entrenchment,[4] which I shall touch on later. Meanwhile the terminological point is simply that projectible predicates are predi-

Reprinted from *Ontological Relativity and Other Essays*, by W. V. O. Quine (New York: Columbia University Press, 1969), pp. 114–138, by permission of the publisher. Copyright © 1969, Columbia University Press.

cates ζ and η whose shared instances all do count, for whatever reason, toward confirmation of $\ulcorner$All ζ are $\eta\urcorner$.

Now I propose assimilating Hempel's puzzle to Goodman's by inferring from Hempel's that the complement of a projectible predicate need not be projectible. "Raven" and "black" are projectible; a black raven does count toward "All ravens are black." Hence a black raven counts also, indirectly, toward "No non-black things are non-ravens," since this says the same thing. But a green leaf does not count toward "All non-black things are non-ravens," nor, therefore, toward "All ravens are black"; "non-black" and "non-raven" are not projectible. "Green" and "leaf" are projectible, and the green leaf counts toward "All leaves are green" and "All green things are leaves"; but only a black raven can confirm "All ravens are black," the complements not being projectible.

If we see the matter in this way, we must guard against saying that a statement $\ulcorner$All ζ are $\eta\urcorner$ is lawlike only if ζ and η are projectible. "All non-black things are non-ravens" is a law despite its non-projectible terms, since it is equivalent to "All ravens are black." Any statement is lawlike that is logically equivalent to $\ulcorner$All ζ are $\eta\urcorner$ for some projectible ζ and η.[5]

Having concluded that the complement of a projectible predicate need not be projectible, we may ask further whether there is *any* projectible predicate whose complement is projectible. I can conceive that there is not, when complements are taken strictly. We must not be misled by limited or relative complementation; "male human" and "non-male human" are indeed both projectible.

To get back now to the emeralds, why do we expect the next one to be green rather than grue? The intuitive answer lies in similarity, however subjective. Two green emeralds are more similar than two grue ones would be if only one of the grue ones were green. Green things, or at least green emeralds, are a kind.[6] A projectible predicate is one that is true of all and only the things of a kind. What makes Goodman's example a puzzle, however, is the dubious scientific standing of a general notion of similarity, or of kind.

The dubiousness of this notion is itself a remarkable fact. For surely there is nothing more basic to thought and language than our sense of similarity; our sorting of things into kinds. The usual general term, whether a common noun or a verb or an adjective, owes its generality to some resemblance among the things referred to. Indeed, learning to use a word depends on a double resemblance: first, a resemblance between the present circumstances and past circumstances in which the word was used, and second, a phonetic resemblance between the present utterance of the word and past utterances of it.

And every reasonable expectation depends on resemblance of circumstances, together with our tendency to expect similar causes to have similar effects.

The notion of a kind and the notion of similarity or resemblance seem to be variants or adaptations of a single notion. Similarity is immediately definable in terms of kind; for, things are similar when they are two of a kind. The very words for "kind" and "similar" tend to run in etymologically cognate pairs. Cognate with "kind" we have "akin" and "kindred." Cognate with "like" we have "ilk." Cognate with "similar" and "same" and "resemble" there are "sammeln" and "assemble," suggesting a gathering into kinds.

We cannot easily imagine a more familiar or fundamental notion than this, or a notion more ubiquitous in its applications. On this score it is like the notions of logic: like identity, negation, alternation, and the rest. And yet, strangely, there is something logically repugnant about it. For we are baffled when we try to relate the general notion of similarity significantly to logical terms. One's first hasty suggestion might be to say that things are similar when they have all or most or many properties in common. Or, trying to be less vague, one might try defining comparative similarity—"a is more similar to b than to c"—as meaning that a shares more properties with b than with c. But any such course only reduces our problem to the unpromising task of settling what to count as a property.

The nature of the problem of what to count as a property can be seen by turning for a moment to set theory. Things are viewed as going together into sets in any and every combination, describable and indescribable. Any two things are joint members of any number of sets. Certainly then we cannot define "a is more similar to b than to c" to mean that a and b belong jointly to more sets than a and c do. If properties are to support this line of definition where sets do not, it must be because properties do not, like sets, take things in every random combination. It must be that properties are shared only by things that are significantly similar. But properties in such a sense are no clearer than kinds. To start with such a notion of property, and define similarity on that basis, is no better than accepting similarity as undefined.

The contrast between properties and sets which I suggested just now must not be confused with the more basic and familiar contrast between properties, as intensional, and sets as extensional. Properties are intensional in that they may be counted as distinct properties even though wholly coinciding in respect of the things that have them. There is no call to reckon kinds as intensional. Kinds can be seen as sets, determined by their members. It is just that not all sets are kinds.

If similarity is taken simple-mindedly as a yes-or-no affair, with no degrees, then there is no containing of kinds within broader kinds. For, as remarked, similarity now simply means belonging to some one same kind. If all colored things comprise a kind, then all colored things count as similar, and the set of all red things is too narrow to count as a kind. If on the other hand the set of all red things counts as a kind, then colored things do not all count as similar, and the set of all colored things is too broad to count as a kind. We cannot have it both ways. Kinds can, however, overlap; the red things can comprise one kind, the round another.

When we move up from the simple dyadic relation of similarity to the more serious and useful triadic relation of comparative similarity, a correlative change takes place in the notion of kind. Kinds come to admit now not only of overlapping but also of containment one in another. The set of all red things and the set of all colored things can now both count as kinds; for all colored things can now be counted as resembling one another more than some things do, even though less, on the whole, than red ones do.

At this point, of course, our trivial definition of similarity as sameness of kind breaks down; for almost any two things could count now as common members of some broad kind or other, and anyway we now want to define comparative or triadic similarity. A definition that suggests itself is this: a is more similar to b than to c when a and b belong jointly to more kinds than a and c do. But even this works only for finite systems of kinds.

The notion of kind and the notion of similarity seemed to be substantially one notion. We observed further that they resist reduction to less dubious notions, as of logic or set theory. That they at any rate be definable each in terms of the other seems little enough to ask. We just saw a somewhat limping definition of comparative similarity in terms of kinds. What now of the converse project, definition of kind in terms of similarity?

One may be tempted to picture a kind, suitable to a comparative similarity relation, as any set which is "qualitatively spherical" in this sense: it takes in exactly the things that differ less than so-and-so much from some central norm. If without serious loss of accuracy we can assume that there are one or more actual things (*paradigm cases*) that nicely exemplify the desired norm, and one or more actual things (*foils*) that deviate just barely too much to be counted into the desired kind at all, then our definition is easy: *the kind with paradigm a and foil b* is the set of all the things to which a is more similar than a is to b. More generally, then, a set may be said to be a *kind* if and only if there are a and b, known or unknown, such that the set is the kind with paradigm a and foil b.

If we consider examples, however, we see that this definition does not give us what we want as kinds. Thus take red. Let us grant that a central shade of red can be picked as norm. The trouble is that the paradigm cases, objects in just that shade of red, can come in all sorts of shapes, weights, sizes, and smells. Mere degree of overall similarity to any one such paradigm case will afford little evidence of degree of redness, since it will depend also on shape, weight, and the rest. If our assumed relation of comparative similarity were just comparative chromatic similarity, then our paradigm-and-foil definition of kind would indeed accommodate redkind. What the definition will not do is distill purely chromatic kinds from mixed similarity.

A different attempt, adapted from Carnap, is this: a set is a kind if all its members are more similar to one another than they all are to any one thing outside the set. In other words, each non-member differs more from some member than that member differs from any member. However, as Goodman showed in a criticism of Carnap,[7] this construction succumbs to what Goodman calls the difficulty of imperfect community. Thus consider the set of all red round things, red wooden things, and round wooden things. Each member of this set resembles each other member somehow: at least in being red, or in being round, or in being wooden, and perhaps in two or all three of these respects or others. Conceivably, moreover, there is no one thing outside the set that resembles every member of the set to even the least of these degrees. The set then meets the proposed definition of kind. Yet surely it is not what anyone means by a kind. It admits yellow croquet balls and red rubber balls while excluding yellow rubber balls.

The relation between similarity and kind, then, is less clear and neat than could be wished. Definition of similarity in terms of kind is halting, and definition of kind in terms of similarity is unknown. Still the two notions are in an important sense correlative. They vary together. If we reassess something a as less similar to b than to c, where it had counted as more similar to b than c, surely we will correspondingly permute a, b, and c in respect of their assignment to kinds; and conversely.

I have stressed how fundamental the notion of similarity or of kind is to our thinking, and how alien to logic and set theory. I want to go on now to say more about how fundamental these notions are to our thinking, and something also about their non-logical roots. Afterward I want to bring out how the notion of similarity or of kind changes as science progresses. I shall suggest that it is a mark of maturity of a branch of science that the notion of similarity or kind finally dissolves, so far as it is relevant to that branch of science. That is, it ultimately submits to analysis in the special terms of that branch of science and logic.

For deeper appreciation of how fundamental similarity is, let us observe more closely how it figures in the learning of language. One learns by *ostension* what presentations to call yellow; that is, one learns by hearing the word applied to samples. All he has to go on, of course, is the similarity of further cases to the samples. Similarity being a matter of degree, one has to learn by trial and error how reddish or brownish or greenish a thing can be and still be counted yellow. When he finds he has applied the word too far out, he can use the false cases as samples to the contrary; and then he can proceed to guess whether further cases are yellow or not by considering whether they are more similar to the in-group or the out-group. What one thus uses, even at this primitive stage of learning, is a fully functioning sense of similarity, and relative similarity at that: *a* is more similar to *b* than to *c*.

All these delicate comparisons and shrewd inferences about what to call yellow are, in Sherlock Holmes's terminology, elementary. Mostly the process is unconscious. It is the same process by which an animal learns to respond in distinctive ways to his master's commands or other discriminated stimulations.

The primitive sense of similarity that underlies such learning has, we saw, a certain complexity of structure: *a* is more similar to *b* than to *c*. Some people have thought that it has to be much more complex still: that it depends irreducibly on *respects*, thus similarity in color, similarity in shape, and so on. According to this view, our learning of yellow by ostension would have depended on our first having been told or somehow apprised that it was going to be a question of color. Now hints of this kind are a great help, and in our learning we often do depend on them. Still one would like to be able to show that a single general standard of similarity, but of course comparative similarity, is all we need, and that respects can be abstracted afterward. For instance, suppose the child has learned of a yellow ball and block that they count as yellow, and of a red ball and block that they do not, and now he has to decide about a yellow cloth. Presumably he will find the cloth more similar to the yellow ball and to the yellow block than to the red ball or red block; and he will not have needed any prior schooling in colors and respects. Carnap undertook to show long ago how some respects, such as color, could by an ingenious construction be derived from a general similarity notion;[8] however, this development is challenged, again, by Goodman's difficulty of imperfect community.

A standard of similarity is in some sense innate. This point is not against empiricism; it is a commonplace of behavioral psychology. A response to a red circle, if it is rewarded, will be elicited again by a pink ellipse more readily than by a blue triangle; the red circle resembles the pink ellipse more than the blue triangle. Without some such prior spacing of qualities, we could never acquire a habit; all stimuli would be equally alike and equally different. These spacings of qualities, on the part of men and other animals, can be explored and mapped in the laboratory by experiments in conditioning and extinction.[9]

Needed as they are for all learning, these distinctive spacings cannot themselves all be learned; some must be innate.

If then I say that there is an innate standard of similarity, I am making a condensed statement that can be interpreted, and truly interpreted, in behavioral terms. Moreover, in this behavioral sense it can be said equally of other animals that they have an innate standard of similarity too. It is part of our animal birthright. And, interestingly enough, it is characteristically animal in its lack of intellectual status. At any rate we noticed earlier how alien the notion is to mathematics and logic.

This innate qualitative spacing of stimulations was seen to have one of its human uses in the ostensive learning of words like "yellow." I should add as a cautionary remark that this is not the only way of learning words, nor the commonest; it is merely the most rudimentary way. It works when the question of the reference of a word is a simple question of spread: how much of our surroundings counts as yellow, how much counts as water, and so on. Learning a word like "apple" or "square" is more complicated, because here we have to learn also where to say that one apple or square leaves off and another begins. The complication is that apples do not add up to an apple, nor squares, generally, to a square. "Yellow" and "water" are mass terms, concerned only with spread; "apple" and "square" are terms of divided reference, concerned with both spread and individuation. Ostension figures in the learning of terms of this latter kind too, but the process is more complex.[10] And then there are all the other sorts of words, all those abstract and neutral connectives and adverbs and all the recondite terms of scientific theory; and there are also the grammatical constructions themselves to be mastered. The learning of these things is less direct and more complex still. There are deep problems in this domain, but they lie aside from the present topic.

Our way of learning "yellow," then, gives less than a full picture of how we learn language. Yet more emphatically, it gives less than a full picture of the human use of an innate standard of similarity, or innate spacing of qualities. For, as remarked, every reasonable expectation depends on similarity. Again on this score, other animals are like man. Their expectations, if we choose so to conceptualize their avoidance movements and salivation and pressing of levers and the like, are clearly dependent on their appreciation of similarity. Or, to put matters in their methodological order, these avoidance movements and salivation and pressing of levers and the like are typical of what we have to go on in mapping the animals' appreciation of similarity, their spacing of qualities.

Induction itself is essentially only more of the same: animal expectation or habit formation. And the ostensive learning of words is an implicit case of induction. Implicitly the learner of "yellow" is working inductively toward a general law of English verbal behavior, though a law that he will never try to state; he is working up to where he can in general judge when an English speaker would assent to "yellow" and when not.

Not only is ostensive learning a case of induction; it is a curiously comfortable case of induction, a game of chance with loaded dice. At any rate this is so if, as seems plausible, each man's spacing of qualities is enough like his neighbor's. For the learner is generalizing on his yellow samples by similarity considerations, and his neighbors have themselves acquired the use of the word "yellow," in their day, by the same similarity considerations. The learner of "yellow" is thus making his induction in a friendly world. Always, induction expresses our hope that similar causes will have similar effects; but when the induction is the ostensive learning of a word, that pious hope blossoms into a forgone conclusion. The uniformity of people's quality spaces virtually assures that similar presentations will elicit similar verdicts.

It makes one wonder the more about other inductions, where what is sought is a generalization not about our neighbor's verbal behavior but about the harsh impersonal world. It is reasonable that our quality space should match our neighbor's, we being birds of a feather; and so the general trustworthiness of induction in the ostensive learning of words was a put-up job. To trust induction as a way of access to the truths of nature, on the other hand, is to suppose, more nearly, that our quality space matches that of the cosmos. The brute irrationality of our sense of similarity, its irrelevance to anything in logic and mathematics, offers little reason to expect that this sense is somehow in tune with the world—a world which, unlike language, we never made. Why induction should be trusted, apart from special cases such as the ostensive learning of words, is the perennial philosophical problem of induction.

One part of the problem of induction, the part that asks why there should be regularities in nature at all, can, I think, be dismissed. *That* there are or have been regularities, for whatever reason, is an established fact of science; and we cannot ask better than that. *Why* there have been regularities is an obscure question, for it is hard to see what would count as an answer. What does make clear sense is this other part of the problem of induction: why does our innate subjective spacing of qualities accord so well with the functionally relevant groupings in nature as to make our inductions tend to come out right? Why should our subjective spacing of qualities have a special purchase on nature and a lien on the future?

There is some encouragement in Darwin. If people's innate spacing of qualities is a gene-linked trait, then the spacing that has made for the most successful inductions will have tended to predominate through natural selection.[11] Creatures inveterately wrong in their inductions have a pathetic but praiseworthy tendency to die before reproducing their kind.

At this point let me say that I shall not be impressed by protests that I am using inductive generalizations, Darwin's and others, to justify induction, and thus reasoning in a circle. The reason I shall not be impressed by this is that my position is a naturalistic one; I see philosophy not as an *a priori* propaedeutic or groundwork for science, but as continuous with science. I see philosophy and science as in the same boat—a boat which, to revert to Neurath's figure as I so often do, we can rebuild only at sea while staying afloat in it. There is no external vantage point, no first philosophy. All scientific findings, all scientific conjectures that are at present plausible, are therefore in my view as welcome for use in philosophy as elsewhere. For me then the problem of induction is a problem about the world: a problem of how we, as we now are (by our present scientific lights), in a world we never made, should stand better than random or coin-tossing chances of coming out right when we predict by inductions which are based on our innate, scientifically unjustified similarity standard. Darwin's natural selection is a plausible partial explanation.

It may, in view of a consideration to which I next turn, be almost explanation enough. This consideration is that induction, after all, has its conspicuous failures. Thus take color. Nothing in experience, surely, is more vivid and conspicuous than color and its contrasts. And the remarkable fact, which has impressed scientists and philosophers as far back at least as Galileo and Descartes, is that the distinctions that matter for basic physical theory are mostly independent of color contrasts. Color impresses man; raven black impresses Hempel; emerald green impresses Goodman. But color is cosmically secondary. Even slight differences in sensory mechanisms from species to species, Smart remarks,[12] can make overwhelming differences in the grouping of things by color. Color is king in our innate quality space, but undistinguished in cosmic circles. Cosmically, colors would not qualify as kinds.

Color is helpful at the food-gathering level. Here it behaves well under induction, and here, no doubt, has been the survival value of our color-slanted quality space. It is just that contrasts that are crucial for such activities can be insignificant for broader and more theoretical science. If man were to live by basic science alone, natural selection would shift its support to the color-blind mutation.

Living as he does by bread and basic science both, man is torn. Things about his innate similarity sense that are helpful in the one sphere can be a hindrance in the other. Credit is due man's inveterate ingenuity, or human sapience, for having worked around the blinding dazzle of color vision and found the more significant regularities elsewhere. Evidently natural selection has dealt with the conflict by endowing man doubly: with both a color-slanted quality space and the ingenuity to rise above it.

He has risen above it by developing modified systems of kinds, hence modified similarity standards for scientific purposes. By the trial-and-error process of theorizing he has regrouped things into new kinds which prove to lend themselves to many inductions better than the old.

A crude example is the modification of the notion of fish by excluding whales and porpoises. Another taxonomic example is the grouping of kangaroos, opossums, and marsupial mice in a single kind, marsupials, while excluding ordinary mice. By primitive standards the marsupial mouse is more similar to the ordinary mouse than to the kangaroo; by theoretical standards the reverse is true.

A theoretical kind need not be a modification of an intuitive one. It may issue from theory full-blown, without antecedents; for instance the kind which comprises positively charged particles.

We revise our standards of similarity or of natural kinds on the strength, as Goodman remarks,[13] of second-order inductions. New groupings, hypothetically adopted at the suggestion of a growing theory, prove favorable to inductions and so become "entrenched." We newly establish the projectibility of some predicate, to our satisfaction, by successfully trying to project it. In induction nothing succeeds like success.

Between an innate similarity notion or spacing of qualities and a scientifically sophisticated one, there are all gradations. Science, after all, differs from common sense only in degree of methodological sophistication. Our experiences from earliest infancy are bound to have overlaid our innate spacing of qualities by modifying and supplementing our grouping habits little by little, inclining us more and more to an appreciation of theoretical kinds and similarities, long before we reach the point of studying science systematically as such. Moreover, the later phases do not wholly supersede the earlier; we retain different similarity standards, different systems of kinds, for use in different contexts. We all still say that a marsupial mouse is more like an ordinary mouse than a kangaroo, except when we are concerned with genetic matters. Something like our innate quality space continues to function alongside the more sophisticated regroupings that have been found by scientific experience to facilitate induction.

We have seen that a sense of similarity or of kinds is fundamental to learning in the widest sense—to language learning, to induction, to expectation. Toward a further appreciation of how utterly this notion permeates our thought, I want now to point out a number of other very familiar and central notions which seem to depend squarely on this one. They are notions that are definable in terms of similarity, or kinds, and further irreducible.

A notable domain of examples is the domain of dispositions, such as Carnap's example of solubility in water. To say of some individual object that it is soluble in water is not to say merely that it always dissolves when in water, because this would be true by default of any object, however insoluble, if it merely happened to be destined never to get into water. It is to say rather that it *would* dissolve if it were in water; but this account brings small comfort, since the device of a subjunctive conditional involves all the perplexities of disposition terms and more. Thus far I simply repeat Carnap.[14] But now I want to point out what could be done in this connection with the notion of kind. Intuitively, what qualifies a thing as soluble though it never gets into water is that it is of the same kind as the things that actually did or will dissolve; it is similar to them. Strictly we can't simply say "*the* same kind," nor simply "similar," when we have wider and narrower kinds, less and more similarity. Let us then mend our definition by saying that the soluble things are the common members of *all* such kinds. A thing is soluble if *each* kind that is broad enough to embrace all actual victims of solution embraces it too.

Graphically the idea is this: we make a set of all the sometime victims, all the things that actually did or will dissolve in water, and then we add just enough other things to round the set out into a kind. This is the water-soluble kind.

If this definition covers just the desired things, the things that are really soluble in water, it owes its success to a circumstance that could be otherwise. The needed circumstance is that a sufficient variety of things actually get dissolved in water to assure their not all falling under any one kind narrower than the desired water-soluble kind itself. But it is a plausible circumstance, and I am not sure that its accidental character is a drawback. If the trend of events had been otherwise, perhaps the solubility concept would not have been wanted.

However, if I seem to be defending this definition, I must now hasten to add that of course it has much the same fault as the definition which used the subjunctive conditional. This definition uses the unreduced notion of kind, which is certainly not a notion we want to rest with either; neither theoretical kind nor intuitive kind. My purpose in giving the definition is only to show the link between the problem of dispositions and the problem of kinds.

As between theoretical and intuitive kinds, certainly the theoretical ones are the ones wanted for purposes of defining solubility and other dispositions of scientific concern. Perhaps "amiable" and "reprehensible" are disposition terms whose definitions should draw rather on intuitive kinds.

In considering the disposition of solubility we observed a link first with the subjunctive conditional and then with the notion of kind. This suggests comparing also the two end terms, so as to see the connection between the subjunctive conditional and the notion of kind. We had then, on the one side, the subjunctive conditional "If x were in water it would dissolve"; and on the other side, in terms of kinds, we had "Each kind that embraces all things that ever get into water and dissolve, embraces x." Here we have equated a sample subjunctive conditional to a sentence about kinds. We can easily enough generalize the equivalence to cover a significant class of subjunctive conditionals: the form "If x were an F then x would be a G" gets equated to "Each kind that embraces all Fs that are Gs embraces x." Notice that the Fs themselves, here, would not be expected to constitute a kind; nor the Gs; nor the Fs which are Gs. But you take the fewest things you can which, added to the Fs which are Gs, suffice to round the set out to a kind. Then x is one of these few additional things; this is the interpretation we get of the subjunctive conditional "If x were an F then x would be a G."

One might try this formula out on other examples, and study it for possible light on subjunctive conditionals more generally. Some further insight into this queer idiom might thus be gained. But let us remember that we are still making uncritical use of the unreduced notion of kind. My purpose, again, is only to show the link between these matters.

Another dim notion, which has intimate connections with dispositions and subjunctive conditionals, is the notion of cause; and we shall see that it too turns on the notion of kinds. Hume explained cause as invariable succession, and this makes sense as long as the cause and effect are referred to by general terms. We can say that fire causes heat, and we can mean thereby, as Hume would have it, that each event classifiable under the head of fire is followed by an event classifiable under the head of heat, or heating up. But this account, whatever its virtues for these general causal statements, leaves singular causal statements unexplained.

What does it mean to say that the kicking over of a lamp in Mrs. Leary's barn caused the Chicago fire? It cannot mean merely that the event at Mrs. Leary's belongs to a set, and the Chicago fire belongs to a set, such that there is invariable succession between the two sets: every member of the one set is followed by a member of the other. This paraphrase is trivially true and too weak. Always, if one event happens to be followed by another, the two belong to *certain* sets between which there is invariable succession. We can rig the sets arbitrarily. Just put any arbitrary events in the first set, including the first of the two events we are interested in; and then in the other set put the second of those two events, together with other events that happen to have occurred just after the other members of the first set.

Because of this way of trivialization, a singular causal statement says no more than that the one event was followed by the other. That is, it says no more if we use the definition just now contemplated; which, therefore, we must not. The trouble with that definition is clear enough: it is the familiar old trouble of the promiscuity of sets. Here, as usual, kinds, being more discriminate, enable us to draw distinctions where sets do not. To say that one event caused another is to say that the two events are of *kinds* between which there is invariable succession. If this correction does not yet take care of Mrs. Leary's cow, the fault is only with invariable succession itself, as affording too simple a definition of general causal statements; we need to hedge it around with provisions for partial or contributing causes and a good deal else. That aspect of the causality problem is not my concern. What I wanted to bring out is just the relevance of the notion of kinds, as the needed link between singular and general causal statements.

We have noticed that the notion of kind, or similarity, is crucially relevant to the notion of disposition, to the subjunctive conditional, and to singular causal statements. From a scientific point of view these are a pretty disreputable lot. The notion of kind, or similarity, is equally disreputable. Yet some such notion, some similarity sense, was seen to be crucial to all learning, and central in particular to the processes of inductive generalization and prediction which are the very life of science. It appears that science is rotten to the core.

Yet there may be claimed for this rot a certain undeniable fecundity. Science reveals hidden mysteries, predicts successfully, and works technological wonders. If this is the way of rot, then rot is rather to be prized and praised than patronized.

Rot, actually, is not the best model here. A better model is human progress. A sense of comparative similarity, I remarked earlier, is one of man's animal endowments. Insofar as it fits in with regularities of nature, so as to afford us reasonable success in our primitive inductions and expectations, it is presumably an evolutionary product of natural selection. Secondly, as remarked, one's sense of similarity or one's system of kinds develops and changes and even turns multiple as one matures, making perhaps for increasingly dependable prediction. And at length standards of similarity set in which are geared to theoretical science. This development is a development away from the immediate, subjective, animal sense of similarity to the remoter objectivity of a similarity determined by scientific hypotheses and posits and constructs. Things are similar in the later or theoretical sense to the degree that they are interchangeable parts of the cosmic machine revealed by science.

This progress of similarity standards, in the course of each individual's maturing years, is a sort of recapitulation in the individual of the race's progress from muddy savagery. But the similarity notion even in its theoretical phase is itself a muddy notion still. We have offered no definition of it in satisfactory scientific terms. We of course have a behavioral definition of what counts, for a given individual, as similar to what, or as more similar to what than to what; we have this for similarity old and new, human and animal. But it is no definition of what it means really for *a* to be more similar to *b* than to *c*; really, and quite apart from this or that psychological subject.

Did I already suggest a definition to this purpose, metaphorically, when I said that things are similar to the extent that they are interchangeable parts of the cosmic machine? More literally, could things be said to be similar in proportion to how much of scientific theory would remain true on interchanging those things as objects of reference in the theory? This only hints a direction; consider for instance the dimness of "how much theory." Anyway the direction itself is not a good one; for it would make similarity depend in the wrong way on theory. A man's judgments of similarity do and should depend on his theory, on his beliefs; but similarity itself, what the man's judgments purport to be judgments of, purports to be an objective relation in the world. It belongs in the subject matter not of our theory of theorizing about the world, but of our theory of the world itself. Such would be the acceptable and reputable sort of similarity concept, if it could be defined.

It does get defined in bits: bits suited to special branches of science. In this way, on many limited fronts, man continues his rise from savagery, sloughing off the muddy old notion of kind or similarity piecemeal, a vestige here and a vestige there. Chemistry, the home science of water-solubility itself, is one branch that has reached this stage. Comparative similarity of the sort that matters for chemistry can be stated outright in chemical terms, that is, in terms of chemical composition. Molecules will be said to *match* if they contain atoms of the same elements in the same topological combinations. Then, in principle, we might get at the comparative similarity of objects *a* and *b* by considering how many pairs of matching molecules there are, one molecule from *a* and one from *b* each time, and how many unmatching pairs. The ratio gives even a theoretical measure of relative similarity, and thus abundantly explains what it is for *a* to be more similar to *b* than to *c*. Or we might prefer to complicate our definition by allowing also for degrees in the matching of molecules; molecules having almost equally many atoms, or having atoms whose atomic numbers or atomic weights are almost equal, could be reckoned as matching better than others. At any rate a lusty chemical similarity concept is assured.

From it, moreover, an equally acceptable concept of kinds is derivable, by the paradigm-and foil definition noted early in this paper. For it is a question now only of distilling purely chemical kinds from purely chemical similarity; no admixture of other respects of similarity interferes. We thus exonerate water-solubility, which, the last time around, we had reduced no further than to an unexplained notion of kind. Therewith also the associated subjunctive conditional, "If this were in water it would dissolve," gets its bill of health.

The same scientific advances that have thus provided a solid underpinning for the definition of solubility in terms of kinds, have also, ironically enough, made that line of definition pointless by providing a full understanding of the mechanism of solution. One can redefine water-solubility by simply describing the structural conditions of that mechanism. This embarrassment of riches is, I suspect, a characteristic outcome. That is, once we can legitimize a disposition term by defining the relevant similarity standard, we are apt to know the mechanism of the disposition, and so by-pass the similarity. Not but that the similarity standard is worth clarifying too, for its own sake or for other purposes.

Philosophical or broadly scientific motives can impel us to seek still a basic and absolute concept of similarity, along with such fragmentary similarity concepts as suit special branches of science. This drive for a cosmic similarity concept is perhaps identifiable with the age-old drive to reduce things to their elements. It epitomizes the scientific spirit, though dating back to the pre-Socratics: to Empedocles with his theory of four elements, and above all to Democritus with his atoms. The modern physics of elementary particles, or of hills in space-time, is a more notable effort in this direction.

This idea of rationalizing a single notion of relative similarity, throughout its cosmic sweep, has its metaphysical attractions. But there would remain still need also to rationalize the similarity notion more locally and superficially, so as to capture only such similarity as is relevant to some special science. Our chemistry example is already a case of this, since it stops short of full analysis into neutrons, electrons, and the other elementary particles.

A more striking example of superficiality, in this good sense, is afforded by taxonomy, say in zoology. Since learning about the evolution of species, we are in a position to define comparative similarity suitably for this science by consideration of family trees. For a theoretical measure of the degree of similarity of two individual animals we can devise some suitable function that depends on proximity and frequency of their common ancestors. Or a more significant concept of degree of similarity might be devised in terms of genes. When kind is construed in terms of any such similarity concept, fishes in the corrected, whale-free sense of the word qualify as a kind while fishes in the more inclusive sense do not.

Different similarity measures, or relative similarity notions, best suit different branches of science; for there are wasteful complications in providing for finer gradations of relative similarity than matter for the phenomena with which the particular science is concerned. Perhaps the branches of science could be revealingly classified by looking to the relative similarity notion that is appropriate to each. Such a plan is reminiscent of Felix Klein's so-called *Erlangerprogramm* in geometry, which involved characterizing the various branches of geometry by what transformations were irrelevant to each. But a branch of science would only qualify for recognition and classification under such a plan when it had matured to the point of clearing up its similarity notion. Such branches of science would qualify further as unified, or integrated into our inclusive systematization of nature, only insofar as their several similarity concepts were *compatible*; capable of meshing, that is, and differing only in the fineness of their discriminations.

Disposition terms and subjunctive conditionals in these areas, where suitable senses of similarity and kind are forthcomimg, suddenly turn respectable; respectable and, in principle, superfluous. In other domains they remain disreputable and practically indispensable. They may be seen perhaps as unredeemed notes; the theory that would clear up the unanalyzed underlying similarity notion in such cases is still to come. An example is the disposition called intelligence—the ability, vaguely speaking, to learn quickly and to solve problems. Sometime, whether in terms of proteins or colloids or nerve nets or overt behavior, the relevant branch of science may reach the stage where a similarity notion can be constructed capable of making even the notion of intelligence respectable. And superfluous.

In general we can take it as a very special mark of the maturity of a branch of science that it no longer needs an irreducible notion of similarity and kind. It is that final stage where the animal vestige is wholly absorbed into the theory. In this career of the similarity notion, starting in its innate phase, developing over the years in the light of accumulated experience, passing then from the intuitive phase into theoretical similarity, and finally disappearing altogether, we have a paradigm of the evolution of unreason into science.

Notes

1. C. G. Hempel 1965, p. 15.

2. Nelson Goodman 1955, p. 74. I am indebted to Goodman and to Burton Dreben for helpful criticisms of earlier drafts of the present paper.

3. Goodman 1955, pp. 82 ff.

4. Ibid., pp. 95 ff.

5. I mean this only as a sufficient condition of lawlikeness. See Donald Davidson 1966.

6. The relevance of kind is noted by Goodman 1955, 1st edition, pp. 119 ff; 2d edition, pp. 121 f.

7. Nelson Goodman 1966, pp. 163 ff.

8. Rudolf Carnap 1967, pp. 141–147.

9. See Quine 1960, pp. 83 ff, for further discussion and references.

10. See Quine 1960, pp. 90–95.

11. This was noted by S. Watanabe on the second page of his 1965.

12. J. J. C. Smart 1963, pp. 68–72.

13. Goodman 1955, pp. 95 ff.

14. Carnap 1936.

3

Pattern Matching as an Essential in Distal Knowing[1]

Donald T. Campbell

To establish the setting and the problem, this paper first deals with Egon Brunswik's concept of distality in terms of behavior theory and evolutionary development. Even here, knowing in science is introduced as in continuity with those modes of knowing on the part of organisms described by biologists and psychologists. The problem is then introduced: How is distal knowing achieved? How are the proximal threads tied in a distal knot? The thesis is advanced that pattern matching is one of the recurrent attributes. This is illustrated first at the level of stereoscopic perception of objects and the coordination of motor behavior. Further illustrations come from the diagnosis of inferred entities in science. Finally, the perspective is used to summarize an emerging consensus among philosophers of science as to the relationship between theory and data.

Joining analytic philosophers since Hume, both scientific knowledge and ordinary knowledge of the common-sense objects of the external world are recognized as analytically unjustified, highly presumptuous, and fallible. This recognition seems basic to both philosophical and psychological approaches to the problem of knowledge. But if to the problem of knowledge, the philosopher answers in a specific instance or in general that "knowledge is impossible," he has answered a different question than was asked. For the question, "How is knowledge possible?" usually implies that knowledge, corrigible though it may be, has in some instances been achieved to a sufficient degree to make the question worth asking. It presumes that instances of valid knowing and of mistake both occur and are in some instances discriminable. How are such discriminations made? How can one identify new instances as "the same" as old ones so that "knowledge" may be applied? How do knowers

Reprinted from *The Psychology of Egon Brunswik*, ed. Kenneth R. Hammond (New York: Holt, Rinehart and Winston, Inc., 1966), pp. 81–106, by permission of CBS College Publishing. Copyright © 1966, Holt, Rinehart and Winston, Inc.

choose between the interpretation of sense data as indicating a new entity versus connoting an old entity from a changed perspective? It is the problem of knowledge at this level to which the present inquiry is addressed.

Distal knowledge means, in particular, knowledge of external objects and events, knowledge of predictable processes reidentifiable as the same, hypothetical knowledge optimally invariant over points of observation and observers. Perhaps in the truest connotations of the word, all knowledge is distal, and our title has a needless redundancy. Perhaps there is no sense in which punctiform raw sense data unidentified as recognizable recurrents, uninterpreted as diagnostic of external events, should be called knowledge.

Both psychology and philosophy are emerging from an epoch in which the *quest for punctiform certainty* seemed the optimal approach to knowledge. To both Pavlov and Watson, single retinal cell activations and single muscle activations seemed more certainly reidentifiable and specifiable than perceptions of objects or adaptive acts. The effort in epistemology to remove equivocality by founding knowledge on particulate sense data and the spirit of logical atomism point to the same search for certainty in particulars. These are efforts of the past, now increasingly recognized to be untenable, yet the quest for punctiform certainty is still a pervasive part of our intellectual background. A preview of the line argument as it relates to the nostalgia for certainty through incorrigible particulars may be provided by the following analogy. Imagine the task of identifying "the same" dot of ink in two newspaper prints of the same photograph. The task is impossible if the photographs are examined by exposing only one dot at a time. It becomes more possible the larger the area of each print exposed. Insofar as any certainty in the identification of a single particle is achieved, it is because a prior identification of the whole has been achieved. Rather than the identification of the whole being achieved through the firm establishment of particles, the reverse is the case, the complex being more certainly known than the elements, neither, of course, being known incorrigibly.

The Operational Distinction Between Distal and Proximal *S-R* Laws

It is today fashionable in the psychology of learning to acknowledge that molar responses and molar stimuli are involved in the empirical regularities upon which behavior theories are based. But usually this is presented as the scientist's arbitrary choice of a convenient level of analysis, rather than in recognition of the empirical fact that it is at a molar level rather than at the molecular level that *S-R* laws can be obtained. This recognition is fundamental

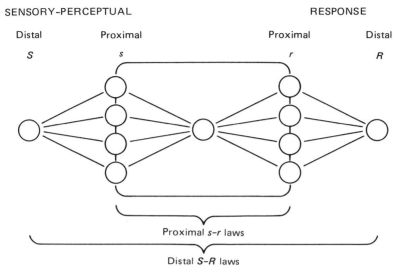

Figure 1.
Brunswik's "lens model." The box represents a conceptual organism, with a sensory-perceptual surface (to the left) and a response surface (to the right). The radial lines indicate the multifarious proximal channels alternatively (vicariously) mediating the distal achievement. On the stimulus side, these could be illustrated by the multiple intersubstitutable proximal cues for distance or for object color, and so forth. On the response side these could be illustrated by the multiple specific muscle contractions by which the rat might depress a lever, or locomote a runway, and so forth.

to Brunswik's similar distinction between the distal and proximal levels. Examination of his "lens model" in Figure 1 will help make this clear.

Brunswik recognized the scientific legitimacy of the search for proximal s-r laws, relationships between single retinal cell activation and specific muscle contraction, for example. However, he summarized psychology's experience with the higher vertebrates by the general induction that such laws did not exist; that when computed, these correlations (between presence-absence of stimulus and presence-absence of muscle contraction over a population of occasions) were of zero magnitude. He did not deny the possibility of discovering such laws in any programmatic or logical sense, and in fact emphasized that the behavioral regularities of the lower animals, such as Uexküll's (1934) sea urchins, were of this proximal sort (Brunswik, 1956, p. 62). For such coelenterates, the activation of a given tactile receptor cell dependably activates a specific muscle. But for man, the significant S-R correlations are to be found at the distal, object-act level, rather than at the proximal level. These significant and impressive (if never perfect) correlations are a major fact that psychological theory must accept. A major self-deception of traditional behaviorisms has been the use of these distal correlations in specious support of theories adequate only to explain proximal ones. A major achievement of Brunswik's perspective is that of maintaining a positivistic, behavioristic orientation without denying the flexible, purposive adaptedness which is characteristic of the perceptual and motor systems of the higher organisms. Smedslund (1953) and Campbell (1954), in defense of a Brunswikian point of view on the problem of "what is learned" and in summary of the research in learning showing the distal character of most learned habits, have emphasized that such distal foci are operationally distinguishable from the proximal.

The achievement of such a point of view meant overcoming special temptations for a person of Brunswik's positivist background. The positivist's militant attack upon vitalism and upon the metaphysical baggage of pseudo-problems made them prone to overlook or deny these less tangible facts of perception and behavior. The particular form that their quest for certainty took was in seeking a certainty of communication, that is, in seeking unequivocally specifiable terms. Proximal stimuli and proximal responses seem much more appealing in this sense than do distal ones. It was Brunswik's achievement to make objective the facts that necessitated the renunciation of this approach to certainty, facts to which many positivists within psychology are still blind. It was his achievement to have retained both his vigorous positivism, and to have harnessed these "organismic" and "vitalistic" facts as positivistically demonstrated laws. His empirical law of distal achievements through vicarious mediation I accept as established, setting the problem for this essay.

Evolutionary Perspective upon Degrees of Distality

In the primitive coelenterate, the nervous system connects each specific tactile sense organ with a specific muscle. The *s-r* reflexes are adaptive, in that the muscle response changes the relationship between the organism and environment (in some instances leading to tenacle withdrawing, in other instances, contraction and grasping, depending on location, and so forth). While these are distal effects, there is but a single means of mediating them—there are no alternative channels for vicarious mediation. Thus at the proximal level, the correlation holds. Higher forms, even locomotor forms, may possibly preserve this proximal consistency. Loeb (1918) described an ingenious mechanical bug with presumed animal counterparts that flexibly tracked a light. The left eye or photocell activated the right hind leg or wheel, and the right eye, the left hind leg. Thus when both eyes were equally stimulated, locomotion was straight ahead toward the light. If the initial orientation was to one side, the eye receiving the greater amount of light activated the opposite side the more, leading the bug to turn in the direction of the light, up to that point where the eyes were equally stimulated.

But the major stable relationships in the world available for organismic exploitation are consistencies adhering to other objects than the organism itself—consistencies adhering to food objects, shelters, predators, locomotor obstacles, throughways, and so forth. Due to the fluctuating illumination and the variable distance of such objects, proximal stimuli are not optimal indicators of these, nor are proximal responses optimal effectors. Somewhere in the evolutionary hierarchy the available distal relationships come to be exploited, and with this comes a renunciation of rigid one-to-one reflexes at the proximal level. Presumably this has been achieved by the evolutionary level at which image-forming eyes appear. The organism at that point tries out the strategy of hypothesizing stable external objects mediately known, or of behaving in a manner consistent with such hypothesizing.

This is awkwardly conveyed on two counts. On the one hand, the statement is atrociously anthropomorphic. On the other, we so unquestioningly assume the existence of specific external objects—objects with a stability independent of our movements—that we find it hard to accept these as merely the hypotheses of a fallible cognitive apparatus, at best mediately known. We find it hard to comprehend an organism that does not live and locomote in a world of objects. Yet this feature of animal life is clearly depenent upon distance receptors and, in any high degree, upon perceptual constancy mechanisms.

S-R consistencies, whether instinctive or habitual, are dependent for their establishment and maintenance upon consistencies in the environment, inasmuch as selective survival or selective reinforcement are essential. Initially, only environmental contingencies at the skin of the organism are involved. At higher stages, environmental contingencies at some remoteness from the skin can be diagnosed, and the diagnostic inference becomes to some degree independent of the position of the observing organism. Since it is ecologically true that these less selfcentered, more "objective" contingencies are stronger statistically (provide better predictions) there is a selection-pressure in evolution leading to their exploitation, and to the increasingly complex perceptual-loco-motor apparatus that makes this possible.

Students of science and epistemology have long found it appropriate to tease out the hidden premises underlying the reasoning of scientists and laymen. These premises are often for convenience stated in a language of conscious contents: the scientist presumes order (or partial order) in nature, he presumes that there are fewer causal laws than there are events, and so forth. These premises are unconscious until thus explicated. It is in a similar vein that I use a conscious experience terminology of "hypothesizing" in discussing the implicit presumptions about the nature of the world built into animals at various evolutionary stages (Lorenz, 1941; Campbell, 1959). These presumptions, these synthetic hypotheses (ontogenetically a priori or a posteriori), increase with the adaptive radius, the range of correspondences of the organism (Spencer, 1896), and represent the increased "knowledge" of the laws of the world, of the "causal texture of the environment." (Tolman & Brunswik, 1935.) In these terms, the proximal-level organism in his inherited reflexes modestly assumes some degree of order, some deviation from pure randomness in his environment. At some later level, his ambitious presumptiveness goes so far as to presume the existence of external objects. At this stage, the organism's cognitive apparatus becomes a diagnoser of external entities and processes. At this stage, the puzzling fact of distality and of purposive behavior emerges in full degree. From the standpoint of an amoeba, this is a wondrous, if very presumptive, procedure.

Continuing the evolutionary paradigm, we can note that the higher the level of development the higher the degree of distality achieved, the greater the magnitude of the Brunswik constancy ratio, and the greater the degree to which external events and objects are known in a manner independent of the point of view of the observer. Thus Brunswik (1928; 1956) found the degree of constancy achieved to be higher in older children than younger ones, reaching a maximum around fourteen or fifteen years of age. Thus Piaget (for example, Flavell, 1963; Piaget, 1957) finds his youngest children failing to reify external objects as having continuing existence and motion when out of sight. With increasing age come not only increasing hypostatization of external objects, but also of increasing presumption of the conservation of weight and volume, as the child more and more imputes to the world stability under transformations of his point of observation. Thus, within the historical span of human experience, the distality of man's knowledge has been increased by learning and reason over that provided by visual perception. Brunswik both emphasized the marvelous constancy mechanisms of the visual and auditory systems, and at the same time spoke of the "stupidity" of the perceptual apparatus relative to thinking in its rigidity and susceptibility to illusion under ecologically atypical conditions (for example, Brunswik, 1934; 1956, pp. 88–92). Piaget provides similar evidence. Man's introduction of measuring rods constructed of relatively inelastic quasi solids has freed his knowledge of objects from the ubiquitous compromise with retinal size found in unaided vision (Brunswik, 1956, p. 88 and *ad passim*).

The course of science has this over-all trend. The intricacies of measuring instruments and laboratory equipment show a development analogous to that of the vertebrate eye. The addition of specific compensating devices and control features lead meter readings to reflect more and more purely the attributes of the object of study, uncontaminated by the irrelevant specifics, vagaries, and rigidities of the measuring instrument. The concept of a compensated or of an automatically self-calibrating instrument, and the need for continually recalibrating a more primitive one, convey the general spirit of this development. (See Wilson, 1952, for specific illustrations.)

Similarly, physical theory has provided in each generation a model of the universe more independent of man's particular position of observation. In the shift from Ptolemy to Kepler this is clear; some see the contributions of relativity and quantum theory and the complementarity principle as reversals in this direction. This is not the position taken here, however. What these developments have done is to convince man that his knowledge of the world is not as completely distal or objective as he had thought, that it is still contaminated by a certain degree of astigmatism (Bachem, 1951), and that there are limitations upon the degree of objective knowledge that he can obtain. But note that in many specifics, if not all, the errors of the Newtonian system become correctible when an Einsteinian relativity is adopted, achieving a greater degree of distality, independence of point of observation, and predictive efficacy than that previously held. Oppenheimer (1956) has presented a parallel development in early science. He contrasts Babylonian astronomy with the later Mediterranean versions of Ptolemy and Copernicus. Babylonian astronomy was able to predict the movement of the heavenly bodies with great accuracy, including such subtleties as the eclipses of the moon, without any model of celestial mechanics. This achievement was the product of centuries of bookkeeping, and was based upon vast libraries of detail from which identical sequences and spatial contingencies could be identified as a base for prediction. The great advantage of the model-building astronomies was not one of accuracy (at least initially) but rather one of library space. The same repertoire of predictions could be encompassed with one one-thousandth of the written records. Similarly, while it is conceivable that instinct or learning provide an animal with a fixed response tendency for each possible proximal pattern of stimulation, the central nervous system storage requirements involved for an animal like ourselves with proximal stimulus receptors numbering in the millions, are such as to argue the economy of the more presumptive strategy of creating an approximate model of the environment as a base of prediction. The phenomenal reality of separate external objects for myself, and reputedly for other men, helps convince me that my near relatives probably use this presumptive strategy.

Tying the Proximal Threads in a Distal Knot

In the laboratory research on thing constancy, the distal thinghood of the object being judged is never in question—rather only some attribute of it—as its size, shape, or distance. Starting from this setting one misses some of the wonder of the achievement that would be more apparent if one examined an instance in which even the positing of a single thing was equivocal. For note, there is always the alternative of inferring several independent causal sources for the several proximal data, rather than inferring a single common source (Heider, 1959).

"Triangulation" is an attractive model (for example, Feigl, 1958; Campbell, 1959). The "lens model" suggests it. From several widely separated proximal points, there is a triangulation upon the distal object, "fixing" it and its distance in a way quite impossible from a single proximal point. Binocular vision can be seen quite literally as such a triangulation.

As Brunswik emphasized, each proximal stimulation is equivocal when interpreted as evidence of a distal event. For each, there is a subinfinity of possible distal events to which it could be witness. We could if we wished add to the lens model a radiation of lines from a heterogeneity of distal events to a single proximal one. How does the cognitive apparatus decide on the distal focus, decide in what distal bundles to tie the proximal particulars? How do the two proximal sources "know" when they are fixing on one single object rather than two separate ones? Or rather, under what conditions do they "presume" one rather than two? The tentative and partial answer is that this is achieved through a pattern matching. The tentative theme of this paper is that such a pattern matching is involved in all instances of distal knowing, including the achievements of scientific theory. In making this suggestion I join many others. For example, it is an important theme in Craik's (1943) *The Nature of Explanation*. Konrad Lorenz has made a similar point in his recent paper on "Gestalt Perception as Fundamental to Scientific Knowledge" (1959), a paper which, like the present one, emphasizes the epistemological significance of the evolution of the perceptual constancies. Bertrand Russell has been particularly explicit.

In Russell's (1948) *Human Knowledge: Its Scope and Limits* he starts out as though writing a summary of epistemological problems for laymen. And in the section on language, he seems little changed from his earlier logical atomism. But in the subsequent parts of the book he is again creatively thinking about the problems that have always troubled him. Particularly in his final section on "The Postulates of Scientific Inference" he offers a synthetic theory of inductive knowledge quite in keeping in spirit with that essayed here. While the list of implicit hypotheses about the nature of the world which he offers differs in particulars from one that I might develop, the general effort is similar.

In his "structural postulate" Russell states the principle with which the present paper deals: "When a number of structurally similar complex events are ranged about a center in regions not widely separated, it is usually the case that all belong to causal lines having their origin in an event of the same structure at the center" (p. 492). His illustrations include multiple copies of photographs, the similar percepts of people viewing a given scene or hearing a given sound, the multiple copies of a given book, the identification of which shadow goes with which man, the assumption of a common culprit in the "brides-in-the-bath" murders, and so forth (Russell, 1948, pp. 460–475).

Stereoscopic Vision

As a first example, let us examine binocular vision via the stereoscope. The stereoscope is ecologically a very unrepresentative sample of possible environments, and is one in which the distal-perceptual apparatus goes awry, in that two separate distal events (the separate pictures each eye views) are misinterpreted as one. In the process, the cues by which oneness is inferred are made more evident.

There are three typical outcomes, if heterogeneous pairs of pictures be allowed: Binocular fusion into a single image, double-image superimposition, and a domination of one eye's content to the exclusion of the other. If one starts out with similar simple line drawings that will fuse, this resolution can be destroyed by making one of the drawings more and more different from the other. If there is little detail in the drawings, the failure of fusion may lead to a superimposition of the two contents. For example, if each side has only two vertical lines, under the fused condition only two are seen. If the separation of the two is greatly increased beyond the capacity of binocular resolution, then three or four lines may be seen. If, on the other hand, each eye's view is rich in detail (as when two photographs are used), lack of common contour in the two pictures results in a total suppression of one or the other. It seems clear that the fusion of the two proximal sources into a distal inference is made possible through a process of pattern matching, and does not occur in the absence of a high degree of pattern similarity. Once this high degree of similarity is present to guide fusion, then minor disparities of the correct kind can produce a distal increment through the inference of the third dimension. But without an overwhelming similarity of pattern, such discrepancies cannot be utilized, as the inference of a single common source does not take place.

The above contrasts the matching of congruent patterns with the condition under which patterns are incompatible. We can draw a similar conclusion by comparing the presence of congruent patterns with the absence of any pattern. Consider the use of the stereoscope in connection with a separate reduction screen for each eye, so that a punctiform view of each image is obtained. Under these conditions, no convergence takes place, even though each eye be viewing positions that would be fused if the total patterns were to be seen. Similarly, triangulation upon one of several distal light sources of heterogeneous distance and location would be impossible in a system consisting of two mechanical eyes each made up of a single photocell. Under such conditions, triangulation would be unusable just because of the unresolvable ambiguity as to whether both eyes were looking at the same source. While pattern identity can be misleading, it seems in this setting to be a minimum essential. The multiple-celledness of the retina becomes an essential requirement. No doubt it is true that the greater the degree of pattern similarity the more certain the fusion and the more inappropriate angles of optical convergence that it will overcome. From the point of view of inductive theory, the more elaborate the pattern, the more statistically unlikely a repetition of it through independent chance events becomes, and hence the more implausible the rival hypothesis of twoness becomes, in competition with the hypothesis of oneness.

Monocular processes of distal inference contain upon examination the same dependence upon pattern, and through the utilization of memory, the assumption that repetitions of pattern in time come from a common source. In Wertheimer's phi phenomenon of perceived movement, where two separate events are presented (under certain conditions of spatial and temporal proximity and sequence), the visual system shows bias toward a single-object interpretation so great that the hypothesis of one object in motion becomes more plausible than that of two discrete events. No doubt this effect is the stronger, and occurs over the wider spatial and temporal intervals, the more elaborate the shared pattern of the two stimuli. The recognition of visual events as similar to past ones, and hence the use of memory at all, is dependent upon pattern similarity, and is unavailable to homogeneous fragments. Similarly for patterns extended in time. (Russell calls these "event structures" as distinct from the spatial patterns or "material structures," 1948, p. 464.) Auditory recognition and memory are obviously dependent upon this. In animal brains at least, it seems probable that memory access or memory search is only possible on the basis of some pattern-matching resonance process (Pringle, 1951). In mechanical brains, all outcome-controlled processes including memory search are based upon a matching process, in the older machines called "comparing relays." The detail of the pattern involved depends upon the magnitude of the alternative set within which equivocality could take place.

"Image" as a Pattern of Object, Guiding Distal Response

So far our focus has been on the perceptual side of distality, on human perceptual performance where verbal response effectively makes the response unproblematic. But in fact, distal responses too show imperfect mediation via equivocal proximal responses. The learned memories or instinctive guides that provide the comparison base against which motor feedback is checked must be quite multidimensional. For this multidimensional thermostat setting, for this "input reference set" as a servosystem engineer might put it, for this blueprint of desired outcomes, or criteria aganist which to check the sensory inputs representing the status quo, the use of the term *template* seems appropriate (for example, Campbell, 1963, pp. 143–144).

Without in any way suggesting how or in what form such a central nervous system record might be carried, it nonetheless seems logically required that there be stored templates or maps for each distal, object-consistent segment of behavior. A further problem enters here. In the servomechanism model in its simplest form, the template operates in terms of feedback *after* response. But such a model does not seem to be complicated enough for the typical guided distal response. For these there seem to be a perceptual search and a perceptual checking of perceptual objects against a template in terms of the discrepancy from which motor responses are guided. For organisms with vision one needs either one template against which both vision and motor feedback are compared, or else separate templates somehow coordinated. The checking of a perceptual pattern against the template (which very obviously must take place even in instinctive behavior, as in the insect recognizing a mate, or the baby chick pecking at grains of wheat) brings us closer to concepts of the storage of behavioral dispositions in terms of *images*. Note Uexküll's (1934) use of the concept of "search image," Tolman's (1948) "cognitive map," and Holst's and Mittelstaedt's "efference copy."(For example, Holst, 1954; Mittelstaedt, 1962; Lorenz, 1959.) Mowrer (1960), and Miller, Galanter, and Pribram (1960) have also been influenced by cybernetic considerations to reintroduce the term *image*. The traditional concept of *schema* as used by Head (1920), Bartlett (1932), and Piaget (for example, Flavell, 1963) has a similar function.

Trial-and-Error of Pattern Matching

In the present writer's previous contributions to a potential "psychology of knowledges processes" or "psychological epistemology," two themes have dominated. One is a perceptual theme (Campbell, 1958; 1959, pp. 172–179; 1964; Campbell & Fiske, 1959) and the other is of a trial-and-error nature

(Campbell, 1956; 1959, pp. 163–172; 1960b). Since many find these two themes incompatible, and since the present paper is in the perceptual vein, it seems well to emphasize that I do not at all see the points of view in disagreement, and do indeed regard both as essential. Distal knowing when involving discovery of new distal objects, or the recognition of old ones from among a set, is a trial-and-error of pattern matchings. The trial-and-error component is, of course, missing in settings in which—through other sources of knowledge—no selection is required. It is often overlooked when actually present due to the utilization of human links in a communication system, whose rapid and subtle processes are assumed but not specified.

Let us consider a possible map-guided postal missile, designed to home on a city and airport via radar pictures. Let us conceive of the system as designed to operate under conditions of ambiguity as to city, distance, and approach angle. For such a system to operate mechanically, there would have to be a trial-and-error of matchings of the current scope reading with a stored criterion map. This would have to include a mechanism for expanding and contracting the current radar picture, shifting it horizontally and vertically, tilting and rotating it, and so forth, comparing it with the criterion under all conditions. Some summation of discrepancy process would be involved, as through the use of a "negative" image of the criterion projected upon the "positive" of current reading, so that when the net reached a low, some guidance-locking impulse was transmitted. While the practical details are overwhelming, and might require a mechanism too large to transport, the general system is possible. In considering such a system, the blind surveying of possibilities (whether systematically, as in a radar beam, or randomly) is an essential process only reduced insofar as already achieved knowledge, and/or reduction of potential equivocalities, is built in.

Probably for our postal missiles such a spatial or "visual" homing system is too expensive and too uncertain. The city maps, for example, might not be distinctive enough. So the engineer would probably be tempted to employ homing on a radio beam. (The problem of contraction of pattern magnitudes with greater distance is avoided, inasmuch as the temporal "spacings" do not expand with distance from source as do the spatial ones.) If we now envisage a purely mechanical system that can "recognize" its own appropriate homing beam from among the inappropriate ones designating different systems, we see that again a pattern matching, and a trial-and-error of pattern matching is involved. Being no electrical engineer, I shall not attempt to indicate an efficient system but merely sketch out a crudely plausible one that makes explicit the problems involved. For a pattern-comparator, let us again use a subtractive procedure of combining energies, with a selector system picking out minimum energies. (Lorenz, 1959, citing Holst, has pointed to the ubiquity of these image-cancellation processes in perceptual phenomena.) Or a resonator generating a derived energy when two inputs maximally matched could be used. The process would be a "selective retention" one in that all inputs picked up would be tried out, only those which happened to resonate being "selected." It would save a lot of hardware if the total system were master-clocked so that the correct homing sender and the criterion model contained within the missile were always in perfect synchrony once the missile came in range. However, "auditory" recognition systems are not usually so restricted. To remove this restriction, a trial-and-error of lags of the criterion pattern is required, such as might be achieved by having multiple resonator units each with a recording of the criterion at a different time of onset. The received input would be blindly matched against all of these, resonance magnitude or over-all pattern similarity measures selecting the optimal one.

In creative knowledge processes involving exploring new areas of knowledge, there is not only a try and fit of extant patterns against some input, but there is also a trial-and-error of novel patterns, novel gestalten, or recenterings (Campbell, 1960b, pp. 389–390).

Pattern Matching in Astronomy

Astronomy, our oldest successful science, deals with the most remote and unknowable of objects. It is, therefore, an appropriate place from which to select samples of the utilizations of pattern matching in science.

Consider first the remarkable assurance with which man assumes that he can identify "the same" star upon successive nights, even with the unaided eye. This is the more remarkable (and the more presumptive) because the stars for such instrumentation are so homogeneous a set of objects as to be mutually indistinguishable. It is further remarkable because a given star is continually changing its location, and because the average star is out of range of observation some three-fourths of the time (that is, when below the horizon, when in ascendance during the daytime, and when eclipsed by clouds). It is the rigid pattern of the so-called "fixed" stars that makes this possible, or which makes this the preferred interpretation. If indeed the stars were transient events, destroyed each dawn and constituted afresh each evening, then the recurrence across the observed ages of "the same" pattern would be a set of coincidences beyond our credulity. If there were indeed permanent stars, but these moved on a time and space scale corresponding to an enlarged Brownian movement, so that each evening a novel pattern were apparent, then astronomy would not have been the first science to emerge, nor would the confident reidentification of "the same" star on successive nights have taken place. If all the visible "stars" had been planets of our sun (a system that we now understand as simpler and more orderly than that of the fixed stars), the manifest pattern would have been so much less obvious and compelling as to have postponed the hypothesis of reidentifiable sameness for many centuries. It was the grid of the "fixed" stars that facilitated the observation of the patterned meanderings of the "wandering" stars, and enabled their reification as stable particulate substantial entities.

Astronomy's entities at this stage were diagnosed almost entirely (except for the sun and the moon) by external pattern. Each star was unidentifiable in isolation. The frame of the other stars, each in itself unidentifiable, provided the identification through its fixed pattern. In the ecology of our normal vertebrate development, most external entities are diagnosed by recurrence of internal pattern. Today with telescopes, we can so identify nearby planets, and potentially with refined spectroscopes extended into the radio frequencies, we may find internal patterns marked enough to justify the hypothesis of stable thing for some of the fixed stars without the crutch of external pattern. The external pattern of the fixed stars is so strong and redundant that minor discrepancies can provide 3-D gains from successive comparisons, and through such triangulations the distances of stars and the movements of the sun itself have been inferred.

The first achievement of radar reflection from Venus (Price, et al., 1959) provides another illustration. It provides a good example because the knowledge process utilized an extremely noisy and fallible channel, and yet was so clear-cut in outcome as to make possible a correction of the prior computations of the distance of the target. Note in ordinary radar (and in television) an interchangeable transition between temporal pattern and spatial pattern, the latter being made possible by the lag in the decay of the phosphorescence on the picture tube. For ordinary uses of radar, the output beam need not be temporally patterned, but can be a constant emission in amplitude and frequency. Its figure-ground patterning comes through the contrasting reflection from object and nonobject as the antenna sweeps and resweeps the area. (A single punctiform and unmoving antenna's reception would be uninterpretable, due to the numerous extraneous sources of radio waves.) For the first radar reflection from Venus, this spatial patterning was not used, as not enough contrast to be visible would have resulted, the small angular size of the target and the small energy reflection being parts of the problem. Instead, a temporal pattern was imposed upon the emitting wave. The reception of a radio telescope antenna focused in the direction of Venus was then searched for a matching pattern. The reflected signal was so weak relative to the radio frequency noise of the background that such pattern matching could only be ascertained by a cross-correlation of broadcast and reception which used two-millisecond pulses, present or absent on a fixed quasi random pattern for four and one-half minutes of transmission. When the cross-correlation was computed with a lag appropriate to the speed of light for the astronomically computed distance, the correlation was not above chance levels. A trial-and-error survey of shorter and longer lags located the optimal lag at a point some 5.0 milliseconds less than expected. At this lag a highly significant cross-correlation repeatedly appeared, indicating a small but significant error in the previous computation of distance. This achievement is a most impressive evidence of the power of pattern matching in identifying recurrences of "the same" thing even when the initial instructions as to "where to look" were in error.

Further Notes on the Ubiquity of Pattern Matching

The above are, of course, but a small fraction of the relevant illustrations that might be drawn of this most ubiquitous ingredient in cognitive achievements. And the present paper is, of course, only one of many appeals for the recognition of its centrality. Acknowledgment should again be made of the important paper by Lorenz (1959) on this topic. Polya (1954), Oppenheimer (1956), and Jones (1957), among others, have called attention to the important role of analogy in scientific thought. Jones has provided a bibliography on the theory of the use of models and analogues and discussions of the concept of similarity under such conditions. The concentration of efforts on pattern recognition in the computer simulation of cognitive process is further testimony to the widespread recognition of the problem (for example, McCulloch and Pitts, 1947; Clark and Farley, 1955; Dineen, 1955; Selfridge, 1955; Unger, 1959; Rosenblatt, 1960; Uhr, 1963).

The Pattern Matching of Scientific Theory and Data: Implications for Operational Definitions and Verification of Theory

Science is the most distal form of knowing. Scientific theories are distal achievements. The processes and entities posited by science (for example, radio stars, neutrinos, atoms, molecules, genes, cells, and so forth) are all very distal objects very mediately known via processes involving highly presumptive pattern matchings at many stages. Such is a summary of the preceding pages. The present section extends this by identifying the over-all relationship between a formal scientific theory and the relevant accumulations of empirical data as one of pattern matching. The resulting interpretation is felt to be compatible with, and to summarize something common among those several modern philosophies of science that have attempted to retain the "posit" and "put-up-or-shut-up" hard-headedness of pragmatism and logical positivism, without making the error of exhaustive-definitional-operationism (Campbell, 1960a). We will but sample from these philosophies, and will not argue here their equivalence upon any grounds other than this one.

It has long been a common property among logical positivisms to describe scientific theory as an internally consistent formal logic (analytically valid) which becomes empirical (gains synthetic truth) when various terms are interpreted in a data language. A variant of this general model is accepted here. The formal theory becomes one "pattern," and against this pattern the various bodies of data are matched, in some overall or total way. These empirical observations provide the other pattern, but somewhat asymmetrically. The data are not required to have an analytical coherence among themselves, and indeed cannot really be assembled as a total except upon the skeleton of theory. In addition, the imperfection or error of the process is ascribed to the data pattern, for any theory-data set regarded currently as "true," and except for quantum theory. Theories "known" to be in need of revision, or accepted only as convenient oversimplifications are conceptually allowed to share the residual matching error. It is as though in the radar reflection from Venus we regarded the known or intended output as the "true" pattern or theory, and the noisy reception as the data. (The asymmetrical conceptual allocation of error between experimental and dependent variables is, however, another problem, receiving explicit treatment in modern statistics.)

This variant of the "interpreted logic" version of logical positivism is in disagreement primarily with those applied variants that have taken an extreme position on "operational definitions." For the "exhaustive-definitional-operationist" if we take his "operational definitions" as defining terms in his formal theory, no error is allowed in the interpretation of theory by data. For him, the admitted imperfection of all scientific theory is located in the strength of the theoretical laws stated, that is, within the kind of relationships which the theory posits. In such a case, it seems doubtful if a formal, analytically consistent theory is possibly utilizing such terms.

While the categorization may seem to fit, Bergmann (1957) should not be identified as an "exhaustive-definitional-operationalist" in any simple manner, for note his criticisms of a similarly extreme operationism (1954) and his condoning of the reification of concepts in physics (1943). Nor should Bridgman (1927), in spite of his temptingly clear expression of this point of view in this quote: "If we have more than one set of operations we have more than one concept, and strictly there should be a separate name to correspond to each different set of operations." (p. 10.) The exposition of this paper will not be hindered by regarding the "exhaustive-definitional-operationalist" as a straw man or ideal type useful in clarifying the issues but not to be identified with the position of any actual philosopher of science. While some have indirectly advocated it when arguing against the errors of other positions, the obvious weaknesses of the position as here presented have probably kept any from direct advocacy.

In contrast to definitional operationism, in the position here advocated the error in matching theory to data is allocated to the imperfect representation of the theoretical concepts by the data series. Where the measurements used by a science have a negligible proportion of error, as in macrophysics and astronomy, the difference in the points of view may be unnoticeable. In any case, focusing the difference upon a decision in the allocation of error makes it obvious that there is no analytically correct choice between the two points of view. As a description of how science has operated, I prefer the present variant, at least as the model of those segments of the physical and biological sciences that have achieved useful formal theory.

Among the logical empiricists, Feigl's critical-realistic version (for example, 1950) is compatible with that here advocated. Hempel (1952, pp. 29–50) states the "interpreted logic" position clearly, and has attempted to preserve the values of operationism without accepting a construct-defining version of it. He calls for operational *interpretations* of scientific terms, allowing these to be partial interpretations. His version of the operationist requirement becomes the requirement that theory be testable, that is, interpretable so that at many points its matching with data be ascertainable. Were he to have explicitly emphasized the inherent mediateness and imperfection of all measurement processes, or to have explicitly recognized the interpretations of theory-terms as fallible, or to have explicitly located the errorfulness on the data side of the matching, his position would be indistinguishable from the one here advocated. Margenau (1950) while not a member of the logical positivist camp has a point of view regarding the relationship between theory and data that is equivalent on these points. So also are judged to be the positions of Popper (1935; 1959), Quine (1953), Hanson (1958), and Kuhn (1962), some aspects of which will be discussed in more detail below.

Note particularly that there are *two* patterns to be compared—that of theory and that of data, even though in an iterative fashion each has developed in contact with the other. This is in disagreement with those views of science in which theory is viewed simply as a summary of data, that is, as the simple product of inductive generalization. Popper (1959) has effectively discredited such a point of view. Hanson (1958) has emphasized this duality through his stress upon the perceptual aspects of relating theory to data, that is, how differences in theory lead scientists to perceive the world differently, how corrections of outmoded theories must await the availability of an alternative theoretical structure. While there is a subjectivist flavor to much of Hanson's protest, descriptively his portrait of science is a pattern matching one. His discussion of Kepler's struggles to match theory and data is of particular value, as also are his detailed citations on the shifts in status of specific scientific constructs from empirical law to analytic tautology. The replacement of an old and unsatisfactory theory by a new one has in many instances the characteristic of a trial-and-error process in which total theoretical systems are tried out, being accepted or rejected as a whole. In practice, no theory that has been judged useful in the past of a science is ever rejected simply upon the basis of its inadequacy of fit to data. Instead, it is only rejected when there is an alternative that fits better to replace it. And the fit of the new theory is not perfect, only better. Kuhn (1962) presents similar episodes in the history of science.

Of course, even for theory in physics, the above description has exaggerated the analytic (logical, mathematical) internal consistency of the theory. As Quine (1953) has pointed out, analytic systems contain hidden empirical assumptions. Where the logical or mathematical form of the theory is not complete, considerable revision of specific terms of a theory is possible without necessitating an over-all accept-reject decision. What is important is the recognition of the two-part, two-patterned nature of the process, and the acceptance or rejection of the theory or model upon the basis of some over-all criterion of fit. This is particularly clear in total-theory shifts in science (Kuhn, 1962). The model of piecemeal theory revision in its extreme form makes the "theory" no theory at all, but simply a restatement of the data in its full complexity. Theory must instead be a separable pattern from data, with the fit to data problematic, otherwise testability, predictive power, and parsimony all are lost.

Fringe Imperfection

It is fundamental to the general epistemology here argued that all knowledge is indirect, that all proximal stimulation is equivocal or fallible as a basis for inferring distal objects. This leads to the rejection of those epistemologies based upon any incorrigible sense data or other phenomenal givens, and a parallel rejection of a purely "proximal" science in which scientific constructs be defined in terms of (exhaustively known through) specific meter readings. Instead, all specific meters are regarded as fallible, corrigible instruments. On theoretical grounds alone, any specific meter can be seen to involve many physical laws other than the construct-relevant one. Keeping these other laws inactive through specific compensations (as in the control of inertial forces in a galvanometer) or through constant conditions is never achieved to perfection. Wilson (1952) in instance after instance provides specific illustrations of such limitations. Yet this obvious fact is apt to be negated implicitly in a *definitional* operationism. This negation is induced by the need to make explicit the essential relationship of scientific theory to experimental data, overdetermined by a psychic need for certainty. The pattern matching model for the fit of theory to data provides an explanation of that essential relationship which nonetheless avoids the assumption of certainty for any of the specific data. The imperfection of fit is conceptualized so that any specific meter reading can be regarded as in error, as judged by the pattern matching that minimizes error in general.

Let us consider a case in which we graph together a set of empirical points and a theoretically derived curve and achieve a good correspondence. Some of the points lie above the line, others below, but in general they fit well, and some lie "exactly" on the line. If there is no systematic deviation, we interpret the point by point deviations where they occur as error, and would expect such error to occur on some of the "perfectly fitting" points were the experiment to be replicated. While an over-all fit has been required, no single observation point has been taken as an infallible operational *definition* of a theoretical value—all rather are partial and fallible operational representations. Were each taken as "operational definitions," the "theory" would have to be multiple parametered enough to fit each point exactly—and if selected upon that basis one would need a new "theory" for each new set of data.

In the pattern matching of theory to data we reduce the fringe of error as much as possible, we center theory in the data points so that the fringe occurs without systematic deviation from theory, and we distribute the fringe of error over all of the observational points, potentially. We may end up saying that one observation was "right on," and that another was probably in error. A priori, however, any of the points could be wrong. It is through such a process that physicists can throw away "wild observations," an impossibility for a rigid operationist (Kruskal, 1960; Campbell, 1964). It is through such a process that physics has been able to refine its measuring instruments, a paradoxical event from the standpoint of exhaustive-definitional-operationism. Physics has at any period assumed that the great bulk of its "knowledge" was correct. From this floating platform of over-all pattern, it has then challenged and reexamined a particular measurement process. As Neurath said "We are like sailors who must rebuild their ship on the open sea" (1932). The "anchoring" of theory to data has not at all been achieved through a *perfect* correspondence at any particular point, but rather through a pattern matching of the two in some over-all way. The matching of the noisy radar reception from Venus with the ideal transmission pattern shows how such a pattern matching process as cross-correlation can powerfully recognize pattern while still distributing the large fringe of error over every data point. Actual statistics for estimating degree of pattern matching are, of course, not generally available, and the estimate of the human eye from graphed results is still the commonest criterion. The correlation coefficient sets a good example, however, by its equitable allocation of error.

Although Quine doubts the value of the traditional analytic-synthetic distinction which it has been convenient to employ here, he states a perspective upon the relation of theory to data quite compatible with that presented here on a number of points, but in particular, in the handling of fringe imperfection:

Taken collectively, science has its double dependence upon language and experience; but this duality is not significantly traceable into statements of science taken one by one. The idea of defining a symbol in use was an advance over the impossible term-by-term empiricism of Locke and Hume. The statement, rather than the term, came with Frege to be recognized as the unit accountable to an empiricist critique. But what I am now urging is that even in taking the statement as a unit we have drawn our grid too finely. The unit of empirical significance is the whole of science.

The totality of our so-called knowledge or beliefs, from the most casual matters of geography and history to the profoundest laws of atomic physics or even of pure mathematics and logic, is a man-made fabric which impinges on experience only along the edges. ... A conflict with experience at the periphery occasions readjustments in the interior of the field. ... But the total field is so undetermined by its boundary conditions, experience, that there is much latitude of choice as to what statements to re-evaluate in the light of any single contrary experience. ... A recalcitrant experience can ... be accommodated by any of various alternative re-evaluations in various alternative quarters of the total system, ... but ... our natural tendency [is] to disturb the total system as little as possible. ... Physical objects are conceptually imported into the situation as convenient intermediaries—not by definition in terms of experience, but simply as irreducible posits. ... Science is a continuation of common sense, and it continues the commonsense expedient of swelling ontology to simplify theory. (Reprinted by permission of the publishers from Willard Van Orman Quine from *A logical point of view*. Cambridge, Mass.: Harvard University Press, Copyright 1953, 1961, by the President and Fellows of Harvard College. Pp. 42–45.)

Confirmation and Falsification of Theory

In the positivists' early effort to root out pseudo problems and metaphysics, they produced a testability criterion of meaning, so stated that confirmability of a proposition through the agreement of theory and data become its typical form. But since theories posit general laws whose verification can only spottily be sampled, and also because of the ambiguity introduced through error in data collection processes, this criterion has been challenged, particularly by Popper (1935; 1959). A strict and rigid form of it shares many of the problems of a definitional operationism, and we may regard it as an unsatisfactory statement of how experimental outcomes strengthen our belief in theory.

Popper has advocated instead a falsifiability criterion, in which a theory becomes scientifically meaningful if it is capable of being falsified by empirical data, and in which a theory becomes the better established the more experimental opportunities for falsification that it has survived and the more exacting these probes. Our established scientific theories at any time are thus those that have been repeatedly exposed to falsification, and have so far escaped being falsified. Because of its evolutionary and selective retention analogies, this criterion has appealed greatly to the present writer. As Popper explicitly recognizes (for example, 1959, pp. 80–81), falsifiability cannot be held too strictly, as every observation refutes theory if carried out to enough decimal points. Instead, it is a selective retention of theories in competition with other theories, with the magnitude of the tolerable fringe of imperfection dependent upon the sharpness of that competition.

Note that in the pattern-matching model, the theoretical pattern is complete and continuous (with the exception of quantum theory), but the data series may be spotty and incomplete. Kepler actually had data on only a few segments of the path of Mars. If the data confirm the pattern insofar as tested, the theoretical pattern as a whole is made more tenable, including the nontested segments of the pattern. The fact that theories go beyond the as-yet-observed would not require the rejection of a confirmation criterion in a pattern-matching model, as it would in a more traditionally inductive empiricism. Further, the selective-survival of theories is now perceived to be a selection taking place *in competition with other extant theories*. As Popper (1959), Hanson (1958), and Kuhn (1962) all make clear, it is the absence of plausible rival hypotheses that establishes one theory as "correct." In cases where there are rival theories, it is the relative over-all goodness of fit that leads one to be preferred to another, not the absolute degree of fit of the better.

Summary

Ordinary and scientific knowledge of the external world is an analytically unjustified, highly presumptuous, and fallible process. As Egon Brunswik has pointed out, the strategy of distal knowing, that is, the positing of external objects mediately known, is characteristic of knowledge processes at all higher levels. In distal knowing, proximal particulars are equivocal and intersubstitutable, raising the problem of how recognition, reidentification, and confirmation are achieved. The thesis of this paper is that in all distal knowing, a pattern-matching process is involved. This thesis is sampled at various levels including visual perception and the diagnosis of specific entities in science. As a model for the fit between scientific theory and data, pattern matching makes data relevant to the acceptance or rejection of theories without committing the error of a definitional operationism. In this, it points to an emerging consensus among philosophers of science, a common denominator among such varied philosophers as Feigl, Hempel, Margenau, Popper, Quine, Hanson, and Kuhn.

Note

1. Supported in part by U.S. Office of Education Project C-998, Contract 3-20-001, under provisions of Title VII of the National Defense Education Act.

4

The Significance of Naturalized Epistemology

Barry Stroud

Naturalized epistemology is the scientific study of perception, learning, thought, language-acquisition, and the transmission and historical development of human knowledge—everything we can find out scientifically about how we come to know what we know. In asking about the *significance* of those investigations I do not mean to be asking the absurd question whether the deliverances of natural science on such matters are true, or correct, or illuminating, or important. I mean to ask: true or correct *as what?* in what specific *ways* illuminating? important *for what?*

I want to ask, in particular, about the relation between the project of naturalized epistemology as Quine conceives it and the more traditional philosophical examination of knowledge it is meant to supplant. The "old" epistemology asked how any of us knows anything at all about the world around us, and it recognized that most of what we know is based somehow on the senses. The problem was given its special philosophical character by certain facts about sense-perception, familiar from antiquity and employed to dramatic effect in Descartes's *First Meditation* and elsewhere, which seem to imply at least the possibility of the world's being quite different in general from the way it is perceived to be. The philosophical problem was then to explain how anyone can know that such a possibility does not obtain, and thereby know what the world is really like, not just the way it is perceived to be. Only then would the possibility of human knowledge have been explained.

Quine says many things about his epistemological program that suggest that it is a fairly direct response to this familiar question. He recommends an investigation into the source of "our general knowledge of the ways of

Reprinted from *Midwest Studies in Philosophy*, vol. VI (Minneapolis: University of Minnesota Press, 1981), pp. 455–471, by permission of the publisher. Copyright © 1981, the University of Minnesota.

physical objects,"[1] and he sees the problem as arising from the undeniable fact that "physical things generally, however remote, become known to us only through the effects which they help to induce at our sensory surfaces."[2] Since "we know external things only mediately through our senses,"[3] the problem is: "given only the evidence of our senses, how do we arrive at our theory of the world?"[4]

Quine's way of raising this question differs from that of the traditional epistemologists in that they tried to isolate a domain of pure sensory data evidentially or epistemically prior to the knowledge of nature that is to be explained, whereas for Quine there is no "implicit sub-basement of conceptualization, or language"[5] in which a basic stream of sense-experience could be grasped. That does not imply that the traditional problem of "bridging a gap between sense data and bodies" was a mere pseudo-problem. For Quine it was "real but wrongly viewed."[6] Even without the mistaken belief in pure data of awareness there remain the same good reasons to inquire into the "sensory or stimulatory background" of our knowledge of the world, "namely, to see how evidence relates to theory, and in what way one's theory of nature transcends any available evidence."[7]

Quine's conception of human knowledge and therefore of his epistemological project shares with earlier philosophers the idea of human knowledge as a combination of two quite general, but distinguishable, factors—the contribution of the world and the contribution of the knowing or perceiving subject. Just as we can distinguish the proteins from the carbohydrates in our material intake while we subsist on an unanalyzed combination of both of them, so:

we can investigate the world, and man as part of it, and thus find out what cues he could have of what goes on around him. Subtracting his cues from his world view, we get man's net contribution as the difference. This difference marks the extent of man's conceptual sovereignty—the domain within which he can revise theory while saving the data.[8]

In carrying out this subtraction we would inevitably come to appreciate the very wide scope of man's "conceptual sovereignty" and thereby discover the extent to which all of science itself is man's "free creation" and is thus to that extent a "put-up job."[9] The subjective contribution of perceiving and knowing subjects will inevitably appear as the overwhelmingly dominant influence on the present state of our general knowledge of the world, given this picture. That is the key to Quine's theory of knowledge.

Although many of the physiological and psychological details are still unknown, Quine thinks we already have the outlines of an answer to the general problem of our knowledge of the world. Considered relative to the irritations at our sensory surfaces, the physical objects we believe in are "posits"; statements of their existence are "far in excess of any available data," past, present, and future.[10] From such "meager traces" as "two dimensional optical projections and various impacts of airwaves on the eardrums and some gaseous reactions in the nasal passages and a few kindred odds and ends,"[11] we somehow arrive at the complex totality of our views about the world.

Our belief in physical objects is therefore a "hypothesis" which we arrive at by the "so-called scientific method."[12] Positing or acknowledging the existence of physical objects differs from the scientist's deliberate and explicit positing of molecules or other theoretical entities only in being "archaic," "unconscious," and "shrouded in prehistory."[13] In each case the point of the hypothesis is the same—to help provide a simpler total "theory" while remaining compatible with as much of the data as possible. And according to Quine the "hypothesis" of physical objects has been eminently successful in that respect. It "has proved more efficacious than other myths as a device for working a manageable structure into the flux of experience";[14] it gives us "the smoothest and most adequate overall account of the world."[15] Each of us acquires that fruitful "hypothesis" when we learn the language of our community. We thereby gradually become masters of the mechanisms of objective reference which enable us to talk of a world of enduring physical objects, and our sensory impacts then dispose us to believe and assert things about an objective physical world. In that way we come to know of physical objects.

This view of the physical world as "hypothetical" or merely "posited" relative to the data of the senses would seem less than satisfactory if it were considered as an answer to the traditional epistemological question raised in, say, Descartes's *First Meditation*. For one thing, scientists explicitly engaged in theory construction do not actually consider and then reasonably reject the "hypothesis," for example, that they are dreaming, or are victims of a mass hallucination or of an evil demon, as the traditional problem requires. And if we ordinary non-scientific mortals arrive at our view of the world by the "scientific method, however amorphous,"[16] then we do not do so by reasonably eliminating such "hypotheses" either. We normally do not even consider, let alone justifiably rule out, those bizarre possibilities. Accordingly, Quine in his positive account does not try to show how we rule out the possibility that the world is completely different in general from the way our sensory impacts and our internal makeup lead us to think of it. But it cannot be that we can afford to ignore this question simply because we know at the outset that that bizarre general "hypothesis" is false or is less likely to be true than the physical object "theory." Whether and how the physical object "hypothesis" *is* better confirmed or known is precisely what is in question when the traditional philosophical problem is raised, so the alleged superiority of the physical object "theory" cannot be taken for granted in demonstrating its superiority. Therefore, there seem to be good reasons for concluding that Quine's naturalistic epistemology does not amount to an answer to the traditional problem of our knowledge of the external world.

Quine would seem to agree with this verdict. On the "doctrinal" issue of "justifying our knowledge of truths of nature in sensory terms," [17] he finds that we have not progressed beyond the plight Hume left us in. "The Humean predicament is the human predicament," [18] he says, enigmatically. If he is referring to the predicament of never being able adequately to justify our knowledge of the physical world on sensory grounds, the predicament that Hume thought we are all in, then presumably no naturalized epistemology, or any other kind of epistemology, could show that we are not in that predicament and that we really can give a positive answer to the traditional philosophical question about our knowledge of the world.

Naturalized epistemology is the empirical, scientific study of human knowledge, and in his "Epistemology Naturalized" Quine concedes an illegitimate circularity in any naturalistic attempt to "validate" or "substantiate" our knowledge of the world.

If the epistemologist's goal is validation of the grounds of empirical science, he defeats his purpose by using psychology or other empirical science in the validation.[19]

However, he continues:

such scruples against circularity have little point once we have stopped dreaming of deducing science from observations. If we are out simply to understand the link between observation and science, we are well advised to use any available information, including that provided by the very science whose links with observation we are seeking to understand.[20]

The illegitimate circularity of relying on one's knowledge of nature in an attempt to "validate" that very knowledge on sensory grounds is obviously no objection to naturalistic investigations in which no such project of "validation" is in question. Naturalized epistemology is to be seen as itself part of psychology and hence part of the very science of nature the sources of which it seeks to understand, but there is nothing viciously, or even unpleasantly, circular about that. So it need not be seen as a shortcoming of Quine's theory, or of any scientific study of how we come to know what we do, that it fails to answer the traditional philosophical question of how we can "validate" all our knowledge of the world and thereby know that the world matches up with the way it is perceived to be.

On the other hand, Quine in *The Roots of Reference* seems to regard something at least very like the traditional problem of "validation" as a real problem and as answerable by a naturalized epistemology. The earlier epistemologists's refusal to rely on psychology and the rest of natural science out of fear of circularity, he says, "was a case of needless logical timidity, even granted the project of substantiating our knowledge of the external world."[21] The challenge to science which the epistemologist must meet is one that arises from within science itself, and on the basis of already acknowledged scientific facts.

Science tells us that our only source of information about the external world is through the impact of light rays and molecules upon our sensory surfaces. Stimulated in these ways, we somehow evolve an elaborate and useful science. How do we do this, and why does the resulting science work so well? These are genuine questions, and no feigning of doubt is needed to appreciate them. They are scientific questions about a species of primates, and they are open to investigation in natural science, the very science whose acquisition is being investigated.[22]

The old epistemologist missed the fact that the skeptical challenge arises from within science itself, and so, Quine thinks, he failed to recognize the strength of his own position.[23] He can rely on any knowledge currently available to him to answer the scientific questions that constitute the challenge to science he is trying to meet. That is the task for the newly "liberated" epistemologist, but for Quine it appears that the new epistemology has not simply changed the subject or left the traditional problem and its apparently inevitable skeptical solution intact. It is rather "an enlightened persistence in the original epistemological problem."[24] If that is so and if the original problem was that of justifying or "validating" our beliefs about the world, it would seem that naturalized epistemology can or should answer the question of "validation." But Quine seems elsewhere to have conceded that it cannot do that.

This difficulty in interpreting the results of naturalized epistemology is perhaps not surprising once we become explicitly aware of the difficulty of gaining a firm sense of what I have called the "significance" of statements or remarks that might seem on the face of them to be answers to the philosophical question about our knowledge but which often turn out not to be. The traditional philosopher asked whether there is an external world, and whether we can know that there is. G. E. Moore, for example, said, "There are external things," and he even thought he could prove their existence. He also asserted in the same way that he knows that external objects exist.[25] And all of us say things every day (e.g., "I know that your glasses are on the table in the next room") which seem to imply the truth of the things Moore asserted. But does 'I know that external objects exist,' as asserted by G. E. Moore, contradict 'No-one knows whether any external objects exist,' as asserted by the traditional philosopher as a result of his investigation of human knowledge?

There is some reason to think that the two assertions do not conflict, that the same form of words is being put to quite different uses in the two cases, and so what Moore and the rest of us say, even if true, or correct, or illuminating, or important, would not be straightforwardly decisive for the philosophical investigation of knowledge. Even if we understood perfectly what Moore and the rest of us say, we would not thereby understand its relation to the traditional epistemological question.

Carnap, Schlick, and other logical positivists would agree.[26] If G. E. Moore, or better still an empirical psychologist, says we know there are physical objects, and even goes on to explain how we know it, it does not follow that he is answering the question that the traditional epistemologist asked, or that he is giving an answer to it which is incompatible with philosophical skepticism. The traditional epistemological question of the reality of the external world and of our knowledge of it was for Carnap and Schlick and other verificationists a meaningless pseudoquestion; no answer to it was empirically confirmable or disconfirmable. That of course does not imply that the empirical psychologists's question about our knowledge of the physical world is meaningless or a pseudo-question. It is a perfectly meaningful question to be answered by empirical investigation. But precisely because it is answerable in that way, its answer could not also be the answer to the philosophical question, which according to the verificationist is meaningless. Although the two sorts of questions and answers might be expressed in the very same English words, they could not be the same questions and answers if verificationism is correct.

For Carnap we must distinguish a philosophical (pseudo-) employment of a form of words from an ordinary or scientific employment of the same words. Kant's claim that the statement 'Objects exist independently of us' is "empirically" true but "transcendentally" false would be another example of the same sort of distinction, not of course unrelated to Carnap's own later view.[27] And no doubt there are others ways of making some such distinction according to which Moore's assertions, and those of the rest of us in everyday and scientific life, can be perfectly legitimate and acceptable without settling one way or the other the traditional philosophical question about our knowledge.[28] The relation between the philosophical investigation of knowledge on the one hand, and everything that goes on in ordinary or scientific life that is presumably its subject matter, on the other, is more puzzling and obscure than has often been supposed. That relation, and the source of its obscurity, is what I am interested in.

How then are we to understand the results that Quine's naturalized epistemology would achieve? Not only does he assert, with Moore, that we do know that there is a world of physical objects; he also tries to explain, in general outline, how we know it. And he offers that explanation in terms of a conception of knowledge as a combination of two quite general, but distinguishable, factors, one objective and one subjective—the contribution of the world and the contribution of the knowing subject. In the rest of this paper I will try to show that (i) given Quine's conception of knowledge, his program of naturalized epistemology cannot answer what appears to be the most general question of how any knowledge at all of the world is possible. That in itself would be no reflection on naturalized epistemology if that question were ill-formed, incoherent, or in some other way illegitimate, but I will also try to show that (ii) there is in Quine no demonstration of the incoherence or illegitimacy of that question. Even if I were right on both counts, no aspersions would have been cast on the empirical study of human knowledge. I would have shown at most that so far there still appears to be a question (and what looks like the most basic question we can ask about our knowledge of the world) which Quine's epistemology does not and cannot answer. The issue is not that of some alleged "limits" of empirical science. I want only to throw light on the way in which the results of a naturalized epistemology would have to be understood if Quine's traditional bipartite conception of knowledge were correct.

Quine's naturalized epistemology is the empirical study of a species of primates or, in the particular case, of an individual human subject in interaction with his environment.

This human subject is accorded a certain experimentally controlled input— certain patterns of irradiation in certain frequencies, for instance—and in the fullness of time the subject delivers as output a description of the three-dimensional external world and its history.[29]

Given Quine's account of our knowledge of the world, in investigating "the relation between the meager input and the torrential output ... we are studying how the human subject of our study posits bodies and projects his physics from his data."[30]

There is nothing mysterious about such a study. We observe a human being and we observe his environment while also observing the "output" he produces in the form of utterances we understand to be about the world around him. Given what we know about his surroundings and the processes of perception, we can try to explain how the "torrential output" to which we have accesss is related to, or produced by, the "meager input" science tells us he is receiving. Knowing what we do about his perceptual mechanisms, we know that what he says about the world far transcends his "input" in the sense that its truth is underdetermined by all the sensory impacts he and everyone else will ever have.[31] In that sense his talk of physical objects is a "hypothesis" that goes beyond the "data." But calling his conception of the world a "posit" or "projection" relative to those sensory impacts is not to malign it or, as Quine says, to "patronize" it.[32] Normally we are in a position to see whether what the subject says about the world around him is in large part true, so there is no unreliability or falsity implied in calling his conception of the world a "posit" or "projection" relative to his "data." If we see that what he says is true, as we usually do, then we do not regard it as a *mere* "posit" or "projection" on his part. We see that his "output" is, generally speaking, accurate, and our only reason for saying he is "positing" or "projecting" at all is that what he says about bodies goes well beyond the meager physical stimulations science tells us he is receiving at his sensory surfaces. But we know it does not go beyond what is actually the case right before his eyes. And that is something we know because we can see what is right before his eyes.

The truth of the subject's beliefs is certainly important for the question whether he *knows* what the world around him is like. That becomes clear if we imagine a second and more unusual situation in which it is possible to find ourselves as experimenters or observers of the human scene. Suppose, as sometimes happens, that we see that there are no bodies at all before the subject, or none of the kinds he says and thinks there are. In that situation, knowing what we do, we would conclude that he does not know what the world around him is like, since his beliefs are false. He would be seen to be *merely* projecting or constructing a world that does not in fact exist as he thinks it does. We might be able to explain how that subject comes to say and believe what he does, but since he does not know what the world around him is like we would not thereby have explained how he knows. Not every explanation of a subject's beliefs is an explanation of knowledge.

But of course the truth of the subject's beliefs, although relevant to the question whether he knows, is not sufficient to settle it. If we explain how he comes to say and believe what he does and if we know that what he says and believes is true, we do not thereby explain how he knows. We must also at least explain how it happens that he is right in his assertions and beliefs. That is a question about how the subject's "projections" or "posits" turn out to be correct, and not just a question about how he comes to make them. Any satisfactory explanation of the origins of the subject's beliefs and of their correctness would show at least that, as we might put it, it is no accident that he gets things right. We would see that the world around him is generally speaking exactly the way he says it is and that its being that way is partly responsible for his saying and believing what he does about it. Many philosophers nowadays would hold that that is enough for knowledge: the subject believes that *p*, he is right, and it is no accident that he is right.[33] On that view an explanation of people's "projections" and of their correctness would explain how we know the science we do, and that is what Quine thinks a naturalized epistemology should explain.

The adequacy of any such "causal" account of knowledge is still questionable at best, and I do not want to go into it further. It is enough for my present purposes that we can and do observe sentient subjects and somehow come to understand how their knowledge is possible. In the two kinds of experimental situations I have imagined so far we can do so because we can observe the subject and his surroundings and investigate the relation between them. We have access to what Quine calls the "torrential output" of the subject and so can identify what he believes, and we can observe the world around him and so can see whether what he believes is true, quite independently of whether it is asserted or accepted as true by him. Only because that is so can we determine whether the subject has true beliefs (or perhaps knowledge) and then explain how that is possible.

So far I have imagined a case in which we recognize that the subject's beliefs are generally true, perhaps not accidentally so, and a case in which we recognize that his beliefs are false and so he does not know. But I now want to introduce another (and eventually a fourth) more unfavorable kind of position it is possible, but not customary, for us to find ourselves in in relation to another perceiving subject. Suppose we find we can observe the subject and can determine his impacts and his "output," but for some reason we are denied access to the surrounding world his remarks are supposed to be about. Perhaps we simply cannot see what is in his environment or perhaps some barrier permanently obstructs our view—in any case we have no information about the world around him. We are restricted to what is happening in the subject himself and to his "output." Obviously we could not then establish that the subject knows what the world around him is like, nor could we even tell whether what he says or believes is in general correct. We would not have access both to his "output" and to the world it is about, so we could not compare them or explain the relation between them. Given only what we would have access to in that situation, we could not go beyond saying, "He projects (or posits or believes or puts it forward) that . . ." We could not assert the much stronger conclusion, "He correctly believes (perhaps knows) that . . ." and so we could not see his view of the world as anything more than a *mere* "projection" or construction from certain stimulations. Even if we could somehow explain how he comes to construct and adopt the "projection" we know he has made (and it is not clear how we could do even that),[34] we would still not be in a position to know whether he is generally speaking right or whether he knows anything about the world around him.

Of course we are fortunately not in that kind of position very often—or not for very long. We move around the barrier and see what is happening on the other side. So the mere possibility of our observation's being restricted in that way poses no threat to the naturalistic study of knowing subjects. I raise it simply as a reminder that there is such a possibility and as an illustration of the truism that we could not explain how someone's knowledge, or even true belief, is possible unless we could observe that person's assertions on the one hand, and observe or otherwise know about the world they are about on the other, and thereby ascertain, independently of his asserting them, whether those assertions about the world are true. But although that is an uncontroversial truism, I think it presents a problem for Quine's conception of naturalized epistemology if it is taken as an answer to what looks like the most general question about human knowledge.

The problem arises because so far we have been considering *other* subjects—those whose interactions with the world we observe—but in order to explain how *anyone* ever comes to know anything about the physical world what is true of other people must somehow be seen to apply to ourselves. Quine tries to generalize it this way:

We are studying how the human subject of our study posits bodies and projects his physics from his data, and we appreciate that our position in the world is just like his. Our very epistemological enterprise, therefore, and the psychology wherein it is a component chapter, and the whole of natural science wherein psychology is a component book—all this is our own construction or projection from stimulations like those we were meting out to our epistemological subject.[35]

So we are to "appreciate that our position in the world is just like" that of the subject who "posits bodies and projects his physics from his data." To put it mildly, I think that is a very difficult thing to do. Or rather, I think we cannot see all our beliefs in the physical world as a "construction or projection from stimulations" in this way while remaining in a position to understand in general how knowledge, or even true belief, about the world is possible. When we try to "appreciate that our position in the world is just like" that of the "positing" or "projecting" subject we have been studying, what sort of view do we get of ourselves and our position? I think that at best[36] we must see ourselves as we see the subject in the third and therefore restricted kind of experimental situation. If we tried to think of *all* our own beliefs as a "construction or projection from stimulations," we would at most have access to what we know to be our assertions or beliefs about the world, but we would not in addition have independent access to the world they are about on the basis of which we could determine whether they are true. We could not compare our beliefs with the world they are about as we can in the normal experimental study of another person. Each of us would find himself with a set of beliefs and dispositions to assert things about the world, and we could of course undergo experiences that would strengthen or alter those dispositions, but those reinforced or newly acquired beliefs themselves would have to be seen in turn as at most some further "projections" from some new but still extremely meager "input." They could not be seen as a source of independent information about the world against which their own truth or the truth of the earlier beliefs could be checked. Therefore, if we follow Quine's instructions and try to see our own position as "just like" the position we can find another "positing" or "projecting" subject to be in, we will have to view ourselves as we view another subject when we can know nothing more than what is happening at his sensory surfaces and what he believes or is disposed to assert.

In the unusually restricted experimental situation we saw that we could not say more than that the subject's assertions and beliefs are *mere* "projections" on his part. We were there restricted to saying only "He posits or believes that . . ." with no way of going on to the stronger verdict "He correctly believes (perhaps knows) that . . ." So in that position we could never come to understand how the subject's knowledge, or even true belief, is possible. And if Quine's account implies that we must find *ourselves* as epistemologists in no better a position with respect to our own beliefs, we can never understand how our own true beliefs are possible either. On Quine's view we could not see ourselves as having knowledge or true beliefs as opposed to merely believing or "projecting" something about a physical world. We could at most hope to explain why we believe or "project" what we do, but since that is never enough in itself to explain how knowledge or true belief is possible we could never get the kind of understanding of our own position that we seek.

In fact a moment's reflection is enough to show that if we did manage to take the view of ourselves that Quine recommends, we would be even worse off than I have imagined so far, and worse off with respect to ourselves than we are even with respect to another subject in the restricted third sort of experimental situation. Strictly speaking, I could no longer see my so-called scientific belief that my beliefs about the physical world are "projections" from impacts at my sensory surfaces as itself anything more than something I believe or "posit" or "project." If I am precluded from seeing any of my beliefs about the physical world as knowledge, or as anything more than a *mere* "projection" on my part, then in particular I must take that attitude to my belief that I am suffering impacts at my sensory surfaces, and indeed to my belief that I have physical sensory surfaces at all. That too is one of my beliefs about a physical world. Even in the restricted situation in which I was denied access to the subject's environment beyond his skin I was at least granted access to his sensory surfaces and therefore to his meager "input." The question of the relation between that meager "input" and the subject's "torrential output" was not fully answerable in that restricted situation, but it arose there from at least some prior knowledge of the physical world on the part of the experimenter. But in my own case I do not even have that. What is unquestioned information about at least part of the physical world in asking the epistemological question about others must be seen in my own case as nothing more than yet another part of an elaborate "projection" about a physical world that I have somehow come to accept. In my own case I have nothing but "output" to work with. And that puts me in an even more restricted situation than the one imagined so far. In relation to another person it would be like standing alone in total darkness and silence and suddenly hearing from somewhere the words "There is a bear," or "Gavagai." Without access to the world I take those words to be about, there is simply no telling whether they express knowledge, or even truth, so there is no way of explaining in that case how knowledge or true belief is possible. If I saw all my own beliefs as "projections" or "posits" from meager "data," I would be in the same position with respect to all my own "output" as I would be to the "output" in that fourth and even more severely restricted situation. My own "output" would for me be no better than whistling in the dark.

Within this very restricted conception of my own position, in which I have access only to my own "output," I might even come to wonder whether and how some of the things I believe in are related to my asserting and believing what I do about a physical world. I believe in impacts at my sensory surfaces, and I believe that my sensory "input" is meager and my "scientific" "output" torrential, and this might strike me as puzzling and in need of explanation. In an effort to understand the relation between "input" and "output," I might appeal to other beliefs of mine, e.g., about psychology, language-learning, physiology—in fact, all of what I regard as natural science—if I believe it and I think it might help. But telling that complicated story would in turn be only a matter of expressing more and more of my elaborate "construction or projection" of a physical world. I could not regard it as an explanation of how my knowledge, or even true belief, about the physical world is possible, and I could not regard the alleged "explanation" itself as part of my *knowledge* as opposed to a story I fully believe and am perhaps unavoidably disposed to tell myself from time to time.

So I think that if we try to ask with complete generality how it is possible for any human being to know anything at all about the physical world, and if we adopt Quine's traditional two-part conception of knowledge as a combination of a subjective and an objective factor, we cannot get a satisfactory answer to that question. On that conception we would have to recognize that countless "theories" could be "projected" from the sensory impacts we receive, so if we do happen to accept one such "theory" it could not be because of any objectively discoverable superiority it enjoys over its competitors. Every competing "theory" is equally compatible with the same meager "data" that make up what Quine thinks of as the objective component, so our selection of one "theory" over others could arise only from some aspect or other of our subjective constitution. And that is precisely what the traditional epistemologist always saw as a threat to our knowledge of the external world. The possibility that our view of the world is nothing more than a *mere* "projection" is what had to be shown not to obtain in order to explain how our knowledge is possible. Unless that challenge has been met, or rejected, we will never understand how our knowledge is possible at all.

It is perhaps worth repeating that I do not suggest that there is anything illegitimate or even questionable—let alone impossible—about a scientific explanation of how human beings know what they do. Nor would I question the full legitimacy of Moore's "common sense" assertion that he knows there are external things, if that assertion is taken as irrelevant to the general question of our knowledge of the external world. The so-called scientific account is equally unassailable for the same reason. Naturalized epistemology is supposed to give us all the discoverable scientific information about human knowledge that there is, so the deliverances of naturalized epistemology will simply be "scientific" analogues of G. E. Moore's "common sense" assertions. Both would have the very same epistemological status, and we should have the same attitude toward them both. If not, if Quine's naturalized epistemology is taken as an answer to the philosophical question of our knowledge of the external world, then I think that for the reasons I have given no satisfactory explanation is either forthcoming or possible.

If naturalized epistemology can potentially yield everything knowable about how knowledge is possible, but still not settle the most general epistemological question, then it will perhaps be felt, with Carnap and Schlick and many others, that that question itself must be illegitimate or incoherent or in some way not fully capable of asking what we naturally try to ask about knowledge when we think about it in the traditional philosophical way. Quine's insistence that the only questions about knowledge arise within science itself and can be answered on the basis of scientific information might look like an expression of some such feeling. He argues that even in familiar skeptical appeals to sensory illusions "the concept of illusion itself rested on science, since the quality of illusion consisted simply in deviation from external scientific reality." [37] If we understand what an illusion is, and hence can use the idea to raise a skeptical challenge to science, only because we already know in general what reality is like, it may seem plausible to argue that since some unquestioned knowledge of reality is needed even to understand the idea of illusion used in raising the challenge in the first place, it follows that no skeptical argument can have completely general force against all of science at once. That would be to undermine the traditional question and its specious universality by showing that a completely general skeptical answer to it would be impossible. It would not be that science can answer the question, but that there is no coherent philosophical question that can be raised.

Arguments of that form tend to place a great deal of weight on precisely what is or is not included in the meaning of such terms as 'illusion,' 'reality,' and so on, or on the logically necessary conditions for their meaningful application. Quine's views about meaning do not put him in a strong position to support any such putatively "transcendental" conclusions. And he explicitly disavows all refutations of that form when he says:

I am not accusing the sceptic of begging the question; he is quite within his rights in assuming science in order to refute science; this, if carried out, would be a straightforward argument by *reductio ad absurdum*. I am only making the point that sceptical doubts are scientific doubts. [38]

The *reductio* in question would presumably proceed as follows: either science is true or it is not; if it is not true then nothing we believe about the physical world amounts to knowledge; if it is true then from what it tells us about perception we can see that we can never tell whether we are perceiving the world as it really is, so once again nothing we believe about the physical world amounts to knowledge. On either assumption we know nothing about the physical world.

If, as Quine says, the skeptic is "quite within his rights" in arguing in this way, then even if "sceptical doubts are scientific doubts" it does not follow that the epistemologist who tries to meet the skeptical challenge raised by those "scientific" doubts can legitimately make free use of the natural science he is trying to account for. Quine says he can. The epistemologist can answer his scientifically created doubts by pursuing a naturalized epistemology. But what support does Quine have for that claim?

Suppose we have asked how any knowledge at all of the physical world is possible, and suppose that we have asked it because of what we take at the outset to be true about the physical world—in particular about the processes of perception. If we then arrived by *reductio* at the general skeptical conclusion which Quine thinks is at least coherent, we would find all our alleged knowledge of the physical world suspect; on either horn of the dilemma none of it could be seen as knowledge. At that point in our investigation surely no scientific "knowledge" could then be unproblematically introduced to meet the skeptical challenge. We would have reached the tentative conclusion that nothing we believe about the physical world amounts to knowledge, so it would then be to no avail to appeal to some of those very beliefs about the physical world in the hope of showing how they all amount to knowledge after all. We would find ourselves precluded from using as independently reliable any part of what we had previously accepted as physical science; whatever we chose would be as open to question as everything else.

So even if "sceptical doubts are scientific doubts" in the sense that the skeptical challenge arises because we originally accept many things as true about the physical world, it does not follow that we can make free use of what we accept as physical science in an attempt to meet that challenge. It is true that if we rely on scientific knowledge in order to understand and recognize illusions in the first place, and therefore in order to appeal to illusions to raise skeptical doubts about science, then if we eventually arrive at a completely general skeptical conclusion about all of science we will have "lost" or "thrown away" the very distinction between illusions and reality that we relied on at the outset to reach that negative conclusion. But that is always the way with arguments by *reductio ad absurdum*. We always "lose" or "throw away" what we started with. I conclude that even if Quine is right in saying that skeptical doubts are "scientific" doubts, the "scientific" source of those doubts has no anti-skeptical force in itself. Nor does it establish the relevance and legitimacy of a scientific epistemology as an answer to the traditional epistemological question. If Quine is confident that a naturalized epistemology can answer the traditional question about knowledge, he must have some other reason for that confidence. He believes that skeptical doubts are scientific doubts, and he believes that in resolving those doubts we may make free use of all the scientific knowledge we possess. But if, as he allows, it is possible for the skeptic to argue by *reductio* to the conclusion that science is not known, then it cannot be that the second of those beliefs (that a naturalized epistemology is all we need) follows from the first.

Until the traditional philosophical question has been exposed as in some way illegitimate or incoherent there will always appear to be an intelligible question about human knowledge in general which, as I have argued, a naturalized epistemology cannot answer. And Quine himself seems committed at least to the coherence of that traditional question by his very conception of knowledge. If objective "input" from the world can always in general be isolated from everything we believe about the world as a result of that "input," it does not seem possible for Quine to expose and therefore defuse or get rid of the traditional question in the right way. The traditional bipartite view of knowledge leaves open the general possibility that the objective world is different from the way we take it to be, and so the question of how we know that that possibility does not obtain will always be in place. If I am right that naturalized epistemology alone cannot answer that question, then what is needed is a convincing repudiation of that alleged possibility or an exposure of its failure to give sense to the traditional philosophical question in such a way that naturalized epistemology cannot answer it. Only then would we be in a position to assert that naturalistic or scientific understanding of human knowledge will give us *everything there is to understand* about human knowledge.

Compare Quine's views with those of Hume, one of Quine's illustrious naturalistic predecessors. Hume certainly endorsed the naturalistic, scientific study of the origins of our beliefs. He too had the traditional conception of knowledge as a combination of an objective and a subjective factor. But he showed, as no one had shown before or since, the fatal consequences of that conception. It implies that we do not know anything about the world and have no more reason to believe one thing about it rather than another. For Hume that remains the real truth about our position, even though we can go on, if we like, to engage in "scientific" investigation and even to give "scientific" explanations of how we come to have the scientific beliefs that we have.[39] But for Hume that "scientific" account could never tell us the whole truth about our position; it is not all there is that can be said about how we get the knowledge we think we have. And the extra news, not covered by science or naturalized epistemology, is not good. For Quine the findings of naturalized epistemology are supposed to be not just the truth but the whole truth about human knowledge. There is supposed to be nothing left out. But if that is so, the general question to which Hume gave such a discouraging answer must make no sense. Science cannot answer it, and if science is all there is that is true, then the question must ask nothing, or at least not what it seems to.

What is needed, then, is some demonstration of the incoherence or illegitimacy of that question. If the operation of defusing that question were successful, the stage would be cleared for naturalized epistemology. That defusing operation would not show that we do know that the objective world is in fact the way we take it to be; so it would not imply that we do know in that way that there is an external world after all. Both skepticism and its apparent negation would have been set aside. But the task of exposing the traditional epistemological question and thereby guaranteeing that all intelligible questions about knowledge *can* be answered by naturalized epistemology alone is not itself part of naturalized epistemology. And it seems to me that it is in that task—in demonstrating that scientific investigation can give us everything we could intelligibly ask for—that the real epistemological progress would be made.[40]

Notes

1. Quine 1960, p. 2.

2. Quine 1960, p. 1.

3. Quine 1960, p. 1.

4. Quine 1974, p. 1.

5. Quine 1960, p. 3.

6. Quine 1974, p. 2.

7. Quine 1969, p. 83.

8. Quine 1960, p. 5.

9. Quine 1974, p. 4.

10. Quine 1960, p. 22.

11. Quine 1974, p. 2.

12. Quine 1960, p. 23.

13. Quine 1960, p. 22.

14. Quine 1951, p. 44.

15. Quine 1960, p. 4.

16. Quine 1960, p.4.

17. Quine 1969a, p. 71.

18. Quine 1969a, p. 72.

19. Quine 1969a, pp. 75–76.

20. Quine 1969a, p. 76. It is not clear from this passage exactly how Quine understands the "doctrinal" question of "justifying our knowledge of nature in sensory terms." Throughout the essay he draws parallels between our knowledge of nature and mathematical knowledge, and perhaps that is why he tends to describe the problem of justifying our beliefs about the physical world as that of "deducing science from observations" or "strictly deriving the science of the external world from sensory evidence" (p. 75) or grounding science upon immediate experience "in a firmly logical way" (p. 74). That leaves it unclear whether he thinks that the "Humean predicament" is simply that of having no deductively sufficient justification for our beliefs about the world from our data, or the apparently much more serious plight of having no sensory

justification at all, deductive or non-deductive. I think Hume thought he had shown that we are in both "predicaments." But our being in the second does not obviously follow from our being in the first. In the essay Quine gives no reason for believing that we are in the second "predicament," and therefore no reason for abandoning the project of justifying our beliefs non-demonstratively or inductively on sensory grounds.

21. Quine 1974, p. 2.

22. Quine 1975, p. 3.

23. Quine 1974, p. 3.

24. Quine 1974, p. 3.

25. Moore 1959.

26. Carnap 1967, pp. 273–287, 325–34, and Schlick 1959b.

27. I have tried to illustrate the importance of some such distinction and the corresponding problems of understanding the "significance" of philosophical scepticism (with explicit consideration of positivistic verificationism) in Stroud 1979. The importance of Kant's distinction between the transcendental and the empirical is discussed in Stroud 1984.

28. The importance of Moore in this connection is best brought out in Clarke 1972.

29. Quine 1969a, pp. 82–83.

30. Quine 1969a, p. 83.

31. To say that a person's beliefs about the world transcend or are underdetermined by the sensory impacts that produce them could mean (i) it does not follow from the fact that he has received those impacts that he believes what he does about the world (his believing what he does is underdetermined) (ii) it does not follow from the fact that he has received those sensory impacts that what he believes about the world is true (the truth of his beliefs is underdetermined). The first appears to be a consequence of the general Humean point that when one event causes another it is still possible for the first to occur without the second. The second reading seems closer to Quine's intention. It appears to amount to the uncontroversial claim that truths about what actually happened at certain human sensory surfaces do not alone imply most other truths about the physical world. But this second reading would also have the consequence that the truth 'Impacts $I_1, I_2, \ldots$ occurred at sensory surfaces $S_1, S_2, \ldots$' is *not* underdetermined by those impacts, even though it is itself a statement about the physical world.

32. Quine 1960, p. 22.

33. Accounts of knowledge or reasonable belief along these lines are now very popular. For some earlier examples, on which much of the subsequent discussion has been based, see, e.g., Goldman 1967; Unger 1967, 1968; Dretske 1971.

34. On Quine's view the origin of linguistic competence and cognitive development is to be found in language-learning; subjects are trained to behave linguistically in ways that come to conform to the general practice prevalent in their linguistic community. If we as experimenters were restricted solely to information about the subject's sensory

impacts, we would not know what the general practices prevalent in his linguistic community were. We would have access to the *effects* of his linguistic community, since everything external that influences a person's speech does so through his sensory surfaces, and we have access to them. But those sensory effects presumably underdetermine every hypothesis about what causes them (in both of the two senses distinguished in note 31). So we could not begin to explain why the subject responds in one way rather than a thousand others compatible with the same impacts. We would have a multitude of his sensory impacts, but we would know nothing about what produced them. Our understanding of how and why our subject "posits" bodies and "projects" his physics from his "data" would therefore be at best extremely limited.

35. Quine 1969a, p. 83.

36. I say "at best" because, even in the restricted, third kind of situation we must rely on independent access at some time or other to the world that the subject's utterances are about if we are even to understand those utterances and thereby identify his beliefs about the world. I argue here that such independent access to the world is not available when we take the experimenter's attitude toward ourselves, so our position with respect to ourselves will be like that of the third kind of experimental situation only if understanding of the utterances is assumed in both cases.

37. Quine 1974, p. 3.

38. Quine 1975, p. 68.

39. I have tried to explain how the pursuit of scientific explanations of natural phenomena, including human behavior, can be incorporated within Hume's skepticism in Stroud 1977, esp. chap. 10.

40. In parts of this paper I am repeating and elaborating suggestions to be found in slightly different form in Stroud 1979.

5   What Is Justified Belief?

Alvin I. Goldman

The aim of this paper is to sketch a theory of justified belief. What I have in mind is an explanatory theory, one that explains in a general way why certain beliefs are counted as justified and others as unjustified. Unlike some traditional approaches, I do not try to prescribe standards for justification that differ from, or improve upon, our ordinary standards. I merely try to explicate the ordinary standards, which are, I believe, quite different from those of many classical, e.g., 'Cartesian', accounts.

Many epistemologists have been interested in justification because of its presumed close relationship to knowledge. This relationship is intended to be preserved in the conception of justified belief presented here. In previous papers on knowledge,[1] I have denied that justification is necessary for knowing, but there I had in mind 'Cartesian' accounts of justification. On the account of justified belief suggested here, it *is* necessary for knowing, and closely related to it.

The term 'justified', I presume, is an evaluative term, a term of appraisal. Any correct definition or synonym of it would also feature evaluative terms. I assume that such definitions or synonyms might be given, but I am not interested in them. I want a set of *substantive* conditions that specify when a belief is justified. Compare the moral term 'right'. This might be defined in other ethical terms or phrases, a task appropriate to meta-ethics. The task of normative ethics, by contrast, is to state substantive conditions for the rightness of actions. Normative ethics tries to specify non-ethical conditions that determine when an action is right. A familiar example is act-utilitarianism, which says an action is right if and only if it produces, or would produce, at least as much net happiness as any alternative open to the agent. These necessary and sufficient conditions clearly involve no ethical notions.

Reprinted from *Justification and Knowledge*, ed. George Pappas (Dordrecht: Reidel, 1979), pp. 1–23, by permission of the publisher. Copyright © 1979, Reidel.

Analogously, I want a theory of justified belief to specify in non-epistemic terms when a belief is justified. This is not the only kind of theory of justifiedness one might seek, but it is one important kind of theory and the kind sought here.

In order to avoid epistemic terms in our theory, we must know which terms are epistemic. Obviously, an exhaustive list cannot be given, but here are some examples: 'justified', 'warranted', 'has (good) grounds', 'has reason (to believe)', 'knows that', 'sees that', 'apprehends that', 'is probable' (in an epistemic or inductive sense), 'shows that', 'establishes that', and 'ascertains that'. By contrast, here are some sample non-epistemic expressions: 'believes that', 'is true', 'causes', 'it is necessary that', 'implies', 'is deducible from', and 'is probable' (either in the frequency sense or the propensity sense). In general, (purely) doxastic, metaphysical, modal, semantic, or syntactic expressions are not epistemic.

There is another constraint I wish to place on a theory of justified belief, in addition to the constraint that it be couched in non-epistemic language. Since I seek an explanatory theory, i.e., one that clarifies the underlying source of justificational status, it is not enough for a theory to state 'correct' necessary and sufficient conditions. Its conditions must also be appropriately deep or revelatory. Suppose, for example, that the following sufficient condition of justified belief is offered: 'If S senses redly at t and S believes at t that he is sensing redly, then S's belief at t that he is sensing redly is justified.' This is not the kind of principle I seek; for, even if it is correct, it leaves unexplained *why* a person who senses redly and believes that he does, believes this justifiably. Not every state is such that if one is in it and believes one is in it, this belief is justified. What is distinctive about the state of sensing redly, or 'phenomenal' states in general? A theory of justified belief of the kind I seek must answer this question, and hence it must be couched at a suitably deep, general, or abstract level.

A few introductory words about my *explicandum* are appropriate at this juncture. It is often assumed that whenever a person has a justified belief, he knows that it is justified and knows what the justification is. It is further assumed that the person can state or explain what his justification is. On this view, a justification is an argument, defense, or set of reasons that can be given in support of a belief. Thus, one studies the nature of justified belief by considering what a person might *say* if asked to defend, or justify, his belief. I make none of these sorts of assumptions here. I leave it an open question whether, when a belief *is* justified, the believer *knows* it is justified. I also leave it an open question whether, when a belief is justified, the believer can *state* or *give* a justification for it. I do not even assume that when a belief is justified there is something 'possessed' by the believer which can be called a 'justification'. I do assume that a justified belief gets its status of being justified from some processes or properties that make it justified. In short, there must be some justification-conferring processes or properties. But this does not imply that there must be an argument, or reason, or anything else, 'possessed' at the time of belief by the believer.

I

A theory of justified belief will be a set of principles that specify truth-conditions for the schema ⌜S's belief in p at time t is justified⌝, i.e., conditions for the satisfaction of this schema in all possible cases. It will be convenient to formulate candidate theories in a recursive or inductive format, which would include (A) one or more base clauses, (B) a set of recursive clauses (possibly null), and (C) a closure clause. In such a format, it is permissible for the predicate 'is a justified belief' to appear in recursive clauses. But neither this predicate, nor any other epistemic predicate, may appear in (the antecedent of) any base clause.[2]

Before turning to my own theory, I want to survey some other possible approaches to justified belief. Identification of problems associated with other attempts will provide some motivation for the theory I shall offer. Obviously, I cannot examine all, or even very many, alternative attempts. But a few sample attempts will be instructive.

Let us concentrate on the attempt to formulate one or more adequate base-clause principles.[3] Here is a classical candidate:

(1)   If S believes p at t, and p is indubitable for S (at t), then S's belief in p at t is justified.

To evaluate this principle, we need to know what 'indubitable' means. It can be understood in at least two ways. First, 'p is indubitable for S' might mean: 'S has no *grounds* for doubting p'. Since 'ground' is an epistemic term, however, principle (1) would be inadmissible on this reading, for epistemic terms may not legitimately appear in the antecedent of a base-clause. A second interpretation would avoid this difficulty. One might interpret 'p is indubitable for S' psychologically, i.e., as meaning 'S is psychologically incapable of doubting p'. This would make principle (1) admissible, but would it be correct? Surely not. A religious fanatic may be psychologically incapable of doubting the tenets of his faith, but that doesn't make his belief in them justified. Similarly, during the Watergate affair, someone may have been so blinded by the aura of the Presidency that even after the most damaging evidence against Nixon had emerged he was still incapable of doubting

Nixon's veracity. It doesn't follow that his belief in Nixon's veracity was justified.

A second candidate base-clause principle is this:

(2)   If S believes p at t, and p is self-evident, then S's belief in p at t is justified.

To evaluate this principle, we again need an interpretation of its crucial term, in this case 'self-evident'. On one standard reading, 'evident' is a synonym for 'justified'. '*Self*-evident' would therefore mean something like 'directly justified', 'intuitively justified', or 'non-derivatively justified'. On this reading 'self-evident' is an epistemic phrase, and principle (2) would be disqualified as a base-clause principle.

However, there are other possible readings of '*p* is self-evident' on which it isn't an epistemic phrase. One such reading is: 'It is impossible to understand *p* without believing it'.[4] According to this interpretation, trivial analytic and logical truths might turn out to be self-evident. Hence, any belief in such a truth would be a justified belief, according to (2).

What does 'it is *impossible* to understand *p* without believing it' mean? Does it mean '*humanly* impossible'? That reading would probably make (2) an unacceptable principle. There may well be propositions which humans have an innate and irrepressible disposition to believe, e.g., 'Some events have causes'. But it seems unlikely that people's inability to refrain from believing such a proposition makes every belief in it justified.

Should we then understand 'impossible' to mean 'impossible in principle', or 'logically impossible'? If that is the reading given, I suspect that (2) is a vacuous principle. I doubt that even trivial logical or analytic truths will satisfy this definition of 'self-evident'. Any proposition, we may assume, has two or more components that are somehow organized or juxtaposed. To understand the proposition one must 'grasp' the components and their juxtaposition. Now in the case of *complex* logical truths, there are (human) psychological operations that suffice to grasp the components and their juxtaposition but do not suffice to produce a belief that the proposition is true. But can't we at least *conceive* of an analogous set of psychological operations even for simple logical truths, operations which perhaps are not in the repertoire of human cognizers but which might be in the repertoire of some conceivable beings? That is, can't we conceive of psychological operations that would suffice to grasp the components and componential-juxtaposition of these simple propositions but do not suffice to produce *belief* in the propositions? I think we can conceive of such operations. Hence, for any proposition you choose, it will possible for it to be understood without being believed.

Finally, even if we set these two objections aside, we must note that self-evidence can at best confer justificational status on relatively few beliefs, and the only plausible group are beliefs in necessary truths. Thus, other base-clause principles will be needed to explain the justificational status of beliefs in contingent propositions.

The notion of a base-clause principle is naturally associated with the idea of 'direct' justifiedness, and in the realm of contingent propositions first-person-current-mental-state propositions have often been assigned this role. In Chisholm's terminology, this conception is expressed by the notion of a '*self-presenting*' state or proposition. The sentence 'I am thinking', for example, expresses a self-presenting proposition. (At least I shall *call* this sort of content a 'proposition', though it only has a truth value given some assignment of a subject who utters or entertains the content and a time of entertaining.) When such a proposition is true for person S at time t, S is justified in believing it at t: in Chisholm's terminology, the proposition is 'evident' for S at t. This suggests the following base-clause principle.

(3)   If p is a self-presenting proposition, and p is true for S at t, and S believes p at t, then S's belief in p at t is justified.

What, exactly, does 'self-presenting' mean? In the second edition of *Theory of Knowledge*, Chisholm offers this definition: "h is self-presenting for S at t = df. h is true at t; and necessarily, if h is true at t, then h is evident for S at t."[5] Unfortunately, since 'evident' is an epistemic term, 'self-presenting' also becomes an epistemic term on this definition, thereby disqualifying (3) as a legitimate base-clause. Some other definition of self-presentingness must be offered if (3) is to be a suitable base-clause principle.

Another definition of self-presentation readily comes to mind. 'Self-presentation' is an approximate synonym of 'self-intimation', and a proposition may be said to be self-intimating if and only if whenever it is true of a person that person believes it. More precisely, we may give the following definition.

(SP)   Proposition p is self-presenting if and only if: necessarily, for any S and any t, if p is true for S at t, then S believes p at t.

On this definition, 'self-presenting' is clearly not an epistemic predicate, so (3) would be an admissible principle. Moreover, there is initial plausibility in the suggestion that it is *this* feature of first-person-current-mental-state proposition—viz., their truth guarantees their being believed—that makes beliefs in them justified.

Employing this definition of self-presentation, is principle (3) correct? This cannot be decided until we define self-presentation more precisely. Since the operator 'necessarily' can be read in different ways, there are different forms of self-presentation and correspondingly different versions of principle (3). Let us focus on two of these readings: a *'nomological'* reading and a *'logical'* reading. Consider first the nomological reading. On this definition a proposition is self-presenting just in case it is nomologically necessary that if p is true for S at t, then S believes p at t.[6]

Is the nomological version of principle (3)—call it '(3_N)'—correct? Not at all. We can imagine cases in which the antecedent of (3_N) is satisfied but we would not say that the belief is justified. Suppose, for example, that p is the proposition expressed by the sentence 'I am in brain-state B', where 'B' is shorthand for a certain highly specific neural state description. Further suppose it is a nomological truth that anyone in brain-state B will ipso facto *believe* he is in brain-state B. In other words, imagine that an occurrent belief with the content 'I am in brain-state B' is realized whenever one is in brain-state B.[7] According to (3_N), any such belief is justified. But that is clearly false. We can readily imagine circumstances in which a person goes into brain-state B and therefore has the belief in question, though this belief is by no means justified. For example, we can imagine that a brain-surgeon operating on S artifically induces brain-state B. This results, phenomenologically, in S's suddenly believing—out of the blue—that he is in brain-state B, without any relevant antecedent beliefs. We would hardly say, in such a case, that S's belief that he is in brain-state B is justified.

Let us turn next to the logical version of (3)—call it '(3_L)'—in which a proposition is defined as self-presenting just in case it is logically necessary that if p is true for S at t, then S believes p at t. This stronger version of principle (3) might seem more promising. In fact, however, it is no more successful than (3_N). Let p be the proposition 'I am awake' and assume that it is logically necessary that if this proposition is true for some person S and time t, then S belives p at t. This assumption is consistent with the further assumption that S frequently believes p when it is false, e.g., when he is dreaming. Under these circumstances, we would hardly accept the contention that S's belief in this proposition is always justified. But nor should we accept the contention that the belief is justified when it is *true*. The truth of the proposition logically guarantees that the belief is *held*, but why should it guarantee that the belief is *justified*?

The foregoing criticism suggests that we have things backwards. The idea of self-presentations is that truth guarantees belief. This fails to confer justification because it is compatible with there being belief without truth. So what seems necessary—or at least sufficient—for justification is that belief should guarantee truth. Such a notion has usually gone under the label of *'infallibility'*, or *'incorrigibility'*. It may be defined as follows.

(INC) · Proposition p is incorrigible if and only if: necessarily, for any S and any t, if S believes p at t, then p is true for S at t.

Using the notion of incorrigibility, we may propose principle (4).

(4) If p is an incorrigible proposition, and S believes p at t, then S's belief in p at t is justified.

As was true of self-presentation, there are different varieties of incorrigibility, corresponding to different interpretations of 'necessarily'. Accordingly, we have different versions of principle (4). Once again, let us concentrate on a nomological and a logical version, (4_N) and (4_L) respectively.

We can easily construct a counterexample to (4_N) along the lines of the belief-state/brain-state counterexample that refuted (3_N). Suppose it is nomologically necessary that if anyone believes he is in brain-state B then it is true that he is in brain-state B, for the only way this belief-state is realized is through brain-state B itself. It follows that 'I am in brain-state B' is a nomologically incorrigible proposition. Therefore, according to (4_N), whenever anyone believes this proposition at any time, that belief is justified. But we may again construct a brain-surgeon example in which someone comes to have such a belief but the belief isn't justified.

Apart from this counterexample, the general point is this. Why should the fact that S's believing p guarantees the truth of p imply that S's belief is justified? The nature of the guarantee might be wholly fortuitous, as the belief-state/brain-state example is intended to illustrate. To appreciate the point, consider the following related possibility. A person's mental structure might be such that whenever he believes that p will be true (of him) a split second later, then p is true (of him) a split second later. This is because, we may suppose, his believing it brings it about. But surely we would not be compelled in such a circumstance to say that a belief of this sort is justified. So why should the fact that S's believing p guarantees the truth of p *precisely at the time of belief* imply that the belief is justified? There is no intuitive plausibility in this suppositon.

The notion of *logical* incorrigibility has a more honored place in the history of conceptions of justification. But even principle (4_L), I believe, suffers from defects similar to those of (4_N). The mere fact that belief in p logically guarantees its truth does not confer justificational status on such a belief.

The first difficulty with (4_L) arises from logical or mathematical truths. Any true proposition of logic or mathematics is logically necessary. Hence, any such proposition p is logically incorrigible, since it is logically necessary that, for any S and any t, if S believes p at t then p is true (for S at t). Now assume that Nelson believes a certain very complex mathematical truth at time t. Since such a proposition is logically incorrigible, (4_L) implies that Nelson's belief in this truth at t is justified. But we may easily suppose that this belief of Nelson is not at all the result of proper mathematical reasoning, or even the result of appeal to trustworthy authority. Perhaps Nelson believes this complex truth because of utterly confused reasoning, or because of hasty and ill-founded conjecture. Then his belief is not justified, contrary to what (4_L) implies.

The case of logical or mathematical truths is admittedly peculiar, since the truth of these propositions is assured independently of any beliefs. It might seem, therefore, that we can better capture the idea of 'belief logically guaranteeing truth' in cases where the propositions in question are *contingent*. With this in mind, we might restrict (4_L) to *contingent* incorrigible propositions. Even this amendment cannot save (4_L), however, since there are counterexamples to it involving purely contingent propositions.

Suppose that Humperdink has been studying logic—or, rather, pseudologic—from Elmer Fraud, whom Humperdink has no reason to trust as a logician. Fraud has enunciated the principle that any disjunctive proposition consisting of at least 40 distinct disjuncts is very probably true. Humperdink now encounters the proposition p, a contingent proposition with 40 disjuncts, the 7th disjunct being 'I exist'. Although Humperdink grasps the proposition fully, he doesn't notice that it is entailed by 'I exist'. Rather, he is struck by the fact that it falls under the disjunction rule Fraud has enunciated (a rule I assume Humperdink is not *justified* in believing). Bearing this rule in mind, Humperdink forms a belief in p. Now notice that p is logically incorrigible. It is logically necessary that if anyone believes p, then p is true (of him at that time). This simply follows from the fact that, first, a person's believing anything entails that he exists, and second, 'I exist' entails p. Since p is logically incorrigible, principle (4_L) implies that Humperdink's belief in p is justified. But surely, given our example, that conclusion is false. Humperdink's belief in p is not at all justified.

One thing that goes wrong in this example is that while Humperdink's belief in p logically implies its truth, Humperdink doesn't *recognize* that his believing it implies its truth. This might move a theorist to revise (4_L) by adding the requirement that S 'recognize' that p is logically incorrigible. But this, of course, won't do. The term 'recognize' is obviously an epistemic term, so the suggested revision of (4_L) would result in an inadmissible base-clause.

II

Let us try to diagnose what has gone wrong with these attempts to produce an acceptable base-clause principle. Notice that each of the foregoing attempts confers the status of 'justified' on a belief without restriction on *why* the belief is held, i.e., on what *causally initiates* the belief or *causally sustains* it. The logical versions of principles (3) and (4), for example, clearly place no restriction on causes of belief. The same is true of the nomological versions of (3) and (4), since nomological requirements can be satisfied by simultaneity or cross-sectional laws, as illustrated by our brain-state/belief-state examples. I suggest that the absence of causal requirements accounts for the failure of the foregoing principles. Many of our counterexamples are ones in which the belief is caused in some strange or unacceptable way, e.g., by the accidental movement of a brain-surgeon's hand, by reliance on an illicit, pseudo-logical principle, or by the blinding aura of the Presidency. In general, a strategy for defeating a noncausal principle of justifiedness is to find a case in which the principle's antecedent is satisfied but the belief is caused by some faulty belief-forming process. The faultiness of the belief-forming process will incline us, intuitively, to regard the belief as unjustified. Thus, correct principles of justified belief must be principles that make causal requirements, where 'cause' is construed broadly to include sustainers as well as initiators of belief (i.e., processes that determine, or help to overdetermine, a belief's continuing to be held.)[8]

The need for causal requirements is not restricted to base-clause principles. Recursive principles will also need a causal component. One might initially suppose that the following is a good recursive principle: 'If S justifiably believes q at t, and q entails p, and S believes p at t, then S's belief in p at t is justified'. But this principle is unacceptable. S's belief in p doesn't receive justificational status simply from the fact that p is entailed by q and S justifiably believes q. If what causes S to believe p at t is entirely different, S's belief in p may well not be justified. Nor can the situation be remedied by adding to the antecedent the condition that S justifiably believes that q entails p. Even if he believes this, and believes q as well, he might not put these beliefs together. He might believe p as a result of some other wholly extraneous, considerations. So once again, conditions that fail to require appropriate causes of a belief don't guarantee justifiedness.

Granted that principles of justified belief must make reference to causes of belief, what kinds of causes confer justifiedness? We can gain insight into this problem by reviewing some faulty processes of belief-formation, i.e., processes whose belief-outputs would be classed as unjustified. Here are some examples: confused reasoning, wishful thinking, reliance on emotional attachment, mere hunch or guesswork, and hasty generalization. What do these faulty processes have in common? They share the feature of *unreliability*: they tend to produce *error* a large proportion of the time. By contrast, which species of belief-forming (or belief-sustaining) processes are intuitively justification-conferring? They include standard perceptual processes, remembering, good reasoning, and introspection. What these processes seem to have in common is *reliability*: the beliefs they produce are generally true. My positive proposal, then, is this. The justificational status of a belief is a function of the reliability of the process or processes that cause it, where (as a first approximation) reliability consists in the tendency of a process to produce beliefs that are true rather than false.

To test this thesis further, notice that justifiedness is not a purely categorical concept, although I treat it here as categorical in the interest of simplicity. We can and do regard certain beliefs as more justified than others. Furthermore, our intuitions of comparative justifiedness go along with our beliefs about the comparative reliability of the belief-causing processes.

Consider perceptual beliefs. Suppose Jones believes he has just seen a mountain-goat. Our assessment of the belief's justifiedness is determined by whether he caught a brief glimpse of the creature at a great distance, or whether he had a good look at the thing only 30 yards away. His belief in the latter sort of case is (*ceteris paribus*) more justified than in the former sort of case. And, if his belief is true, we are more prepared to say he *knows* in the latter case than in the former. The difference between the two cases seems to be this. Visual beliefs formed from brief and hasty scanning, or where the perceptual object is a long distance off, tend to be wrong more often than visual beliefs formed from detailed and leisurely scanning, or where the object is in reasonable proximity. In short, the visual processes in the former category are less reliable than those in the latter category. A similar point holds for memory beliefs. A belief that results from a hazy and indistinct memory impression is counted as less justified than a belief that arises from a distinct memory impression, and our inclination to classify those beliefs as '*knowledge*' varies in the same way. Again, the reason is associated with the comparative reliability of the processes. Hazy and indistinct memory impressions are generally less reliable indicators of what actually happened; so beliefs formed from such impressions are less likely to be true than beliefs formed from distinct impressions. Further, consider beliefs based on inference from ob-served samples. A belief about a population that is based on random sampling, or on instances that exhibit great variety, is intuitively more justified than a belief based on biased sampling, or on instances from a narrow sector of the population. Again, the degree of justifiedness seems to be a function of reliability. Inferences based on random or varied samples will tend to produce less error or inaccuracy than inferences based on non-random or non-varied samples.

Returning to a categorical concept of justifiedness, we might ask just *how* reliable a belief-forming process must be in order that its resultant beliefs be justified. A precise answer to this question should not be expected. Our conception of justification is *vague* in this respect. It does seem clear, however, that *perfect* reliability isn't required. Belief-forming processes that *sometimes* produce error still confer justification. It follows that there can be justified beliefs that are false.

I have characterized justification-conferring processes as ones that have a 'tendency' to produce beliefs that are true rather than false. The term 'tendency' could refer either to *actual* long-run frequency, or to a 'propensity', i.e., outcomes that would occur in merely *possible* realizations of the process. Which of these is intended? Unfortunately, I think our ordinary conception of justifiedness is vague on this dimension too. For the most part, we simply assume that the 'observed' frequency of truth versus error would be approximately replicated in the actual long-run, and also in relevant counterfactual situations, i.e., ones that are highly 'realistic', or conform closely to the circumstances of the actual world. Since we ordinarily assume these frequencies to be roughly the same, we make no concerted effort to distinguish them. Since the purpose of my present theorizing is to capture our ordinary conception of justifiedness, and since our ordinary conception is vague on this matter, it is appropriate to leave the theory vague in the same respect.

We need to say more about the notion of a belief-forming '*process*'. Let us mean by a 'process' a *functional operation* or procedure, i.e., something that generates a *mapping* from certain states—'inputs'—into other states—'outputs'. The outputs in the present case are states of believing this or that proposition at a given moment. On this interpretation, a process is a *type* as opposed to a *token*. This is fully appropriate, since it is only types that have statistical properties such as producing truth 80% of the time; and it is precisely such statistical properties that determine the reliability of a process. Of course, we also want to speak of a process as *causing* a belief, and it looks as if types are incapable of being causes. But when we say that a belief is caused by a given process, understood as a functional procedure, we may interpret this to mean that it is caused by the particular *inputs* to the process (and by the intervening events 'through which' the functional procedure carries the inputs into the output) on the occasion in question.

What are some examples of belief-forming 'processes' construed as functional operations? One example is reasoning processes, where the inputs include antecedent beliefs and entertained hypotheses. Another example is functional procedures whose inputs include desires, hopes, or emotional states of various sorts (together with antecedent beliefs). A third example is a memory process, which takes as input beliefs or experiences at an earlier time and generates as output beliefs at a later time. For example, a memory process might take as input a belief $at\ t_1$ that Lincoln was born in 1809 and generate as output a belief $at\ t_n$ that Lincoln was born in 1809. A fourth example is perceptual processes. Here it isn't clear whether inputs should include states of the environment, such as the distance of the stimulus from the cognizer, or only events within or on the surface of the organism, e.g., receptor stimulations. I shall return to this point in a moment.

A critical problem concerning our analysis is the degree of generality of the process-types in question. Input-output relations can be specified very broadly or very narrowly, and the degree of generality will partly determine the degree of reliability. A process-type might be selected so narrowly that only one instance of it ever occurs, and hence the type is either completely reliable or completely unreliable. (This assumes that reliability is a function of *actual* frequency only.) If such narrow process-types were selected, beliefs that are intuitively unjustified might be said to result from perfectly reliable processes; and beliefs that are intuitively justified might be said to result from perfectly unreliable processes.

It is clear that our ordinary thought about process-types slices them broadly, but I cannot at present give a precise explication of our intuitive principles. One plausible suggestion, though, is that the relevant processes are *content-neutral*. It might be argued, for example, that the process of *inferring p whenever the Pope asserts p* could pose problems for our theory. If the Pope is infallible, this process will be perfectly reliable; yet we would not regard the belief-outputs of this process as justified. The content-neutral restriction would avert this difficulty. If relevant processes are required to admit as input beliefs (or other states) with *any* content, the aforementioned process will not count, for its input beliefs have a restricted propositioned content, viz., '*the Pope* assert *p*'.

In addition to the problem of 'generality' or 'abstractness' there is the previously mentioned problem of the '*extent*' of belief-forming processes. Clearly, the causal ancestry of beliefs often includes events outside the organism. Are such events to be included among the 'inputs' of belief-forming processes? Or should we restrict the extent of belief-forming processes to '*cognitive*' events, i.e., events within the organism's nervous system? I shall choose the latter course, though with some hesitation. My general grounds for this decision are roughly as follows. Justifiedness seems to be a function of how a cognizer deals with his environmental input, i.e., with the goodness or badness of the operations that register and transform the stimulation that reaches him. ('Deal with', of course, does not mean *purposeful* action; nor is it restricted to *conscious* activity.) A justified belief is, roughly speaking, one that

results from cognitive operations that are, generally speaking, good or successful. But 'cognitive' operations are most plausibly construed as operations of the
cognitive faculties, i.e., 'information-processing' equipment *internal* to the
organism.

With these points in mind, we may now advance the following base-clause
principle for justified belief.

(5)   If S's believing p at t results from a reliable cognitive belief-forming
process (or set of processes), then S's belief in p at t is justified.

Since 'reliable belief-forming process' has been defined in terms of such
notions as belief, truth, statistical frequency, and the like, it is not an epistemic
term. Hence, (5) is an admissible base-clause.

It might seem as if (5) promises to be not only a successful base clause, but
the only principle needed whatever, apart from a closure clause. In other
words, it might seem as if it is a necessary as well as a sufficient condition of
justifiedness that a belief be produced by reliable cognitive belief-forming
processes. But this is not quite correct, give our provisional definition of
'reliability'.

Our provisional definition implies that a reasoning process is reliable only if
it generally produces beliefs that are true, and similarly, that a memory process
is reliable only if it generally yields beliefs that are true. But these requirements are too strong. A reasoning procedure cannot be expected to produce
true belief if it is applied to false premises. And memory cannot be expected to
yield a true belief if the original belief it attempts to retain is false. What we
need for reasoning and memory, then, is a notion of *'conditional reliability'*. A
process is conditionally reliable when a sufficient proportion of its output-
beliefs are true *given that its input-beliefs are true*.

With this point in mind, let us distinguish *belief-dependent* and *belief-
independent* cognitive processes. The former are processes *some* of whose
inputs are belief-states.[9] The latter are processes *none* of whose inputs are
belief-states. We may then replace principle (5) with the following two
principles, the first a base-clause principle and the second a recursive-clause
principle.

(6_A)   If S's belief in p at t results ('immediately') from a belief-independent
process that is (unconditionally) reliable, then S's belief in p at t is justified.

(6_B)   If S's belief in p at t results (''immediately'') from a belief-dependent
process that is (at least) conditionally reliable, and if the beliefs (if any) on
which this process operates in producing S's belief in p at t are themselves
justified, then S's belief in p at t is justified.[10]

If we add to (6_A) and (6_B) the standard closure clause, we have a complete
theory of justified belief. The theory says, in effect, that a belief is justified if

and only it is '*well-formed*', i.e., it has an ancestry of reliable and/or condition-ally reliable cognitive operations. (Since a dated belief may be over-determined, it may have a number of distinct ancestral trees. These need not all be full of reliable or conditionally reliable processes. But at least one ancestral tree must have reliable or conditionally reliable processes throughout.)

The theory of justified belief proposed here, then, is an *Historical* or *Genetic* theory. It contrasts with the dominant approach to justified belief, an ap-proach that generates what we may call (borrowing a phrase from Robert Nozick) '*Current Time-Slice*' theories. A Current Time-Slice theory makes the justificational status of a belief wholly a function of what is true of the cognizer *at the time* of belief. An Historical theory makes the justificational status of a belief depend on its prior history. Since my Historical theory emphasizes the reliability of the belief-generating processes, it may be called '*Historical Reliabilism*'.

The most obvious examples of Current Time-Slice theories are 'Cartesian' Foundationalist theories, which trace all justificational status (at least of contingent propositions) to current mental states. The usual varieties of Coherence theories, however, are equally Current Time-Slice views, since they too make the justificational status of a belief wholly a function of *current* states of affairs. For Coherence theories, however, these current states include all other beliefs of the cognizer, which would not be considered relevant by Cartesian Foundationalism. Have there been other Historical theories of justi-fied belief? Among contemporary writers, Quine and Popper have Historical epistemologies, though the notion of 'justification' is not their avowed *ex-plicandum*. Among historical writers, it might seem that Locke and Hume had Genetic theories of sorts. But I think that their Genetic theories were only theories of ideas, not of knowledge or justification. Plato's theory of recollec-tion, however, is a good example of a Genetic theory of knowing.[11] And it might be argued that Hegel and Dewey had Genetic epistemologies (if Hegel can be said to have had a clear epistemology at all).

The theory articulated by (6_A) and (6_B) might be viewed as a kind of 'Foundationalism,' because of its recursive structure. I have no objection to this label, as long as one keeps in mind how different this 'diachronic' form of Foundationalism is from Cartesian, or other 'synchronic' varieties of, Foundationalism.

Current Time-Slice theories characteristically assume that the justificational status of a belief is something which the cognizer is able to know or determine at the time of belief. This is made explicit, for example, by Chisholm.[12] The Historical theory I endorse makes no such assumption. There are many facts about a cognizer to which he lacks 'privileged access', and I regard the justificational status of his beliefs as one of those things. This is not to say that a cognizer is necessarily ignorant, at any given moment, of the justificational status of his current beliefs. It is only to deny that he necessarily has, or can get, knowledge or true belief about this status. Just as a person can know without knowing that he knows, so he can have justified belief without knowing that it is justified (or believing justifiably that it is justified.)

A characteristic case in which a belief is justified though the cognizer doesn't know that it's justified is where the original evidence for the belief has long since been forgotten. If the original evidence was compelling, the cognizer's original belief may have been justified; and this justificational status may have been preserved through memory. But since the cognizer no longer remembers how or why he came to believe, he may not know that the belief is justified. If asked now to justify his belief, he may be at a loss. Still, the belief *is* justified, though the cognizer can't demonstrate or establish this.

The Historical theory of justified belief I advocate is connected in spirit with the causal theory of knowing I have presented elsewhere.[13] I had this in mind when I remarked near the outset of the paper that my theory of justified belief makes justifiedness come out closely related to knowledge. Justified beliefs, like pieces of knowledge, have appropriate histories; but they may fail to be knowledge either because they are false or because they founder on some other requirement for knowing of the kind discussed in the post-Gettier knowledge-trade.

There is a variant of the Historical conception of justified belief that is worth mentioning in this context. It may be introduced as follows. Suppose S has a set B of beliefs at time t_0, and some of these beliefs are *un*justified. Between t_0 and t_1 he reasons from the entire set B to the conclusion p, which he then accepts at t_1. The reasoning procedure he uses is a very sound one, i.e., one that is conditionally reliable. There is a sense or respect in which we are tempted to say that S's belief in p at t_1 is 'justified'. At any rate, it is tempting to say that the *person* is justified in believing p at t. Relative to his antecedent cognitive state, he did as well as could be expected: the *transition* from his cognitive state at t_0 to his cognitive state at t_1 was entirely sound. Although we may acknowledge this brand of justifiedness—it might be called '*Terminal-Phase Reliabilism*'—it is not a kind of justifiedness so closely related to knowing. For a person to know proposition p, it is not enough that the *final phase* of the process that leads to his belief in p be sound. It is also necessary that some entire history of the process be sound (i.e., reliable or conditionally reliable).

Let us return now to the Historical theory. In the next section of the paper, I shall adduce reasons for strengthening it a bit. Before looking at these reasons, however, I wish to review two quite different objections to the theory.

First, a critic might argue that *some* justified beliefs do not derive their justificational status from their causal ancestry. In particular, it might be argued that beliefs about one's current phenomenal states and intuitive beliefs about elementary logical or conceptual relationships do not derive their justificational status in this way. I am not persuaded by either of these examples. Introspection, I believe, should be regarded as a form of retrospection. Thus, a justified belief that I am 'now' in pain gets its justificational status from a relevant, though brief, causal history.[14] The apprehension of logical or conceptual relationships is also a cognitive process that occupies time. The psychological process of 'seeing' or 'intuiting' a simple logical truth is very fast, and we cannot introspectively dissect it into constituent parts. Nonetheless, there are mental operations going on, just as there are mental operations that occur in *idiots savants*, who are unable to report the computational processes they in fact employ.

A second objection to Historical Reliabilism focuses on the reliability element rather than the causal or historical element. Since the theory is intended to cover all possible cases, it seems to imply that for any cognitive process C, if C is reliable in possible world W, then any belief in W that results from C is justified. But doesn't this permit easy counterexamples? Surely we can imagine a possible world in which wishful thinking is reliable. We can imagine a possible world where a benevolent demon so arranges things that beliefs formed by wishful thinking usually come true. This would make wishful thinking a reliable process in that possible world, but surely we don't want to regard beliefs that result from wishful thinking as justified.

There are several possible ways to respond to this case and I am unsure which response is best, partly because my own intuitions (and those of other people I have consulted) are not entirely clear. One possibility is to say that in the possible world imagined, beliefs that result from wishful thinking *are* justified. In other words we reject the claim that wishful thinking could never, intuitively, confer justifiedness.[15]

However, for those who feel that wishful thinking couldn't confer justifiedness, even in the world imagined, there are two ways out. First, it may be suggested that the proper criterion of justifiedness is the propensity of a process to generate beliefs that are true *in a non-manipulated environment*, i.e., an environment in which there is no purposeful arrangement of the world either to accord or conflict with the beliefs that are formed. In other words, the suitability of a belief-forming process is only a function of its success in 'natural' situations, not situations of the sort involving benevolent or malevolent demons, or any other such manipulative creatures. If we reformulate the theory to include this qualification, the counterexample in question will be averted.

Alternatively, we may reformulate our theory, or reinterpret it, as follows. Instead of construing the theory as saying that a belief in possible world *W* is justified if and only if it results from a cognitive process that is reliable in *W*, we may construe it as saying that a belief in possible world *W* is justified if and only if it results from a cognitive process that is reliable *in our world*. In short, our conception of justifiedness is derived as follows. We note certain cognitive processes in the actual world, and form beliefs about which of these are reliable. The ones we believe to be reliable are then regarded as justification-conferring processes. In reflecting on hypothetical beliefs, we deem them justified if and only if they result from processes already picked out as justification-conferring, or processes very similar to those. Since wishful thinking is not among these processes, a belief formed in a possible world *W* by wishful thinking would not be deemed justified, even if wishful thinking is reliable *in W*. I am not sure that this is a correct reconstruction of our intuitive conceptual scheme, but it would accommodate the benevolent demon case, at least if the proper thing to say in that case is that the wishful-thinking-caused beliefs are unjustified.

Even if we adopt this strategy, however, a problem still remains. Suppose that wishful thinking turns out to be reliable *in the actual world*![16] This might be because, unbeknownst to us at present, there is a benevolent demon who, lazy until now, will shortly start arranging things so that our wishes come true. The long-run performance of wishful thinking will be very good, and hence even the new construal of the theory will imply that beliefs resulting from wishful thinking (in *our* world) are justified. Yet this surely contravenes our intuitive judgment on the matter.

Perhaps the moral of the case is that the standard format of a 'conceptual analysis' has its shortcomings. Let me depart from that format and try to give a better rendering of our aims and the theory that tries to achieve that aim. What we really want is an *explanation* of why we count, or would count, certain beliefs as justified and others as unjustified. Such an explanation must refer to our *beliefs* about reliability, not to the actual *facts*. The reason we *count* beliefs as justified is that they are formed by what we *believe* to be reliable belief-forming processes. Our beliefs about which belief-forming processes are reliable may be erroneous, but that does not affect the adequacy of the explanation. Since we *believe* that wishful thinking is an unreliable belief-forming process, we regard beliefs formed by wishful thinking as unjustified. What matters, then, is what we *believe* about wishful thinking, not what is *true* (in the long run) about wishful thinking. I am not sure how to express this point in the standard format of conceptual analysis, but it identifies an important point in understanding our theory.

III

Let us return, however, to the standard format of conceptual analysis, and let us consider a new objection that will require some revisions in the theory advanced until now. According to our theory, a belief is justified in case it is caused by a process that is in fact reliable, or by one we generally believe to be reliable. But suppose that although one of S's beliefs satisfies this condition, S has no reason to believe that it does. Worse yet, suppose S has reason to believe that his belief is caused by an *un*reliable process (although *in fact* its causal ancestry is fully reliable). Wouldn't we deny in such circumstances that S's belief is justified? This seems to show that our analysis, as presently formulated, is mistaken.

Suppose that Jones is told on fully reliable authority that a certain class of his memory beliefs is almost all mistaken. His parents fabricate a wholly false story that Jones suffered from amnesia when he was seven but later developed *pseudo*-memories of that period. Though Jones listens to what his parents say and has excellent reason to trust them, he persists in believing the ostensible memories from his seven-year-old past. Are these memory beliefs justified? Intuitively, they are not justified. But since these beliefs result from genuine memory and original perceptions, which are adequately reliable processes, our theory says that these beliefs are justified.

Can the theory be revised to meet this difficulty? One natural suggestion is that the actual reliability of a belief's ancestry is not enough for justifiedness; in addition, the cognizer must be *justified in believing* that the ancestry of his belief is reliable. Thus one might think of replacing (6_A), for example, with (7). (For simplicity, I neglect some of the details of the earlier analysis.)

(7) If S's belief in p at t is caused by a reliable cognitive process, and S justifiably believes at t that his p-belief is so caused, then S's belief in p at t is justified.

It is evident, however, that (7) will not do as a base clause, for it contains the epistemic term 'justifiably' in its antecedent.

A slightly weaker revision, without this problematic feature, might next be suggested, viz.,

(8) If S's beief in p at t is caused by a reliable cognitive process, and S believes at t that his p-belief is so caused, then S's belief in p at t is justified.

But this won't do the job. Suppose that Jones believes that his memory beliefs are reliably caused despite all the (trustworthy) contrary testimony of his parents. Principle (8) would be satisfied, yet we wouldn't say that these beliefs are justified.

Next, we might try (9), which is stronger than (8) and, unlike (7), formally admissible as a base clause.

(9)   If S's belief in p at t is caused by a reliable cognitive process, and S believes at t that his p-belief is so caused, and this meta-belief is caused by a reliable cognitive process, than S's belief in p at t is justified.

A first objection to (9) is that it wrongly precludes unreflective creatures— creatures like animals or young children, who have no beliefs about the genesis of their beliefs—from having justified beliefs. If one shares my view that justified belief is, at least roughly, *well-formed* belief, surely animals and young children can have justified beliefs.

A second problem with (9) concerns its underlying rationale. Since (9) is proposed as a substitute for (6_A), it is implied that the reliability of a belief's own cognitive ancestry does not make it justified. But, the suggestion seems to be, the reliability of a *meta-belief*'s ancestry confers justifiedness on the first-order belief. Why should that be so? Perhaps one is attracted by the idea of a 'trickle-down' effect: if an $n + 1$-level belief is justified, its justification trickles down to an n-level belief. But even if the trickle-down theory is correct, it doesn't help here. There is no assurance from the satisfaction of (9)'s antecedent that the meta-belief itself is *justified*.

To obtain a better revision of our theory, let us re-examine the Jones case. Jones has strong evidence against certain propositions concerning his past. He doesn't *use* this evidence, but if he *were* to use it properly, he would stop believing these propositions. Now the proper use of evidence would be an instance of a (conditionally) reliable process. So what we can say about Jones is that he *fails* to use a certain (conditionally) reliable process that he could and should have used. Admittedly, had he used this process, he would have 'worsened' his doxastic states: he would have replaced some true beliefs with suspension of judgment. Still, he couldn't have known this in the case in question. So, he failed to do something which, epistemically, he should have done. This diagnosis suggests a fundamental change in our theory. The justificational status of a belief is not only a function of the cognitive processes *actually* employed in producing it; it is also a function of processes that could and should be employed.

With these points in mind, we may tentatively propose the following revision of our theory, where we again focus on a base-clause principle but omit certain details in the interest of clarity.

(10)   If S's belief in p at t results from a reliable cognitive process, and there is no reliable or conditionally reliable process available to S which, had it been used by S in addition to the process actually used, would have resulted in S's not believing p at t, then S's belief in p at t is justified.

There are several problems with this proposal. First, there is a technical problem. One cannot use an additional belief-forming (or doxastic-state-forming) process *as well as* the original process if the additional one would result in a different doxastic state. One wouldn't be using the original process at all. So we need a slightly different formulation of the relevant counter-factual. Since the basic idea is reasonably clear, however, I won't try to improve on the formulation here. A second problem concerns the notion of *'available'* belief-forming (or doxastic-state-forming) processes. What is it for a process to be 'available' to a cognizer? Were scientific procedures 'available' to people who lived in pre-scientific ages? Furthermore, it seems implausible to say that all 'available' processes ought to be used, at least if we include such processes as gathering *new* evidence. Surely a belief can sometimes be justified even if additional evidence-gathering would yield a different doxastic attitude. What I think we should have in mind here are such additional processes as calling previously acquired evidence to mind, assessing the implications of that evidence, etc. This is admittedly somewhat vague, but here again our ordinary notion of justifiedness is vague, so it is appropriate for our analysans to display the same sort of vagueness.

This completes the sketch of my account of justified belief. Before concluding, however, it is essential to point out that there is an important use of 'justified' which is not captured by this account but can be captured by a closely related one.

There is a use of 'justified' in which it is not implied or presupposed that there is a *belief* that is justified. For example, if S is trying to decide whether to believe p and asks our advice, we may tell him that he is 'justified' in believing it. We do not thereby imply that he *has* a justified *belief*, since we know he is still suspending judgement. What we mean, roughly, is that he *would* or *could* be justified if he were to believe p. The justificational status we ascribe here cannot be a function of the causes of S's believing p, for there is no belief by S in p. Thus, the account of justifiedness we have given thus far cannot explicate *this* use of 'justified'. (It doesn't follow that this use of 'justified' has no connection with causal ancestries. Its proper use may depend on the causal ancestry of the cognizer's cognitive state, though not on the causal ancestry of his believing p.)

Let us distinguish two uses of 'justified': an *ex post* use and an *ex ante* use. The *ex post* use occurs when there exists a belief, and we say *of that belief* that it is (or isn't) justified. The *ex ante* use occurs when no such belief exists, or when we wish to ignore the question of whether such a belief exists. Here we say of the *person*, independent of his doxastic state vis-à-vis p, that p is (or isn't) suitable for him to believe.[17]

Since we have given an account of *ex post* justifiedness, it will suffice if we can analyze *ex ante* justifiedness in terms of it. Such an analysis, I believe, is ready at hand. *S* is *ex ante* justified in believing *p* at *t* just in case his total cognitive state at *t* is such that from that state he could come to believe *p* in such a way that this belief would be *ex post* justified. More precisely, he is *ex ante* justified in believing *p* at *t* just in case a reliable belief-forming operation is available to him such that the application of that operation to his total cognitive state at *t* would result, more or less immediately, in his believing *p* and this belief would be *ex post* justified. Stated formally, we have the following:

(11)   Person *S* is *ex ante* justified in believing *p* at *t* if and only if there is a reliable belief-forming operation available to *S* which is such that if *S* applied that operation to his total cognitive state at *t*, *S* would believe *p* at *t*-plus-delta (for a suitably small delta) and that belief would be *ex post* justified.

For the analysans of (11) to be satisfied, the total cognitive state at *t* must have a suitable causal ancestry. Hence, (11) is implicitly an Historical account of *ex ante* justifiedness.

As indicated, the bulk of this paper was addressed to *ex post* justifiedness. This is the appropriate analysandum if one is interested in the connection between justifiedness and knowledge, since what is crucial to whether a person *knows* a proposition is whether he has an actual *belief* in the proposition that is justified. However, since many epistemologists are interested in *ex ante* justifiedness, it is proper for a general theory of justification to try to provide an account of that concept as well. Our theory does this quite naturally, for the account of *ex ante* justifiedness falls out directly from our account of *ex post* justifiedness.[18]

Notes

1. Goldman 1967, 1975, 1976.

2. Notice that the choice of a recursive format does not prejudice the case for or against any particular theory. A recursive format is perfectly general. Specifically, an explicit set of necessary and sufficient conditions is just a special case of a recursive format, i.e. one in which there is no recursive clause.

3. Many of the attempts I shall consider are suggested by material in William Alston 1971.

4. Such a definition (though without the modal term) is given, for example, by W. V. Quine and J. S. Ullian 1970, p. 21. Statements are said to be self-evident just in case "to understand them is to believe them".

5. Chisholm 1977, p. 22.

6. I assume, of course, that 'nomologically necessary' is *de re* with respect to '*S*' and '*t*' in this construction. I shall not focus on problems that may arise in this regard, since my primary concerns are with different issues.

7. This assumption violates the thesis that Davidson calls 'The Anomalism of the Mental'. Cf. Davidson 1970. But it is unclear that this thesis is a necessary truth. Thus, it seems fair to assume its falsity in order to produce a counterexample. The example neither entails nor precludes the mental-physical identity theory.

8. Keith Lehrer's example of the gypsy lawyer is intended to show the in-appropriateness of a causal requirement. (See Lehrer 1974, pp. 124–125.) But I find this example unconvincing. To the extent that I clearly imagine that the lawyer fixes his belief solely as a result of the cards, it seems intuitively wrong to say that he *knows*—or has a *justified belief*—that his client is innocent.

9. This definition is not exactly what we need for the purposes at hand. As Ernest Sosa points out, introspection will turn out to be a belief-dependent process since sometimes the input into the process will be a belief (when the introspected content is a belief). Intuitively, however, introspection is not the sort of process which may be merely conditionally reliable. I do not know how to refine the definition so as to avoid this difficulty, but it is a small and isolated point.

10. It may be objected that principles (6_A) and (6_B) are jointly open to analogues of the lottery paradox. A series of processes composed of reliable but less-than-perfectly-reliable processes may be extremely unreliable. Yet applications of (6_A) and (6_B) would confer justifiedness on a belief that is caused by such a series. In reply to this objection, we might simply indicate that the theory is intended to capture our ordinary notion of justifiedness, and this ordinary notion has been formed without recognition of this kind of problem. The theory is not wrong *as* a theory of the ordinary (naive) conception of justifiedness. On the other hand, if we want a theory to do more than capture the ordinary conception of justifiedness, it might be possible to strengthen the principles to avoid lottery-paradox analogues.

11. I am indebted to Mark Pastin for this point.

12. Cf. Chisholm 1977, pp. 17, 114–116.

13. Cf. Goldman 1967. The reliability aspect of my theory also has its precursors in earlier papers of mine on knowing: Goldman 1975, 1976.

14. The view that introspection is retrospection was taken by Ryle, and before him (as Charles Hartshorne points out to me) by Hobbes, Whitehead, and possibly Husserl.

15. Of course, if people in world *W* learn *inductively* that wishful thinking is reliable, and regularly base their beliefs on this inductive inference, it is quite unproblematic and straightforward that their beliefs are justified. The only interesting case is where their beliefs are formed *purely* by wishful thinking, without using inductive inference. The suggestion contemplated in this paragraph of the text is that, in the world imagined, even pure wishful thinking would confer justifiedness.

16. I am indebted here to Mark Kaplan.

17. The distinction between *ex post* and *ex ante* justifiedness is similar to Roderick Firth's distinction between *doxastic* and *propositional* warrant. See Firth 1978.

18. Research on this paper was begun while the author was a fellow of the John Simon Guggenheim Memorial Foundation and of the Center for Advanced Study in the Behavioral Sciences. I am grateful for their support. I have received helpful comments and criticism from Holly S. Goldman, Mark Kaplan, Fred Schmitt, Stephen P. Stich, and many others at several universities where earlier drafts of the paper were read.

6

Beyond Foundationalism
and the Coherence Theory

Hilary Kornblith

One of the legacies of positivist epistemology is a tendency to divorce epistemological questions from psychological questions. Epistemology is a normative
discipline; it is concerned, among other things, with questions about how
reasoning ought to proceed. Such questions can be answered, we are told,
independently of investigation into the processes that in fact occur when
reasoning takes place. Questions about justified belief are thus "translated"
from the mental realm—'What kinds of transitions between mental states
make for justified belief?'—to the logical realm—'What kinds of arguments
are "good" arguments?'. This approach to epistemological questions pervades
much of contemporary philosophy.

I believe that this approach is mistaken. The approach I favor, a psychological approach to questions about knowledge and justification, is the naturalized epistemology of W. V. Quine and Alvin Goldman.[1] In this paper, I will
explore the implications of this approach for questions about justification,
and, in particular, for the debate between foundationalists and coherence
theorists.

Foundationalism and the coherence theory of justification may be viewed as
two sides of a Kantian antinomy. Arguments for each view are predominantly
negative; they are arguments for the claim that the opposing view is untenable.
When the best available argument for a view is that competing views are
untenable, one is left with the suspicion that a different conclusion would
have been reached had one only considered the competing positions in a
different order. More importantly, this suggests that the competing views may
rest on a common false presupposition.

I do not believe that the standard objections to either foundationalism or the
coherence theory have been adequately addressed. If I am correct in this, then

Reprinted from *The Journal of Philosophy* LXXII (October 1980): 597–612, by permission of the publisher. Copyright © 1980, *The Journal of Philosophy*.

it is worth considering whether there are other possible views about the nature of justification. I will argue that foundationalism and the coherence theory share a common false presupposition and that this lies in their anti-psychological approach to epistemological questions. Once this false pre-supposition is rejected, the insights of both foundationalism and the coherence theory may be joined in a single unified theory of justification.

Knowledge and Justified Belief

The standard account of knowledge is that knowledge is some sort of justified, true belief. This account is often presented as a rival to causal theories of knowledge. Causal theorists of knowledge believe that knowledge is reliably produced true belief. This, we are told, leaves justification out of the picture.

I do not believe that this way of presenting the causal theory of knowledge is correct. Causal theorists of knowledge do not deny that knowledge is some sort of justified true belief; they merely give a nonstandard account of what it is for a belief to be justified. They claim that a belief is justified just in case it is caused by a reliable process. Self-styled justified-true-belief theorists of knowl-edge typically give a quite different account of justification.

This may sound like a merely terminological dispute, but I do not believe that it is. The notion of justification was not invented by philosophers. Answers to questions about justification play an important action-guiding role. It is thus important to develop a theory that tells us what justification is. Causal theorists of knowledge are not exempt from this task. I do not believe, however, that they have tried to avoid dealing with it.

The claim that knowledge requires justified true belief is a mere truism. What is controversial is the proper analysis of the notion of justification. There are two ways in which one might try to go about giving an analysis of justification. One is to tackle this problem directly; the other is to try to give an account of knowledge. A proper account of knowledge will include an account of justification. This must be true, unless the truism that knowledge requires justified belief is false. In claiming that knowledge is reliably produced true belief, causal theorists of knowledge are thus not abandoning the notion of justification, but rather committing themselves to a reliabilist account of justification.[2]

It is thus worth pointing out that there is room for dispute about what justification consists in. This is important because there is a standard account of justification which is so widely accepted—indeed, so widely taken for granted—that its merits as a theory of justification are rarely examined. This is especially unfortunate, I believe, because the standard account is false.

The Arguments-on-Paper Thesis

The standard account of what it is to be justified in believing a proposition is an apsychological account. If such an account is correct, questions about justification amount to nothing more than questions about the quality of various sorts of arguments. I will thus call the view that underlies the standard account the *arguments-on-paper thesis*.

Let us suppose that, for any person, it is possible, at least in principle, to list all the propositions that person believes. The arguments-on-paper thesis is just the view that a person has a justified belief that a particular proposition is true just in case that proposition appears on the list of propositions that person believes, and either it requires no argument, or a good argument can be given for it which takes as premises certain other propositions on the list.[3] Crucial to this explanation of the arguments-on-paper thesis is the notion of a "good argument." Foundationalism and the coherence theory of justification provide us with rival accounts of what it is to be a "good argument."

On the foundationalist version of the thesis, some of the propositions on the list of propositions one believes will have a special epistemic status: these propositions will be such that, if a person believes one of them, that person is justified in that belief. It has been widely held that some propositions are incorrigible; they are known if they are believed. If there are any incorrigible propositions, these propositions have the required epistemic status. There may be some propositions, however, that are not incorrigible and yet have the required status. Let us suppose that all propositions that have the required special epistemic status are starred whenever they occur on the list of propositions a person believes. The foundationalist will now provide us with a list of rules of inference. It is then claimed that a proposition requires no argument if and only if it is starred, and that an argument for a proposition is a good one just in case all its premises are starred and all the rules that must be applied to get from the premises to the conclusion are on the appropriate list. Various claims are often made for the epistemic status of the rules of inference, but we need not be concerned with these here.

Coherence theorists suppose that there are no starred propositions. The coherentist thus makes different claims about what makes for a good argument. It is claimed that there is a relation, call it C, which a proposition might bear to a set of propositions and which is such that, if a proposition appears on the list of propositions a person believes and bears C to the set of all the remaining propositions on that list, this provides a good argument for that proposition. In keeping with the spirit of the arguments-on-paper thesis, C must of course be definable solely in terms of relations among propositions.

The Psychological Turn

There are familiar objections against both foundationalism and the coherence theory, as presented above. Against foundationalism, it has been argued that there are no propositions the content of which guarantees that anyone who believes them is justified in believing them; in short, there are no starred propositions.[4] Against the coherence theory, it has been argued that the mere fact that a set of propositions cohere with one another is no evidence of their truth; in short, there is no such relation as C.[5] In response to these objections, various epicycles have been added to both foundationalist and coherentist accounts, but I do not believe that these objections have ever been answered.

I would therefore like to propose an account alternative to both foundationalism and the coherence theory, and here I have in mind not just a rival account of what it is to be a good argument, but rather an account that rejects the framework common to both of these theories. In this section, I will argue that the arguments-on-paper thesis is false;[6] in the following sections, I will develop an account that avoids the standard objections to both foundationalism and the coherence theory.

Consider Alfred. Alfred justifiably believes that p and justifiably believes that if p then q; he also believes that q. Is Alfred justified in believing that q?

Notice, first, that if the arguments-on-paper thesis is true, then, on any reasonable foundationalist or coherentist account, Alfred is justified in believing q. Foundationalists must allow that Alfred is justified in believing q, for it must surely be allowed that modus ponens is on the list of rules available for constructing good arguments.[7] Since Alfred is justified in believing p and if p then q, there are "good" arguments available for each of these propositions, and, given that modus ponens is an available rule, an acceptable argument for q is easily constructed. Similarly, coherence theorists will surely grant that a proposition that follows from others by modus ponens coheres with them, and thus, they too must insist that Alfred is justified in believing q.

It is clear, however, that Alfred need not be justified in believing q. Alfred may well be aware that he believes that p and that if p then q, and yet fail to believe that q on these grounds. If Alfred has a strong distrust of modus ponens, and yet believes q because he likes the sound of some sentence that expresses the proposition that q, then surely Alfred is not justified in believing that q. Nor will it do to suggest that this problem can be cleared up if we merely stipulate that Alfred must also believe that if p and if p and q, then q; for the same problem arises all over again.

Alfred is justified in believing that q only if his belief that q *depends* on his beliefs that p, and if p then q. The notion of belief dependence cannot be accounted for in terms of the contents of the various beliefs held. The arguments-on-paper thesis is thus false.

In rejecting the arguments-on-paper thesis, we must take a psychological turn.[8] The notion of belief dependence must be accounted for by looking at the belief states of persons and, in particular, at the relations among them. Questions about the justification of beliefs are thus intimately tied to questions about the sorts of processes responsible for the presence of those beliefs. This is the first step toward a naturalized epistemology, and the failure of the arguments-on-paper thesis shows that it is a step we must take.

I will not attempt to give an account of what it is for one belief to depend on another. I will, however, adopt the following working hypothesis: if one belief depends on another, the former must be *causally* dependent on the latter; one belief cannot depend on another when the two are causally independent. This suggestion, I believe, allows us to recognize an important insight of foundationalism.

The Hierarchical Structure of Justification

That causal dependence is a necessary condition of belief dependence leads immediately to the conclusion that the structure of belief dependence is hierarchical. The argument for this conclusion is nothing more than the familiar *regress argument*, an argument frequently advanced by foundationalists.

Consider some person's justified belief that *p*. What might make a person justified in having such a belief? Either that belief is not justified, even in part, by its dependence on other beliefs, or there is a set of beliefs *B* such that *p* is justified in virtue of its dependence on the members of *B*. We may now ask of each of the members of *B* whether that belief is justified in virtue of its dependence on other beliefs, and so on. A tree structure results.

Clearly, it is not possible, in tracing the source of a belief's justification in this way, that one should come across an unjustified belief; a belief cannot be justified in virtue of its dependence on an unjustified belief. There are then three possibilities. Either (1) at least one branch of the tree will be made up of infinitely many distinct justified beliefs; (2) there will be no branches made up of infinitely many distinct beliefs, but at least one branch, in effect, will turn back on itself; that is, there will be some branch that forms a closed circle; or (3) all branches will be finite in length and contain no circles; all branches will terminate with what we shall call a *terminal belief*—a belief that is not justified in virtue of its dependence on other beliefs.

The fact that belief dependence requires causal dependence guarantees that justificatory trees fall into the last of these three categories. Consider the causal chain of events that accounts for a person's holding a particular belief. A complete explanation of the presence of a belief will include a complete description of this chain of events. There must be a first belief on this causal chain; thus, there must be a belief on any such chain which is justified, though not justified in virtue of its dependence on any other beliefs. It therefore follows that each justified belief is either such that, though justified, it is not justified in virtue of its dependence on any other beliefs, or such that it is justified, ultimately, in virtue of its dependence on beliefs which, though justified, are not justified in virtue of their dependence on other beliefs.[9]

I have said nothing about the content of terminal beliefs, for I am interested not so much in their content as in their existence. If the view championed by J. J. Gibson,[10] that perception is detection, is correct, terminal beliefs are perceptual beliefs. On the other hand, the view that perception is hypothesis, favored by R. L. Gregory,[11] would suggest that perceptual beliefs are not typically terminal. I will briefly sketch each of these two views.

Gibson's view gives foundationalists a good part of what they have always wanted. If Gibson is correct, the causal chain of events that leads to the production of a perceptual belief typically does not itself include any believings. Perceptual beliefs, when justified, are thus typically not justified in virtue of their dependence on other beliefs.

Gregory, on the other hand, claims that if we examine the etiology of a perceptual belief we will typical find that it is dependent on other previously acquired beliefs, many of which are also perceptual. These, in turn, will also typically depend on other previously held beliefs; and so on. Of course the position that all beliefs are causally dependent on previously held beliefs is incoherent, and this is not the position that Gregory holds. If Gregory is right, however, then if we trace the etiology of a typical perceptual belief we will find that it is dependent on many beliefs that were acquired in the past, and perhaps as long ago as early childhood.

There is no need for me to enter this psychological controversy. I wish only to argue that some beliefs must be terminal, and each justified belief must either be terminal or be dependent on terminal beliefs. Although this conclusion sounds very much like foundationalism, it is important to emphasize the contrast between foundationalism and the view I am defending here. The argument just given demonstrates the existence of terminal beliefs; it does not demonstrate the existence of what foundationalists have called "self-justifying beliefs." First, it should be noted that this argument does not in any way suggest that terminal beliefs are justified in virtue of their content, nor does it suggest that a belief that is terminal at one time must be terminal at another. Moreover, it does not show that a belief might not depend on itself; this argument in no way precludes the possibility that, in tracing the etiology of a belief, it should be discovered that an agent's holding the belief that p at time t is dependent, in part, on his holding the belief that p at some time earlier than t. Most importantly, however, the justificatory trees that have been described are nothing more than trees of belief dependence. Although justification is clearly in part a matter of belief dependence, this is not to say that there is nothing more to justification than belief dependence.[12] Indeed I will argue that relations among beliefs other than those captured by the justificatory trees just described play a crucial role in making beliefs justified.

The Role of Background Beliefs

I have argued thus far that part of what determines whether a particular person is justified in holding a particular belief at a particular time is the process responsible for the presence of that belief in that person at that time.[13] Such processes, however, are not the sole determinants of justification.

Consider the following example. Joe and Moe are both looking at a bowl of fruit, and this causes both Joe and Moe to believe that there is an apple in front of them. Let us suppose that the psychological processes responsible for the presence of these beliefs in Joe and Moe are the same, and thus the tree diagram illustrating the beliefs (if any) upon which Moe's belief that there is an apple in front of him depends is the same as the corresponding diagram for Joe. Let us suppose further that Joe also believes that he is myopic and, thus, that if the basket of fruit in front of him were artificial fruit, he would not be able to tell at this distance; Moe has no such belief. In spite of Joe's belief that he cannot distinguish what is in front of him from artificial fruit, Joe still believes that he is looking at a genuine apple.[14]

In this circumstance, Moe is justified in believing that there is an apple in front of him, but Joe is not. Since the processes that produced their beliefs are the same, something other than the process responsible for the presence of their beliefs must be involved in determining whether they are justified. In this case, it is quite clear what this additional factor is. Although the process responsible for the presence of Joe's belief would ordinarily be adequate for justification, it is not adequate for justification given Joe's background beliefs—beliefs which do not appear on the justificatory tree tracing the etiology of the belief in question. In determining whether a process is adequate for justification, we must examine not only features intrinsic to the process itself, but also background beliefs which may play no part at all in the process. A belief's justificatory status is thus a function of (at least) the process responsible for its presence, as well as the background beliefs had by the agent at the time in question.

The importance of background beliefs should not be underestimated. It has sometimes been suggested that some beliefs, though not incorrigible, are justified independently of their relations to other beliefs.[15] This cannot, however, be true. As long as a belief is not incorrigible, its justificatory status will vary not only with changes in the process responsible for its presence but also with changes in background beliefs. Thus, for any given belief-forming process, there will always be background beliefs that would make that process inadequate for justification. *All nonincorrigible beliefs are thus justified, in part, in virtue of their relations to other beliefs.* The qualification is unnecessary, of course, if there are no incorrigible beliefs. I have nothing to add to the arguments available against the existence of incorrigible beliefs, and since there is a growing consensus that such beliefs do not exist, I will take for granted in what follows that the justificatory status of all beliefs has been shown to depend, in part, on other beliefs.

Beyond Foundationalism and the Coherence Theory

Foundationalists have argued that the structure of belief dependence is hierarchical; that some beliefs, though justified, are not dependent on others; and that all other justified beliefs must ultimately be dependent on these. If the argument I have given [previously] is correct, foundationalists are correct about all these points.

Coherence theorists have argued that no belief is justified independently of its relations to other beliefs. This claim too is vindicated by the account I offer. Although there must be some beliefs such that an account of the process responsible for their presence does not involve other beliefs, an account of what makes these processes adequate for justification must involve other beliefs. A complete account of what makes a particular belief justified will always involve beliefs other than the one in question.

Foundationalists have argued that the coherence theory of justification "cuts justification off from the world." Justified beliefs are beliefs that, in some sense or other, are likely to be true. A proper theory of justification must therefore explain in what sense it is that justified beliefs are likely to be true. Since it is the way the world is which makes beliefs true or false, a proper theory of justification must explain what it is about justified beliefs which makes it likely that they should "match up" with the way the world is. The outline of a theory of justification which I have offered explicitly makes room for such an account. Any adequate account of the features of belief-producing processes that make for justified belief must surely indicate the relation between these processes and the world. The fact that the account offered is a causal account requires that, in filling in the outline offered, the connection between justified beliefs and the world must be included.

Coherence theorists have argued that foundationalism is not plausible unless foundationalists can come up with some plausible candidates for foundational (or "starred," as I have called them) beliefs, and that no such plausible candidates have ever been offered. Though I have not made any suggestions about which beliefs might be terminal, this does not leave me vulnerable to the coherence theorist's objection. Foundationalists have made quite elaborate claims for the epistemic status of foundational beliefs; I make no such claims for the superficially similar terminal beliefs of my account. What makes a belief terminal at a particular time is simply that the chain of events responsible for its presence does not include any believings. There can be little doubt that there are such beliefs, though nothing short of a psychological theory of the mechanisms involved in belief acquisition will tell us what they are. Needless to say, I am not prepared to offer such a theory.

I thus hope that the outline of a theory of justified belief which I have offered incorporates those features of foundationalism and the coherence theory which have made each of these views attractive and yet avoids those features which have made each of these views unacceptable. Let me close this section with a brief discussion of the notion of *epistemic priority*.

Some philosophers have suggested that there is a special class of beliefs that are "epistemically prior" to other beliefs; it has sometimes been claimed that this special class might consist of beliefs about one's present state of mind, or, alternatively, about medium-sized physical objects. I believe that claims about epistemic priority are to be understood as claims about the relative position of beliefs on the justificatory trees described above. In these terms, we may distinguish among a number of different theses about epistemic priority.

The following is a very weak claim about epistemic priority. There is some class of beliefs that tend to be epistemically prior—i.e., lower in justificatory trees—than some other class of beliefs. This claim is clearly true. Consider the class of beliefs about medium-sized physical objects and the class of beliefs about subatomic particles. Beliefs in the former class tend to occur lower in justificatory trees than beliefs in the latter class; beliefs about subatomic particles tend to depend on beliefs about medium-sized physical objects, rather than vice versa. This is of course compatible with the claim that, for example, if the structure of human sense organs were different, the epistemic ordering of these two classes might have been different. It is also compatible with the claim that some beliefs about subatomic particles are epistemically prior to some beliefs about medium-sized physical objects.

Foundationalists have argued for a stronger claim about epistemic priority:

the class of beliefs that are in fact terminal must be terminal; the class of beliefs that are in fact epistemically prior to other beliefs must be epistemically prior to other beliefs. I think this view is plausible only if the terminal beliefs are incorrigible. Let us suppose that there is a terminal belief t that is not incorrigible. Since t is not incorrigible, there is some evidence e which one might obtain that t is false. Let us suppose that one comes to believe e, and on this basis one gives up one's belief that t. Let us further suppose that e is later discovered to be misleading evidence and that one thus comes to believe t again, this time on the basis of one's belief that e is misleading. Thus, although t was once a terminal belief, it now no longer is. Since such a chain of events might occur, no (nonincorrigible) terminal belief is necessarily terminal. The fact that one belief is epistemically prior to another at a particular time does not in any way guarantee that the order of epistemic priority will not shift at a later time.

Most importantly, it should be pointed out again that the fact that a certain class of beliefs is terminal at a particular time, and thus epistemically prior to all other beliefs at that time, does not show that what makes these beliefs justified has nothing to do with other beliefs higher up in the tree. In spite of the "foundational" structure of justificatory trees, no beliefs are justified independently of their relations to other beliefs.

Reliabilism

The outline of a theory of justification which I have presented is neutral on the question of what makes a belief-forming process adequate for justification. For the purposes of this paper, namely, to extract the elements of truth from foundationalism and the coherence theory and combine them in a unified theory of justification, it is unnecessary to take a stand on this question. Nevertheless, there is only one theory currently in the field which addresses this question, *reliabilism*, and it will thus be worth while to see how my outline looks in reliabilist dress.[16]

Reliabilism is the view that knowledge is reliably produced true belief, and thus that justified belief is reliably produced belief. This view is presented in what is now a *locus classicus* of reliabilism, Alvin Goldman's "Discrimination and Perceptual Knowledge"[17]:

What kinds of causal processes or mechanisms must be responsible for a belief if that belief is to count as knowledge? They must be mechanisms that are, in an appropriate sense, "reliable." Roughly, a cognitive mechanism or process is reliable if it not only produces true beliefs in actual situations, but would also produce true beliefs, or at least inhibit false beliefs, in relevant counterfactual situations (771).

In presenting my account of justification in reliabilist terms, I will follow Goldman's analysis closely.

A belief-producing process is reliable just in case it tends to produce true beliefs in actual situations as well as in counterfactual situations that are relevant alternatives to the actual situation. A belief is justified just in case the process responsible for its presence is reliable.

Given an epistemic agent, a proposition, and a time at which that agent believes that proposition, the determinants of the relevant alternatives to that proposition, for that agent, at that time, fall into two categories: the way the world is, and the way the agent believes the world to be. Goldman does not offer an account of how relevant alternatives are determined, nor is such an account available in the literature. In spite of this, it will be useful to see how, in particular cases, relevant alternatives are determined.

Let us bring Joe and Moe back to center stage. Joe, it will be remembered, believes that there is an apple in front of him in spite of the fact that he believes that if he were looking at artificial fruit he would be unable to tell the difference. Joe's belief that he is looking at an apple is thus clearly unjustified. How do we account for this within the Goldman framework?

The process that produces Joe's belief, we have supposed, is a standard perceptual process. This is a perfectly respectable belief-forming process, but it is not adequate for justification unless it tends to produce true beliefs in both actual and relevant counterfactual situations. Joe's belief that he cannot tell the difference between genuine and artificial fruit at this distance makes a certain counterfactual situation relevant that would otherwise not be relevant: namely the situation in which he is actually looking at artificial fruit. The process that produced Joe's belief in the actual situation would tend to produce false beliefs in this relevant counterfactual situation, and thus Joe is unjustified in believing that he sees an apple. Since what makes this counterfactual situation relevant is Joe's belief about his myopia and since Moe does not have a similar belief, this counterfactual situation is not relevant for Moe. The process that produced Moe's belief, namely, the very same process that produced Joe's, is reliable because it tends to produce true beliefs in actual situations as well as in those which are relevant for Moe. Moe thus has a justified belief.

It might seem, in light of this example, that the relevant alternatives for justification should be determined only by the way the agent believes the world to be, and not also by the way the world is. Nevertheless, situations outside the agent's doxastic realm may serve to determine relevant alternatives. Just as there are cases of morally culpable ignorance, there are cases of epistemically culpable ignorance. Had Moe been frequently fooled by artificial fruit before, he would be no more justified than Joe. The way the world is thus enters in determining relevant alternatives.

Alternatively, it might be argued that one needn't take into account the way the world is believed to be in order to determine relevant alternatives. It might be argued that all the facts about justification which can be accounted for by allowing an agent's beliefs to determine some of the relevant alternatives can equally well be accounted for by by-passing the agent's beliefs and looking only at certain facts about the way the world is. Beliefs thus play no role in the determination of relevant alternatives.

This argument is a non sequitur. Consider a particular belief that seems to determine a particular relevant alternative, e.g., Joe's belief that he is myopic. Now consider the causal chain that leads to the production of Joe's belief. This chain of events surely determines that the situation in which Joe is looking at artificial fruit is a relevant alternative to the actual situation. The only reason that this chain of events determines the relevant alternative, however, is that it also determines that Joe will come to believe he is unable to tell the difference between artificial fruit and genuine fruit from this distance. Chains of events that do not thus determine Joe's belief will not determine relevant alternatives.

Relevant alternative situations are thus determined, in part, by an agent's beliefs, and questions of justification are determined by the tendency of the process responsible for the presence of a belief to produce true beliefs in relevant alternative situations. I have urged that all justified beliefs must either be or depend on beliefs that do not depend on others, simply because there must be some first belief involved in any belief-forming process. Nevertheless, no belief is justified independently of its relations to other beliefs; for in order be justified a belief must be produced by a process that tends to produce true beliefs in relevant counterfactual situations, and relevance is always determined, in part, by an agent's beliefs. Concessions are thus made to both foundationalism and the coherence theory.

It is a short step from a reliabilist account of justified belief to a reliabilist account of knowledge, for knowledge is merely reliably produced true belief. Here, however, we "up the ante" in setting the standards of reliability adequate for knowledge. A process must tend to produce true beliefs in a wider range of counterfactual circumstances if it is to be sufficiently reliable for knowledge than if it is to be merely reliable enough for justified belief. A single example should make this point clear.

Alphonse is looking at a bowl of fruit and, as a consequence, comes to believe that there is an apple in front of him. Alphonse is terribly myopic, although he's never had any reason to believe this, and if the apple in front of him were made of wax, Alphonse wouldn't notice the difference. In this situation, Alphonse's belief that there is an apple in front of him is surely justified—he does not realize that he is myopic, and his ignorance is not culpable—but he does not have knowledge. Here it seems that the fact that Alphonse is myopic determines a relevant alternative as regards knowledge, but not as regards justification.

The determinants of the relevant alternatives as regards justification are thus the class of the agent's beliefs, as well as a subclass of the true propositions about the world apart from the agent's beliefs. The determinants of the relevant alternatives as regards knowledge are the class of the agent's beliefs as well as a larger subclass of the true propositions about the world.

This concludes my outline of a theory of justification. Many questions remain open. Most obviously, it remains to be shown how relevant alternatives are determined, and a great deal remains to be said about terminal beliefs. Nevertheless I hope this sketch serves to focus questions about the nature of justification in a more productive way than the endless battle between foundationalists and coherence theorists might have suggested was possible.

Notes

An earlier version of this paper was presented to colloquia at the Universities of Pittsburgh, Michigan, Cornell and UCLA; versions more like the present one were read at the University of Delaware and the University of Vermont. I have received helpful comments from Kristin Guyot, Harold Hodes, Patricia Kitcher, George Sher, Nicholas Sturgeon, and William Wilcox, Jr. Sydney Shoemaker, Carl Ginet, and Richard Boyd have given me extensive comments on numerous drafts. I am especially indebted to Philip Kitcher.

1. See especially Quine 1969a, 1969b; and Goldman 1976, 1979.

2. In Goldman 1975, Goldman suggested that the causal theory of knowledge amounts to an account of knowledge without justification. In his more recent Goldman 1979, he insists that a causal theory of knowledge brings with it a causal theory of justification.

3. The following is a representative sampling of those who have held the arguments-on-paper thesis in this century, with references: Ayer 1974, p. 63; Chisholm 1957, p. 16; Chisholm 1977, p. 109; Chisholm 1976, pp. 182–3; Cornman 1978, p. 230; Firth 1965 passim; Firth 1969 passim; Ginet 1975, p. 52; Lehrer 1974, p. 17; Lewis 1946, pp. 265–314; Neurath 1959, p. 203; Pastin 1976a, p. 575; Pastin 1976b, passim; Pollock 1974, pp. 33–39; Popper 1979, p. 6; Russell 1912, p. 134; Russell 1948, p. 155; Sellars 1963, p. 169; Sosa 1978, p. 188.

4. See, e.g., Sellars 1963, pp. 127–196; Williams 1977, pp. 25–59.

5. Lewis 1969, p. 128.

6. Similar arguments have been offered by Harman 1973, pp. 24–33; Stroud 1979; Goldman 1979.

7. This assumption is used only for purposes of illustration. Foundationalists must accept some rules of inference, and, if modus ponens is not among these, an analogous example can be constructed making use of one of the accepted rules. Similarly, for coherence theorists, the assumption is unnecessary.

8. Lehrer 1974, pp. 124–5, has resisted this move. He presents an example that purports to show that the psychological turn should not be taken. In their simplest form, examples of the type Lehrer offers presuppose that a person's reason for holding a certain belief must always be tied to the reason for which the belief was acquired; this presupposition is false. When this presupposition is not made, it is not obvious that Lehrer's intuitions about the example are correct.

9. One might try to escape this conclusion by arguing that the notion of belief, like that of baldness, is vague. If the notion of belief were vague in this way, this would undermine my argument. I know of no reason for thinking, however, that this is so. We make use of the notion of belief in explaining action. If such explanations were to break down with further investigation of the etiology of action, we might have to conclude that the notion of belief is as vague as that of baldness. There is no reason yet, however, to draw this conclusion.

10. Gibson 1966.

11. Gregory 1970.

12. Sydney Shoemaker and Richard Boyd argued with me relentlessly to get me to see this point. I would never have come to see it if not for discussions with Philip Kitcher.

13. I am very much indebted in this section, as I am throughout the paper, to Goldman 1979.

14. Joe is, of course, being irrational; but this is surely possible.

15. This view has come to be known as "modest foundationalism". See e.g., Firth 1969; Pastin 1976b.

16. This is not quite true. There is also the account offered in Harman 1973.

17. Reliabilism is also defended in Armstrong 1973.

7

A Priori Knowledge

Philip Kitcher

"A priori" has been a popular term with philosophers at least since Kant distinguished between a priori and a posteriori knowledge. Yet, despite the frequency with which it has been used in twentieth century philosophy, there has been little discussion of the concept of apriority.[1] Some writers seem to take it for granted that there are propositions, such as the truths of logic and mathematics, which are a priori; others deny that there are any a priori propositions. In the absence of a clear characterization of the a priori/a posteriori distinction, it is by no means obvious what is being asserted or what is being denied.

"A priori" is an epistemological predicate. What is *primarily* a priori is an item of knowledge.[2] Of course, we can introduce a derivative use of "a priori" as a predicate of propositions:[3] a priori propositions are those which we could know a priori. Somebody might protest that current practice is to define the notion of an a priori proposition outright, by taking the class of a priori propositions to consist of the truths of logic and mathematics (for example). But when philosophers allege that truths of logic and mathematics are a priori, they do not intend merely to recapitulate the definition of a priori propositions. Their aim is to advance a thesis about the epistemological status of logic and mathematics.

To understand the nature of such epistemological claims, we should return to Kant, who provided the most explicit characterization of a priori knowledge: "we shall understand by a priori knowledge, not knowledge which is independent of this or that experience, but knowledge absolutely independent of all experience."[4] While acknowledging that Kant's formulation sums

Reprinted from *The Philosophical Review* LXXVI (1980): 3–23, by permission of the author and the publisher. Copyright © 1980, *The Philosophical Review*.

up the classical notion of apriority, several recent writers who have discussed the topic have despaired of making sense of it.[5] I shall try to show that Kant's definition can be clarified, and that the concept of a priori knowledge can be embedded in a naturalistic epistemology.

II

Two questions naturally arise. What are we to understand by "experience"? And what is to be made of the idea of independence from experience? Apparently, there are easy answers. Count as a person's experience the stream of her sensory encounters with the world, where this includes both "outer experience," that is, sensory states caused by stimuli external to the body, and "inner experience," that is, those sensory states brought about by internal stimuli. Now we might propose that someone's knowledge is independent of her experience just in case she could have had that knowledge whatever experience she had had. To this obvious suggestion there is an equally obvious objection. The apriorist is not ipso facto a believer in innate knowledge: indeed, Kant emphasized the difference between the two types of knowledge. So we cannot accept an analysis which implies that a priori knowledge could have been obtained given minimal experiences.[6]

Many philosophers (Kant included) contend both that analytic truths can be known a priori and that some analytic truths involve concepts which could only be acquired if we were to have particular kinds of experience. If we are to defend their doctrines from immediate rejection, we must allow a minimal role to experience, even in a priori knowledge. Experience may be needed to provide some concepts. So we might modify our proposal: knowledge is independent of experience if any experience which would enable us to acquire the concepts involved would enable us to have the knowledge.

It is worth noting explicitly that we are concerned here with the *total* experience of the knower. Suppose that you acquire some knowledge empirically. Later you deduce some consequences of this empirical knowledge. We should reject the suggestion that your knowledge of those consequences is independent of experience because, at the time you perform the deduction, you are engaging in a process of reasoning which is independent of the sensations you are then having.[7] As Kant recognized,[8] your knowledge, in cases like this, is dependent on your total experience: different total sequences of sensations would not have given you the premises for your deductions.

Let us put together the points which have been made so far. A person's experience at a particular time will be identified with his sensory state at the time. (Such states are best regarded physicalistically in terms of stimulation of sensory receptors, but we should recognize that there are both "outer" and "inner" receptors.) The total sequence of experiences X has had up to time t is *X's life at t*. A life will be said to be *sufficient for X for p* just in case X could have had that life and gained sufficient understanding to believe that p. (I postpone, for the moment, questions about the nature of the modality involved here.) Our discussion above suggests the use of these notions in the analysis of a priori knowledge: X knows a priori that p if and only if X knows that p and, given any life sufficient for X for p, X could have had that life and still have known that p. Making temporal references explicit: at time t X knows a priori that p just in case, at time t, X knows that p and, given any life sufficient for X for p, X could have had that life at t and still have known, at t, that p. In subsequent discussions I shall usually leave the temporal references implicit.

Unfortunately, the proposed analysis will not do. A clear-headed apriorist should admit that people can have empirical knowledge of propositions which can be known a priori. However, on the account I have given, if somebody knows that p and if it is possible for her to know a priori that p, then, apparently, given any sufficiently rich life she could know that p, so that she would meet the conditions for a priori knowledge that p. (This presupposes that modalities "collapse," but I don't think the problem can be solved simply by denying the presupposition.) Hence it seems that my account will not allow for empirical knowledge of propositions that can be known a priori.

We need to amend the analysis. We must differentiate situations in which a person knows something empirically which could have been known a priori from situations of actual a priori knowledge. The remedy is obvious. What sets apart corresponding situations of the two types is a difference in the ways in which what is known is known. An analysis of a priori knowledge must probe the notion of knowledge more deeply than we have done so far.

III

We do not need a general analysis of knowledge, but we do need the *form* of such an analysis. I shall adopt an approach which extracts what is common to much recent work on knowledge, an approach which may appropriately be called "the psychologistic account of knowledge."[9] The root idea is that the question of whether a person's true belief counts as knowledge depends on whether the presence of that true belief can be explained in an appropriate fashion. The difference between an item of knowledge and mere true belief turns on the factors which produced the belief; thus the issue revolves around the way in which a particular mental state was generated. It is important to emphasize that, at different times, a person may have states of belief with the same content, and these states may be produced by different processes. The claim that a process produces a belief is to be understood as the assertion that the presence of the current state of belief is to be explained through a description of that process. Hence the account is not committed to supposing that the original formation of a belief is relevant to the epistemological status of later states of belief in the same proposition.[10]

The question of what conditions must be met if a belief is to be explained in an appropriate fashion is central to epistemology, but it need not concern us here. My thesis is that the distinction between knowledge and true belief depends on the characteristics of the process which generates the belief, and this thesis is independent of specific proposals about what characteristics are crucial. Introducing a useful term, let us say that some processes *warrant* the beliefs they produce, and that these processes are *warrants* for such beliefs. The general view of knowledge I have adopted can be recast as the thesis that X knows that p just in case X correctly believes that p and X's belief was produced by a process which is a warrant for it. Leaving the task of specifying the conditions on warrants to general epistemology, my aim is to distinguish a priori knowledge from a posteriori knowledge. We discovered above that the distinction requires us to consider the ways in which what is known is known. Hence I propose to reformulate the problem: let us say that X knows a priori that p just in case X has a true belief that p and that belief was produced by a process which is an *a priori warrant* for it. Now the crucial notion is that of an a priori warrant, and our task becomes that of specifying the conditions which distinguish a priori warrants from other warrants.

At this stage, some examples may help us to see how to draw the distinction. Perception is an obvious type of process which philosophers have supposed *not* to engender a priori knowledge. Putative a priori warrants are more controversial. I shall use Kant's notion of pure intuition as an example. This is not to endorse the claim that processes of pure intuition are a priori warrants, but only to see what features of such processes have prompted Kant (and others) to differentiate them from perceptual processes.

On Kant's theory, processes of pure intuition are supposed to yield a priori mathematical knowledge. Let us focus on a simple geometrical example. We are supposed to gain a priori knowledge of the elementary properties of triangles by using our grasp on the concept of triangle to construct a mental picture of a triangle and by inspecting this picture with the mind's eye.[11] What are the characteristics of this kind of process which make Kant want to say that it produces knowledge which is independent of experience? I believe that Kant's account implies that three conditions should be met. The same type of process must be *available* independently of experience. It must produce *warranted* belief independently of experience. And it must produce *true* belief independently of experience. Let us consider these conditions in turn.

According to the Kantian story, if our life were to enable us to acquire the appropriate concepts (the concept of a triangle and the other geometrical concepts involved) then the appropriate kind of pure intuition would be available to us. We could represent a triangle to ourselves, inspect it, and so reach the same beliefs. But, if the process is to generate *knowledge* independently of experience, Kant must require more of it. Given any sufficiently rich life, if we were to undergo the same type of process and gain the same beliefs, then those beliefs would be warranted by the process. Let us dramatize the point by imagining that experience is unkind. Suppose that we are presented with experiments which are cunningly contrived so as to make it appear that some of our basic geometrical beliefs are false. Kant's theory of geometrical knowledge presupposes that if, in the circumstances envisaged, a process of pure intuition were to produce geometrical belief then it would produce warranted belief, despite the background of misleading experience.

So far I have considered how a Kantian process of pure intuition might produce warranted belief independently of experience. But to generate *knowledge* independently of experience, a priori warrants must produce warranted *true* belief in counterfactual situations where experiences are different. This point does not emerge clearly in the Kantian case bacause the propositions which are alleged to be known a priori are taken to be necessary, so that the question of whether it would be possible to have an a priori warrant for a false belief does not arise. Plainly, we could ensure that a priori warrants produce warranted *true* belief independently of experience by declaring that a priori warrants only warrant necessary truths. But this proposal is unnecessarily strong. Our goal is to construe a priori knowledge as knowledge which is independent of experience, and this can be achieved, without closing the case against the contingent a priori, by supposing that, in a counterfactual situation in which an a priori warrant produces belief that p then p. On this account, a priori warrants are ultra-reliable; they never lead us astray.[12]

Summarizing the conditions that have been uncovered, I propose the following analysis of a priori knowledge.

(1) X knows a priori that p if and only if X knows that p and X's belief that p was produced by a process which is an a priori warrant for it.

(2) α is an a priori warrant for X's belief that p if and only if α is a process such that, given any life e, sufficient for X for p, then

  (a) some process of the same type could produce in X a belief that p

(b) if a process of the same type were to produce in X a belief that p then it would warrant X in believing that p

(c) if a process of the same type were to produce in X a belief that p then p.

It should be clear that this analysis yields the desired result that, if a person knows a priori that p then she could know that p whatever (sufficiently rich) experience she had had. But it goes beyond the proposal of §II in spelling out the idea that the knowledge be obtainable in the same way. Hence we can distinguish cases of empirical knowledge of propositions which could be known a priori from cases of actual a priori knowledge.

IV

In this section, I want to be more explicit about the notion of "types of processes" which I have employed, and about the modal and conditional notions which figure in my analysis. To specify a process which produces a belief is to pick out some terminal segment of the causal ancestry of the belief. I think that, without loss of generality, we can restrict our attention to those segments which consist solely of states and events internal to the believer.[13] Tracing the causal ancestry of a belief beyond the believer would identify processes which would not be available independently of experience, so that they would violate our conditions on a priori warrants.

Given that we need only consider psychological processes, the next question which arises is how we divide processes into types. It may seem that the problem can be sidestepped: can't we simply propose that to defend the apriority of an item of knowledge is to claim that that knowledge was produced by a psychological process and that *that very process* would be available and would produce warranted true belief in counterfactual situations where experience is different? I think it is easy to see how to use this proposal to rewrite (2) in a way which avoids reference to "types of processes." I have not adopted this approach because I think that it shortcuts important questions about what makes a process the same in different counterfactual situations.

Our talk of processes which produce belief was originally introduced to articulate the idea that some items of knowledge are obtained in the same way while others are obtained in different ways. To return to our example, knowing a theorem on the basis of hearing a lecture and knowing the same theorem by following a proof count, intuitively, as different ways of knowing the theorem. Our intuitions about this example, and others, involve a number of different principles of classification, with different principles appearing in different cases. We seem to divide belief-forming processes into types by considering content of beliefs, inferential connections, causal connections, use of perceptual mechanisms and so forth. I suggest that these principles of classification probably do not give rise to one definite taxonomy, but that, by using them singly, or in combination, we obtain a number of different taxonomies which we can and do employ. Moreover, within each taxonomy, we can specify types of processes more or less narrowly.[14] Faced with such variety, what characterization should we pick?

There is probably no privileged way of dividing processes into types. This is not to say that our standard principles of classification will allow *anything* to count as a type. Somebody who proposed that the process of listening to a lecture (or the terminal segment of it which consists of psychological states and events) belongs to a type which consists of itself and instances of following a proof, would flout *all* our principles for dividing processes into types. Hence, while we may have many admissible notions of types of belief-forming processes, corresponding to different principles of classification, some collections of processes contravene all such principles, and these cannot be admitted as genuine types.[15]

My analysis can be read as issuing a challenge to the apriorist. If someone wishes to claim that a particular belief is an item of a priori knowledge then he must specify a segment of the causal ancestry of the belief, consisting of states and events internal to the believer, and type-identity conditions which conform to some principle (or set of principles) of classification which are standardly employed in our divisions of belief-forming processes (of which the principles I have indicated above furnish the most obvious examples). If he succeeds in doing this so that the requirements in (2) are met, his claim is sustained; if he cannot, then his claim is defeated.

The final issue which requires discussion in this section is that of explaining the modal and conditional notions I have used. There are all kinds of possibility, and claims about what is possible bear an implicit relativization to a set of facts which are held constant.[16] When we say, in (2), that, given any sufficiently rich life, X could have had a belief which was the product of a particular type of process, should we conceive of this as merely logical possibility or are there some features of the actual world which are tacitly regarded as fixed? I suggest that we are not just envisaging any logically possible world. We imagine a world in which X has similar mental powers to those he has in the actual world. By hypothesis, X's experience is different. Yet the capacities for thinking, reasoning, and acquiring knowledge which X possesses as a member of *homo sapiens* are to remain unaffected: we want to say that X, *with the kinds of cognitive capacities distinctive of humans*, could have undergone processes of the appropriate type, even if his experiences had been different.[17]

Humans might have had more faculties for acquiring knowledge than they actually have. For example, we might have had some strange ability to "see" what happens on the other side of the Earth. When we consider the status of a particular type of process as an a priori warrant, the existence of worlds in which such extra faculties come into play is entirely irrelevant. Our investigation focuses on the question of whether a particular type of process would be available to a person with the kinds of faculties people actually have, not on whether such processes would be available to creatures whose capacities for acquiring knowledge are augmented or diminished. Conditions (2(b)) and (2(c)) are to be read in similar fashion. Rewriting (2(b)) to make the form of the conditional explicit, we obtain: for any life e sufficient for X for p and for any world in which X has e, in which he believes that p, in which his belief is the product of a process of the appropriate kind, and *in which X has the cognitive capacities distinctive of humans*, X is warranted in believing that p. Similarly, (2(c)) becomes: for any life e sufficient for X for p and for any world in which X has e, in which he believes that p, in which his belief is the product of a process of the appropriate kind, *and in which X has the cognitive capacities distinctive of humans*, p. Finally, the notion of a life's being sufficient for X for p also bears an implicit reference to X's native powers. To say that a particular life enables X to form certain concepts is to maintain that, given the genetic programming with which X is endowed, that life allows for the formation of the concepts.

The account I have offered can be presented more graphically in the following way. Consider a human as a cognitive device, endowed initially with a particular kind of structure. Sensory experience is fed into the device and, as a result, the device forms certain concepts. For any proposition p, the class of experiences which are sufficiently rich for p consists of those experiences which would enable the device, with the kind of structure it actually has, to acquire the concepts to believe that p. To decide whether or not a particular item of knowledge that p is an item of a priori knowledge we consider whether the type of process which produced the belief that p is a process which would have been available to the device, with the kind of structure it actually has, if different sufficiently rich experiences had been fed into it, whether, under such circumstances, processes of the type would warrant belief that p, and would produce true belief that p.

Seen in this way, claims about apriority are implicitly indexical, in that they inherit the indexical features of "actual." [18] If this is not recognized, use of "a priori" in modal contexts can engender confusion. The truth value of "Possibly, X knows a priori that p" can be determined in one of two ways: we may consider the proposition expressed by the sentence at our world, and inquire whether there is a world at which that proposition is true; or we may ask whether there is a world at which the sentence expresses a true proposition. Because of the covert indexicality of "a priori," these lines of investigation may yield different answers. I suspect that failure to appreciate this point has caused trouble in assessing theses about the limits of the a priori. However, I shall not pursue the point here.[19]

V

At this point, I want to address worries that my analysis is too liberal, because it allows some of our knowledge of ourselves and our states to count as a priori. Given its Kantian psychologistic underpinnings, the theory appears to favor claims that some of our self-knowledge is a priori. However, two points should be kept in mind. Firstly, the analysis I have proposed can only be applied to cases in which we know enough about the ways in which our beliefs are warranted to decide whether or not the conditions of (2) are met. In some cases, our lack of a detailed account of how our beliefs are generated may mean that no firm decision about the apriority of an item of knowledge can be reached. Secondly, there may be cases, including cases of self-knowledge, in which we have no clear pre-analytic intuitions about whether a piece of knowledge is a priori.

Nevertheless, there are some clear cases. Obviously, any theory which implied that I can know a priori that I am seeing red (when, in fact, I am) would be suspect. But, when we apply my analysis, the unwanted conclusion does not follow. For, if the process which leads me to believe that I am seeing red (when I am) can be triggered in the absence of red, then (2(c)) would be violated. If the process cannot be triggered in the absence of red, then, given some sufficiently rich experiences, the process will not be available, so that (2(a)) will be violated. In general, knowledge of any involuntary mental state—such as pains, itches or hallucinations—will work in the same way. Either the process which leads from the occurrence of pain to the belief that I am in pain can be triggered in the absence of pain, or not: if it can, (2(c)) would be violated, if it cannot, then (2(a)) would be violated.

This line of argument can be sidestepped when we turn to cases in which we have the power, independently of experience, to put ourselves into the appropriate states. For, in such cases, one can propose that the processes which give us knowledge of the states cannot be triggered in the absence of the states themselves *and* that the processes are always available because we can always put ourselves into the states.[20] On this basis, we might try to conclude that we have a priori knowledge that we are imagining red (when we are) or thinking of Ann Arbor (when we are). However, the fact that such cases do not fall victim to the argument of the last paragraph does not mean that we are compelled to view them as cases of a priori knowledge. In the first place, the thesis that the processes through which we come to know our imaginative feats and our voluntary thoughts cannot be triggered in the absence of the states themselves requires evaluation—and, lacking detailed knowledge of those processes, we cannot arrive at a firm judgment here. Secondly, the processes in question will be required to meet (2(b)) if they are to be certified as a priori warrants. This means that, whatever experience hurls at us, beliefs produced by such processes will be warranted. We can cast doubt on this idea by imagining that our experience consists of a lengthy, and apparently reliable, training in neurophysiology, concluding with a presentation to ourselves of our own neurophysiological organization which appears to show that our detection of our imaginative states (say) is slightly defective, that (we always make mistakes about the contents of our imaginings. If this type of story can be developed, then (2(b)) will be violated, and the knowledge in question will not count as a priori. But, even if it cannot be coherently extended, and even if my analysis does judge our knowledge of states of imagination (and other "voluntary" states) to be a priori, it is not clear to me that this consequence is counterintuitive.

In fact, I think that one can make a powerful case for supposing that *some* self-knowledge is a priori. At most, if not all, of our waking moments, each of us knows of herself that she exists.[21] Although traditional ideas to the effect that self-knowledge is produced by some "non-optical inner look" are clearly inadequate, I think it is plausible to maintain that there are processes which do warrant us in believing that we exist—processes of reflective thought, for example—and which belong to a general type whose members would be available to us independently of experience.[22] Trivially, when any such process produces in a person a belief that she exists that belief is true. All that remains, therefore, is to ask if the processes of the type in question inevitably warrant belief in our own existence, or whether they would fail to do so, given a suitably exotic background experience. It is difficult to settle this issue conclusively without a thorough survey of the ways in which reflective belief in one's existence can be challenged by experience, but perhaps there are Cartesian grounds for holding that, so long as the belief is the product of reflective thought, the believer is warranted, no matter how wild his experience may have been. If this is correct, then at least some of our self-knowledge will be a priori. However, in cases like this, attributions of apriority seem even less vulnerable to the criticism that they are obviously incorrect.

At this point we must consider a doctrinaire objection. If the conclusion of the last paragraph is upheld then we can know some contingent propositions a priori.[23] Frequently, however, it is maintained that only necessary truths can be known a priori. Behind this contention stands a popular argument.[24] Assume that a person knows a priori that p. His knowledge is independent of his experience. Hence he can know that p without any information about the kind of world he inhabits. So, necessarily p.

This hazy line of reasoning rests on an intuition which is captured in the analysis given above. The intuition is that a priori warrants must be ultra-reliable: if a person is entitled to ignore empirical information about the type of world she inhabits then that must be because she has at her disposal a method of arriving at belief which guarantees *true* belief. (This intuition can be defended by pointing out that if a method which could produce false belief were allowed to override experience, then we might be blocked from obtaining knowledge which we might otherwise have gained.) In my analysis, the intuition appears as (2(c)).[25]

However, when we try to clarify the popular argument we see that it contains an invalid step. Presenting it as a *reductio*, we obtain the following line of reasoning. Assume that a person knows a priori that p but that it is not necessary that p. Because p is contingent there are worlds at which p is false. Suppose that the person had inhabited such a world and behaved as she does at the actual world. Then she would have had an a priori warrant for a false belief. This is debarred by (2(c)). So we must conclude that the initial supposition is erroneous: if someone really does know a priori that p then p is necessary.

Spelled out in this way, the argument fails. We are not entitled to conclude from the premise that there are worlds at which p is false the thesis that there are worlds at which p is false *and* at which the person behaves as she does at the actual world. There are a number of propositions which, although they could be false, could not both be false and also believed by us. More generally, there are propositions which could not both be false and also believed by us in particular, definite ways. Obvious examples are propositions about ourselves and their logical consequences: such propositions as those expressed by tokens of the sentences "I exist," "I have some beliefs," "There are thoughts," and so forth. Hence the attempted *reductio* breaks down and allows for the possibility of a priori knowledge of some contingent propositions.

I conclude that my analysis is innocent of the charge of being too liberal in ascribing to us a priori knowledge of propositions about ourselves. Although it is plausible to hold that my account construes some of our self-knowledge as a priori, none of the self-knowledge it takes to be a priori is clearly empirical.

Moreover, it shows how a popular argument against the contingent a priori is flawed, and how certain types of contingent propositions—most notably propositions about ourselves—escape that argument. Thus I suggest that the analysis illuminates an area of traditional dispute.

VI

I now want to consider two different objections to my anslysis. My replies to these objections will show how the approach I have developed can be further refined and extended.

The first objection, like those considered above, charges that the analysis is too liberal. My account apparently allows for the possibility that a priori knowledge could be gained through perception. We can imagine that some propositions are true at any world of which we can have experience, and that, given sufficient experience to entertain those propositions, we could always come to know them on the basis of perception. Promising examples are the proposition that there are objects, the proposition that some objects have shapes, and other, similar propositions. In these cases, one can argue that we cannot experience worlds at which they are false and that any (sufficiently rich) experience would provide perceptual warrant for belief in the propositions, regardless of the specific content of our perceptions. If these points are correct (and I shall concede them both, for the sake of argument), then perceptual processes would qualify as a priori warrants. Given any sufficiently rich experience, some perceptual process would be available to us, would produce warranted belief and, *ex hypothesi,* would produce warranted *true* belief.

Let us call cases of the type envisaged cases of *universally empirical* knowledge. The objection to my account is that it incorrectly classifies universally empirical knowledge as a priori knowledge. My response is that the classical notion of apriority is too vague to decide such cases: rather, this type of knowledge only becomes apparent when the classical notion is articulated. One could defend the classification of universally empirical knowledge as a priori by pointing out that such knowledge requires no particular type of experience (beyond that needed to obtain the concepts, of course). One could oppose that classification by pointing out that, even though the content of the experience is immaterial, the knowledge is still gained by perceiving, so that it should count as a posteriori.

If the second response should seem attractive, it can easily be accommodated by recognizing a stronger and a weaker notion of apriority. The weaker notion is captured in (1) and (2). The stronger adds an extra requirement: no process which involves the operation of a perceptual mechanism is to count as an a priori warrant.

At this point, it is natural to protest that the new condition makes the prior analysis irrelevant. Why not define a priori knowledge outright as knowledge which is produced by processes which do not involve perceptual mechanisms? The answer is that the prior conditions are not redundant: knowledge which is produced by a process which does not involve perceptual mechanisms need not be independent of experience. For the process may fail to generate warranted belief against a backdrop of misleading experience. (Nor may it generate true belief in all relevant counterfactual situations.) So, for example, certain kinds of thought-experiments may generate items of knowledge given a particular type of experience, but may not be able to sustain that knowledge against misleading experiences. Hence, if we choose to exclude universally empirical knowledge from the realm of the a priori in the way suggested, we are building on the analysis given in (1) and (2), rather than replacing it.

A different kind of criticism of my analysis is to accuse it of revealing the emptiness of the classical notion of apriority. Someone may suggest that, in exposing the constraints on a priori knowledge, I have shown that there could be very little a priori knowledge. Although I believe that this suggestion is incorrect, it is worth pointing out that, even if it is granted, my approach allows for the development of weaker notions which may prove epistemologically useful.

Let me first note that we can introduce approximations to a priori knowledge. Suppose that A is any type of process all of whose instances culminate in belief that p. Define the *supporting class* of A to be that class of lives, e, such that, (a) given e, some process in A could occur (and so produce belief that p), (b) given e, any process in A which occurred would produce warranted true belief that p. (Intuitively, the supporting class consists of those lives which enable processes of the type in question to produce knowledge.) The *defeating class* of A is the complement of the supporting class of A within the class of lives which are sufficient for p. A priori warrants are those processes which belong to a type whose defeating class is null. But we can be more liberal, and allow approximations to a priori knowledge by considering the size and/or nature of the defeating class. We might, for example, permit the defeating class to contain those radically disruptive experiences beloved of sceptics. Or we can define a notion of *contextual* apriority by allowing the defeating class to include experiences which undermine "framework principles." [26] Or we may employ a concept of *comparative* apriority by ordering defeating classes according to inclusion relations. Each of these notions can serve a useful function in delineating the structure of our knowledge.

VII

Finally, I want to address a systematic objection to my analysis. The approach I have taken is blatantly psychologistic. Some philosophers may regard these psychological complications as objectionable intrusions into epistemology. So I shall consider the possibility of rival apsychologistic approaches.

Is there an acceptable view of a priori knowledge which rivals the Kantian conception? The logical positivists hoped to understand a priori knowledge without dabbling in psychology. The simplest of their proposals was the suggestion that X knows a priori that p if and only if X believes that p and p is analytically true.[27]

Gilbert Harman has argued cogently that, in cases of factual belief, the nature of the reasons for which a person believes is relevant to the question of whether he has knowledge.[28] Similar considerations arise with respect to propositions which the positivists took to be a priori. Analytic propositions, like synthetic propositions, can be believed for bad reasons, or for no reasons at all, and, when this occurs, we should deny that the believer knows the propositions in question. Assume, as the positivists did, that mathematics is analytic, and imagine a mathematician who comes to believe that some unobvious theorem is true. This belief is exhibited in her continued efforts to prove the theorem. Finally, she succeeds. We naturally describe her progress by saying that she has come to know something she only believed before. The positivistic proposal forces us to attribute knowledge from the beginning. Worse still, we can imagine that the mathematician has many colleagues who believe the theorem because of dreams, trances, fits of Pythagorean ecstasy, and so forth. Not only does the positivistic approach fail to separate the mathematician after she has found the proof from her younger self, but it also gives her the same status as her colleagues.

A natural modification suggests itself: distinguish among the class of analytic truths those which are elementary (basic laws of logic, immediate consequences of definitions, and, perhaps, a few others), and propose that elementary analytic truths can be known merely by being believed, while the rest are known, when they are known a priori, by inference from such truths. Even this restricted version of the original claim is vulnerable. If you believe the basic laws of logic because you have learned them from an eminent mathematician who has deluded himself into believing that the system of *Grundgesetze* is consistent and true, then you do not have a priori knowledge of those laws. Your belief in the laws of logic is undermined by evidence which you do not currently possess, namely the evidence which would expose your teacher as a misguided fanatic. The moral is obvious: apsychologistic approaches to a priori knowledge fail because, for a priori knowledge as for factual knowledge, the reasons for which a person believes are relevant to the question of whether he knows.

Although horror of psychologizing prevented the positivists from offering a defensible account of a priori knowledge, I think that my analysis can be used to articulate most of the doctrines that they wished to defend. Indeed, I believe that many classical theses, arguments and debates can be illuminated by applying the analysis presented here. My aim has been to prepare the way for investigations of traditional claims and disputes by developing in some detail Kant's conception of a priori knowledge. "A priori" has too often been a label which philosophers could attach to propositions they favored, without any clear criterion for doing so. I hope to have shown how a more systematic practice is possible.

Notes

I am grateful to several members of the Department of Philosophy at the University of Michigan for their helpful comments on a previous version of this paper, and especially to Alvin Goldman and Jaegwon Kim for their constructive suggestions. I would also like to thank Paul Benacerraf, who first interested me in the problem of characterizing a priori knowledge, and prevented many errors in early analyses. Above all, I am indebted to Patricia Kitcher and George Sher, who have helped me to clarify my ideas on this topic. Patricia Kitcher's advice on issues in the philosophy of mind relevant to §V was particularly valuable.

1. There are some exceptions. Passing attention to the problem of defining apriority is given in Pollock 1974, chapter 10; Swinburne 1975, esp. pp. 238–241; Erwin 1974, especially pp. 593–597. The inadequacy of much traditional thinking about apriority is forcefully presented in Kripke 1971, especially pp. 149–151, and Kripke 1972, especially pp. 260–264.

2. See Kripke 1971, 1972.

3. For ease of reference, I take propositions to be the objects of belief and knowledge, and to be what declarative sentences express. I trust that my conclusions would survive any successful elimination of propositions in favor of some alternative approach to the objects of belief and knowledge.

4. Kant 1787, B2–3.

5. See Pollock 1974; Swinburne 1975; Erwin 1974.

6. Someone might be tempted to propose, conversely, that all innate knowledge is a priori (cf. Swinburne 1975, p. 239). In Kitcher 1978, I have argued that there may well be no innate knowledge and that, if there were any such knowledge, it would not have to be a priori.

7. Pollock 1974, p. 301, claims that we can only resist the suggestion that this knowledge is independent of experience by complicating the notion of experience. For the reason given in the text, such desperate measures seem to me to be unnecessary.

8. See the example of the man who undermines the foundations of his house, Kant 1787, B3.

9. Prominent exponents of this approach are Alvin Goldman, Gilbert Harman and David Armstrong. See Goldman 1967, 1975, 1976, 1979; Harman 1973; Armstrong 1973.

10. Psychologistic epistemologies are often accused of confusing the context of discovery with the context of justification. For a recent formulation of this type of objection, see Lehrer 1974, pp. 123 ff. I have tried to show that psychologistic epistemology is not committed to mistakes with which it is frequently associated in Kitcher 1979. I shall consider the possibility of an apsychologistic approach to apriority in §VII below.

11. More details about Kant's theory of pure intuition can be found in my paper Kitcher 1975, especially pp. 28–33.

12. For further discussion of this requirement and the possibility of the contingent a priori, see §V below.

13. For different reasons, Goldman proposes that an analysis of the general notion of warrant (or, in his terms, justification) can focus on psychological processes. See section 2 of Goldman 1979.

14. Consider, for example, a Kantian process of pure intuition which begins with the construction of a triangle. Should we say that a process of the same type must begin with the construction of a triangle of the same size and shape, a triangle of the same shape, any triangle, or something even more general? Obviously there are many natural classifications here, and I think the best strategy is to suppose that an apriorist is entitled to pick any of them. Strictly, the sets which do not constitute types are those which violate correct taxonomies. In making present decisions about types, we assume that our current principles of classification are correct. If it should turn out that those principles require revision then our judgments about types will have to be revised accordingly.

16. For a lucid and entertaining presentation of this point, see Lewis 1976, pp. 149–151.

17. Of course, X might have been more intelligent, that is, he might have had better versions of the faculties he has. We allow for this type of change. But we are not interested in worlds where X has extra faculties.

18. The idea that "actual" is indexical is defended by David Lewis in Lewis 1970. In van Fraassen 1977, Bas van Fraassen puts Lewis' ideas about "actual" in a general context. The machinery which van Fraassen presents in that paper can be used to elaborate the ideas of the present paragraph.

19. Jaegwon Kim has pointed out to me that, besides the "species-relative" notion of apriority presented in the text, there might be an absolute notion. Perhaps there is a class of propositions which would be knowable a priori by any being whom we would count as a rational being. Absolute a priori knowledge would thus be that a priori knowledge which is available to all possible knowers.

20. In characterizing pain as an involuntary state one paragraph back I may seem to have underestimated our powers of self-torture. But even a masochist could be defeated by unkind experience: as he goes to pinch himself his skin is anesthetized.

21. I shall ignore the tricky issue of trying to say exactly what is known when we know this and kindred things. For interesting explorations of this area, see Casteneda 1967, 1968; Perry 1977, 1979. The issue of how to represent the content of items of self-knowledge may force revision of the position taken in footnote 3 above: it may not be possible to identify objects of belief with meanings of sentences. Although such a revision would complicate my analysis, I don't think it would necessitate any fundamental modifications.

22. This presupposes that our knowledge of our existence does not result from some special kind of "inner sensation." For, if it did, different lives would deprive us of the warrant.

23. Kripke 1971, 1972 has attempted to construct examples of contingent propositions which can be known a priori. I have not tried to decide here whether his examples are successful, since full treatment of this question would lead into issues about the analysis of the propositions in question which are well beyond the scope of the present paper. For a discussion of some of the difficulties involved in Kripke's examples, see Donnellan 1977.

24. Kripke seems to take this to be the main argument against the contingent a priori. See Kripke 1972, p. 263.

25. As the discussion of this paragraph suggests, there is an intimate relation between my requirements (2(b)) and (2(c)). Indeed, one might argue that (2(b)) would not be met unless (2(c)) were also satisfied—on the grounds that one cannot allow a process to override experience unless it guarantees truth. The subsequent discussion will show that this type of reasoning is more complicated than appears. Hence, although I believe that the idea that a priori warrants function independently of experience does have implications for the reliability of these processes, I have chosen to add (2(c)) as a separate condition.

26. This notion of contextual apriority has been used by Hilary Putnam. See, for example, Putnam 1975a, 1978, especially p. 154.

27. See Ayer 1936, chapter IV and Schlick 1959a, especially p. 224.

28. Harman 1973, chapter 2; see also Goldman 1979, section 1.

8 Truth and Confirmation

Michael Friedman

Ideally, there is a close connection between confirmation and truth. Theories that are well confirmed tend to be true, or at least *approximately* true. Theories that are disconfirmed tend to be false. It would seem that some such nice connection between confirmation and truth must exist if scientific method is to be justified as a rational activity. For one of the important ends of scientific method is the construction of theories that are true, or at least approximately true. Obviously, then, scientific method will be an effective means to this end only if it does indeed tend to produce true, or at least approximately true, theories. Of course, this is not sufficient to justify scientific method as a rational activity, if only because scientific method has other important ends besides the construction of true theories: for example, to produce theories that have a lot of explanatory power. However, assuming (as I will here) that the construction of true theories is *one* important end of scientific method, such a connection between confirmation and truth is clearly necessary.

Now I don't know whether there really is this kind of relationship between confirmation and truth, whether scientific method really does tend to produce true theories (from now on I will omit the qualification about *approximate* truth). What I hope to do in this paper is to see what must be the case *if* such a connection between confirmation and truth is to exist. In particular, what must theories of confirmation and theories of truth look like, and how must they fit together, if we are to have such a desirable connection? Balancing the demands of theories of confirmation and theories of truth against one another in this way produces some, to my mind, interesting results: first, that a theory of confirmation must itself be an empirical science, that it must appeal to facts about the actual world; second, that a theory of truth must go beyond the usual Tarskian format, that it must contain in addition something like a causal theory of reference.

Reprinted from *The Journal of Philosophy* LXXVI (July 1979): 361–382, by permission of the author and the publisher. Copyright © 1979, *The Journal of Philosophy*.

I

What does traditional philosophy of science have to say about the connection between confirmation and truth? According to one view, which I will call the *positivist* view, the connection is remarkably simple: (i) theories are confirmed by their true observational consequences; (ii) theories are true if all their observational consequences are true. This view explains the notion of truth for theories in terms of the relatively unproblematic notion of truth for observation sentences. Further, it promises to give us the desired relationship between confirmation and truth: the better a theory is confirmed—that is, the larger the set of its true observational consequences—the closer it is to being true.

Unfortunately, this kind of view is faced with two immediate, and devastating, objections. First, although it tells us what it is for an entire theory to be true, it cannot supply a workable notion of truth for individual sentences of a theory. Given that our theories contain nonobservational sentences,[1] there can be two theories, T and T', both of which have all true observational consequences, even though, for some nonobservational sentence S, S belongs to T and the negation of S belongs to T'. Consequently, we cannot extend our definition of truth to individual sentences by requiring that a sentence be true just in case it is an element of a true theory; for this would result in both S and its negation being true.

Hence, the positivist view fails to define an even minimally adequate notion of truth. However, even if its definition of truth were formally satisfactory, it would still fail to deliver the promised connection between truth and confirmation. The positivist definition tells us that if *all* the observational consequences of a theory are true then the theory itself is true. Does it follow that theories that are confirmed—that is, *some* of whose observational consequences are true—tend to be true? Not at all. Most theories that have some true observational consequences do *not* have all true observational consequences. So the mere fact that a theory is confirmed does not make it probable or likely that it is true; it shows simply that its truth is still possible. The positivist view tells us that when all the evidence is in, when all the observational consequences of our theory have been checked, we will know whether the theory is true or false. It tells us absolutely nothing about the likelihood of our theory being true when less than all the evidence is in. Therefore, it really tells us nothing useful about confirmation at all, since *our* situation is always that all the evidence is not yet in.

A second type of view, which I will call the *Peircean* view, also tries to ensure a connection between scientific method and truth by giving a special *definition* of truth. According to this view, a sentence is true just in case it belongs to the unique theory that scientific method will arrive at "in the limit" when all the evidence is in. Waiving questions about the existence and uniqueness of its "limiting" theory, the Peircean view avoids some of the problems that beset the positivist view. That is, assuming existence and uniqueness, there can be only one true theory. Consequently, we are not faced with the possibility of a sentence and its negation both being true. Note, however, that unless the "limiting" theory is complete, it will not be the case that each sentence *or* its negation is true.

Thus, the Peircean notion of truth is more satisfactory from a formal point of view than the positivist notion. Nevertheless, the connection between truth and confirmation which it establishes is just as useless. We know, again by definition, that the theory produced by scientific method when all the evidence is in is true. What about the theories that scientific method produces when less than all the evidence is in? We are told nothing at all about the relation between *these* theories (which are all the theories *we* will ever know) and the ideal "limiting" theory. For all we know, all these theories are arbitrarily far from the "limiting" theory and are arbitrarily far, therefore, from the truth. Once one has defined truth as what scientific method arrives at "in the limit," it is easy to start picturing scientific method as gradually and steadily climbing closer and closer to the truth. However, just as on the positivist view, no gradual and steady *convergence* toward truth is guaranteed by the Peircean definition; it guarantees, merely, that truth is there waiting at the end.

The basic problem facing both the positivist view and the Peircean view can be brought out most clearly, I think, by examining the more sophisticated account of confirmation offered by Hans Reichenbach. By giving a highly idealized and specific model of confirmation, Reichenbach was able to achieve the same type of connection between truth and confirmation—a guarantee of truth in the "long run"—without having to give a special definition of truth. On both the positivist view and the Peircean view, on the other hand, we are given only the vaguest description of confirmation. A guarantee of truth in the "long run" is achieved only by redefining the word 'true'.

According to Reichenbach, we should think of scientific method in the following idealized way. The hypotheses we are trying to confirm are all about the relative frequencies of kinds of events in particular sequences of events. We are interested in hypotheses like 'The relative frequency of heads in a given sequence of tosses of a coin is $\frac{1}{2}$', 'The relative frequency of black ravens in a given sequence of ravens is 1', etc. Now, in general, the sequence in question will be infinite; so what we are really interested in are *limits* of relative frequencies. Given a sequence of events (for example, coin tossings), $e_1, e_2, e_3, \ldots$, and a property F of interest (for example, the property of coming up heads), form the sequence of relative frequencies, $s_1, s_2, s_3, \ldots$, where s_n is the relative frequency of Fs among the first n es, that is, the number of Fs in the set $\{e_1, e_2, \ldots, e_n\}$ divided by n. What we are interested in knowing, on Reichenbach's model, is the number

$$p = \lim_{n \to \infty} s_n$$

if it exists. (If the sequence of events is finite, p is just the ordinary relative frequency of Fs in the sequence.)

Such, according to Reichenbach, is the object of scientific method. The method itself proceeds as follows: Given a sequence of events and a property F of interest, we assume that our *evidence* consists of the relative frequency of Fs in an initial segment of the sequence. For example, we've observed ten tosses of a coin and noted that half of them so far have come up heads. Our problem is to say what the relative frequency will be if we continue the sequence. How do we infer this from the given evidence? First, we arbitrarily pick a small positive number ε. It doesn't matter what number we pick, as long as we use the same number for every inference we make about this particular sequence. Given an initial segment $e_1, e_2, \ldots, e_n$ of our sequence and the relative frequency s_n of Fs so far, we infer that $s_n - \varepsilon < p < s_n + \varepsilon$; that is, we infer that p—the eventual limiting relative frequency—lies within ε of s_n—the observed relative frequency.

What can we say about the tendency of this method of inference to lead to true beliefs? On Reichenbach's view we can say something very strong, namely that, if truth is there to be found at all, if the limit of the relative frequency of Fs actually exists, our method will eventually find it. More precisely, there is a number N such that the inferences we make after observing N or more elements of the sequence all have true conclusions. This follows directly from the definition of 'limit'. For recall that

$$p = \lim_{n \to \infty} s_n \text{ iff } \quad \text{for every positive } \varepsilon, \text{ there exists an } N, \text{ such that,}$$
$$\text{for all } m \geqslant N, s_n - \varepsilon < p < s_m + \varepsilon.$$

That is, if p really is the limit, then, for every positive ε no matter how small, there comes a point in the sequence of relative frequencies such that all later relative frequencies lie within ε of p. Thus, no matter which ε we pick to begin with, there will be a point N such that all inferences made after observing N or more elements (all of which have conclusions of the form '$s_m - \varepsilon < p < s_m + \varepsilon$' with $m \geqslant N$) are correct.

Reichenbach's account of the connection between truth and confirmation, like the accounts given by the positivist view and the Peircean view, establishes a connection in the "long run": scientific method is guaranteed to produce true hypotheses if we wait long enough. Reichenbach's account, however, has several advantages over the other two views. First, as noted above, it is not necessary to give any special redefinition of the notion of truth. Reichenbach can simply rely on our intuitive understanding that a statement of the form '$s_m - \varepsilon < p < s_m + \varepsilon$' is true just in case p really does lie within ε of s_m. Second, we don't have to wait until *all* the evidence is in. We know that there is a *finite* number N—which may, of course, be very large—such that the inferences based on the evidence of the first N members of our sequence are guaranteed of true conclusions. We are guaranteed of true conclusions, provided a limit exists at all, at some point considerably before we have examined all the elements of our sequence. Thus, unlike the positivist view and the Peircean view, Reichenbach's account gives us genuine *convergence* toward truth.

Nevertheless, it seems to me that Reichenbach's view does not really overcome the basic problem—which is a problem for all "long run" justifications, whether the "long run" is infinite or finite. We know that scientific method will produce truth at some point, but (i) we have no idea where the happy point, the point of convergence, occurs, and (ii) we have no idea what the connection between scientific method and truth is before the point of convergence; before the point of convergence our hypotheses may be arbitrarily far from the truth. In particular, we don't know whether the inferences we actually do make, or even whether the inferences that are physically possible for us to make, occur before or after the point of convergence. So, for all we know, all the inferences we ever actually make, and even all physically possible inferences, may have no likelihood whatever of having true conclusions. In other words, although Reichenbach's method converges, it doesn't necessarily converge in the class of actual (or even physically possible) inferences.

This difficulty is highlighted if we notice, as Reichenbach himself immediately points out, that there are infinitely many different methods of inference which all lead to truth in the "long run" in the very same sense. To see this, observe that if $c_1, c_2, c_3, \ldots$ is any sequence of positive numbers such that

$$\lim_{n \to \infty} c_n = 0$$

then the method that concludes that p lies within ε of $s_n + c_n$ on evidence s_n will eventually find the true limit p (if it exists) in exactly the same sense as the method that concludes that p lies within ε of s_n. This, of course, is because

$$\lim_{n\to\infty} (s_n + c_n) = \lim_{n\to\infty} s_n$$

Reichenbach's method is just a special case in this more general class of *convergent* methods, the special case when $c_n = 0$.

Now all these convergent methods—methods that conclude that p lies within ε of $s_n + c_n$ (with $\lim_{n\to\infty} c_n = 0$) on evidence s_n—agree in the "long run," and this fact may lead one to conclude that the choice of one method from among them does not really matter. This, however, would be to underestimate drastically the severity of the problem. For, given any particular piece of evidence—that a coin has come up heads 95% of the time in 1000 tosses, say—the different convergent methods yield arbitrarily divergent conclusions. One method will say that the eventual limiting relative frequency of heads is about .95; another will say that it is .05; a third will say that it is .50, etc. In short, any inference from any evidence is licensed by some convergent method. And we are given no reason to think that any one convergent method is better than any of the others.

Reichenbach himself thought there was a reason to prefer the value $c_n = 0$:

Now it is obvious that a system of wagers of the more general type may have advantages. The "correction" c_n may be determined in such a way that the resulting wager furnishes even at an early stage of the series a good approximation of the limit p. The prophesies of a good clairvoyant would be of this type. On the other hand, it may happen also that c_n is badly determined, i.e., the convergence is delayed by the correction. If the term c_n is arbitrarily formulated, we know nothing about the two possibilities. The value $c_n = 0$— i.e., the inductive method—is therefore the value of the smallest risk; any other determination may worsen the convergence. This is a practical reason for preferring the inductive principle.[2]

But it is clear that the situation with respect to the relative riskiness of the value $c_n = 0$ and any other value is perfectly symmetrical. Granted, any other value may worsen the convergence, may lead to true conclusions at a later point, when compared to $c_n = 0$. Equally, however, the value $c_n = 0$ may worsen the convergence when compared to any other value. A priori, there is no way of knowing which value, including the value $c_n = 0$, will lead to convergence soonest. A priori, all values of c_n are equally risky.

How, then, can one value of c_n, one particular convergent method, be superior to the others? I think the answer is obvious: a method is superior if, when it is used in the inferences we actually do make, it leads to true conclusions sooner and more often than the other methods. And which method actually enjoys this kind of superiority depends on empirical facts: facts about the distribution of observed and unobserved relative frequencies. To take an absurdly simple example, suppose we are living in a world containing a single sequence of eight coin tossings. Suppose we never actually observe more than the first four tossings (the coin is tossed by a machine), and the distribution of heads looks like this is the entire sequence:

H T H T H H H H

The relative frequency of heads in the observed portion of the sequence is $\frac{1}{2}$, but the true relative frequency is $\frac{3}{4}$. In this simple world, the method that takes $c_n = 1/n$ does better than the method $c_n = 0$. $c_n = 1/n$ yields the true value $\frac{1}{2} + \frac{1}{4} = \frac{3}{4}$ on the evidence we actually observe; $c_n = 0$ yields the incorrect value $\frac{1}{2}$. In general, the value $c_n = 0$ works better in worlds in which the distribution of relative frequencies is uniform as between the observed and the unobserved parts; other values of c_n work better in worlds that are not so uniform.[3]

If this is correct, if the superiority of an inductive method consists in its propensity to produce true conclusions in the class of actual or physically possible inferences, it follows that "long run" justifications are completely beside the point. If a method does not tend to produce true conclusions in the inferences we actually make, or even in the inferences we (physically) could make, why should its properties in the "long run" be of any interest to us? Conversely, if a method does tend to produce true conclusions when used in actual inferences, we should prefer it, regardless of its behavior "in the limit"—which may, after all, be physically impossible for us to reach. Conclusion: "long run" justifications, whether of the simple definitional type characteristic of the positivist and Peircean views or of the more sophisticated Reichenbachian type, do not provide us with the kind of connection that we want between confirmation and truth. They do not and cannot show that scientific method tends to produce true theories in actual practice.

II

The moral that I would like to draw from the failure of "long run" justifications, then, is this: What needs to be shown is that scientific method tends to produce true hypotheses not "in the limit" or when all the evidence is in, but in the class of actual and physically possible inferences. Further, I would like to suggest that we explain what it is for a method to tend toward truth in the class of actual and physically possible inferences, in terms of the existence of *statistical laws* of the form:

For all S, the probability that S is true, given that S is accepted (rejected) by method M is r.

Thus, we can say that a method *M* is *reliable* if

For all *S* and *R*, if *M* rejects *R* in favor of *S*, then the probability that *S* is true is greater than the probability that *R* is true.

(If *M* attaches a numerical degree of belief *p* to *S*, we can say that *M* is reliable just in case the probability that *S* is true, given that *M* assigns value *p* to *S*, is *p*.) In other words, although a reliable method does not necessarily produce true conclusions, or even conclusions with a high probability of truth, it does *tend* toward truth: as time goes on, the conclusions that it accepts acquire ever increasing probabilities of truth. My suggestion is that it is the task of confirmation theory to show that the methods scientists actually use are reliable in this sense.

   This suggestion calls for a few words of explanation. First, since we are concerned with statistical laws, the kind of probability at issue is objective or physical probability, not epistemic probability. We are requiring that there be a lawlike statistical correlation between the property of being reached by *M* and the property of being true, in the very same sense in which there is a lawlike statistical correlation between being a radium atom in a particular state and emitting radiation during a given interval of time, between tosses of a fair coin and the property of coming up heads, between smoking and lung cancer, etc. Such lawlike statistical correlations hold independently of our knowledge that they hold; just as lawlike *universal* correlations hold independently of our knowledge that they hold. Second, such a statistical law should not be confused with the statement

r% of the sentences accepted (rejected) by actual applications of *M* are true.

In a sense, the corresponding statistical law is both stronger and weaker than a statement about actual relative frequencies. It is stronger because the statement about actual relative frequencies may be merely accidental and not hold as a matter of law. It is weaker because the statistical law can be true even if the actual relative frequency is arbitrarily far from *r*. Thus, for example, a method can be reliable in my sense even if all its actual applications lead to false conclusions. It seems to me, however, that this is as it should be. What we are interested in is the lawlike correlation between our method and truth, not in the—perhaps merely accidental—distribution of actual true and false conclusions. This is just to say that we are interested in the class of actual and physically possible inferences, not merely in the class of actual inferences.

   How is confirmation theory to arrive at such statistical laws connecting our inductive methods and truth? How are we to establish the reliability of scientific method? The way to proceed, I think, is to try to *derive* the reliability of our inductive methods from our psychological and physical theories, our theories about how the human mind arrives at beliefs through interaction with its environment. For the reliability of our inductive methods, if indeed they are reliable, depends on general facts relating the process of belief acquisition to events in the world. Thus, for example, the reliability of the regularities we follow in coming to hold simple perceptual beliefs depends on two factors: (i) general connections between perceptual beliefs and sensory stimulation; (ii) general connections between sensory stimulation and physical objects. Very roughly, I am usually right when I assent to 'There is a table in front of me' as a result of sensory stimulation, because such stimulation is usually due to the presence of a table. Since the reliability of an inductive method depends in this way on general connections between the mind and the world, the way to establish the reliability of an inductive method is to appeal to our best theories of the mind and the world, our best psychological and physical theories.

Now, of course, on this type of view the justification that confirmation theory provides for scientific method is in an important sense circular. For we derive the reliability of scientific method from theories that are themselves the product of scientific method. In appealing to general facts about the actual world, confirmation theory has to depend on the very methods it is attempting to justify. And, of course, it is the desire to avoid precisely this kind of circularity that motivates philosophers to look for an a priori justification of scientific method: a connection between scientific method and truth which does not depend on facts about the actual world. Such is the nature of the connection between scientific method and truth provided by the positivist view, the Peircean view, and Reichenbach's view. In looking for a connection between scientific method and truth only "in the limit" or in the "long run" we avoid the appeal to empirical facts about the reliability of scientific method in actual practice. However, if I am right, this kind of circularity is both necessary and inevitable. Can we say anything to make it more palatable?

First, one should appreciate just how hopeless the idea of an a priori justification of scientific method is. The impossibility of such a justification follows, it seems to me, from two simple and fundamental facts: (i) there has to be some kind of link between justification and truth; a justification of scientific method must say something about its propensity to lead to truth; (ii) scientific method is not logically guaranteed of reaching true conclusions; it is an incurably nondeductive method. There is no inductive method that is more reliable in every logically possible world than every other method; consequently, there is no method that is a priori best, there is no method that is a priori the most reliable. We have to know facts about the actual world if we are to know which method is best; and we have to know facts about the actual world to know even that any given method has any chance at all of leading to truth. This is why attempts to justify induction by appealing to the *meaning* of 'justified' or of 'rational' or of 'inference' are so unsatisfying. No such facts about meaning (if indeed they exist) can guarantee that there is any connection at all between inductive inference and truth. It is not very comforting to be told that scientific method is justified or rational in virtue of the meaning of 'justified' or the meaning of 'rational', if, for all we know, we inhabit a world in which scientific method has no chance whatever of producing true conclusions.

Second, although the justification we obtain by deriving the reliability of scientific method from general facts about the actual world is undoubtedly circular, it is not necessarily *viciously* circular. That is, the procedure I envision is certainly not *guaranteed* of success. Just because the facts about the world that we appeal to in attempting to justify scientific method are themselves obtained by scientific method, it by no means follows that these facts will actually justify scientific method, that they will entail its reliability. For all we know, the theories produced by our inductive methods will eventually undermine the reliability of those very methods. And, in fact, some skeptically minded philosophers have argued that this is the situation in which we find ourselves. Some philosophers, for example, have claimed that science shows that material objects never, or almost never, have the properties that they seem to have in ordinary perceptual contexts. According to these philosophers, then, the regularities we follow in coming to hold ordinary perceptual beliefs are completely unreliable. As Russell puts it: "Naive realism leads to physics, and physics, if true, shows that naive realism is false. Therefore, naive realism, if true, is false; therefore, it is false." [4] Russell neglects to point out that this kind of situation would cast doubt on physics as well as naive realism, since physics is itself inferred from naive-realist perceptual beliefs. As I see it, an important task of scientific epistemology is to show that science does not undermine its own evidential base in this way. Our task, in Quine's words, is to "defend science from within, against its self-doubts." [5]

Finally, it is helpful to compare the problem of justifying inductive methods of inference with the problem of justifying deductive methods of inference. How do we justify our deductive methods? In particular, how do we establish a connection between deductive inference and truth? Ideally, we proceed as follows. First, we give a syntactic description of the class of deductive arguments: a definition of a syntactic consequence relation that, we hope, holds between two sentences of our language just in case the second is deductively inferable from the first. Second, we define a semantic consequence relation that holds between two sentences just in case every interpretation of the nonlogical vocabulary of the language that makes the first sentence true also makes the second sentence true. Third, we try to prove a completeness theorem that establishes the equivalence of the syntactic and the semantic consequence relations. This procedure furnishes a justification of our deductive methods of inference in the following sense. It shows that every deductive inference that is captured by our syntactic description is in fact truth-preserving, that if the premises of such an argument are true, the conclusion is also. And it gives us a reason to think that our syntactic description does indeed capture all deductive inferences—or, at any rate, that it captures all deductive inferences that we are willing to call correct.

It is obvious that this procedure is also in an important sense circular. In proving the desired completeness theorem, we have to use the very methods of deductive inference that we are attempting to justify. In proving the soundness of *modus ponens*, for example, we have to use an argument that is, in effect, itself just an instance of *modus ponens*. However, it is just as obvious, I think, that our procedure does nonetheless provide an important kind of justification for deductive methods of inference. It shows that there is a desirable harmony between the methods we use in practice and our conception of what the point of those methods is, namely, preservation of truth from premises to conclusion. And, just as in the case of inductive methods, we have no guarantee in advance that this kind of harmony exists. The completeness theorem, therefore, accomplishes something significant despite its circularity.

Moreover, following an extremely illuminating discussion by Michael Dummett,[6] we should observe that the purpose of justifying deductive inference in this way is not to persuade someone who rejects our deductive methods to adopt them. Rather, it is to explain to ourselves why our deductive methods are good methods to use. The kind of circularity exhibited by the completeness theorem detracts from its usefulness in the former case but not in the latter. I think the situation with inductive inference is similar. The aim of confirmation theory is not to persuade someone who rejects our inductive methods to adopt them. Rather, it is to explain to ourselves what is so good about the methods we actually employ. And, again, the circularity exhibited by the kind of empirical approach to confirmation theory that I am suggesting presents no obstacle to *this* goal. On the contrary, if I am right, this approach represents the only possible way to achieve it.

III

We saw above that formal demands coming from the side of semantics or the theory of truth place constraints on the possible connections between scientific method and truth which confirmation theory can hope to establish. Thus, for example, the positivist view is unsatisfactory, because it relies on a notion of truth according to which a sentence and its negation can both be true. Similarly, the Peircean view is unsatisfactory, because, unless we have some guarantee that the ideal "limiting" theory is complete, it will not be the case that each sentence or its negation is true. In this section I would like to see whether the demands of confirmation theory place any analogous constraints on the theory of truth. In particular, does asking confirmation theory to derive *reliability statements*: statements of the form

For all S, the probability that S is true, given that S is accepted (rejected) by method M, is r.

from our psychological and physical theories, have any implications for the theory of truth? I will argue that this requirement on confirmation theory does indeed have such implications, that it can be satisfied only if the theory of truth includes something like a causal theory of reference.

Before proceeding with the argument, it will be helpful to have before us examples of the two kinds of semantic theories we will be discussing: a theory of truth without a theory of reference (this, of course, is the kind that Tarski himself actually constructed) and a theory of truth that includes a theory of reference. For simplicity, let us suppose that the language we are giving a theory of has the structure of a first-order quantificational language; that it has a finite number of primitive one-place predicates $'P_1'$, $'P_2'$, ... , $'P_n'$; a finite number of individual constants $'a_1'$, $'a_2'$, ... , $'a_m'$; an infinite number of variables $'x_1'$, $'x_2'$, $'x_3'$, ... ; and that the well-formed formulas of the language are built up from these and the primitive logical symbols $'\sim'$, $'\vee'$, $'\exists'$ $'('$, $')'$ in the usual way. Call this language L. We will give our two theories of truth in a metalanguage M^L for L which consists of English, plus corner quotes, plus L *itself*. In addition, α will be an assignment of objects to the terms—the variables and individual constants—of L; and $\alpha(v/d)$ will be the assignment that assigns the object d to the variable v and agrees with α on all other terms of L.

T1 will be a theory of truth without a theory of reference. We construct T1 by adding a two-place predicate 'sat' to M^L which relates assignments to formulas of L. The axioms of T1 are:

1.1 $\alpha('a_1') = a_1$
1.2 $\alpha('a_2') = a_2$
$\vdots$ $\vdots$

1.m $\alpha('a_m') = a_m$
2.1 α sat $\ulcorner P_1 t \urcorner$ iff $P_1 \alpha(t)$
2.2 α sat $\ulcorner P_2 t \urcorner$ iff $P_2 \alpha(t)$
$\vdots$ $\vdots$

2.n α sat $\ulcorner P_n t \urcorner$ iff $P_n \alpha(t)$

3. α sat $\ulcorner \sim f \urcorner$ iff α does not sat f
4. α sat $\ulcorner f \vee g \urcorner$ iff α sat f or α sat g
5. α sat $\ulcorner \exists v f \urcorner$ iff for some object d, $\alpha(v/d)$ sat f

where f, g are formulas of L, t is a term of L, and v is a variable of L. Finally, we define a one-place predicate 'Tr' in M^L by

6. $\mathrm{Tr}\,(f)$ iff every α sat f

T2 will be a theory of truth that includes a theory of reference. It consists of two parts. First, we add a two-place predicate 'sat' as above, plus two additional two-place predicates from the theory of reference: 'Den', which relates individual constants of L to the objects they denote; and 'Ap', which relates predicates of L to the objects in their extensions. As axioms we take:

1. $\alpha(c) = d$ iff Den (c,d)
2. α sat $\ulcorner Ft \urcorner$ iff Ap $(F, \alpha(t))$

where c is an individual constant and F a predicate; and 3–6 exactly as in T1. Second, we add a body of general truths about the relations Den and Ap: a theory of reference.[7] Of course, neither I nor anyone else actually has such a theory, and that is one reason the idea of settling for T1 is attractive. Nevertheless, I will try to show that patience would be a better strategy.

What does the difference between T1 and T2 amount to? Let us call axioms 3–6, which are common to the two theories, the *induction axioms*; the remaining axioms, on which T1 and T2 differ, the *basis axioms*. The basis axioms of T1 are all singular assertions, one for each particular individual constant of L and each particular primitive predicate of L. The basis axioms of T2, on the other hand, generalize over all individual constants of L and all primitive predicates of L, respectively. The significance of this kind of distinction is clarified if we compare T1 and T2 to an even simpler theory of truth, T3. T3 is constructed by adding a single one-place predicate 'Tr' to M^L, and for each sentence (formula with no free variables) S of L an axiom of the form:[8]

Tr ('S') iff S

Thus, T3, unlike T1 and T2, has an infinite number of axioms.

The difference between T2 and T1 is analogous to the difference between T1 and T3. T3 contains no general assertions involving Tr, just an infinite number of singular assertions about particular sentences of L; whereas T1 allows us to make general assertions involving Tr and the logical vocabulary of L. Thus, in T1 (plus a bit of concatenation theory) we can prove:

For all sentences S and R Tr $(\ulcorner S \vee R \urcorner)$ iff Tr (S) or Tr (R)

but in T3 we can prove only, for each particular S and R,

$$\text{Tr}('S \vee R') \text{ iff } \text{Tr}('S') \text{ or } \text{Tr}('R')$$

Similarly, T1 contains no general assertions involving the primitive predicates of L and sat; just n singular assertions, one for each particular predicate. T2, on the other hand, in virtue of the general truths in its (as yet unknown) theory of reference, can contain such general assertions about the primitive predicates of L.

The advantage that T1 enjoys over T3—the fact that T1 contains generalizations where T3 contains just the instances of such generalizations—allows us to derive desirable general laws about truth in T1 which are not derivable in T3. We can prove in T1 such general laws as

For all S, either $\text{Tr}(S)$ or $\text{Tr}(^\ulcorner \sim S^\urcorner)$

and

For all S, $\text{Tr}(^\ulcorner S \vee \sim S^\urcorner)$.

Most importantly, in T1 plus concatenation theory, we can prove a general soundness theorem:

For all S and R, if $S \vdash R$ and $\text{Tr}(S)$, then $\text{Tr}(R)$.

where $\vdash$ is the usual syntactic consequence relation. In T3, on the other hand, even together with concatenation theory, there is no hope of deriving a general soundness theorem. We can derive at most particular instances of the theorem. This, then, is one clear virtue of inductive Tarski-style theories of truth as compared to *purely* disquotational theories like T3. A Tarski-style theory is necessary if we wish to justify deductive inference by appealing to the fact that it preserves truth.

I suggest that T2 enjoys an analogous advantage over T1 with respect to the justification of inductive inference. If one wishes to justify inductive inference in the way I sketched above—by deriving reliability statements about our inductive methods—then a Tarski-style theory of truth is insufficient: a theory of reference is needed. For note first that a reliability statement is a general assertion, a statement of a statistical law. But the only general assertions contained in T1 concern the interaction of 'Tr' and 'sat' with the logical vocabulary of L; T1 makes no general claims about the nonlogical vocabulary of L. Reliability statements, however, if true at all, are not true simply in virtue of general facts about the logical vocabulary of L; they depend on general facts about the nonlogical vocabulary of L as well. Furthermore, reliability statements, if true at all, depend largely on facts of physics and psychology, on how the world is and how the human mind interacts with the world. To derive reliability statements, therefore, we need some way of connecting up our physical and psychological theories with our semantic theories. We need general laws connecting physics and psychology with the theory of truth; and it is precisely this kind of generality that a theory of reference attempts to provide. On the other hand, it is difficult to see how a Tarski-style theory of truth can be connected up with physics and psychology in any general way, since it contains only a list of singular assertions in its basis, one for each individual constant and one for each predicate. It provides no mechanism, therefore, by which general laws from other disciplines can have implications for semantics.

Now this point about generality is important; but, by itself, it is not very informative unless we know what *kind* of general laws are supposed to be contained in our theory of reference. For mere generality is far too easy to come by. To see this, observe that we can even transform T1 into a theory that generalizes over primitive expressions by the following trivial expedient:

1. Den (c,d) iff $c = $ 'a_1' and $d = a_1$ or $c = $ 'a_2' and $d = a_2$ or ... or
   $\quad\quad c = $ 'a_m' and $d = a_m$
2. Ap (F,d) iff $F = $ 'P_1' and $P_1 d$ or $F = $ 'P_2' and $P_2 d$ or ... or
   $\quad\quad F = $ 'P_n' and $P_n d$

These two axioms are indeed *general* assertions about the nonlogical vocabulary of L. Nevertheless, they clearly do not take us beyond the disquotational spirit of T1, and they are not the sort of assertions one has in mind when one speaks of a genuine *theory* of reference. We are faced, therefore, with two large questions: What sort of assertions do make up a genuine theory of reference? Why should one prefer such assertions to trivial disquotational theories? [9]

Unfortunately, I have relatively little to say about the first question. What I have in mind is the kind of causal theory of reference that has been sketched, for example, by Hilary Putnam.[10] This kind of theory looks for physical and psychological mechanisms that relate the acquisition and use of expressions of L to features in the environment of speakers of L. The hope is to explain reference in terms of such physical and psychological mechanisms: a predicate of a certain general type (for example, a natural-kind word) has an object in its extension if that object bears the "right sort" of causal relation to the history of the predicate's acquisition and use. The obvious model here is the causal theory of perception. Just as the causal theory of perception determines the objects of perception by causal relations between those objects and perceptual activities, the causal theory of reference hopes to determine the objects of belief generally by similar (?) relations between those objects and linguistic activities.

What is important for our present purposes is that this kind of theory is historical or genetic. To determine the referent of an expression it looks "backward" to features of the environment that bear the "right sort" of causal relation to the use of the expression. As such, this kind of theory is to be distinguished not only from trivial disquotational theories, but also from what one might call *charity-based* theories of reference. Charity-based theories are teleological rather than genetic; instead of looking "backward" for causal mechanisms, they look "forward" to the theory of the world that speakers of L eventually construct. The idea is to assign referents in such a way that we maximize (roughly) the number of *true* sentences of this theory.[11] Of course, there is a very close relationship between charity-based theories and disquotational theories. A disquotational theory is the optimal charity-based theory for one's *own* language: it maximizes the number of sentences of one's own theory that are true (according to that very theory).

Why should one prefer causal or genetic theories of reference to both disquotational and charity-based theories? The above point about generality is insufficient to explain such a preference, because all three kinds of theory can be formulated in general terms. However, if we recall our earlier discussion of circularity, an interesting explanation emerges: a causal theory of reference is the only kind of theory that can figure in a justification of inductive inference which is not *viciously* circular. The "justification" provided by a charity-based theory, for example, is obviously viciously circular. Given that it is possible to assign referents in accordance with the principle of charity, we can easily prove in our semantics that most of the theory to be "justified" is in fact true. But this procedure puts no significant constraints on that theory; indeed, it can be carried out completely and optimally for any theory that is merely consistent. The "justification" provided by disquotational theories is similarly defective. On the basis of such a theory, together with the rest of our theory of the world, we can easily prove that each sentence of our theory of the world is true. (If this theory is finitely axiomatizable, we can even prove the general claim that all sentences in our theory of the world are true.) But again, this procedure puts no constraints at all on what our theory of the world must be like; it can be carried out for any theory whatsoever.

By contrast, the requirement that we derive reliability statements from our general theory of the world plus a causal theory of reference does put a significant constraint on our theory. It requires our theory to contain a detailed general description of how the mind interacts with its environment, on the basis of which our processes of belief acquisition can be shown to tend toward truth. There is no guarantee in advance that we can find any interesting general relations between the mind and its environment, nor, even if we can, that it will turn out that our theories are true or even tend toward truth. This is because a causal theory of reference, unlike the other two theories, specifies the referents of terms by considerations that are independent of the truth or falsehood of the sentences we happen to accept. The great virtue of this kind of theory is that it leaves open the *possibility* that most (or all) of our beliefs are false. For, if we can show nonetheless that our beliefs are true or at least tend toward truth, we will have accomplished something significant. Unlike the other two theories, a causal theory of reference allows our over-all theory of the world to have genuine self-critical power and, therefore, genuine potential for self-justification as well.

IV

To illustrate these points, let us consider the problem of saying when a generalization is confirmed by its instances. Under what conditions is a sentence of the form $\ulcorner \forall v(Fv \to Gv) \urcorner$ confirmed by the observed truth of a conjunction of instances of the form $\ulcorner (Fc \,\&\, Gc) \urcorner$? From the present point of view, the problem is to find a relation between sentences $C(S, R)$ such that if S is a generalization and R is a conjunction of its instances, we can derive a statistical law of the form:

(*) For all S and R, the probability that S is true given that R is observed to be true and $C(S, R)$, is p.

We can then say that S is confirmed by R if p is sufficiently large, large compared with competing generalizations, for example.

It was the hope of philosophers of science in the logical positivist tradition to characterize C in a purely syntactic or logical way, to describe the confirmation relation by appealing only to the logical forms of the sentences involved.[12] For example, on the simplest possible model, we just say that S and R have the required forms:

$C(S, R)$ iff there are predicates F, G such that $S = \ulcorner \forall v(Fv \to Gv) \urcorner$
            and R is a conjunction of sentences of the form $\ulcorner (Fc \,\&\, Gc) \urcorner$.

However, a purely syntactic approach was shown to be inadequate by the work of Nelson Goodman. Goodman shows that, for every generalization of the form $\ulcorner \forall v(Fv \to Gv) \urcorner$ that has true observed instances of the form $\ulcorner (Fc \,\&\, Gc) \urcorner$, there is a second generalization $\ulcorner \forall v(F'v \to G'v) \urcorner$—containing grue-like predicates—which is incompatible with the first and which also has true observed instances of the form $\ulcorner (F'c \,\&\, G'c) \urcorner$. The two generalizations bear exactly the same logical and syntactic relations to their observed instances, but they are not both confirmed by their instances. From the present point of view, this is not at all surprising, because, as I noted above, there is no hope of deriving reliability statements on the basis of logical and syntactic information alone. Accordingly, Goodman's examples show that the method of inference on which $C(S,R)$ is defined purely syntactically is simply not reliable.

What we need to add to the characterization of the confirmation relation is some information about the *predicates* occurring in our generalization. Goodman's work suggests that there is a class of predicates, the *projectible* predicates, such that generalizations in which only projectible predicates occur are confirmed by their instances, whereas generalizations in which nonprojectible predicates occur are not.[13] In other words, we want to modify the above syntactic characterization of confirmation to:

$C(S,R)$ iff there are *projectible* predicates F, G such that $S = \ulcorner \forall v(Fv \to Gv) \urcorner$
and R is a conjunction of sentences of the form $\ulcorner (Fc \,\&\, Gc) \urcorner$.

But which predicates are projectible? On Goodman's view they are the entrenched predicates, the predicates that have been frequently used in actual inductive inferences. This account, however, although it may be correct, leaves too much unexplained. By itself, it gives us no hint of why it is *better* to make inferences with projectible predicates rather than nonprojectible predicates.[14]

From the present point of view, Goodman's definition of 'projectible' is a good example of a charity-based strategy. The projectible predicates are just those which appear in *our* inductive inferences and, therefore, in the generalizations that *we* accept. Following out this kind of strategy, we can define 'projectible' by

(P) Proj (F) iff $F = \,'P_1'$ or $F = \,'P_2'$ or ... or $F = \,'P_k'$.

where $'P_1'$, $'P_2'$, ... , $'P_k'$ are the predicates occurring in our accepted generalizations. We can then use (P), together with those same generalizations, to derive something very like (*) from T1. The trouble with this strategy, of course, is that it makes it far too easy to establish reliability. Since we have given no *independent* specification of the class of projectible predicates, all the generalizations we actually accept are automatically justified. A justification of scientific method based on (P) and T1 *is* viciously circular: the requirement that we derive reliability statements of the form (*) from T + (P) + T1, where T is the rest of our theory of the world, puts no significant constraints on T.

The alternative suggestion is that we try to define 'projectible' in a manner independent of the generalizations we actually accept; we specify the projectible predicates in terms of the history of their acquisition, for example. We then use a causal theory of reference—a general theory of how physical and psychological mechanisms relate predicates with such-and-such a history of acquisition to features of the environment of such-and-such a kind—together with the rest of our theory of the world, to show that inductive inferences to generalizations whose vocabulary is limited to projectible predicates are in fact reliable. This strategy, unlike the above charity-based strategy, is circular but not viciously so. The requirement that we derive reliability statements of the form (*) from T + T2, where T2 contains a causal theory of reference, does put a significant constraint on T. Furthermore, I can think of no plausible way of achieving this result without something like a causal theory of reference. Conclusion: if one wants a nontrivial naturalistic justification of inductive inference one needs a nontrivial naturalistic semantics.

V

The upshot of my discussion is that both semantic theories and theories of confirmation have to be much more empirical than most philosophers have supposed. Confirmation theory has to appeal to statistical correlations between the methods of inference scientists actually employ and the physical environment. Semantic theory has to appeal to causal relations between the learning and use of words and their referential properties. Neither kind of theory can be purely formal in the way that the study of deductive logic is formal, and neither kind of theory, therefore, can be developed exclusively by philosophers or by philosopher-logicians. It seems to me that this is one important reason many philosophers have been so reluctant to pursue the point of view outlined here. This is one reason theories of confirmation that do not appeal to the actual probability of success or failure and semantic theories that don't involve a naturalistic notion of reference have been so popular. If my dignosis is correct, however, these kinds of theories prevent us from establishing precisely the connection between confirmation theory and semantics that is necessary for the justification of scientific method. By jealously guarding the purity of our subject matter we rob our theories of explanatory power; we leave ourselves unable to explain why scientific method is a rational activity.

Notes

An earlier version of this paper was presented at a Tufts University philosophy of science colloquium in April 1976. I am indebted to Hartry Field and Hilary Putnam for helpful conversations and general inspiration. I am also grateful to the editors of the *Journal of Philosophy* for forcing me to clarify and (I hope) improve my argument.

1. This is the heart of the problem, of course. It is the failure of attempts to define theoretical vocabulary explicitly in observational terms (à la Carnap's *Aufbau*) that leads to the collapse of this kind of positivism.

2. Reichenbach 1938, p. 355.

3. A similar point can be made with respect to more sophisticated classes of inductive methods: e.g., Carnap's λ-continuum. The λ-continuum is characterized as follows: Let h_F be the hypothesis that the next observed object will have property F, where F is an element of a partition of the universe (a class of mutually exclusive and jointly exhaustive properties). Let e be the statement that s_F out of s already observed objects have property F. The different confirmation functions c_λ satisfy

$$c_\lambda(h_F,e) = \frac{s_F + \lambda/K}{s + \lambda}$$

where K is the size of our partition. (i) For every finite λ, c_λ is convergent in (almost) Reichenbach's sense: as $s \to \infty$, $c_\lambda(h_F,e) \to \lim_{s\to\infty} s_F/s$. (ii) For small (compared with s) λ, $c_\lambda(h_F,e) \approx s_F/s \approx 1/K$. Thus, the larger λ we choose, the more reluctant we are to extrapolate from our observed samples. Smaller values of λ work better in worlds in which observed samples (of almost any size) tend to be representative of the entire universe. Larger values of λ work better in worlds in which observed samples (unless they are very big) tend not to be so representative.

4. Russell 1965, p. 13.

5. Quine 1974, p. 3.

6. Dummett 1973.

7. Note that it is really such a body of *general truths* about Den and Ap that distinguishes T2 from T1. If we like, we can add the *predicates* Den and Ap to T1 by the definitions T2: 1–2. I will have a bit more to say below about the *kind* of general truths that belong in such a theory of reference.

8. In this schema " '*S*' " is not a name for the letter '*S*'; rather, it is the result of enclosing the sentence *S* of *L* in quotation marks. Instead of " '*S*' " I could have more accurately, but less perspicuously, written " '"' $\cap$ *S* $\cap$ '"'."

9. It is not enough to complain that the disquotational theories *are* trivial—cf. Field 1972, where the distinction between T1 and T2 is first clearly set out (note that my T2 is Field's T1, and vice-versa)—for the notion of reference might just be a trivial notion; it might have no serious explanatory role. In this paper I am trying to suggest that there *is* an important explanatory role for the notion of reference.

10. Cf. Putnam 1975b.

11. Cf. Donald Davidson's use of the principle of charity, e.g., in Davidson 1973. I am indebted to the editors of the *Journal of Philosophy* for suggesting that such charity-based theories be considered and for the basic idea of the criticism to follow.

12. The classical treatments are Carnap 1936; and Hempel 1945. A recent contribution to this tradition is Glymour 1975.

13. Here, and in what follows, I ignore various technical niceties: that, for Goodman, 'projectible' applies to generalizations not predicates; that we should consider *pairs* of predicates rather than *single* predicates; *etc*. These complications do not affect my main point.

14. Of course, Goodman explicity rejects the demand for this kind of explanations; cf. Goodman 1965, pp. 98–9. This is because he is took quick to assume that a circular explanation of the kind suggested here is as good as no explanation at all.

9

Précis of *Knowledge and the Flow of Information*

Fred I. Dretske

Knowledge and the Flow of Information (Dretske 1981; henceforth *Knowledge*) is an attempt to develop a philosophically useful theory of information. To be philosophically useful the theory should: (1) preserve enough of our common understanding of information to justify calling it a theory *of* information; (2) make sense of (or explain its failure to make sense of) the theoretically central role information plays in the descriptive and explanatory efforts of cognitive scientists; and (3) deepen our understanding of the baffling place of mind, the chief consumer of information, in the natural order of things.

A secondary motive in writing this book, and in organizing its approach to philosophical problems around the notion of information, was to build a bridge, if only a terminological one, to cognitive science. Even if we don't have the same problems (psychologists are no more interested in Descartes's Demon than philosophers are in Purkinje's twilight shift), we have the same subject, and both sides could profit from improved communication.

In pursuit of these ends, it was found necessary to think of information as an *objective* commodity, as something whose existence (as information) is (largely) independent of the interpretative activities of conscious agents. It is common among cognitive scientists to regard information as a creation of the mind, as something we conscious agents assign to, or impose on, otherwise meaningless events. Information, like beauty, is in the eye of the beholder. For philosophical purposes though, this puts things exactly backward. It assumes what is to be explained. For we want to know what this interpretative ability amounts to, why some physical systems (typically, those with brains) have this capacity and others do not. What makes *some* processors of information (persons, but not television sets) sources of meaning? If we *begin* our study by populating the world with fully developed cognitive systems, systems that can

Reprinted from *The Behavioral and Brain Sciences* 6 (1983): 55–63, by permission of the publisher. Copyright © 1983, Cambridge University Press.

transform "meaningless" stimuli into thoughts, beliefs, and knowledge (or whatever is involved in interpretation), we make the analysis of information more tractable, perhaps, but only by abandoning it as a tool in our quest to understand the nature of cognitive phenomena. We merely postpone the philosophical questions.

Part I of *Knowledge* develops a semantic theory of information, a theory of the propositional *content* of a signal (events, structure, or state of affairs). It begins by rehearsing some of the elementary ideas of the mathematical theory of communication (Shannon & Weaver 1949). This theory, though developed for quite different purposes, and though having (as a result) only the remotest connection (some would say *none*) with the kinds of cognitive issues of concern to this study, does, nonetheless, provide a key that can be used to articulate a semantical theory of information. Chapters 2 and 3 are devoted to *adapting* and *extending* this theory's account of an information source and channel into an account of how much information a *particular* signal carries about a source and what (if any) information this is.

Part II applies this theory of information to some traditional problems in epistemology: knowledge, skepticism, and perception. Knowledge is characterized as information-produced belief. Perception is a process in which incoming information is coded in analog form in preparation for further selective processing by cognitive (conceptual) centers. The difference between seeing a duck and recognizing it *as* a duck (seeing *that* it is a duck) is to be found in the different way information about the duck is coded (analog vs. digital).

Part III is devoted to an information—theoretic analysis of what has come to be called our propositional attitudes—in particular, the belief that something is so. Belief, the *thinking* that something is so, is characterized in terms of the instantiation of structures (presumably neural) that have, through learning, acquired a certain information-carrying role. Instances of these structures (the types of which are identified as concepts) sometimes fail to perform satisfactorily. This is false belief.

Information

The mathematical theory of communication (Cherry 1951; Shannon & Weaver 1949) is concerned with certain statistical quantities associated with "sources" and "channels." When a certain condition is realized at a source, and there are other possible conditions that might have been realized (each with its associated probability of occurring), the source can be thought of as a generator of information. The ensemble of possibilities has been reduced to a single reality, and the amount of information generated is a function of these possibilities and their associated probabilities. The die is cast. Any one of six faces might appear uppermost. A "3" appears. Six possibilities, all (let us say) equally likely, have been reduced to one. The source, in this case the throw of the die, generates 2.6 bits of information ($\log_2 6 = 2.6$).

But more important (for my purposes and for the purpose of understanding *communication*) is the measure of how much information is transmitted from one point to another, how much information there is at point r (receiver) about what is transpiring at s (source). Once again, communication theory is concerned with the statistical properties of the "channel" connecting r and s, because, for most engineering purposes, it is this channel whose characteristics must be exploited in designing effective coding strategies. The theory looks at a statistical quantity that is a certain weighted average of the conditional probabilities of all signals that can be transmitted from s to r. It does not concern itself with the individual events (the particular signals) except as a basis for computing the statistical functions that define the quantities of interest.

I skip over these matters rather lightly here, because it should be obvious that, insofar as communication theory deals with quantities that are statistical *averages* (sometimes called *entropy* to distinguish them from real information), it is *not* dealing with information as it is ordinarily understood. For information as it is ordinarily understood, and as it must figure in semantic and cognitive studies, is something associated with, and *only* with, individual events (signals, structures, conditions). It is only the particular signal (utterance, track, print, gesture, sequence of neural discharges) that has a content that can be given propositional expression (the content, message, or information carried by the signal). *This* is the relevant commodity in semantic and cognitive studies, and content—*what* information a signal carries— cannot be averaged. All one can do is average *how much* information is carried. There is no meaningful average for the information that my grandmother had a stroke and that my daughter is getting married. If we can say *how much* information these messages represent, then we can speak about their average. But this tells us nothing about *what* information is being communicated. Hence, the quantities of interest in engineering—and, of course, some psychophysical contexts (Attneave 1959; Garner 1962; Miller 1953)—are not the quantities of interest to someone, like myself, concerned to develop an account of *what* information travels from source to receiver (object to receptor, receptor to brain, brain to brain) during communication.

Nevertheless, though communication theory has its attention elsewhere, it does, as Sayre (1965) and others have noted, highlight the relevant objective relations on which the communication of genuine information depends. For what this theory tells us is that the amount of information at *r* about *s* is a function of the *degree of lawful* (*nomic*) *dependence* between conditions at these two points. If two conditions are statistically independent (the way the ringing of *your* telephone is independent of the ringing of *mine*), then the one event carries no information about the other. When there is a lawful regularity between two events, statistical or otherwise, as there is between your dialing my number and my phone's ringing, then we can speak of one event's carrying information about the other. And, of course, this is the way we *do* speak. The ring *tells me* (informs me) that someone is calling my number, just as fingerprints carry information about the identity of the person who handled the gun, tracks in the snow about the animals in the woods, the honeybee's dance about the location of nectar, and light from a distant star about the chemical constitution of that body. Such events are pregnant with information, because they depend, in some lawfully regular way, on the conditions about which they are said to carry information.

If things are working properly, the ringing of my phone *tells* me that someone has dialed my number. It delivers this piece of information. It does *not* tell me that your phone is ringing, even if (coincidentally) your phone happens to be ringing at the same time. Even if *A* dials *B*'s number whenever *C* dials *D*'s number (so that *D*'s phone rings *whenever A* dials *B*'s number), we cannot say that the ringing of *D*'s phone carries information about *A*'s dialing activites—*not* if this "correlation" is a mere coincidence. We cannot say this, because the correlation, being (by hypothesis) completely fortuitous, does not affect the conditional *probability* of *A*'s dialing *B*'s number, given that *D*'s phone is ringing. Of course, if we *know* about this (coincidental) correlation (though *how* one could know about its *persistence* is beyond me), we can predict one event from a knowledge of the other, but this doesn't change the fact that they are statistically independent. If I correctly describe your future by consulting tea leaves, this is not genuine communication *unless* the arrangement of tea leaves somehow depends on what you are going to do, in the way a barometer depends on meteorological conditions and, therefore, indirectly on the impending weather. To deny the existence of mental telepathy is not to deny the possibility of improbable cooccurrences (between what *A* thinks and what *B* thinks *A* is thinking); it is, rather, to deny that they are manifestations of *lawful* regularities.

Communication theory only makes sense if it makes sense to talk about the probability of certain specific conditions given certain specific signals. This is so because the quantities of interest to communication theory are statistical functions of these probabilities. It is this *presupposed* idea that I exploit to develop an account of a signal's content. These conditional probabilities determine how much, and indirectly *what*, information a particular signal carries about a remote source. One needs only to stipulate that the content of the signal, the information it carries, be expressed by a sentence describing the condition (at the source) on which the signal depends in some regular, lawful way. I express this theoretical definition of a signal's (structure's) informational content (Chapter 3, p. 65) in the following way:

A signal *r* carries the information that *s* is *F* = The conditional probability of *s*'s being *F*, given *r* (and *k*), is 1 (but, given *k* alone, less than 1)

My gas gauge carries the information that I still have some gas left, if and only if the conditional probability of my having some gas left, given the reading on the gauge, is 1. For the same reason, the discharge of a photoreceptor carries the information that a photon has arrived (perhaps a photon of a certain wavelength), and the pattern of discharge of a cluster of ganglion cells carries the information that there is a sharp energy gradient (a line) in the optic array (Lindsay & Norman 1972; Rumelhart 1977). The following comments explain the main features of this definition.

1. There are, essentially, three reasons for insisting that the value of the conditional probability in this definition be 1—nothing less. They are:

a. If a signal could carry the information that *s* was *F* while the conditional probability (of the latter, given the former) was less than 1 (.9 say), then the signal could carry the information that *s* was *F* (probability = .91), the information that *s* was *G* (probability = .91), but *not* the information that *s* was *F and G* (because the probability of their *joint* occurrence might be less than .9). I take this to be an unacceptable result.

b. I accept something I call the xerox principle: If *C* carries the information that *B*, and *B*'s occurrence carries the information that *A*, then *C* carries the information that *A*. You don't *lose* information about the original (*A*) by perfectly reproduced copies (*B* of *A* and *C* of *B*). Without the transitivity this principle describes, the *flow* of information would be impossible. If we put the threshold of information at anything less than 1, though, the principle is violated. For (using the same numbers) the conditional probability of *B*, given *C*, could be .91, the conditional probability of *A*, given *B*, also .91, but the conditional probability of *A*, given *C*, less than .9. The noise (equivocation, degree of nomic *in*dependence, or nonlawful relation) between the end points of this communication channel is enough to break communication, even though every link in the chain passes along the information to its successor. Somehow the information fails to get through, despite the fact that it is nowhere lost.

c. Finally, there is no nonarbitrary place to put a threshold that will retain the intimate tie we all intuitively feel between knowledge and information. For, if information about s's being F can be obtained from a signal that makes the conditional probability of this situation only (say) .94, then information loses its cognitive punch. Think of a bag with 94 red balls and 6 white balls. If one is pulled at random (probability of red = .94), can you *know* (just from the fact that it was drawn from a bag with that composition of colored marbles) that it was red? Clearly not. Then why suppose you have the information that it is red?

The only reason I know for *not* setting the required probability this high is worries (basically skeptical in character) that there are no (or precious few) conditional probabilities of 1—hence, that no information is ever communicated. I address these worries in Chapter 5. They raise issues (e.g., the idea of a "relevant alternative") that have received some attention in recent epistemology.

2. The definition captures the element that makes information (in contrast, say, to meaning) an important *epistemic* commodity. No structure can carry the information that s is F unless, in fact, s is F. False information, misinformation, and (grimace!) disinformation are not varieties of information—any more than a decoy duck is a kind of duck. A glance at the dictionary reveals that information is related to intelligence, news, instruction, and knowledge—things that have an important connection to *truth*. And so it should be with any theoretical approximation to this notion. Information *is* an important commodity: We buy it, sell it, torture people to get it, and erect booths to dispense it. It should not be confused with meaning, despite some people's willingness to speak of anything (true, false, or meaningless) stored on a magnetic disk as information.

3. Information, as defined above, is an objective commodity, the sort of thing that can be delivered to, processed by, and transmitted from instruments, gauges, computers, and neurons. It is something that can be *in* the optic array,[1] on the printed page, carried by a temporal configuration of electrical pulses, and stored on a magnetic disk, and it exists there *whether or not anyone appreciates this fact or knows how to extract it*. It is something that was in this world before we got here. It was, I submit, the raw material out of which minds were manufactured.

The parenthetical k occurring in the definition above (and explained below) relativizes information to what the receiver already knows (if anything) about the possibilities at the source, but this relativization does not undermine the essential objectivity of the commodity so relativized (MacKay 1969). We still have the flow of information (perhaps not so much) without conscious agents who know things, but without a lawfully regular universe (no matter how much knowledge we assign the occupants), no information is ever communicated.

4. A signal's informational content is not unique. There is, generally speaking, no *single* piece of information in a signal or structure. For anything that carries the information that *s* is a square, say, also carries the information that it is a rectangle, a parallelogram, *not* a circle, a circle *or* a square, and so on. If the acoustic pattern reaching my ears carries the information that the doorbell is ringing, and the ringing of the bell carries the information that the doorbell button is being pressed, then the acoustic pattern also carries the information that the doorbell button is being pressed (xerox principle). The one piece of information is *nested* in the other. This, once again, is as it should be. The linguistic meaning of an utterance may be unique (distinguishable, for instance, from what it implies), but not the information carried by that utterance. Herman's statement that he won't come to my party means, simply, that he won't come to my party. It doesn't mean (certainly not in any linguistically relevant sense of "meaning") that he doesn't like me or that he can speak English, although his utterance may well carry these pieces of information.

5. The definition of a signal's informational content has been relativized to *k*, what the receiver (in the event that we are talking about a communication system in which the receiver—organism or computer—already has knowledge about the possible conditions existing at the source) already knows. This is a minor concession to the way we think and talk about information. The *k* is dischargeable by recursive applications of the definition. So, for instance, if I receive the information that your knight is *not* on KB-3 (by some signal), this carries the information that it *is* on KB-5, *if* I already know that the other possible positions to which your knight could have moved are already occupied by your pieces. To someone lacking such knowledge, the same signal does not carry this information (though it still carries the information that your knight is not on KB-3). The less we know, the more pregnant with information must be the signals we receive if we are to learn.

6. There is, finally, the important fact, already mentioned, that the informational content of a signal is a function of the *nomic* (or law-governed) relations it bears to other conditions. Unless these relations are what philosophers like to call "counterfactual supporting" relations (a symptom of a background, lawful regularity), the relations in question are not such as to support an assignment of informational content (Dretske 1977). The reason my thermometer carries information about the temperature of *my* room (the information *that* it is 72°F. in the room), but not about your room though both rooms are at the same temperature, is that (given its location) the registration of my thermometer is such that it *would not* read 72°F. *unless* my room was at this temperature. This isn't true of your room.

This fact helps explain an (otherwise puzzling) feature of information and, ultimately, of the cognitive attitudes that depend on it (belief, knowledge). For it is by virtue of this fact that a structure (some neural state, say) can carry the information that *s* (a distal object) is *F* (spherical) without carrying the information that *s* is *G* (plastic), even though (let us suppose) all spheres (in the relevant domain) are plastic. If the fact that all spheres are plastic is sheer accident, not underwritten by any lawful constraint, then the neural state might depend on *s*'s being spherical without depending, in the same way, on its being plastic. Another way of expressing this fact (dear to the heart of philosophers) is to say that the informational content of a structure exhibits *intentional* properties. By saying that it exhibits intentional properties, I mean what philosophers typically mean by this technical term: that the informational content of a signal or structure (like the content of a belief, a desire, or knowledge) depends, not only on the reference (extension) of the terms used in its sentential expression, but on their *meaning* (intension). That is, in the sentential expression of a structure's informational content, one cannot substitute coreferring (i.e., referring to the same thing, coextensional) expressions without (possible) alteration in content. Just as a belief that this man is my cousin differs from a belief that he is Susan's husband, despite the fact that Susan's husband *is* my cousin (these expressions have the same reference), the information (as defined above) that he is my cousin differs from the information that he is Susan's husband. A signal can carry the one piece of information without carrying the other.

We have, then, an account of a signal's informational content that exhibits a degree of intentionality. We have, therefore, an account of information that exhibits some of the attributes we hope eventually to be able to explain in our account of our cognitive states. Perhaps, that is, one can know that *s* is *F* without knowing that *s* is *G*, despite the fact that all *F*s are *G*, *because* knowledge requires information, and one *can* get the information that *s* is *F* without getting the information that it is *G*. If intentionality is "the mark of the mental," then we already have, in the physically objective notion of information defined above (even without *k*), the traces of mentality. And we have it in a form that voltmeters, thermometers, and radios have. What distinguishes us from these more pedestrian processors of information is not our occupation of intentional states, but the sophisticated way we process, encode, and utilize the information we receive. It is our *degree* of intentionality (see Part III).

Knowledge

Knowledge is defined (Chapter 4) as information-caused (or causally sustained) belief. The analysis is restricted to perceptual knowledge of contingent states of affairs (conditions having an informational measure of something greater than 0) of a *de re* form: seeing (hence, knowing) that this (the perceptual object) is blue, moving, a dog, or my grandmother.

This characterization of knowledge is a version of what has come to be called the "regularity analysis" of knowledge (Armstrong 1973; Dretske 1969; 1971). It is an attempt to get away from the philosopher's usual bag of tricks (justification, reasons, evidence, etc.) in order to give a more realistic picture of what perceptual knowledge is. One doesn't need reasons, evidence, or rational justification for one's belief that there is wine left in the bottle, if the bottle is sitting in good light directly in front of one. One can *see* that it is still half-full. And, rightly or wrongly, I wanted a characterization that would at least allow for the possibility that animals (a frog, rat, ape, or my dog) could know things without my having to suppose them capable of the more sophisticated intellectual operations involved in traditional analyses of knowledge.

What can it mean to speak of information as causing anything—let alone causing a belief? (The analysis of belief, the propositional attitude most often taken as the subjective component of knowledge, is postponed until Part III.) Assuming that belief is some kind of internal state with a content expressible as *s* is *F*, this is said to be caused by the information that *s* is *F*, if and only if those physical properties of the signal by virtue of which it carries this information are the ones that are causally efficacious in the production of the belief. So, for instance, not just any knock on the door tells you it is your friend. The (prearranged) signal is three quick knocks, followed by a pause, and then another three quick knocks. It is that particular signal, that particular temporal pattern, that constitutes the information-carrying property of the signal. The amplitude and pitch are irrelevant. When it is this pattern of knocks that causes you to believe that your friend has arrived, then (it is permissible to say that) the *information* that your friend has arrived causes you to believe he has arrived. The knocks might also frighten away a fly, cause the windows to rattle, and disturb the people upstairs. But what has these effects is not the information, because, presumably, the fly would have been frightened, the windows rattled, and the neighbors disturbed by *any* sequence of knocks of roughly the same amplitude). Hence, the information is not the cause.

In most ordinary situations, there is no explanatory value in talking about the information (in an event) as the cause of something, because there is some easily identifiable physical (nonrelational) property of the event that can be designated as the cause. Why talk of the information (that your friend has arrived) as the cause, when it is clear enough that it is the particular temporal patterns of knocks (or acoustic vibrations) that was the effective agent?

The point of this definition is not to *deny* that there are physical properties of the signal (e.g., the temporal pattern of knocks in the above example) that cause the belief, but to say *which* of these properties must be responsible for the effect if the resultant belief is to qualify as knowledge.[2] If the belief that your friend has arrived is caused by the knock, but the pattern of knocks is irrelevant, then (assuming that someone else could be knocking at your door), though you are caused to believe it by the knock on the door, you do not *know* your friend has arrived. Those properties of the signal that carry the information (that your friend has arrived) are not the ones that are causally responsible for your belief.

The need to speak in this more abstract way—of information (rather than the physical event carrying this information) as the cause of something— becomes much more compelling as we turn to more complex information processing systems. For we then discover that there are an indefinitely large number of different sensory inputs, having no identifiable physical (nonrelational) property in common, that all have the same cognitive outcome. The only way we can capture the relevant causal regularities is by retreating to a more abstract characterization of the cause, a characterization in terms of its relational (informational) properties. We often do this sort of thing in our ordinary descriptions of what we see. Why did he stop? He could see that he was almost out of gas. We speak here of the information (that he was almost out of gas) that is contained in (carried by) the fuel gauge pointer and *not* the fuel gauge pointer itself (which, of course, is what we actually see), because it is a property of this pointer (its position, not its size or color) carrying this vital piece of information that is relevantly involved in the production of the belief. We, as it were, ignore the messenger bringing the information (the fuel gauge indicator) in order to focus on what information the messenger brings. We also ignore the infinite variety of optical inputs (all of varying size, shape, orientation, intensity) in order to focus on the information they carry. Often we have no choice. The only thing they have in common is the information they bear.[3]

A belief that *s* is *F* may not itself carry the information that *s* is *F* just because it is caused by this information (thereby qualifying as knowledge). A gullible person may believe almost anything you tell him—for example, that there are three elephants in your backyard. His beliefs may not, as a result, have any reliable relation to the facts (this is why we don't believe him when he tells us something). Yet this does not prevent him from knowing something he observes firsthand. When he *sees* the elephants in your backyard, he *knows* they are there, whatever other signal (lacking the relevant information) might have caused him to believe this. If the belief is caused by the appropriate information, it qualifies as knowledge whatever *else* may be capable of causing it.

This definition of knowledge accords, I think, with our ordinary, intuitive judgments about when someone knows something. You can't know that Jimmy is home by seeing him come through the door, if it could be his twin brother Johnny. Even if it is extremely unlikely to be Johnny (for Johnny rarely comes home this early in the afternoon), as long as this remains a relevant possibility, it prevents one from seeing (hence, knowing) *that* it is Jimmy (though one may be caused to *believe* it is Jimmy). The information that it is Jimmy is missing. The optical input is equivocal.

Furthermore, this account of knowledge neatly avoids some of the puzzles that intrigue philosophers (and bore everyone else to death). For example, Gettier-like difficulties (Gettier 1963) arise for any account of knowledge that makes knowledge a product of some justificatory relationship (having good evidence, excellent reasons, etc.) that *could* relate one to something false. For on all these accounts (unless special ad hoc devices are introduced to prevent it), one can be justified (in a way appropriate to knowledge) in believing something that is, in fact, false (hence, not know it); also know that Q (which happens to be true) is a logical consequence of what one believes, and come to believe Q as a result. On some perfectly natural assumptions, then, one is justified (in a way appropriate to knowledge) in believing the truth (Q). But one obviously doesn't *know* Q is true. This is problem for justificational accounts. The problem is evaded in the information—theoretic model, because one can get into an appropriate justificational relationship to something false, but one cannot get into an appropriate informational relationship to something false.

Similarly, the so-called lottery paradox (Kyburg 1961; 1965) is disarmed. If one could know something without the information (as here defined), one should be able to know *before the drawing* that the 999,999 eventual losers in a (fair) lottery, for which a million tickets have been sold, are going to lose. For they all *are* going to lose, and one knows that the probability of each one's (not, of course, *all*) losing is negligibly less than 1. Hence, one is perfectly justified in believing (truly) that each one is going to lose. But, clearly, one cannot know this. The paradox is avoided by acknowledging what is already inherent in the information—theoretic analysis—that one cannot know one is going to lose in such a lottery no matter how many outstanding tickets there may be. And the reason one cannot is (barring a fixed drawing) the information that one is going to lose is absent. There remains a small, but nonetheless greater than 0, amount of equivocation for each outcome.

There are further, technical advantages to this analysis (discussed in Chapter

4), but many will consider these advantages purchased at too great a price. For the feeling will surely be that one never gets the required information. *Not* if information requires a conditional probability of 1. The stimuli are *always* equivocal to some degree. Most of us know about Ames's demonstrations, Brunswik's ecological and functional validities, and the fallibility of our own sensory systems. If knowledge requires information, and information requires 0 equivocation, then precious little, if anything, is ever known.

These concerns are addressed in Chapter 5, a chapter that will prove tedious to almost everyone but devoted epistemologists (i.e., those who take skepticism seriously). An example will have to suffice to summarize this discussion.

A perfectly reliable instrument (or one *as* reliable as modern technology can make it) has its output reliably correlated with its input. The position of a mobile pointer on a calibrated scale carries information about the magnitude of the quantity being measured. Communication theorists would (given certain tolerances) have no trouble in describing this as a noiseless channel. If we ask about the conditional probabilities, we note that these are determined by regarding certain parameters as fixed (or simply ignoring them). The spring *could* weaken, it *could* break, its coefficient of elasticity *could* fluctuate unpredictably. The electrical resistance of the leads (connecting the instrument to the apparatus on which measurements are being taken) *could* change. Error would be introduced if any of these possibilities was realized. And who is to say they are not *possibilities?* There *might* even be a prankster, a malevolent force, or a god who chooses to interfere. Should all these possibilities go into the reckoning in computing the noise, equivocation, and information conveyed? To do so, of course, would be to abandon communication theory altogether. For this theory requires for its application a system of fixed, stable, enduring conditions *within* which the degree of covariation in other conditions can be evaluated. If every logical possibility is deemed a possibility, then everything is noise. Nothing is communicated. In the same manner, if everything is deemed a *thing* for purposes of assessing the emptiness of containers (dust? molecules? radiation?), then no room, pocket, or refrigerator is ever empty. The framework of fixed, stable, enduring conditions within which one reckons the flow of information is what I call "channel conditions." Possible variations in these conditions are excluded. They are what epistemologists call "irrelevant alternatives" (Dretske 1970; Goldman 1976).

And so it is with our sensory systems. Certainly, in some sense of the word *could*, Herman, a perfectly normal adult, could be hallucinating the entire football game. There is no logical contradiction in this supposition; it is the same sense in which a voltmeter's spring *could* behave like silly putty. But this is not a sense of *could* that is relevant to cognitive studies or the determination of what information these systems are capable of transmitting. The probability of these things happening is set at 0. If they remain possibilities in some sense, they are not possibilities that affect the flow of information.

This discussion merely accentuates the way our talk of information *presupposes* a stable, regular world in which some things can be taken as fixed for the purpose of assessing the covariation in other things. There is here a certain arbitrary or pragmatic element (in what may be taken as permanent and stable enough to qualify as a channel condition), but this element (it is argued) is precisely what we find when we put our cognitive concepts under the same analytical microscope. It is not an objection to regarding the latter as fundamentally information-dependent notions.

Perception

Perception itself is often regarded as a cognitive activity: a form of recognizing, identifying, categorizing, distinguishing, and classifying the things around us (R. N. Haber 1969). But there is what philosophers (at least *this* philosopher) think of as an *extensional* and an *intensional* way of describing our perceptions (Dretske 1969). We see the duck (extensional: a concrete noun phrase occurs as object of the verb) and we recognize it (see it) as a duck—see *that* it is a duck (intensional: typically taking a factive nominal as complement of the verb). Too many people (both philosophers and psychologists) tend to think about perception *only* in the latter form, and in so doing they systematically ignore one of the most salient aspects of our mental life: the *experiences* we have when we see, hear, and taste things. The experience in question, the sort of thing that occurs in you when you see a duck (without necessarily recognizing it *as* a duck), the internal state without which (though you may be looking at the duck) you don't *see* the duck, is a stage in the processing of sensory information in which information about the duck is coded in what I call analog form, in preparation for its selective utilization by the cognitive centers (where the *belief* that it is a duck may be generated).

To describe what object you see is to describe what object you are getting information about; to describe what you recognize it as (see it to be) is to describe what information (about that object) you have succeeded in cognitively processing (e.g., that it is a duck). You can see a duck, get information *about* a duck, without getting, let alone cognitively processing, the information that it is a duck. Try looking at one in dim light at such a distance that you can barely see it. To confuse seeing a duck with recognizing it (either as a duck or as something else) is simply to confuse sentience with sapience.

Our experience of the world is rich in information in a way that our consequent beliefs (if any) are not. A normal child of two can *see* as well as I can (probably better). The child's experience of the world is (I rashly conjecture) as rich and as variegated as that of the most knowledgeable adult. What is lacking is a capacity to exploit these experiences in the generation of reliable beliefs (knowledge) about what the child sees. I, my daughter, and my dog can all see the daisy. I see it as a daisy. My daughter sees it simply as a flower. And who knows about my dog?

There are severe limits to our information-processing capabilities (Miller 1956), but most of these limitations affect our ability to cognitively process the information supplied in such profusion by our sensory systems (Rock 1975). More information *gets in* than we can manage to digest and get out (in some appropriate response). Glance around a crowded room, a library filled with books, or a garden ablaze with flowers. How much do you see? Is all the information embodied in the sensory representation (experience) given a cognitive form? No. You saw 28 people in a single brief glance (the room was well lit, all were in easy view, and none was occluded by other objects or people). Do you believe you saw 28 people? No. You didn't count and you saw them so briefly that you can only guess. That there were 28 people in the room is a piece of information that was contained *in* the sensory representation without receiving the kind of cognitive transformation (what I call digitalization) associated with conceptualization (belief). This homely· example illustrates what is more convincingly demonstrated by masking experiments with brief visual displays (Averback & Coriell 1961; Neisser 1967; Sperling 1960).

Although it is misleading to put it this way, our sensory experience encodes information in the way a photograph encodes information about the scene at which the camera is pointed. This is *not* to say that our sensory experience is pictorial (consists of sounds, sights, smells,.etc.). I don't think there are daisy replicas inside the head, although I *do* think there is information about—and in *this* sense a representation of—daisies in the head. Nor do I mean to suggest (by the picture metaphor) that we are *aware of* (somehow perceive) these internal sensory representations. On the contrary, what we perceive (what we are aware *of*) are the things represented by these internal representations (not the representations themselves), the things *about which* they carry information (see section on "The Objects of Perception" in Chapter 6).

I see a red apple in a white bowl surrounded by a variety of other objects. I recognize it as an apple. I come to believe that it is an apple. The belief has a content that we express with the words, "That is an apple." The content of this belief does not represent the apple as red, as large, or as lying next to an orange. I may have (other) beliefs about these matters, but the belief in question abstracts from the concreteness of the sensory representation (icon, sensory information store, experience) in order to represent it simply as an apple. However, these additional pieces of information *are* contained in the sensory experience of the apple. As Haber and Hershenson (1973) put it (in commenting on a specific experimental setup), "It appears as if all of the information in the retinal projection is available in the iconic storage, since the perceiver can extract whichever part is asked for."

In passing from the sensory to the cognitive representation (from seeing the apple to realizing that it is an apple), there is a systematic stripping away of components of information (relating to size, color, orientation, surroundings), which makes the experience of the apple the phenomenally rich thing we know it to be, in order to feature *one* component of this information—the information that it is an apple. Digitalization (of, for example, the information that *s* is an apple) is a process whereby a piece of information is taken from a richer matrix of information in the sensory representation (where it is held in what I call "analog" form) and featured to the exclusion of all else. The difference between the analog and digital coding of information is illustrated by the way a picture of an apple (that carries the information that it is an apple) differs from a statement that it is an apple. Both represent it *as* an apple, but the one embeds this information in an informationally richer representation. Essential to this process of digitalization (the essence of conceptualization) is the *loss* of this excess information.

Digitalization is, of course, merely the information—theoretic version of stimulus generalization. Until information is deleted, nothing corresponding to recognition, classification, or identification has occurred. Nothing distinctively cognitive or conceptual has occurred. To design a pattern-recognition routine for a digital computer, for example, is to design a routine in which information *inessential* to *s*'s being an instance of the letter A (information about its specific size, orientation, color) is systematically discarded (treated as noise) in the production of some single type of internal structure, which, in turn, will produce some identificatory output label (Uhr 1973). If all the computer could do was pass along the information it received, it could not be credited with recognizing anything at all. It would not be responding to the essential sameness of different inputs. It would be merely a sophisticated transducer. Learning, the acquisition of concepts, is a process whereby we acquire the ability to extract, in this way, information from the sensory representation. Until that happens, we can see but we do not believe.

Belief

The content of a belief, what we believe when we believe (think) that something is so, can be either true or false. If we think of beliefs as internal representations (as I do), then these representations must be capable of *mis* representing how things stand. This is one aspect of intentionality.

Furthermore, if two sentences, S_1 and S_2, mean something different, then the belief we express with S_1 is different from the belief we express with S_2. Believing that a man is your brother is different from believing that he is my uncle (even if your brother is my uncle), because the sentences "He is your brother" and "He is my uncle" mean something different. A difference in meaning is sufficient, not necessary, for a difference in corresponding beliefs. The belief you express with the words "I am sick" is different from the belief I express with these words, despite the fact that the words mean the same thing. They have a different reference. This is a second aspect of intentionality.

But beliefs not only have a content exhibiting these peculiar intentional characteristics; they also, in association with desires, purposes, and fears, help to determine behavior. They are, if we can trust our ordinary ways of thinking, intentional entities with a hand on the steering wheel (Armstrong 1973).

It is the purpose of Part III to give a unified, information—theoretic account of these entities. The account is incomplete in a number of important ways, but the underlying purpose is to exhibit the way meanings (insofar as these are understood to be the conceptual contents of our internal states) are developed out of informational contents.

We have already seen (Chapter 3) the way information-bearing structures have a content (the information they carry—e.g., that s is F) exhibiting traces of intentionality. But this is only what I call the first order of intentionality. If two properties are lawfully related in the right way, then no signal can carry information about the one without carrying information about the other. No structure can have the (informational) content that s is F without having the (informational) content that s is G, if it turns out that nothing *can* be F without being G. This is the first respect in which the informational content of a structure fails to display the degree of intentionality of a belief (we can certainly believe that s is F without believing that s is G, despite the nomic connection between F and G).

The second respect in which information-carrying structures are ill prepared to serve as beliefs, despite their possession of content, is that, as we have seen, nothing can carry the information that s is F, nothing can have this informational content, unless, in fact, s *is* F. But we can certainly believe that something is so without its being so.

Without the details, the basic strategy in Part III is quite simple. Consider a map. What makes the symbols on a map *say* or *mean* one thing, not another? What makes a little patch of blue ink on a map mean that there is a body of water in a specific location (whether or not there actually *is* a body of water there)? It seems that it acquires this meaning, this content, by virtue of the information-carrying *role* that that symbol (in this case, a *conventionally* selected and used sign) plays in the production and use of maps. The symbol *means* this because that is the information it was designed to carry. In the case of maps, of course, the flow of information from map-maker to map-user is underwritten by the executive fidelity of the map-makers. A type of structure, in this case blue ink, means there is water there, even though particular instances of that (type of) structure may, through ignorance or inadvertence, fail to carry this information. Misrepresentation becomes possible, because instances (tokens) of a structure (type) that has been assigned (and in this sense has acquired) an information-carrying role may fail to perform in accordance with that role. The instances mean what they do by virtue of their being instances of a certain *type*, and the structure type gets its meaning from its (assigned) communicative function.

Neural structures, of course, are not conventionally assigned an information-carrying role. They are not, in this sense, symbols. Nevertheless, they acquire such a role, I submit, during their development in learning (concept acquisition). In teaching a child what a bird is, for example, in giving the child this concept (so that the youngster can subsequently have beliefs to the effect that this is a bird, that is not), we expose the child to positive and negative instances of the concept in question (with some kind of appropriate feedback) in order to develop a sensitivity to the kind of information (that s is a bird) that defines the concept. When the child can successsfully identify birds, distinguish them from other animals (how this actually happens is, as far as I am concerned, a miracle), we have created something in the child's head that responds, in some consistent way, to the information that something is a bird. When the learning is successful, we have given the pupil a new concept, a new capacity, to exploit in subsequent classificatory and identificatory activities. If the child then sees an airplane and says "bird," this stimulus has triggered another token of a structure type that was developed to encode the information that the perceptual object was a bird (thereby representing it *as* a bird). We have a case of misrepresentation, a false belief.[4]

But we still have not captured the full intentionality of beliefs. In teaching our child the concept *water*, for instance, why say that the structure that develops to encode information about water is not, instead, a structure that was developed to encode information about the presence of oxygen atoms? After all, any incoming signal that carries the information that s is water carries (nested in it) the information that s has oxygen atoms in it (since there is a lawful regularity between something's being water and its having oxygen atoms in it).

The answer to this question is, of course, that the child has *not* developed a sensitivity to the information that *s* has oxygen atoms in it just because the pupil has been taught to respond positively to signals *all* of which carry that information. This can easily be demonstrated by testing the child with samples that are not water but do have oxygen atoms in them (rust, air, etc.). The crucial fact is that, although every signal to which the child is taught to respond positively carries information about the presence of oxygen atoms, it is not the properties of the signal carrying *this* information to which the child has acquired a sensitivity. Recall, it is those properties of the signal that are causally responsible for the child's positive response that define what information he is responding to and, hence, what concept he has acquired when he has completed his training. These properties (if the training was reasonably successful) are those carrying the information that the substance is water (or some approximation thereto—as time goes by, the concept may be refined, its information-response characteristics modified, into something more nearly resembling our mature concept of water).

Concept acquisition (of this elementary, ostensive sort) is essentially a process in which a system acquires the capacity to extract a piece of information from a variety of sensory representations *in* which it occurs. The child sees birds in a variety of colors, orientations, activities, and shapes. The sensory representations are infinitely variegated. To learn what a bird is is to learn to recode this analogically held information (that *s* is a bird) into a single form that can serve to determine a consistent, univocal response to these diverse stimuli. Until such structures have been developed, or unless we come into this world with them preformed (see the discussion of innate concepts in Chapter 9), nothing of cognitive significance has taken place.

Notes

1. Though I am sympathetic to some of the (earlier) views of the late James Gibson (1950; 1966), and though some of my discourse on information (e.g., its availability in the proximal stimulus) is reminiscent of Gibson's language, this work was not intended as support for Gibason's views—certainly not the more extravagant claims (1979). If criticized for getting Gibson wrong, I will plead "no contest". I wasn't trying to get him right. If we disagree, so much the worse for one of us at least.

2. This is not so much a denial of Fodor's (1980) formality condition as it is an attempt to say *which* syntactical (formal) properties of the representations must figure in the computational processes if the resulting transformations are to mirror faithfully our ordinary ways of describing them to terms of their semantic relations.

3. I skip here a discussion of information's *causally sustaining* a belief. The idea is simply that one may already believe something when one receives the relevant supporting

information. In this case, the belief is not caused or produced by the information. It nonetheless—after acquisition of the relevant information—qualifies as knowledge if it is, later, causally sustained by this information.

4. In my eagerness to emphasize the way conceptual content is determined by etiological factors (the information-response characteristics of the internal structures) and to contrast it with the (behavioristically inspired) functionalist account (where *what* you believe is largely determined by the kind of output it produces), I seriously misrepresented (in Chapter 8) Dennett's 1969 position. Dennett stresses, as I do, the importance of the way these internal structures *mediate* input and output. He does, however, trace their ultimate significance, meaning, or content to the kind of (appropriate) behavior they produce.

10

Judgmental Heuristics and Knowledge Structures

Richard Nisbett and Lee Ross

The most characteristic thing about mental life, over and beyond the fact that one apprehends the events of the world around one, is that one constantly goes beyond the information given.

Jerome Bruner

The perceiver, as Bruner (1957) recognized, is not simply a dutiful clerk who passively registers items of information. Rather, the perceiver is an active interpreter, one who resolves ambiguities, makes educated guesses about events that cannot be observed directly, and forms inferences about associations and causal relations. In this chapter we explore the strategies that permit and encourage the perceiver to "go beyond the information given, " that is, to venture beyond the most immediate implications of the data. We sketch some of the "knowledge structures" applied to understanding the world. These range from broad propositional theories about people in general to more schematic representations of objects, events, and actors. These structures house the person's generic knowledge and preconceptions about the world and provide the basis for quick, coherent, but occasionally erroneous interpretations of new experience.

Before discussing these structures, we will introduce the reader to the "availability heuristic" and the "representativeness heuristic"—two simple judgmental strategies on which people seem to rely, and by which they sometimes are misled, in a variety of inferential tasks. In so doing, the chapter introduces the reader to a set of extraordinarily important contributions by Daniel Kahneman and Amos Tversky (1972, 1973, in press; Tversky & Kahneman, 1971, 1973, 1974). . . .

Reprinted form *Human Inference: Strategies and Shortcomings of Social Judgment*, by Richard Nisbett and Lee Ross (Englewood Cliffs, N.J.: Prentice-Hall, Inc., 1983), pp. 17–42, by permission of the publisher. Copyright © 1983, Prentice-Hall, Inc.

The heuristics to be explored are relatively primitive and simple judgmental strategies. They are not irrational or even nonrational. They probably produce vastly more correct or partially correct inferences than erroneous ones, and they do so with great speed and little effort. Indeed, we suspect that the use of such simple tools may be an inevitable feature of the cognitive apparatus of any organism that must make as many judgments, inferences, and decisions as humans have to do. Each heuristic or, more properly, the misapplication of each heuristic, does lead people astray in some important inferential tasks. . . . It is the misuse of the heuristics—their application in preference to more normatively appropriate strategies—that we will emphasize.

Although we characterize the heuristics as "judgmental strategies," the term is misleading in that it implies a conscious and deliberate application of well-defined decision rules. The heuristics to be explored should be distinguished from straightforward computational or judgmental "algorithms" (such as the method for finding square roots or deciding whether one's bridge hand merits an opening bid), which generally are explicit and invariant both in the criteria for their use and the manner of their application. The intuitive psychologist probably would not assent to, much less spontaneously express, any general formulation of either heuristic. Instead, the utilization of the heuristics is generally automatic and nonreflective and notably free of any conscious consideration of appropriateness. As we shall see, the heuristics are not applied in a totally indiscriminate fashion. In many contexts in which a given heuristic would promote error, people refrain from using it and probably could articulate why its use would be foolish. On other logically equivalent and equally unpropitious occasions, people readily apply the same heuristic and may even attempt to justify its use.

The Availability Heuristic

When people are required to judge the relative frequency of particular objects or the likelihood of particular events, they often may be influenced by the relative *availability* of the objects or events, that is, their accessibility in the processes of perception, memory, or construction from imagination (cf. Tversky & Kahneman 1973). Such availability criteria often will prove accurate and useful. To the extent that availability is actually associated with objective frequency, the availability heuristic can be a useful tool of judgment. There are many factors uncorrelated with frequency, however, which can influence an event's immediate perceptual salience, the vividness or completeness with which it is recalled, or the ease with which it is imagined. As a result, the availability heuristic can be misleading.

Availability Biases in Frequency Estimation

Let us proceed first by introducing and then exploring in some detail three judgmental tasks for which application of the availability heuristic might lead one to biased estimates of the relative frequency of various objects or events. The first two examples are hypothetical. . . .

1. A pollster who asks a sample of American adults to estimate the "percentage of the work force who are currently unemployed" finds an "egocentric bias." That is, currently unemployed workers tend to overestimate the rate of unemployment, but currently employed workers tend to underestimate it.

2. An Indiana businessman confides to a friend, "Did you ever notice how many Hoosiers become famous or important? Look anywhere—politics, sports, Hollywood, big business, even notorious bank robbers—I couldn't guess the exact figures, but I bet we Hoosiers have far more than our fair share on just about any list in *Who's Who*."

3. A group of subjects consistently errs in judging the relative frequency of two kinds of English words. Specifically, they estimate the number of words beginning with particular letters (for example, *R* or *K*) to be greater than the number of words with those letters appearing third, although words of the latter type actually are far more numerous.

Examples 1 and 2 seem to present common and familiar errors, although one might not immediately recognize the role of availability factors in producing them. In fact, some readers might hasten to cite motivational or even "psychodynamic" factors that could induce unemployed workers to overestimate the commonness of their plight or that could prompt proud Indiana residents to exaggerate their share of the limelight. Example 3 seems less intuitively obvious and at first seems quite unconnected to the other two examples. Nevertheless, the chief source of error in all three cases seems to us to be the availability heuristic.

Consider Example 1, about estimates of unemployment. Here the bias in subjective availability can be traced to a bias in initial sampling. Unemployed people are more likely to know and meet other unemployed people than are job-holders, and vice versa. The reasons for such a sampling bias are hardly mysterious: The unemployed individual is likely to share the neighborhood, socioeconomic background, and occupation of other jobless individuals. He also is likely to encounter other unemployed people in such everyday endeavors as job-hunting, visiting employment agencies, collecting unemployment benefits, and shopping at stores offering cut-rate prices or easy credit. Indeed, he even may seek out such individuals for social comparison, information exchange, or general commiseration. Thus, to the extent that the unemployed person relies upon the sample generated by his personal experience, he will be misled about the commonness of unemployment. In the same manner, employed people, who are apt to live, work, and shop near one another, are apt to err in the opposite direction.

It is important to emphasize that the people in this hypothetical example would not be compelled to rely upon biased availability criteria in estimating the frequency of unemployment. They could try to recall media presentations of data, could apply some popular rule of thumb ("When there's an energy shortage, jobs disappear"), or could employ some more appropriate "sampling procedure" ("How many people have I seen lining up outside my neighborhood unemployment office on the first of the month this year as compared with last year?"). They even could attempt to compensate for the biases distorting their samples of available data ("Hardly anyone I know is jobless, but of course, I don't get to meet many unemployed people, do I? I guess I'd better adjust my estimate upward!"). Indeed, it is quite likely that some people *would* avoid availability criteria or at least would attempt the necessary adjustments. Throughout this book, however, we present experimental evidence showing that simple, tempting, availability criteria are used in contexts in which availability and frequency are poorly correlated and are used without appropriate adjustments for the factors that bias subjective experience.

Now let us consider Example 2, about the relative prominence of Indiana natives. The Hoosier's egocentric estimate clearly contains some of the same features as in our initial example. That is, people from Indiana are disproportionately likely to know or hear about famous fellow Hoosiers. Beyond such biases in initial exposure, however, this example introduces the potential influence of additional biases in *storage*. When a national sportscaster says "Myra Swift of Grandville, Indiana and Mary Speed of Bigtown, Florida won gold medals in the Olympics yesterday," it is the accomplishment of his fellow Hoosier that the Indiana businessman is more likely to notice and to remember. Accordingly, the sample of famous people he subsequently can recall from memory will reflect biases at the "storage" stage as well as at the sampling stage.

Biases in exposure, attention, and storage can arise, of course, from many factors besides the kinship between the perceiver and the object.... For instance, oddity or newsworthiness could accomplish the same end. Thus, people from all states might overestimate the number of very big, very small, very young, very pretty, or very hirsute Olympic gold medalists because such factors would bias the rater's likelihood of sampling, storing, and recalling the pertinent instances.

Example 3, about estimates of the frequency of the letter R in the first versus the third position, is subtler. In fact, readers who try the experiment themselves may find that they make the same incorrect assessments of relative frequency as did the original subjects. Once again, an inappropriate application of the availability criterion is the source of the difficulty. Like the subjects in Tversky's and Kahneman's (1973) demonstration, the reader probably finds that instances of words beginning with R are easier to generate spontaneously (at least in a casual first attempt) than are instances of words that have R as their third letter. But the differences in ease of generation do not reflect corresponding differences in word frequency. Any truly *random* sample of English words would reveal words beginning with R to be much *less* common than words with R as their third letter. The relative difficulty of generating words like "care," "street," and "derail," may give interesting hints of the storage and retrieval of one's vocabulary, but it says virtually nothing about objective word frequencies.

An analogy may be instructive here: In a quick search of the library, one would find it easier to find books by authors named Woolf than by authors named Virginia, or to find books about Australia than books by authors born in Australia. Such differences obviously would indicate little about the relative frequencies of such books in the library's collection. Instead, they would reflect the library's system for referencing books and granting access to them. By the same token, first letters apparently are more useful cues than third letters are for referencing and permitting access to the items in one's personal word collection. Once again, the use of criteria other than the subjective ease of generation (or, alternatively, recognition of relevant biases and adequate compensation) could lead people to a more accurate estimate.

Availability of Event Relationships and of Causal Explanations

Kahneman's and Tversky's work has been largely on the use of the availability heuristic in judgments involving the frequency or probability of individual events. Other research indicates that subjective availability may influence judgments of *relationships* between events, particularly *causal* relationships.

Jones's and Nisbett's (1972) account of the divergent causal interpretations of actors and observers—from which observers cite "dispositional" factors (traits, abilities, attitudes, etc.) to explain behaviors and outcomes that the actors themselves attribute to "situational" factors—is one case in point. For example, the actor who gives a dollar to a beggar is apt to attribute his behavior to the sad plight of the beggar, but the observer of the behavior is apt to attribute it to the actor's generosity. From the actor's perspective, it is the constantly changing features of the environment that are particularly salient or "available" as potential causes to which his behavior can be attributed. From the observer's perspective, the actor is the perceptual "figure" and the situation merely "ground," so that the actor himself provides the most available causal candidate. Indeed, by altering actors' and observers' perspectives through videotape replays, mirrors, or other methods, one can correspondingly alter the actors' and observers' causal assessments (cf. Arkin & Duval 1975; Duval & Wicklund 1972; Regan & Totten 1975; Storms 1973).

Subsequent research by a number of investigators, most notably Taylor and her associates (for example, Taylor & Fiske 1975, 1978), has demonstrated a more general point regarding availability and causal assessment. It appears that almost *any* manipulation that focuses the perceiver's attention on a potential cause, for example, on a particular participant in a social interaction, affects causal assessment. Whether the attentional manipulation is achieved by a blunt instruction about which participant to watch, subtle variations in seating arrangement, or by "solo" versus "nonsolo" status of, for example, female or black participants, the person made disproportionately "available" to onlookers is seen to be a disproportionately potent causal agent. (See also McArthur & Post 1977; McArthur & Solomon 1978.)

Availability effects also may account for other biases involving perceived causality. Consider Fischhoff's (1975; Fischhoff & Beyth 1975) reports on the subjective certainty of hindsight knowledge. These reports show that outcomes often seem in retrospect to have been inevitable. This may be because the antecedents and causal scenarios that "predicted" such outcomes have far greater "after-the-fact" availability than do antecedents or scenarios that predicted alternative outcomes that did not in fact occur. In a similar vein, Ross, Lepper, Strack, and Steinmetz (1977) demonstrated that *explaining* why some event is consistent with known preceding events (for example, explaining the suicide of a clinical patient whose case history one has examined) tends to increase the subjective likelihood that the event actually did occur. Again the relevant mechanism appears to be the availability heuristic. The explanation creates a particular causal scenario, and its causal factors are disproportionately available to the perceiver when predictions are made later.

In both hindsight and explanation, the subjective ease of generation appears to be important. The subjects seem to respond not only to the mere presence of potential causal scenarios but also to the relative ease with which they were detected or invented. People probably implicitly assume this subjective ease of generation to be somehow symptomatic of the scenario's likelihood or of the explanation's aptness.

Appropriate and Inappropriate Applications of the Availability Heuristic

An indiscriminate use of the availability heuristic clearly can lead people into serious judgmental errors. It is important to reemphasize that in many contexts perceptual salience, memorability, and imaginability may be relatively un-biased and therefore well correlated with true frequency, probability, or even causal significance. In such cases, of course, the availability heuristic often can be a helpful and efficient tool of inference.

The same jobless individuals whose estimates of unemployment rates were distorted by the availability heuristic could make a reasonably accurate estimate of the preponderance of oak trees to maple trees in their neighbor-hood by using the same strategy. In estimating the frequencies of various types of trees, the individual's personal experiences and subsequent recollections would constitute generally unbiased samples. Similarly, the Indiana resident who was misled by the disproportionate availability of instances of famous fellow Hoosiers might have fared quite well if the same heuristic had been applied in estimating the success of German Olympians relative to Italian Olympians. Furthermore, the "ease of generation" criterion would have helped rather than hindered Tversky's and Kahneman's subjects if the experimental task had been to estimate the relative frequencies either of a) words beginning with *R* versus words beginning with *L*, or b) words with *R* versus *L* in the third position. In either of these cases, differences in the relative ease of generation would have reflected differences in frequency quite accurately.

The normative status of using the availability heuristic, and the pragmatic utility of using it, thus depend on the judgmental domain and context. People are not, of course, totally unaware that simple availability criteria must sometimes be discounted. For example, few people who were asked to estimate the relative number of moles versus cats in their neighborhood would con-clude "there must be more cats because I've seen several of them but I've never seen a mole." Nevertheless, as this book documents, people often fail to distinguish between legitimate and superficially similar, but illegitimate, uses of the availability heuristic.

The Representativeness Heuristic

The second judgmental heuristic to be introduced is one which Kahneman and Tversky (1972, 1973; Tversky & Kahneman 1974) termed the *representative-ness* heuristic. This heuristic involves the application of relatively simple resemblance or "goodness of fit" criteria to problems of categorization. In making a judgment, people assess the degree to which the salient features of the object are representative of, or similar to, the features presumed to be characteristic of the category.

In the following sections we try to provide a coherent grouping of examples. It should be emphasized, however, that our classification system is neither exhaustive nor theoretically derived. We also should note that we make no attempt to specify the precise criteria by which individuals calculate the representativeness of one object or event to another. (For the interested reader, a recent but already classic paper by Tversky, 1977, takes a first step in this direction by introducing a formal theory of similarity judgments.)

Judgments of the Degree to Which Outcomes Are Representative of Their Origins

People often are required to predict some outcome or judge the likelihood of some event on the basis of information about the "generating process" that produced it. On such occasions, the judgment is likely to reflect the degree to which the specified outcome represents its origin. Let us consider an example adapted from one used by Kahneman and Tversky (1972):

Subjects are asked to assess the relative likelihood of three particular sequences of births of boys (B) and girls (G) for the next six babies born in the United States. These sequences are i) BBBBBB, ii) GGGBBB, iii) GBBGGB.

According to the conventional probability calculation, the likelihood of each of these sequences is almost identical. (Actually, the first sequence is slightly more likely than either the second or third sequence, since male births are slightly more common than female births. The latter two sequences are simply different orderings of identical, independent events.) Subjects who rely upon their intuitions and upon the representativeness criteria which guide such intuitions, are apt to regard the GBBGGB sequence as far more likely than either of the other two. In doing so, they are responding to what they know about the population of babies and about the processes of "generation," that is, that each birth is a "random" event in which the probability of "boy" and "girl" are nearly equal. Only the GBBGGB sequence is "representative" of the generating process. The GGGBBB sequence seems too "orderly" to represent a random process. The BBBBBB sequence satisfies the criteria even less: It captures neither the randomness of the birth process nor the equal sex distribution of the population from which the six births were "sampled."

The representativeness heuristic also accounts for the familiar "gamblers' fallacy." After observing a long run of "red" on a roulette wheel, people believe that "black" is now due, because the occurrence of black would make the overall sequence of events more representative of the generating process than would the occurrence of another red. In a similar vein, any researcher who has ever consulted a random number table for an unbiased ordering of events has probably felt that the result was somehow insufficiently "representative" of a chance process, that it contained suspiciously orderly sequences, suspiciously long runs, suspicious overrepresentations or underrepresentations of particular numbers early or late in the sequence, and so forth (cf. Tversky & Kahneman 1971).

Judgments of the Degree to Which Instances Are Representative of Categories

Many everyday judgments require people to estimate the likelihood that some object or event with a given set of characteristics is an instance of some designated category or class. Typically, the judgments are made in relative terms, that is, is Event X more likely to be an instance of Class A or of Class B? Consider the following problem, which is similar in form to those in the empirical work by Kahneman and Tversky. . . .

The present authors have a friend who is a professor. He likes to write poetry, is rather shy, and is small in stature. Which of the following is his field: (a) Chinese studies or (b) psychology?

Those readers who quickly and confidently predicted "psychology" probably applied some version, whether sophisticated or crude, of conventional statistical canons. We congratulate these readers. We suspect, however, that many readers guessed "Chinese studies," or at least seriously considered that such a guess might be reasonable. If so, they probably were seduced by the representativeness heuristic. Specifically, they assessed the relative "goodness of fit" between the professor's personality profile and the predominant features of their stereotypes of Sinologists and psychologists. Finding the fit better for the former than for the latter, they guessed the professor's field to be Chinese studies.

In succumbing to the lure of the representativeness heuristic, what the reader likely has overlooked or not appreciated is some relevant category *baserate* information. Let the reader who guessed "Chinese studies" now reconsider that guess in light of the relative numbers of psychologists and Sinologists in the population. Then consider the more restricted population of people likely to be friends of the authors, who themselves are psychologists. Surely *no* reader's implicit personality theory of the strength of association between academic discipline and the professor's various characteristics, that is, poetry-writing, shyness, and slightness of stature, warrants overriding such base-rate considerations.

Errors in problems of the Sinologist/psychologist variety may reflect that the judge has been led to answer the wrong question or, more specifically, to ponder the wrong conditional probability. The judge seems to be responding to the question "How likely is it that a psychologist (versus a Sinologist) would resemble the personal profile provided?" when the actual question posed is "How likely is someone resembling the personality profile to be a psychologist (versus a Sinologist)?" The representativeness heuristic leads people to give a similar answer to the two questions, since it entails consideration only of the resemblance of the two occupational stereotypes to the given personality description. The error is the failure to consider the relevant base rates or marginal probabilities, a consideration which is irrelevant to the first question but critical to the second. Although a much higher proportion of Sinologists than of psychologists may fit the profile, there would still be a much greater *absolute* number of psychologists than of Sinologists who fit it, because of the vastly greater number of psychologists than of Sinologists in the population. . . .

Judgments of the Degree to Which Antecedents Are Representative of Consequences

Earlier we contended that the availability of causal candidates, or of causal scenarios linking outcomes to potential antecedents, influences assessments of causality. We contend that representativeness criteria also may be important to such inferences. That is, a person who is required to account for some observed action or outcome may search the list of *available* antecedents for those that seem to be the most *representative* "causes" of the known "consequences."

Simple resemblance criteria appear to influence causal assessment just as they influence judgments of the representativeness of outcomes to origins or instances to classes. . . . Sometimes the resemblance criterion is used in a crude and unsophisticated way, as it is in primitive medical beliefs attributing a particular illness to an environmental agent with features resembling the illness. Sometimes its influence is less patent, as in the preference for motivational causes in explaining events with strong motivational or affective consequences or the preference for complicated, multifaceted causes for complicated, multifaceted outcomes.

Generally, the use of the representativeness heuristic in causal assessment is more than a simple comparison of the features of effects with those of their potential causes. Normally, people also use *theories* or general *knowledge* of the particular antecedents likely to cause or explain given outcomes and of the specific outcomes likely to follow given antecedents. A person's belief that the cause of Egypt's diplomatic initiative toward Israel was an heroic vision of Egypt's leader rather than economic exigency does not reflect merely a crude assessment of the similarity between historic gestures and heroic visions. Instead, such assessments reflect judgments of the similarity of known effects and potential causes to tacit or explicit models of cause-and-effect relations in international conduct. Application of the representativeness heuristic to the assessment of causality thus ranges from the crude and questionable requirement that potential causes resemble effects, to normatively proper strategies based on a comparison of the similarity of observed effects and potential causes to generalized cause-and-effect models in the given domain.

Appropriate and Inappropriate Applications of the Representativeness Heuristic

Even more than the availability heuristic, the representativeness heuristic is a legitimate, indeed absolutely essential, cognitive tool. Countless inferential tasks, especially those requiring induction or generalization, depend on deciding what class or category of event one is observing; such judgments inevitably hinge upon assessments of resemblance or representativeness (cf. Tversky 1977). Even in our examples, the use of the representativeness heuristic produced errors only because it was overapplied or misapplied while normatively important criteria were overlooked. Let us briefly reconsider each of those examples.

In the case of the representativeness of the outcome to the origin, the problem is clearly one of overapplication. The insight that the features of the sample ought to resemble those of the population or the generating process is generally valid. It leads people to recognize that an all-male or an all-white jury is more likely to reflect a biased selection procedure than will a jury with a more proportionate representation of the overall population. It also leads people to cry foul when a politician's cronies seem to enjoy a disproportionate share of good luck in their transactions with local or state agencies. Unfortunately, when people's understanding of the generating process and its implications is deficient—as when there are misconceptions about randomness—the representativeness heuristic will mislead.

In the second example, the Sinologist/psychologist problem, people are foiled mainly because important information is neglected, that is, the relevant base rates are ignored. In many circumstances, of course, such information is absent, and the representativeness heuristic has no serious contender. In other circumstances, base-rate information may have little practical significance. Sometimes the feature-matching process results in a category determination with a probability near 1.0, and when features are as powerfully diagnostic as that, there is little practical need to consider base rates. For example, in the Sinologist/psychologist problem, if the profile were extended to include the information that the person speaks Chinese, knows no statistics, and has never heard of B. F. Skinner, the relevance of base-rate frequencies would dwindle to triviality. There are also occasions when representativeness criteria can be used directly without violating normative standards because the base rates or marginal probabilities are approximately equal. If the Sinologist/psychologist problem were altered to a decision between a sociologist and an historian, the representativeness heuristic would serve the judge quite well, providing that the relevant occupational stereotypes had at least some validity.

Knowledge Structures: Theories And Schemas

We have discussed some of the judgmental strategies that people use in a variety of social inference tasks. Often, however, people's understanding of the rapid flow of continuing social events may depend less on such judgmental procedures than on a rich store of general knowledge of objects, people, events, and their characteristic relationships. Some of this knowledge may be represented as beliefs or *theories*, that is, reasonably explicit "propositions" about the characteristics of objects or object classes. (For example: Joe is kind to small animals. Rotarians are public spirited. Adult neuroses have their "origin" in childhood trauma. Decision makers prefer minimax strategies.) People's generic knowledge also seems to organized by a variety of less "propositional," more *schematic*, cognitive structures (for example, the knowledge underlying one's awareness of what happens in a restaurant, one's understanding of the Good Samaritan parable, or one's conception of what an introvert is like). To describe such knowledge structures, psychologists refer to a growing list of terms, including "frames" (Minsky 1975), "scripts" (Abelson 1976; Schank & Abelson 1977), "nuclear scenes" (Thomkins 1979), and "prototypes" (Cantor & Mischel 1977, in press), in addition to the earlier and more general term "schemas" (Bartlett 1932; Piaget 1936; also Rumelhart 1976).

In the following discussion we largely forsake any attempt at classifying or defining the possible structures. (See Schank & Abelson 1977, Abelson 1978, and Taylor & Crocker 1980.) We do, however, observe the distinction between beliefs or theories that can be summarized in one or more simple propositions, and other more schematic structures. Both types of knowledge structures are important because they provide an interpretative framework for the lay scientist—one that resolves ambiguity and supplements the information "given" with much "assumed" information.

Theories and Their Impact

... [Here] we restrict ourselves to emphasizing the role of lay psychological theory first in the application of the representativeness heuristic and then in a variety of attributional judgments. The types of theories to be considered vary from the relatively narrow generalizations that people make about particular individuals or groups, to the broadest conceptions of human nature and the determinants of human behavior.

Theory-based Judgments of Representativeness

As we noted earlier, assessments of representativeness often depend less on simple similarity criteria than on more sophisticated "theories" of the types of attributes and events that occur together, or that cause each other. For example, scandal in a parliamentary government is a "respresentative" cause of an impending election. When a scandal occurs we expect an election and when an election is called we are apt to cite any previous scandal as a contributing cause. The reason for such judgments clearly is not in the relative similarity of the outstanding features of political scandals and parliamentary elections. Rather, the judgment reflects one's adherence to a pair of "theoretical" propositions, first, that scandals weaken governments and second, that weakened governments in parliamentary democracies often must go to the electorate for a vote of confidence. Sometimes, as we shall see, the preconceptions governing causal inferences and likelihood assessments may best be regarded not as a set of propositions but as a schema or "script" (cf. Abelson 1976) in which a succession of "scenes" is linked in a single coherent structure—for example, accusations, denials, fresh accusations, limited acknowledgments of bad judgment and mendacity, resignations, and a final emotional appeal by the political leader for support at the polls.

People rely upon an enormous number of such theories, which are derived from personal experience and from the accumulated wisdom of one's culture, to decide on the representativeness of causes and effects, outcomes and outcome-generating processes, and objects and classes. The costs and benefits of relying upon such specific prior theories, rather than collecting and analyzing further data, for instance, depend both on the accuracy of the theories and on the feasibility of employing other, more empirical procedures.

Global Theories and Situational Versus Dispositional Attribution

Perhaps the most significant and far-reaching of the intuitive scientist's theories are those addressing the general causes of human behavior. These theories determine the meaning we extract from social interaction, and, in large measure, they determine the way we behave in response to the actions of our fellows. For example, the lay scientist, like the professional psychologist, believes that rewards for particular behaviors increase the subsequent likelihood of such behaviors and that punishment decreases their likelihood. The lay scientist, like the professional, believes that people's behavior is guided by plans and goals and believes that people seek to maximize pleasure and minimize pain. Such tacit, "global" theories, as well as many more specific theories, including theories about specific individuals or classes of individuals, govern our understanding of behavior—our causal explanations of past behavior and our predictions of future behavior.

There has been surprisingly little research on those beliefs and theories shared by the mass of people in our culture. Heider (1958) was perhaps the first to emphasize their importance, and Abelson (1968) was the first (and very nearly the only) investigator to attempt to study them empirically. What little research has been done on people's theories has focused on individual differences in the beliefs and theories. Christie and Geis (1970), for example, identified a set of cynical views about human nature that characterizes the highly "Machiavellian" individual and explains his success in manipulating his more trusting peers. Even more relevant to present concerns, Rotter and others (Rotter 1966; Collins 1974; Crandall, Katkovsky, & Crandall 1965; Lefcourt 1972) investigated general inclinations toward internal versus external explanations (that is, personal effort and ability versus the vicissitudes of chance) in accounting for personal and social outcomes. More recently, Seligman (1975), discussed the part that people's theories of the controllability of outcomes and of the causes of success and failure may have in the clinical syndrome of depression.

The most general and encompassing lay theory of human behavior—so broadly applied that it might more aptly be termed a "metatheory"—is the assumption that behavior is caused primarily by the enduring and consistent dispositions of the actor, as opposed to the particular characteristics of the situation to which the actor responds. Throughout this book we refer to what Ross (1977a, 1978; Ross & Anderson 1980) called the "fundamental attribution error"—the tendency to attribute behavior exclusively to the actor's dispositions and to ignore powerful situational determinants of the behavior. [Later] we argue that such errors are determined partially by perceptual factors. Such errors probably are also prompted partially by domain-specific theories, for example: "Successful people are ambitious and motivated"; "People who hurt others' feelings are rude and not well 'brought up.'" But in large measure the error, we suspect, lies in a very broad proposition about human conduct, to wit, that people behave as they do because of a general disposition to behave in the way that they do.

It is difficult to prove that people adhere to anything like an overarching "general theory" of'the relative impact of dispositional versus situational factors. There is reason to suspect, nevertheless, that a rather general, "dispositionalist theory" is shared by almost everyone socialized in our culture. Certainly, it is a part of the world view of the so-called Protestant ethic that one's virtues and successes ultimately reflect one's worthiness and, conversely, that one's vices and failings reflect one's unworthiness. According to this view, good or bad luck, accidents of birth, and situational adversities may forestall matters but one's fate will eventually mirror one's character, and one's personal traits and abilities will ultimately prevail over circumstances. This message is as present in Henry Fielding's novels as it is in Horatio Alger's sentimental doggerel. It is the set of beliefs which Max Weber (1904) long ago identified as a precondition for the rise of capitalism, and it is consistent with the many philosophical positions that have assigned central roles to the concepts of personal responsibility and free will. The "dispositionalist theory," in short, is thoroughly woven into the fabric of our culture. Not surprisingly, therefore, children growing up in our culture come to hold an increasingly dispositional view of the causes of behavior (Ross, Turiel, Josephson, & Lepper 1978).

The opposite view, the "situationalist" position, does not lack advocates. It is espoused by most contemporary experimental social psychologists, behaviorists, and role-theory sociologists. (In a sense, the view is also part of the economic determinism of classical Marxism.) This alternative view, which was perhaps first explicitly articulated by Lewin (1935), maintains that behavior is understood best in terms of states and intentions that are themselves the product of those situational stimuli pertinent to the individual at the moment of action. Such a view garners support, . . . from two sources: One is the failure of researchers to demonstrate anything like the cross-situational consistency in behavior demanded by the dispositionalist view (cf. Hartshorne & May 1928; Newcomb 1929; and more generally Mischel 1968). The second source of support for the situationalist position is in the many studies that demonstrate that seemingly insubstantial manipulations of situational factors can control behavior dramatically and can greatly restrict individual differences. The mass of people may be seen to act in ways that seem either cowardly or brave, honest or dishonest, prejudiced or unprejudiced, or apathetic or concerned, depending on the situational constraints and opportunities present at the time of action.

We do not wish to imply that the evidence massively or unambiguously supports a situationalist view. The recent "metatheory shift" in the social sciences, like all such metatheory shifts or new "paradigms" (Kuhn 1962) is currently quite underdetermined by the available data. Perhaps the chief evidence supporting the situationalist view is the continuing ability of social scientists, even those who subscribe to the situationalist view, to be surprised by evidence both of the lack of individual consistency in dispositional tendencies and of the power of manifestly "weak" situational factors to control behavior.

Whether it is the layperson's metatheory or the social scientist's that is correct (cf. Bem & Allen 1974, Bem & Funder 1978), the metatheory exerts a pronounced influence on people's judgments of the causes and meanings of behavior. Often, as we will demonstrate, this marked dispositional bias can be shown to be incorrect.

Schemas, Scripts, and Personae

To understand the social world, the layperson makes heavy use of a variety of knowledge structures normally not expressed in propositional terms and possibly not stored in a form even analogous to propositional statements. In describing these cognitive strutures we shall use the generic designation "schema" and will comment in detail about only two types of schemas—event-schemas, or "scripts," and person-schemas, or "personae."

The most basic type of schema is probably that which underlies the use of common concepts or categories such as *dog, tree* or *chair*, or concepts of far greater or lesser generality (*animals, flora,* and *furniture,* or *Airedales, Ponderosa pines,* and *Chippendales*). In recent years there has been an explosion of interest in and research on people's use of categories, and we cannot digress to summarize this important and ever-expanding literature. Let us note merely that the "classic" view of a category, one that entails clearly specified boundaries and a set of defining characteristics necessary to and sufficient for category membership, has come under increasingly devastating attack (cf. Wittgenstein 1953; Rosch 1978; Tversky 1977). Gradually it has been supplanted by a more lenient and catholic view—one that allows ambiguous boundaries, recognizes a variety of differing bases for assessing category membership, and permits individual members to differ in their prototypicality. What both the traditional and newer views have in common is the notion that the category and the concept underlying it form an important basis for inference. That is, once the criteria for applying the concept have been met, the concept user readily assigns a number of additional characteristics to the entity. For example, upon deciding on the basis of a particular animal's appearance that it is a "dog," one makes the inferential leaps that it is trainable, capable of loyalty, able to bark, and likely to chase cats but is unlikely to climb trees, purr, or wash its coat.

In principle one could speak of a dog "schema," or even an Airedale schema or an animal schema. In practice, however, the term "schema" has come to be differentiated from the term "concept." Since its introduction in the 1930s by Bartlett (1932) and by Piaget (1936), the term "schema" has been used more and more to refer to those mental structures having a *dynamic* or *relational* aspect. For example, Piaget refers to a "thumb-sucking" schema and a "conservation" schema, both of which, despite the enormous difference in their level of abstractness, have dynamic relationships among the schema's components. In the former, the schema is a kind of mental summary of the sensory, cognitive, and motor experiences in a sequence of actions involving body parts. In the latter, the schema represents experiential knowledge of the relationship between mass and volume (or number and position) and the outcomes likely to result from various action sequences involving a fixed mass of material (or a fixed number of objects).

Kelly (1972b) introduced to the attribution literature the notion of a causal schema. Kelley used the term to refer primarily to a highly abstract, content-free notion of the formal relations among causes and effects. He proposed that people possess in very abstract and general form the notions of sufficiency and necessity in causal relations. This distinction underlies a number of specific causal schemas, such as the single necessary cause schema (in which the existence of the effect carries with it the certainty that a particular cause was present) and the multiple sufficient cause schema (in which the existence of the effect implies the possibility of each of several causes). There also are more complicated general schemas. For example, people may have a "discounting" schema: Given an effect capable of being produced by several causes and certain knowledge of the operation of a particular cause, people reduce their subjective probability that each of the other sufficient causes was operative. People also may possess an inhibitory cause schema: Given knowledge of the existence of a factor operating to block the occurrence of the effect, people infer that one or more facilitative causes were unusually powerful.

Though we are not confident that people actually possess such content-free causal schemas, we will use the term occasionally, to refer primarily to causal-analytic strategies that people do *not* seem to understand or to use in situations in which they would be helpful.

Scripts

The lexicons of cognitive social psychology and artificial intelligence recently were enriched by the introduction of the "script" concept (Abelson 1976,

1978; Schank & Abelson 1977). A script is a type of schema in which the related elements are social objects and events involving the individual as actor or observer. Unlike most schemas, scripts generally are event sequences extended over time, and the relationships have a distinctly causal flavor, that is, early events in the sequence produce or at least "enable" the occurrence of later events. A script can be compared to a cartoon strip with two or more captioned "scenes," each of which summarizes some basic actions that can be executed in a range of possible manners and contexts (for instance, the "restaurant script" with its "entering," "ordering," "eating," and "exiting" scenes). Alternatively, a script can be represented as a computer program with a set of tracks, variables, relationships, operations, subroutines, loops, and the like, which are "instantiated" with particular values for any particular application of the script. Thus, the restaurant script has a coffee shop track, a Chinese restaurant track, a cafeteria track, perhaps even a McDonald's track. The variable representing the decor may take on the value "fancy" or "crummy." The waiter values include "polite," "surly," and "bad enough to prompt a complaint." Exiting entails the operational options "pay waiter" or "pay cashier," and so forth.

Scripts can vary in many ways. They can be highly abstract, culturally pervasive, and may owe their existence only slightly to direct personal experience (for example, the script that links "temptation," "transgression," and "retribution"). Or they may be highly concrete, idiosyncratic, and directly tied to experience (for example, the scripted episode in which Daddy comes home from work, asks Mommy what's for dinner, she gets annoyed and sulks and, depending on what his day has been like, he either apologizes or gets angry too). The importance of scripts to the intuitive scientist lies in the speed and ease with which they make events (or secondhand accounts of events) readily comprehensible and predictable. Their potential cost, as always, is the possibility of erroneous interpretations, inaccurate expectations, and inflexible modes of response.

Personae

Central to any dramatic script is the *dramatis personae*, or cast of characters. Indeed, to specify the characters is often sufficient to convey much of the action of the script (for example, "the prostitute with the heart of gold and the scholarly but naive young man" or "the crusty but benign older physician and the hot-headed, idealistic young surgeon").

Social judgments and expectations often are mediated by a class of schemas which we shall term "personae," that is, cognitive structures representing the personal characteristics and typical behaviors of particular "stock characters." Some personae are the unique products of one's own personal experience (good old Aunt Mary, Coach Whiplasch). Others are shared within the culture or subculture (the sexpot, the earth-mother, the girl-next-door, the redneck, the schlemiel, the rebel-without-a-cause). Many of the shared personae are borrowed from fiction (Shakespeare's tortured Hamlet or television's bigoted Archie Bunker) or even from the popularized professional jargon of psychology and psychiatry (the authoritarian, the "Type A" personality, the anal-compulsive).

Our store of personae is augmented further by metaphors drawn from the animal kingdom and from the many occupational roles in our society. Animal or occupational personae are apt to be very simple and "concept-like," primarily highlighting a limited set of physical or behavioral characteristics. Hence, we readily understand, and are apt to be strongly influenced by, remarks like, "What do you see in that big *ox*," or "I wouldn't trust that *viper* if I were you," or "He wants you to be his Haldeman," or "Surgeon Blochit is a real butcher" (or, alternatively, "Butcher Phelps is a real surgeon").

In each instance the persona constitutes a knowledge structure which, when evoked, influences social judgments and behaviors. Once the principal features or behaviors of a given individual suggest a particular persona, subsequent expectations of and responses to that individual are apt to be dictated in part by the characteristics of the persona.

The concept of a persona is not essentially different from that of a stereotype. We prefer the term "persona," however, because it lacks the pejorative implications of the term "stereotype," which has been used to describe culturally shared, indeed hackneyed, notions of particular groups of people. The persona is also similar to the notion of a "person-prototype," proposed and investigated by Cantor and Mischel (1977, in press).

Availability, Representativeness, and the Arousal of Knowledge Structures

The notion that the layperson's experience, understanding, and inferences are structured by a great and varied store of schemas is intuitively satisfying. Indeed, it has become increasingly clear to theorists working in almost all areas of psychology that the schema construct is a cornerstone of psychological theory (Neisser 1976). Workers in social interaction (Berne 1964; Goffman 1959), personality and psychopathology (G. Kelly 1955, 1958), visual perception (Minsky 1975), and especially in language comprehension and artificial intelligence (Abelson 1978; Bobrow & Collins 1976; Bower, Black & Turner in press; Rumelhart, 1976; Rumelhart & Ortony 1976; Schank 1975) all have made essentially the same point—that objects and events in the phenomenal world are almost never approached as if they were *sui generis* configurations but rather are assimilated into preexisting structures in the mind of the perceiver.

Unfortunately, the increasing conviction that schemas exist and are important has not been accompanied by a commensurate increase in our knowledge of them. There still is little evidence that might clarify their properies or define the type of work they perform. Most critical of all, perhaps, is our ignorance of the conditions of their instigation and use. In 1961, De Soto wrote of our "crippling ignorance of the dynamics of schema arousal" (p. 22), and a decade later Kelley (1972b) was obliged to echo De Soto's complaint. Recently, however, matters have begun to improve. For instance, Markus (1977) showed that the speed with which information about the self is processed may be predicted by the presence or absence of schematic self-concepts or "self-schemas." Similarly, Cantor's and Mischel's work (1977, in press) documented the biasing effects of person schemas or "prototypes" on the interpretation of ambiguous information and the recall of specific details about people.

Perhaps the most encouraging development for the question of schema arousal is the theoretical one in Kahneman's and Tversky's work on heuristics. It is obvious that a schema can be aroused only if it exists in the person's long-term repertoire of schemas. What is not so obvious is that the *acute or transient availability* of a schema also may be an important determinant of its application to a particular instance. Two recent experiments support this possibility.

Higgins, Rholes, and Jones (1977) asked subjects to read a brief paragraph describing a young man and then to evaluate him on a number of dimensions. The young man was described as having many risky hobbies, having a high opinion of his abilities, having limited relationships with other people, and being unlikely to change his mind or turn back from a chosen course of action. Before reading about the young man, subjects had participated in a "learning experiment" in which some were exposed to the words "adventurous," "self-confident," "independent," and "persistent," and some were exposed to the words "reckless," "conceited," "aloof," and "stubborn." Subjects exposed to the positive words later evaluated the young man more highly than did those exposed to the negative words. (Subjects exposed to equally positive or negative but conceptually irrelevant words were uninfluenced.) As Higgins and colleagues suggest, this effect is most likely mediated by the transient availability of different concepts or "personae."

Hornstein, LaKind, Frankel, and Manne (1975) performed an experiment with similar implications. Before playing a prisoner's dilemma game, subjects were left seated in a waiting room listening to what they believed was a piped-in radio program. The music was interrupted for a "human interest" story. In one instance this was a heart-warming account of someone who offered a kidney to someone whom he did not know who was in need of a transplant. In another instance, subjects heard a ghastly account of an urban atrocity. The vignette had pronounced effects on subsequent strategy in the prisoner's dilemma game. Subjects who had heard the heart-warming vignette played the game in a much more cooperative way than did those who had heard the horror. The authors argued persuasively (and with data) against a mood interpretation of the subsequent behavior. Instead, it seems likely that it was an acute manipulation of the availability of different personae or "schemas for the human race" that accounted for the results ("most people are basically decent and kind" versus "it's dog eat dog out there").

It seems equally clear that the representativeness heuristic takes part in the selection of schemas. Indeed, the similarity of the data at hand to some stored representation of objects and events always has been presumed to be the chief determinant of schema arousal and application. But it also seems likely that purely incidental and irrelevant features of the stimulus may prompt the arousal of schemas tagged with similar incidental features. Thus, we have it on the testimony of Colonel House (May 1973) that, on the eve of World War I, President Woodrow Wilson was anguishing over the possibility of war with *Great Britain*. Why? Because, as on the eve of the War of 1812, the British were illegally searching American ships and, as Wilson agonized to House, "Madison and I are the only Princeton men to become President" (!) Apparently, the "search-ships/war with England" schema was a representative one for Wilson in part because of the irrelevant surface detail of the alma mater of the incumbent president.

Availability and representativeness determinants of schema arousal appear to be the probable focal guides of future research in this area. It will be fascinating to see whether these determinants operate in a normatively appropriate way, or whether, as in the Wilson anecdote, they operate so as to leave us at the mercy of arbitrary and incidental features of stimuli and structures.

Appropriate and Inappropriate Utilization of Knowledge Structures

It would be even more foolish to criticize people's general tendency to employ schemas and other knowledge structures than it would be to criticize their general tendency to rely on the availability and representativeness heuristics. Indeed, the primary reason for the widespread acceptance of the notion of schematic knowledge structures is that it is almost impossible to imagine how mental life could be managed without them. In a world characterized by recurrent stimuli presenting important functional equivalencies, any cognitive system that places a premium on minimizing computing time and effort must take advantage of such redundancy by storing generic concepts, events, event-sequences, and the like.

Despite the important efficiencies that accure to the schema user, there seems little doubt there often are serious costs as well. Schemas are apt to be overused and misapplied, particularly to the social sphere, and they are apt to be used when other, less rapid and intuitive methods of judgment would fully merit the additional time and effort required.

In the physical world, stimuli categorized in a particular way, or events interpreted in terms of a given schema, may be similar to an extent rarely true in the social domain. In many important respects, it is only a slight overstatement to say that "if you've seen one oak tree, you've seen them all." The number of properties necessary to define uniquely many types of physical objects is highly limited. As a consequence, the number of properties of a particular object that must be perceived in order to place the object in its correct category also is limited. Moreover, once a physical object has been placed in some conceptual category, one can usually disregard much of the information that dicated the categorization (that is, information specifying exactly how, when, and under what observation conditions a particular tree satisfied the requirements for assignment to the "oak" category). Most important of all, classification of a physical object usually permits one to adduce or predict confidently additional properties of the object. Thus, once an object is correctly characterized as an oak tree, it is nearly certain that the tree will provide shade and acorns, that its wood will be hard and burn slowly, that all its leaves will drop in the fall, and so on.

It is quite different in the social domain, in which the observed properties are less diagnostic, in which the number of properties suggestive of a given category are not so sharply delineated, and in which the number of properties that can be inferred confidently, given correct categorization of the object, is very small. To appreciate these differences, let us note how the categorization of a person as a "bigot" differs form the categorization of an object as an oak tree. First, the number of properties that might indicate bigotry is, for all practical purposes, infinite, and information about the circumstances in which a particular person satisfied the "bigot" criterion can be ignored or forgotten only at one's peril. Similarly, the number of properties dicated by the categorization of someone as a bigot is large only in proportion to the naiveté of the perceiver. Few characteristics or behaviors can be confidently assumed about any particular "bigot." Schemas in the social domain rarely are more than rough outlines and tentative guides for perception and behavior. When they are relied on heavily, there are bound to be inferential errors and misguided actions.

E. R. May, in his fascinating book entitled *"Lessons" of the Past* (1973), presented some thought-provoking examples of erroneous political judgments and policies that seem to have originated in the overutilization or misapplication of particular schemas. For example, May describes how a schema, which might be termed the "Munich Conference" script, exerted an undue influence on the thinking of politicians (most notably President Lyndon Johnson), who invoked the specter of the infamous "Munich Conference" to defend the aggressiveness of their military policy or the intransigence of their diplomacy. These politicians seem to have been influenced greatly by— or perhaps hoped to influence the public and their potential detractors through—a particularly vivid, historic script. The script has two scences or vignettes, *"The Political Compromise,"* in which one yields to a power-hungry and unprincipled foe, and *"The Military Consequence,"* in which one's country or that of one's ally is subsequently overrun by the foe. To the extent that politicians rely on such historical scripts, they may be unduly dogmatic and constrained and may be unresponsive to features that ought to distinguish a current political decision from an historical one. They may even be unduly responsive to prominent but superficial considerations of script representativeness, that is, the Munich script may be particularly likely to be evoked if the foreign leader requests the conference in his own country rather than on neutral grounds or if he has a small moustache!

A "persona" can mislead as badly as a script can, as other examples from May's book show. President Harry Truman, a man not given to speaking kindly of all whom he met, demonstrated a peculiar willingness to trust his wartime ally, Joseph Stalin. His personal correspondences reveal a surprising source of this trust. To Truman, Stalin evoked the persona of Tom Pendergast, his former Missouri benefactor. Pendergast was a ruthless and corrupt political kingmaker, but he had always been completely trustworthy in his relations with Truman. Apparently because some of Stalin's characteristics were representative of the Pendergast persona, Truman seemed to feel that other Pendergast characteristics also could be assumed—specifically, trustworthiness in matters relating to Truman.

To May's examples of schema-induced errors in the judgment of politicians, we add one related to us by Dorwin Cartwright. Cartwright told us that spokesmen for the pure sciences, lobbying for financial aid in the postwar period of the late forties and early fifties, effectively argued that the technological innovations of World War II had "depleted the stockpile of basic knowledge." Congressmen, accustomed to arguments about the depletion of stockpiles and the need for replenishing them, apparently accepted the idea that the "basic knowledge stockpile" was one of those depleted. The "stockpile" concept, as applied to basic scientific knowledge, is not entirely invalid, that is, the more knowledge the better, the more money and effort spent, the faster it will grow, and so on. But the "depletion" schema is invalid and highly misleading. For heavy use of basic scientific knowledge, far from exhausting the "stockpile," makes it grow.

Our examples so far have been of the misapplication of particular schemas when more cautious and critical application of the same schemas would have served the intuitive scientist quite well. It is possible, however, to describe particular conceptual categories, scripts, or personae that are so lacking in foundation and predictive value that they almost invariably serve the user badly. Many racial or ethnic stereotypes fit this designation. The Volvo-Saab "thought experiment" described in chapter 1 is another example. [Editor's note: The thought experiment is as follows. You have decided to buy either a Volvo or a Saab. On looking in *Consumer Reports*, you find that Volvo is the more reliable car, and so you decide to buy the Volvo. Your brother-in-law then details his many problems with a single Volvo. What is the likely effect of this new information on your decision?] The brother-in-law's litany of mechanical woes derives its impact, in part, from its ability to evoke the familiar "lemon" schema that haunts most propective car buyers. Such a schema invites the assumption that mechanical difficulties are not distributed in a normal curve but that there is instead a distinct "bump" at the high-difficulty end of the continuum. It is doubtful that there is such a bump, and if there is not then it is clearly counterproductive to direct one's efforts toward avoiding a mythical lemon when one's efforts could be better directed toward obtaining a car with the best overall record for trouble-free performance. But even if the lemon schema is true, the anecdote about the brother-in-law's Volvo provides far less evidence about the distribution of lemons across car makes than do drab statistical surveys of repair records.

An example of inappropriate schema usage that may hit even closer to home is the behavior of the typical faculty committee charged to select students for a graduate program. A letter of recommendation for Elsa Doud may note that Ms. Doud was shy in Professor Smith's class at Ohio State. Doud's shyness and "midwesternness" may call to mind Priscilla Frimp, another shy midwestern woman who never made it through the program. The Frimp persona may then be used as a basis to reject Doud. Any reliance on personae in such a situation is utterly without foundation. The only currently valid grounds for predicting graduate performance seem to be the candidate's GRE (Graduate Record Examination) scores, grades, research experience, quality of undergraduate institution, and evaluations in letters of recommendation. Of course, if the anti-Doud professor wishes to construct a shyness measure and can show that it is related to quality of graduate performance, then the professor may administer this measure to the entire pool of applicants and reject those scoring high on it. If an interaction among shyness, sex, and region of the country is found, such that shyness is particularly crippling to the performance of midwestern females, then a lower cutoff point on the shyness scale may be set for midwestern females than for male or female students from other parts of the country. Unless the professor is willing to perform the requisite validation research, however, any persona ruminations should be kept out of the student selection procedure.

Inferential Adjustment And Its Limitations

In this chapter we described some inferential strategies on which the lay scientist seems to rely in forming judgments of the social world. There were two common themes in our observations. The first and more obvious—that people's errors and insights are intimately linked together and are typically a matter of appropriate versus inappropriate application of a given heuristic, theory, or schema—was reiterated often enough that we trust it needs no reemphasis. There was a second and less obvious theme that merits some elaboration. At several points we emphasized that it is not only people's eagerness to apply simple heuristics and immediately available knowledge structures that leads to grief; it is also the failure to make necessary *adjustments* of initial judgments. That is, once a simple heuristic or schema has been used, subsequent considerations fail to exert as much impact as common sense or normative considerations might dictate that it should.

Some simple, direct demonstrations of inadequate adjustment or "anchoring" effects were provided in work by Tversky and Kahneman (1974). In one study, for example, subjects were asked to adjust an arbitrary initial estimate of the percentage of African countries in the United Nations. Those starting with "anchors" of 10 percent and 65 percent produced "adjusted" estimates of 25 percent and 45 percent, respectively. The same anchoring effects were demonstrated with initial "estimates" dictated by the subject's own previous spin of a roulette wheel! Even though it would have been obvious to the subjects that these "starting points" were wholly arbitrary and unrelated to the judgment task, they nevertheless had an influence on final estimates.

Our present contention is essentially an extension of Tversky's and Kahneman's point about the effects of a cognitive "anchor." That is, once subjects have made a first pass at a problem, the initial judgment may prove remarkably resistant to further information, alternative modes of reasoning, and even logical or evidential challenges. Attempts to integrate new information may find the individual surprisingly "conservative," that is, willing to yield ground only grudgingly and primed to challenge the relevance, reliability, or authority of subsequent information or logical consideration. As a result, the method of first choice—and we believe heuristics and schemas to be such methods of first choice—may have disproportionate impact, while other methods (notably, methods considering pallid base lines, mitigating situational factors, possible sources of unreliability in the data, and the like) have relatively little impact.

Summary

The chapter describes two of the general tools that people use to "go beyond the information given," judgmental heuristics and knowledge structures.

The availability heuristic is used to judge the frequency and likelihood of events and event-relations. Since the availability of remembered events is sometimes biased at the stage of sampling, sometimes at the stage of encoding and storage, and sometimes at the stage of retrieval, frequency and likelihood estimates often will be biased correspondingly.

The representativeness heuristic is used to estimate the likelihood of some state of affairs given knowledge of some other state of affairs, for example, the likelihood that an object is a member of some category because it has certain characteristics. Such judgments are based on the perceived similarity of the known characteristics of the object to the presumed essential characteristics of the category. The heuristic sometimes misleads because, in some circumstances, notably when diagnosticity is low or category base rates differ widely, mere similarity is an unreliable guide to likelihood.

In addition to heuristics, people use certain knowledge structures in approaching judgment tasks. These include relatively propositional structures such as theories and beliefs, and more schematic structures like scripts and personae. These knowledge structures are invaluable aids to understanding social events, but they may mislead to the extent that they are poor representations of external reality and to the extent that they preclude attention to the details of the actual object at hand.

The judgmental heuristics may prove to be the primary determinants of the arousal and application of the various knowledge structures. Availability of a given structure, including transient, arbitrary increments in its availability, may increase the likelihood of its application. The representativeness of a given structure, including the similarity of quite superficial and incidental features of the stimulus to features of the structure, may be a chief determinant of the arousal and application of a given structure.

It is emphasized that it is not the existence of heuristics and knowledge structures that can be criticized but rather, their overuse, misuse, and use in preference to more appropriate strategies. Even when more appropriate strategies are subsequently employed for a given judgmental task, the undue influence of the simpler, more intuitive strategies may persist.

11

Epistemics: The Regulative Theory of Cognition

Alvin I. Goldman

I wish to advocate a reorientation of epistemology. Lest anyone maintain that the enterprise I urge is not epistemology at all (even part of epistemology), I call this enterprise by a slightly different name: *epistemics*. Despite this terminological concession, I believe that the inquiry I advocate is significantly continuous with traditional epistemology. Like much of past epistemology, it would seek to regulate or guide our intellectual activities. It would try to lay down principles or suggestions for how to conduct our cognitive affairs. The contrast with traditional epistemology—at least "analytic" epistemology of the twentieth century—would be its close alliance with the psychology of cognition. The basic premise of epistemics is that one cannot give the best advice about intellectual operations without detailed information about mental processes. Since these processes are most illuminatingly studied by cognitive psychology, epistemics would go hand in hand with empirical investigation of our "information-processing" mechanisms.[1]

Before it can select and recommend intellectual procedures, epistemics must identify a suitable set of goals or outcomes which these procedures should realize. Let us postpone the question of the nature of these goals, however, since the need for a greater alliance of epistemology and psychology can be identified independently of the choice of goals. At any rate, there is a range of different but plausible goals that would all lend themselves to the same rationale.

What then are the grounds for the alliance of epistemology and psychology? There are three such grounds. First, traditional epistemology has usually employed too simple a model of our cognitive life. For one thing, its conceptual or classificatory resources have been too weak and impoverished. Epistemological principles have standardly addressed themselves to what "beliefs" (or

Reprinted from *The Journal of Philosophy* LXXV (October 1978) : 509–523, by permission of the author and the publisher. Copyright © 1978, *The Journal of Philosophy*.

other doxastic attitudes, such as subjective probabilities) one should have under various circumstances. From a psychological perspective, however, this sort of mental classification is too coarse-grained, as I shall argue below. Furthermore, epistemology's simplistic mental scheme has given it an overly restrictive purview of the methods that might be used to improve our cognitive "outputs." Experimental psychology promises to enrich our model of mental processes, and, thereby, provide a more fruitful framework within which regulative epistemology may be conducted.

Second, advice in matters intellectual, as in other matters, should take account of the agent's capacities. There is no point in recommending procedures that cognizers cannot follow or prescribing results that cognizers cannot attain. As in the ethical sphere, 'ought' implies 'can'. Traditional epistemology has often ignored this precept. Epistemological rules often seem to have been addressed to "ideal" cognizers, not human beings with limited information-processing resources. Epistemics wishes to take its regulative role seriously. It does not want to give merely idle advice, which humans are incapable of following. This means it must take account of the powers and limits of the human cognitive system, and this requires attention to descriptive psychology.

Third, it is appropriate for a regulative enterprise to be concerned with the flaws or defects of the system in question. To improve a tennis player's game, it is wise to begin by identifying his bad habits. To improve a political system, it is well to concentrate on its most palpable shortcomings. Analogously, if we wish to raise our intellectual performance, it behooves us to identify those traits which are most in need of improvement. We should examine our native cognitive proclivities, to see how well they operate in the absence of special training or coaching. What kinds of mistakes, if any, are we likely to make? Answers to this sort of question—which can best come from empirical psychology—can help us formulate a genuinely useful set of guidelines for the direction of the mind.

I

Let us explore these three considerations in greater detail. First, what is impoverished about traditional epistemological classifications? What is too coarse-grained about the concept of "belief," for example, and how can cognitive psychology provide more fine-grained concepts?

A sample epistemological rule of a traditional sort might have the following form: "When in circumstances of type C, believe a proposition of type p." How should such an injunction be interpreted? Philosophers have distinguished an "occurrent" and a "dispositional" sense of 'belief'. In psychological terms, these denote, respectively, some sort of conscious event and some sort of storage in memory. If we say that S believes dispositionally at time t that $2 + 2 = 4$, we mean not that S is consciously thinking of this proposition at t, but that he is prepared at t to retrieve it from memory. Yet memory traces differ in accessibility. How easy must it be to recall an item from memory if it is to count as "believed"?

Consider the proposition "The man I met at lunch is named 'Prescott'." Suppose that, when I probe my memory with the question, "What's the name of the man I met at lunch?," I draw a total blank. On the other hand, if someone were to mention the name 'Prescott', I would immediately recognize it as the name of the man I met at lunch. In short, I have "recognition memory" for the name, but I can't retrieve it in "free recall." Given these facts, do I *believe* the foregoing proposition? How we answer this question is not really important for my purposes. The crucial point is that there are alternative strengths of memory storage, or degrees of accessibility from memory, far more complex than the ordinary term 'belief' suggests. An adequate epistemology would offer a richer array of classifications.

Analytical epistemology has not only ignored the complexity of memory storage and retrieval; it has not even paid systematic attention to the simpler distinction between occurrent and dispositional belief. Yet this is critical from a regulative point of view. There is quite a difference between the injunction to entertain a given proposition actively and the injunction to keep it in ("long-term") memory at a given time. Since there are severe limits on the number of propositions we can consciously entertain at a given moment, it is pointless to enjoin a cognizer to keep *all* propositions he is warranted in believing in conscious thought. Epistemological rules must be carefully honed, to reflect these differences in status.[2]

A traditional principle which ignores the foregoing distinctions is the *total-evidence requirement*. According to this principle, the credence it is rational to give to a statement at a given time is a function of the total evidence then "available."[3] What is meant by "available"? Does it mean only those items which immediately come to mind when you entertain the statement? Does it include, in addition, items you can retrieve with effortful search? Does it even include items for which you have "recognition memory" only? The term 'available' is obviously ambiguous, and this renders the requirement too unclear for actual application. How much effortful search of memory, if any, are you supposed to undertake when trying to make a "doxastic decision" vis-à-vis a given proposition?

Admittedly, the distinctions I have here been drawing *might* be made independently of experimental psychology. But in fact it is the detailed study of memory mechanisms which has prompted the distinction between "recognition" memory and "free recall." This illustrates how psychological investigation can refine our mentalistic conceptual scheme.

The restricted set of *methods* considered by analytical epistemology may be illustrated by Roderick Chisholm's *Theory of Knowledge*.[4] On page 15, Chisholm suggests an "intellectual requirement" to the effect that, for any proposition a person considers, he should *"try his best to bring it about"* that he believes the proposition if and only if it is true. What kinds of methods should a person employ in order to satisfy this requirement? Chisholm doesn't pose this question in a general way, but his own "epistemic principles" seem designed to fill this bill. They indicate the appropriateness of belief or suspension of judgment in propositions as a function of certain current beliefs of the cognizer. Thus, they are somewhat analogous to principles of reasoning. But this class of principles is a very narrow class. If one is really going to *try one's best* to bring about the specified goal, many other methods might be used which Chisholm completely ignores.

One kind of method for getting at truths is to employ one's spatial imagination. Recent psychological work supports the intuitive idea that much mental processing involves "iconic" representations. Presented with certain geometrical problems, for example, a person is likely to try to solve them by "mental rotation" of an imagined stimulus.[5] Spatial imaging is a legitimate cognitive method generally ignored by twentieth-century epistemologists, who have concentrated on purely "logical" procedures, construed either linguistically or propositionally.

Another relevant "method" is to employ mnemonic techniques to prevent forgetting. We frequently learn a truth at one time only to forget it later. Yet if we take Chisholm's requirement seriously, we should try our best to avert such forgetting. Again, this problem is ignored by most analytical epistemology, though classical philosophers such as Aristotle were mindful of it.[6] Since mnemonic techniques are often proposed by cognitive psychologists working on memory,[7] the epistemological bearing of this psychological work is straightforward.

II

Let me turn to the second rationale for infusing psychology into epistemology: to take account of our limited capacities. The aim of epistemics is the genuine improvememt of intellectual practice. This means that epistemic advice or rules must be capable of being followed. We may distinguish *ideal* and *executable* rules. The former specify ideal courses of action, or ideal ends, which human beings may or may not be able to realize. The latter specify courses of action that can actually be executed, given only some minimum of resources all normal humans possess. Epistemics ultimately aims at formulating executable rules or principles.

The orientation of much analytical epistemology has been quite different. Epistemological rules have often ignored human capacities, either because they were aimed at "ideal" cognizers or because they were formulated with no consideration of executability. Consider the rules of deductive closure and (non-)inconsistency:

(DC)   At any time, believe all the logical consequences of whatever you believe.
(INC)   Do not believe, at any time, all members of an inconsistent set of propositions.

Since any set of beliefs has infinitely many consequences, but people are incapable of having infinitely many beliefs, (DC) is nonexecutable. Since there is no effective procedure for determining inconsistency, there is nothing humans can do to guarantee conformity with (INC). Hence, it too is nonexecutable.

Althoguh (DC) and (INC) are themselves nonexecutable, it might seem easy to derive executable rules from them, by simply prescribing the resolute *attempt* to satisfy them. This would yield the following principles:

(T-DC)   Try your best to bring it about, at any time, that you believe all the logical consequences of whatever you believe.
(T-INC)   Try your best to bring it about that you do not believe, at any time, all members of any inconsistent set of propositions.

Assuming these rules are executable, are they *acceptable* rules? What would be involved in actually conforming to (T-DC) and (T-INC)? A person would expend all his conscious energy tracing the logical consequences of his beliefs and worrying about their possible inconsistency. This would be an all-consuming mental occupation. Is that a reasonable allocation of limited cognitive resources? Surely not. Someone who uses all his information-processing time and equipment in these tasks will acquire little or no "new" information, e.g., information about dangers in his current environment. At any rate, he will acquire far *less* information of this kind than if he pays more attention to the current environment. The same point holds of a Bayesian theorist's prescription continually to (try to) adjust subjective probabilities so as to preserve a còherent credence function. *Some* concern with logical and probabilistic relations is doubtless appropriate; but total preoccupation with logical or probabilistic relations is a misdirected employment of scarce attentional resources.[8]

I do not deny the epistemological relevance of logic (or probability theory). Truths of logic, both model-theoretic and proof-theoretic, will clearly be useful in helping to formulate epistemic advice. (One plausible bit of epistemic counsel is to study logic—and statistics.) But past epistemologists have often exaggerated the connection between logic and epistemology. Logic alone cannot directly generate epistemic principles. This is so for three reasons. First, epistemic principles should reflect a set of cognitive desiderata, which balance, for example, the relative importance of increasing true belief as compared with avoiding error. Logic cannot determine these desiderata. Second, epistemic principles should take account of the constraints under which cognizers operate, and this goes beyond the scope of logic. Third, precise epistemic principles would indicate "where" and "how" to represent information, e.g., in conscious thought or memory, imagistically or propositionally. Nothing like this can be derived from the truths of logic.

Now if epistemic principles are to be executable, the psychological operations they prescribe must presumably be subject to (direct) voluntary control. In light of this, it is ironic that epistemologists have so often suggested principles that enjoin "doxastic attitudes"; for assent and suspension of judgment are dubious candidates for the sphere of the voluntary. Contrary to Descartes's doctrine of "doxastic voluntarism," which holds that judgment and suspension of judgment are subject to the will, I believe we have little or no direct control over doxastic attitudes. I cannot, for example, simply choose to believe that there is an elephant in my study. I can choose to imagine this, or to write it down, or to repeat it to myself, or even to act as if it were true. But I cannot simply decide to go ahead and believe it.[9] Similarly, if the evidence and my inference patterns incline me to accept one of two scientific hypotheses, I cannot simply choose to believe the other one instead. I may thus be incapable of following any rule that instructs me to accept the other hypothesis.[10]

Although belief and nonbelief (in any of their more determinate psychological manifestations) may not be subject to direct control, they are certainly subject to *indirect* influence by means of (other) psychological operations that *are* under voluntary control. Part of the task of epistemics is to identify these "command variables" and see how they influence doxastic attitudes. In my opinion, *attention* constitutes the most important cognitive process largely under voluntary control. By directing perceptual attention we can influence our evidence and, thereby, our doxastic attitudes. By directing internal attention we can influence the problems and hypotheses we pursue, which also influences our doxastic attitudes.

Let me return to the topic of memory, which again illustrates how traditional epistemology ignores our limited capacities. Philosophy of science standardly assumes that we remember *individual* observed events and draw inferences from the totality of such data recalled at a given time. But psychological research suggests a different story: that it is not only, or even primarily, individual events that we store in memory, but organized "constructions" of "summaries" of past events. More specifically, we often store experience in terms of representative, typical, or average cases, sometimes called *prototypes* or *schemata*. This is indicated by experiments of J. J. Franks and J. D. Bransford in which subjects were shown cards with simple geometric figures. They then received test cards that included not only figures they had actually seen, but prototypes not previously presented. Subjects "recognized" the prototypes more readily than patterns they had actually seen! Apparently, they had formed memory schemata of typical patterns, and found it easy to "match" the prototype cards to these schemata.[11]

Other evidence suggests that, once schemata are formed, they are not easily changed by subsequent events. One often doesn't notice discrepant events at all; and, if the prototype *is* updated by new instances, the updating process is quite conservative. A comfortably lodged prototype or general impression is only slightly influenced by new observations. This is apparent from studies on impression-formation, which show that early data ("first impressions") affect judgment more than later data. When subjects are given a series of descriptive adjectives about a person, adjectives early in the list influence their over-all opinion more than later adjectives.[12]

It is tempting to dismiss these facts and simply urge people to remember individual events, not general impressions. But we simply *can't* remember *all* individual observations. Moreover, the tendency to form prototypes, and to have these prototypes affect the attention given to new instances, is doubtless a deep-seated feature of our cognitive equipment. This feature may lead to error or bias, and that is something with which epistemics should be concerned. But this concern must manifest itself in a realistic acknowledgment of our mnemonic powers and limits, not mere disdain for them.

III

These remarks already initiate the third part of our rationale for the psychologization of epistemology: the importance of recognizing flaws or defects in our native cognitive system. Recent work in cognitive social psychology and the psychology of judgment has focused on such flaws or defects.

As a first example, consider Richard E. Nisbett's suggestion of a significant difference in impact between "vivid" or "concrete" information as compared with "pallid" or "abstract" material. E. Borgida and Nisbett gave undergraduate subjects some course-evaluation information and invited them to state their own choices for future enrollment. Some subjects received written summaries of all previous enrôllees' evaluations, whereas others heard evaluations of only a few individuals, but in *face-to face* contact. It was found that abstract summary information had little impact on course choices, whereas concrete, first-hand contact had substantial impact.[13]

What makes certain information more "vivid" or "salient" than other information (e.g., statistical data) is not clear. It may reflect the relative strength of perception-related processes, i.e., imagistic modes of representation. Alternatively, it may be due to the relative ease with which stories or "scripts" are encoded and retained.[14] In any case, the relative weight of such factors in native thought needs to be assessed, and if this is a defect in our equipment, we must worry about how to obviate or accommodate it.

The underutilization of statistical data was initially stressed by Amos Tversky and Daniel Kahneman.[15] Subsequently, they attempt to explain this fact, among others, by the domination of "causal schemata" in human cognition.[16] They argue that there is a natural tendency to search for causal mechanisms and to neglect information that doesn't lend itself to causal interpretation. More specifically, two propensities are suggested. First, if event X is perceived as a potential *cause of* event Y, its impact on one's judgment of Y's probability is greater than if X is merely a potential *effect* of Y. This is illustrated by a study in which people were given the following problem:

In a survey of high-school seniors in a city, the height of boys was compared to the height of their fathers. In which prediction would you have greater confidence?
(a) The prediction of the father's height from the son's height
(b) The prediction of the son's height from the father's height
(c) Equal confidence

Since the distribution of height is essentially the same in successive generations, the correct answer is "Equal." But 111 subjects chose answer (b), 24 chose (c), and 15 chose (a). Apparently, this is because people tend to see a "causal mechanism" leading from father's height to son's height, but not conversely. The second propensity suggested by Tversky and Kahneman is that data that can be interpreted as either a potential cause or effect has more weight than purely distributional data. Preoccupation with causal theories is what accounts, on their view, for the unwarranted neglect of statistical information.

In their earlier paper[17] Tversky and Kahneman suggested three other biased heuristics that affect our probability judgments: *representativeness, anchoring,* and *availability*. *Representativeness* is illustrated by people's answers to questions about the probability that event *A* originates from process *B*, or resembles *B*. For example, in considering tosses of a coin for heads or tails, people (wrongly) consider the sequence H-T-H-T-T-H to be more likely than the sequence H-H-H-T-T-T, which does not appear random, and also more likely than the sequence H-H-H-H-T-H, which does not represent the fairness of the coin.

Anchoring is a phenomenon in which probability estimates are biased toward arbitrary initial values. For example, people were asked to estimate the percentage of African countries in the U.N. Before doing so, a number between 0 and 100 was determined by spinning a wheel in their presence. The subjects were asked to make their estimate by moving upward or downward from the given number. Different groups were given different initial values, and these arbitrary numbers had a marked effect on estimates. The median estimates were 25 and 45 for groups that received starting points of 10 and 65 respectively.

In making judgments, we frequently employ examples encountered in the past. Because of how we file or code information in memory, however, certain examples are more readily *available* than others, i.e., come to mind with greater ease. Suppose you are asked whether it is more probable that a randomly selected English word *begins* with 'r' or has 'r' in the *third* position. You are likely to try to recall words in each category and assess the probability by the number in each class that come to mind. But, since we tend to code words in memory in terms of first rather than third letters, availability from memory is not a reliable guide to the real probability.

Another arena for the detection of flaws is hypothesis formation. Problem-solvers often get into rigid "ruts" or "loops": they keep returning to hypotheses in fixed categories and cannot get outside these categories. Experimental subjects who have just solved problems requiring *position* hypotheses have an extremely difficult time with a very simple problem whose solution involves *size* rather than *position*.[18] Apparently, which hypotheses one frames or generates is heavily influenced by previous hypotheses *available* from memory. One tends to think of hypotheses that have succeeded in analogous problem situations, especially *recent* ones.

These empirical facts suggest tips for how to improve our hypothesis-generating performance.[19] Such improvement would seem to be a suitable topic for epistemology. Under the positivist conception of epistemology, however, hypothesis formation is excluded. Epistemology is to be the "logic" of science, and, since there is no "logic" of discover, hypothesis formation falls outside the pale. This conception of epistemology, I maintain, is unduly restrictive. Contrary to Carl Hempel's apparent position,[20] advice on hypothesis formation can be considered epistemological, even if it doesn't provide *mechanical* criteria for getting appropriate hypotheses. Heuristic suggestions for how to get out of loops is a legitimate part of epistemology, or at least of epistemics.

IV

My threefold rationale for infusing psychology into epistemology has concentrated on *mental* operations, where the relevance of psychology is fairly straightforward. It must be conceded, however, that intellectual activity is not purely mental. The solution of intellectual problems often involves (a) speech, (b) writing things down, either in words, diagrams, or formulas, (c) physical manipulation of experimental apparatus, and (d) physical interaction with machines and devices, such as computers, calculators, and abaci. Much intellectual improvement arises from learning and using appropriate procedures for these kinds of activities. For these reasons, epistemics cannot be concerned with psychological matters exclusively. Still, even these physical activities are intimately connected with the mental. First, the *purpose* of employing physical aids, such as diagrams or other inscriptions, is ultimately to guide one's psychological states, i.e., to produce *belief* or *understanding* (in any of their specific psychological manifestations). Second, one needs appropriate mental operations to *guide* these physical activities. Which activities should be executed? When? And in what order? These pose problems for the *mind*, problems of the structure and retrieval of plans and subroutines, to which psychology is clearly relevant.

Psychology can also play a role in determining the long-run effect on the mind of various kinds of training. How does critical discussion, for example, or imaginative play, improve mental habits? In general, some of the best advice epistemics can give is to engage in non-(purely-)mental activities that gradually mold one's cognitive traits.[21]

V

Although I have stressed the role of psychology in epistemics, it is evident that epistemic advice cannot be derived from empirical science alone (or from empirical science plus logic). Epistemics assumes that cognitive operations should be assessed instrumentally: given a choice of cognitive procedures, those which would produce the best set of *consequences* should be selected. This means, however, that epistemics must identify a relevant class of "intrinsically valuable" consequences and establish a *rank-ordering* of different sets of these consequences. What is the appropriate class of such consequences?

Some epistemologists might suggest that the proper aim of a cognizer (as such) is to have *justified* doxastic attitudes. Considered as the sole aim of cognition, this is too narrow, at least as justifiedness is usually construed. Typically, justificational status is assessed relative to the evidence actually possessed and the hypotheses actually considered. This means that a cognizer's beliefs can be justified no matter how good or bad his evidence-gathering and hypothesis-generating practices. The criterion of justifiedness does not evaluate these practices. Intuitively, however, such practices are of great intellectual significance. If they cannot be assessed by the standard of justifiedness, then meeting this standard is not the sole end of cognition.

Second it is doubtful that justifiedness is the *final* end of cognition. As I argue elsewhere,[22] justified belief is (roughly) belief formed by cognitive operations that tend to lead to truth. This suggests the more plausible view that justifiedness has value only because of its conduciveness to truth.

Consider then the view that the aim of cognition is the acquisition of truth, i.e., true belief. This must immediately be supplemented by the aim of avoiding error (otherwise one might simply try to believe all propositions, including their contradictories). But how should truth acquisition be weighted as compared with error avoidance? Second, is it only true *belief*—i.e., "acceptance" or full assent—that has (intrinsic) value? This allows no value to subjective probabilities, or qualified acceptances of truths. Third, we have already seen that so-called "belief" is ambiguous as between conscious assent and various forms of memory storage. What weights are to be assigned to such disparate mental lodgings for a given truth?

To resolve these and other problems, one might try a different approach to cognitive ends. One might suggest that the ultimate end of cognition is the *solution of problems,* where a problem is construed as how to attain a goal, whether the goal be intellectual—e.g., finding the answer to a question—or practical—e.g., finding a doctor in a foreign city. Cognitive practices have instrumental value to the extent that they lead to solutions of problems, i.e., attainment of goals. One virtue of this perspective is that it would explain the value of true as opposed to false belief, since truth facilitates goal attainment better than falsehood in all but a few, nonstandard cases. Second, no general weighting of truth acquisition versus error avoidance is needed. Their relative importance depends on the problem at hand. Third, *acceptance* of a truth is not the only good doxastic state. High subjective probabilities vis-à-vis truths also promote goal attainment. Fourth, there is no need for a general formula that weights the value of conscious versus stored beliefs. One should employ whichever patterns of information storage and retrieval best promote attainment of goals. Next, we generally prize *rapid* truth-acquisition techniques. This can be explained by the fact that many goals involve temporal constraints, which speedy techniques help to satisfy. Sixth, the goal-attainment approach can assign appropriate values to different kinds of mental representations. Imagistic representations are suitable for solving certain problems; others are best solved with purely semantic representations.

The problem-solving approach obviously faces difficulties, to which I cannot address myself here. Nor do I mean to commit epistemics to this particular answer to the question of epistemic ends. I propose it only tentatively and illustratively, as one alternative with certain attractions.

VI

Epistemics would not cover all the territory epistemology has covered in the past. It would not, for example, deal with the analysis of knowledge, or with the attempt to answer skepticism. But, to the extent that epistemology has tried to be normative or prescriptive (and it hasn't always been clear about what it was doing), I propose epistemics as an appropriate framework.

The framework presupposes a "contextualist" position of the sort championed, for example, by W. V. Quine. In studying and criticizing our cognitive procedures, we should use whatever powers and procedures we antecedently have and accept. There is no starting "from scratch"; to transcend any cognitive weaknesses, we must use cognitive operations to decide what to do. There is no logical guarantee of success, but that is more than can reasonably be expected.

My conception of epistemics resembles some earlier epistemological standpoints. Descartes's *Regulae* had a similar motivation, and Spinoza's scheme for the improvement of the understanding is very close to the program of epistemics.[23] More generally, pre-twentieth-century epistemology was often interwoven with psychology, as readers of Locke, Berkeley, and especially Hume will recognize. In the twentieth century, philosophers like John Dewey, Karl Popper, and Quine have defended psychologistic conceptions of epistemology.[24] A return to these traditions is especially timely now, when cognitive psychology has renewed prestige and promises to enhance our understanding of fundamental cognitive processes. A few psychologists have begun to detect a convergence between their interests and those of epistemology.[25] I have here tried to lay a foundation for a conception of epistemology that would effect a rapprochement between it and cognitive psychology.

Notes

Research leading to this paper was begun under fellowships from the John Simon Guggenheim Memorial Foundation and the Center for Advanced Study in the Behavioral Sciences. I am grateful for their support. For helpful comments and criticisms on earlier versions, I am especially indebted to Holly S. Goldman, Allan Gibbard, Louis E. Loeb, Richard E. Nisbett, and Stephen P. Stich.

1. Actually my conception of epistemics is broader than these remarks suggest. It would comprehend *social* as well as *individual* dimensions of cognition. It would concern itself with the interpersonal and institutional processes that affect the creation, transmission, and reception of information, misinformation, and partial information. Like the sociology of knowledge, it would study not only organized science, but situational and institutional forces that affect the social dissemination or inhibition of knowledge. In the present paper, however, I restrict myself to "individual epistemics," which treats the individual cognizer and his cognitive system.

2. For further discussion of these points, see Goldman 1978.

3. Cf. Carnap 1950, p. 211, and Hempel 1965, p. 64.

4. Chisholm 1977.

5. Cf. Shepard and Metzler 1971; and Cooper and Shepard 1973.

6. See Sorabji 1972.

7. Cf. Klatzky 1975, chapters 5, 10, and 13.

8. Other deficiencies of (T-INC) have been noted in the literature. For example, anyone who believes that some of his beliefs are false has an inconsistent set of beliefs. But it isn't clear he should try to rid himself of this inconsistency.

9. Pascal appreciated this fact. He did not advise acquisition of faith by simply willing it. He counseled a *life* of "holy water and sacraments," which would indirectly lead to faith.

10. However, if I am persuaded, using others of my cognitive propensities, that the rule is correct, this may *cause* me to believe in accordance with the rule. Even this is not generally true, though. I may be persuaded that the gambler's fallacy is a fallacy and yet continue to have expectations that exemplify it.

11. Franks and Bransford 1971. See also Bransford and Franks 1971.

12. Cf. Posner 1973, p. 82. Also see the discussion of "perseverance" in Ross 1977.

13. Borgida and Nisbett 1977. Cf. Nisbett, Borgida, Crandall and Reed 1976.

14. On the notion of a "script", see Schank and Abelson 1977.

15. Tversky and Kahneman 1974.

16. Tversky and Kahneman 1977.

17. Tversky and Kahneman 1974.

18. Cf. Levine 1971. The original idea of "functional fixedness" or "problem-solving set" is due to Duncker 1945 and A. S. Luchins 1942.

19. See Posner 1973, ch. 7, and Wickelgren 1974, ch. 4.

20. Cf. Hempel 1965, pp. 5–6.

21. My conception of individual epistemics comprehends not only the *self*-regulation of cognitive processes but also the *third-person* control of cognitive traits. In the latter domain, epistemics would interface with the theory of education.

22. Goldman 1979.

23. Spinoza 1951. Cf. especially pp. 10–12.

24. For Quine's views, see Quine 1969a, 1969b. Quine, however, seems interested mainly in explaining the genesis of our beliefs. Thus, his project is more positive than normative. This is equally true of the Empiricists, of course.

25. Cf. Nisbett and Ross 1980. A different psychological orientation is represented by Donald T. Campbell's writings on evolutionary epistemology. Cf. Campbell 1974.

12

Positive versus Negative Undermining in Belief Revision

Gilbert Harman

I am going to compare two competing theories of reasoning or, as I prefer to say, two competing theories of (reasoned) belief revision. I prefer to speak of belief revision rather than reasoning because the theories I am going to talk about are meant to apply as well to the decision to stop believing something one has previously believed as to the decision to start believing something new. The term "reasoning" may suggest inferring something new from premises one previously accepts and I do not want to restrict the comparison to that case. I will be concerned with reasoning as a way of changing one's view both by addition and by subtraction. Indeed I shall try to show that the difference between the theories I will discuss is clearest when the issue is whether to *stop* believing something.

I would really prefer to call these theories theories of "change in view" to allow for changes in plans and intentions as well as changes in beliefs. But I will for the most part restrict discussion to the case of changing one's beliefs.

I will call the theories I am concerned with the "foundations theory of belief revision" and the "coherence theory of belief revision," respectively, since there are similarities between these theories and certain philosophical theories of justification sometimes called "foundations" and "coherence" theories (Sosa 1980; Pollock 1980). But the theories I am concerned with are not precisely the same as the corresponding philosophical theories of justification, which are not normally presented as theories of belief revision. Actually, I am not sure what such theories of justification are supposed to be concerned with. So, although I will be using the *term* "justification" in what follows, as well as the terms "coherence" and "foundations," I do not claim that my use of any of these terms is the same as its use in these theories of justification. I mean to be raising a new issue, not discussing an old one.

Reprinted, with additions, from *NOUS* 18 (1984): 39–50, by permission of the author and the editor of *NOUS*. Copyright © 1984, *NOUS*. Will appear in *Change in View*, by Gilbert Harman, forthcoming (Cambridge, Massachusetts: The MIT Press).

The key point in what I am calling the *foundations* theory is that some of one's beliefs "depend on" others for their "justification"; these other beliefs may depend on still others, until one gets to foundational beliefs that do not depend on any further beliefs for their justification. In this theory, reasoning or belief revision should consist, first, in subtracting any of one's beliefs that do not now have a satisfactory justification and, second, in adding new beliefs that either need no justification or are justified on the basis of other justified beliefs one has.

On the other hand, according to what I am calling the *coherence* theory, it is not true that one's beliefs have, or ought to have, the sort of justificational structure required by the foundations theory. For one thing, in this view beliefs do not usually require any sort of justification at all. Justification is taken to be required only if one has a special reason to doubt a particular belief. Such a reason might consist in a conflicting belief or in the observation that one's beliefs could be made more "coherent," that is, more organized or simpler or less ad hoc, if the given belief were abandoned (and perhaps certain other changes were made). According to the coherence theory, belief revision should involve minimal changes in one's beliefs in a way that sufficiently increases overall coherence.

In this paper I will elaborate these two theories in order to compare them with actual reasoning and intuitive judgments about such reasoning. As I have already said, it turns out that the theories are most easily distinguished by the conflicting advice they occasionally give concerning whether one should *give up* a belief P from which many other of one's beliefs have been inferred, when P's original justification has to be abandoned. Here a surprising contrast seems to emerge—"is" and "ought" seem to come apart. The foundations theory seems, at least at first, to be more in line with our intuitions about how people *ought* to revise their beliefs; the coherence theory is more in line with what people *actually do* in such situations. Intuition seems strongly to support the foundations theory over the coherence theory as an account of what one is *justified* in doing in such cases; but *in fact* one will tend to act as the coherence theory advises.

After I explain this, I will go on to consider how this apparent discrepancy might be resolved. I will conclude by suggesting that the coherence theory is normatively correct after all, despite initial appearances.

Taking each of these theories in turn, I begin with the foundations theory.

The Foundations Theory of Belief Revision

The basic principle of the foundations theory, as I will interpret it, is that one's beliefs have a justificational structure, some serving as reasons or justifications for others, these justifying beliefs being more basic or fundamental for justification than the beliefs they justify.

The justifications are *prima facie* or defeasible. The foundations theory allows, indeed insists, that one can be justified in believing something *P* and then come to believe something else that undermines one's justification for believing *P*. In that case one should stop believing *P*, unless one has some further justification that is not undermined.

I say "unless one has some further justification," because, in this view, a belief may have more than one justification. To be justified, a belief must have *at least* one justification, but it may have more than one. That is, if a belief in *P* is to be justified, it is required, either that *P* be a foundational belief whose intrinsic justification is not defeated, or that there be at least one undefeated justification of *P* from other beliefs one is justified in believing. If one believes *P* and it happens that all of one's justifications for believing *P* come to be defeated, one is no longer justified in continuing to believe *P* and one should subtract *P* from one's beliefs.

Furthermore, and this is very important, if one comes not to be justified in continuing to believe *P* in this way, then not only is it true that one must abandon belief in *P* but justifications one has for other beliefs are also affected if these justifications appeal to one's belief in *P*. Justifications appealing to *P* must be abandoned when *P* is abandoned. If that means further beliefs are left without justification, then these beliefs too must be dropped, along with any justifications appealing to them. So there will be a chain reaction when one loses justification for a belief on which other beliefs depend for their justification. (This is worked out in more detail for an artificial intelligence system in Doyle [1979, 1980].)

Now, it is an important aspect of the foundations theory of reasoning that justifications cannot legitimately be circular. *P* cannot be part of one's justification for *Q*, while *Q* is part of one's justification for *P*, (unless one of these beliefs has a different justification that does not appeal to the other belief).

The foundations theory also disallows infinite justifications. It does not allow *P* to be justified by appeal to *Q*, which is justified by appeal to *R*, and so on forever. Since justification cannot be circular, this means justification must eventually come to an end in beliefs that themselves, either need no justification, or are justified but not by appeal to other beliefs. Let us say that such basic or foundational beliefs are "intrinsically" justified.

For our purposes, it does not matter exactly which beliefs are taken to be intrinsically justified in this sense. Furthermore, I emphasize that the foundations theory allows for situations in which a basic belief has its intrinsic justification defeated by one or more other beliefs, just as it allows for situa-

in which the justification of one belief in terms of other beliefs is defeated by still other beliefs one has. Foundationalism, as I am interpreting it anyway, is not committed to the *incorrigibility* of basic beliefs.

A belief is a basic belief if it has an intrinsic justification which does not appeal to other beliefs. A basic belief may also have one or more nonintrinsic justifications which do appeal to other beliefs. So a basic belief can have its intrinsic justification defeated and still remain justified as long as it retains at least one justification that is not defeated.

The existence of basic beliefs follows from the restrictions against circular and infinite justifications. Infinite justifications are to be ruled out because a finite creature can only have a finite number of beliefs, or at least only a finite number of *explicit beliefs*, whose content is explicitly represented in the brain. (Explicit beliefs do not have to be conscious as long as there is somewhere in the brain or mind an explicit representation of the content of the belief.)

Now, in believing various things explicitly, one believes various other things *implicitly*; one's belief in these further matters is implicit in one's explicitly believing what one believes. For example in virtue of one's explicit beliefs about arithmetic one will implicitly believe that $1002 + 3 = 1005$. And there might well be infinitely many such implicit beliefs, since infinitely many things may be obviously implied by, and therefore implicit in, what one explicitly believes. But in the first instance what one believes is what one believes explicitly, and so what one is justified in believing depends entirely on what one is justified in believing explicitly. To consider whether one's implicit beliefs are justified is to consider whether one is justified in believing the explicit beliefs on which the implicit beliefs depend. A justification for a belief that appeals to other beliefs must always appeal to things one believes explicitly. Since one has only finitely many explicit beliefs, there are only finitely many beliefs that can be appealed to for purposes of justification, and so infinite justifications are ruled out.

So much then for the foundations theory. Let me turn now to the coherence theory.

The Coherence Theory of Belief Revision

The coherence theory is a *conservative* theory in a way the foundations theory is not. The coherence theory supposes one's present beliefs are justified just as they are in the absence of special reasons to change them, where changes are allowed only to the extent that they yield sufficient increases in coherence.This is a striking difference from the foundations theory. The foundations theory takes one to be justified in continuing to believe something

tions only if one has a special reason to continue to accept that belief. The coherence theory, on the other hand, takes one to be justified in continuing to believe something as long as one has no special reason to stop believing it.

According to the coherence theory, if one's beliefs are incoherent in some way, either because of outright inconsistency or perhaps because of simple *ad hoc*ness, then one should try to make minimal changes in those beliefs in order to eliminate the incoherence. More generally, small changes in one's beliefs are justified to the extent these changes add to the coherence of one's beliefs.

For our purposes, we do not need to be too specific as to exactly what coherence involves, except to say it includes not only consistency but also a network of relations among one's beliefs, especially relations of implication and explanation.

It is important that coherence competes with conservatism. It is as if there are two aims or tendencies of reasoned revision, one being to maximize coherence, the other to minimize change. Both tendencies are important. Without conservatism, one would be led to reduce one's beliefs to the single Parmenidean thought that all is one. Without the tendency towards coherence, we would have what Peirce (1877) called "the method of tenacity," in which one holds to one's initial convictions no matter what evidence may accumulate against them.

According to the coherence theory, the assessment of a challenged belief is always holistic. Whether such a belief is justified depends on how well it fits together with everything else one believes. If one's beliefs are coherent, they are mutually supporting. All of one's beliefs are, in a sense, equally fundamental. In the coherence theory there are not the asymmetrical justification relations among one's beliefs that there are in the foundations theory. It can happen in the coherence theory that P is justified because of the way it coheres with Q and Q is justified because of the way it coheres with P. In the foundations theory, such a pattern of justification would be ruled out by the restriction against circular justification. But there is nothing wrong with circular justification in the coherence theory, especially if the circle is a large one!

Here then is a brief sketch of the coherence theory. I turn now to testing these theories against our intuitions about cases. This raises an immediate problem for the coherence theory.

An Objection to the Coherence Theory: Karen's Aptitude Test

The problem is that, contrary to what is assumed in the coherence theory, there do seem to be asymmetrical justification relations among one's beliefs.

Consider Karen, who has taken an aptitude test and has just been told her results show she has a considerable aptitude for science and music, but little aptitude for history and philosophy. This news does not correlate perfectly with her previous grades. She had previously done very well, not only in physics, for which her aptitude scores are reported to be high, but also in history, for which her aptitude scores are reported to be low. Furthermore, she had previously done poorly, not only in philosophy, for which her aptitude scores are reported to be low, but also in music, for which her aptitude scores are reported to be high.

After carefully thinking over these discrepancies, Karen concludes (1) her reported aptitude scores accurately reflect and are explained by her actual aptitudes, so (2) she has an aptitude for science and music and no aptitude for history and philosophy, so (3) her history course must have been an easy one, and (4) she did not work hard enough in the music course. She decides (5) to take another music course but not take any more history.

It seems quite clear that, after Karen reaches these conclusions, some of her beliefs are based on others. Her belief that the history course was very easy depends for its justification on her belief that she has no aptitude for history, a belief which depends in turn for its justification on her belief that she got a low score for history aptitude in her aptitude test. There is not a dependence in the other direction. For example, her belief about her aptitude test score in history is not based on her belief that she has no aptitude for history or her belief that the history course was an easy one.

This asymmetry would seem to conflict with the coherence theory which denies there are such relations of asymmetrical dependency among one's beliefs.

It might be suggested on behalf of the coherence theory, that the relevant relations here are merely *temporal* or *causal* relations. We can agree that Karen's belief about the outcome of her aptitude test precedes and is an important cause of her belief that the history course she took was a very easy one, without our having to agree that a relation of dependence or justification holds or ought to hold among these two beliefs once the new belief has been accepted.

In order to test this suggestion, it is sufficient to tell more of Karen's story. Some days later she is informed that the report about her aptitude scores was incorrect! The scores reported were those of someone else whose name was confused with hers. Unfortunately, her own scores have now been lost. How should Karen revise her views, given this new information?

The foundations theory says she should abandon all beliefs whose justifications depend in part on her prior belief about her aptitude test scores. The only exception is for beliefs for which she can now find another and independent justification which does not depend on her belief about her aptitude test scores. She should continue to believe only those things she would have been justified in believing if she had never been given the false information about those scores. The foundations theory says this because it does not accept a principle of conservatism. The foundations theory does not allow that a belief might acquire justification simply by being believed.

Let us assume that, if Karen had not been given the false information about her aptitude test scores, she could not have reasonably reached any of the conclusions she did reach about her aptitudes in physics, history, philosophy, and music; and let us also assume that without those beliefs, Karen could not have reached any of her further conclusions about the courses she has already taken. Then, according to the foundations theory, Karen should abandon her beliefs about her relative aptitudes in these subjects; and she should give up her belief that the history course she took was very easy, as well as her belief that she did not work hard enough in the music course. She should also reconsider her decisions to take another course in music and not take any more history courses.

Now, the coherence theory does not automatically yield the same advice that the foundations theory gives about this case. Karen's new information does produce a loss of overall coherence in her beliefs, since she can no longer coherently suppose that her aptitudes in science, music, philosophy, and history are in any way responsible for the original report she received about the results of her aptitude test. So she must abandon that particular supposition about the explanation of the original report of her scores. Still, there is considerable coherence among the beliefs she inferred from this false report. For example, there is a connection between her belief that she has little aptitude for history, her belief that her high grade on the history course was the result of the course's being an easy one, and her belief that she will not take any more courses in history. There are similar connections between her beliefs about her aptitudes in other subjects, how well she did in courses in those subjects, and her plans for the future in those areas. Let us suppose Karen inferred a great many other things that we haven't mentioned from that original report so there are a great many beliefs involved here. Abandoning all of these beliefs is costly from the point of view of conservatism, which says to minimize change. Let us suppose it turns out that there are so many of these beliefs, and they are so connected with each other and with other things Karen believes, that the coherence theory implies Karen should retain all these new beliefs even though she must give up her beliefs about the explanation of the report of her aptitude scores.

Then the foundations theory says Karen should give up all these beliefs, while the coherence theory says Karen should retain them. Which theory is right about what Karen ought to do? Almost everyone who I have asked about this issue sides with the foundations theory: Karen should not retain any beliefs she inferred from the false report of her aptitude test scores that she would not have been justified in believing in the absence of that false report. That does seem to be the intuitively right answer. The foundations theory is in accordance with our intuitions about what Karen *ought* to do in a case like this. The coherence theory is not.

Belief Perseverance

But now I must remark on an important complication, to which I have already referred. In fact, Karen would almost certainly keep her new beliefs! That is what people actually do in situations like this. Although the foundations theory gives intuitively satisfying advice about what Karen *ought* to do in such a situation, the coherence theory is more in accord with what people actually do!

To document the rather surprising facts here, let me quote at some length from a recent survey article (Ross and Anderson 1982, pp. 147–149), which speaks of

the dilemma of the social psychologist who has made use of deception in the course of an experiment and then seeks to debrief the subjects who had been the target of such deception. The psychologist reveals the totally contrived and inauthentic nature of the information presented presuming that this debriefing will thereby eliminate any effects such information might have exerted upon the subjects' feelings or beliefs. Many professionals, however, have expressed public concern that such experimental deception may do great harm that is not fully undone by conventional debriefing procedures.

The authors go on to describe experiments designed to "explore" what they call "the phenomenon of belief perseverance in the face of evidential discrediting." In one experiment,

Subjects first received continuous false feedback as they performed a novel discrimination task (i.e., distinguishing authentic suicide notes from fictitious ones) ... [Then] the actor ... received a standard debriefing session in which he learned that his putative outcome had been predetermined and that his feedback had been totally unrelated to actual performance ... Every subject was led to explicitly acknowledge his understanding of the nature and purpose of the experimental deception.

Following this total discrediting of the original information, the subjects completed a dependent variable questionnaire dealing with the actors' performance and abilities. The evidence for postdebriefing impression perseverance was unmistakable ... On virtually every measure ... the totally discredited initial outcome manipulation produced significant "residual" effects upon actors' ... assessments ....

Follow-up experiments have since shown that a variety of unfounded personal impressions, once induced by experimental procedures, can survive a variety of total discrediting procedures. For example, Jennings, Lepper, and Ross ... have demonstrated that subjects' impressions of their ability at interpersonal persuasion (having them succeed or fail to convince a confederate to donate blood) can persist after they have learned that the initial outcome was totally inauthentic. Similarly, ... two related experiments have shown that students' erroneous impressions of their "logical problem solving abilities" (and their academic choices in a follow-up measure two months later) persevered even after they had learned that good or poor teaching procedures provided a totally sufficient explanation for the successes or failures that were the basis for such impressions.

Other studies first manipulated and then attempted to undermine subjects' theories about the functional relationship between two measured variables: the adequacy of firefighters' professional performances and their prior scores on a paper and pencil test of risk perference. ... such theories survived the revelations that the cases in question had been totally fictitious and the different subjects had, in fact, received opposite pairings of riskiness scores and job outcomes ... Over 50% of the initial effect of the "case history" information remained after debriefing.

In summary [the authors conclude] it is clear that beliefs can survive ... the total destruction of their original evidential bases.

It is therefore quite likely that Karen will continue to believe many of the things she inferred from the false report about her aptitude test scores. She will continue to believe these things even after learning that the report was false.

The Habit Theory of Belief

I now want to consider why this is likely to be so. Why is it so hard for subjects to be debriefed? Why do people retain conclusions they have drawn from evidence that is now discredited?

One possibility is that belief is a kind of habit. This would be an implication of behaviorism, the view that beliefs and other mental attitudes are habits of behavior. Of course, behaviorism is not currently fashionable. But the suggestion that beliefs are habits might be correct even apart from behaviorism. The relevant habits need not be overt behavioral habits. They might be habits of thought. Perhaps, to believe that P is to be disposed to *think* that P under certain conditions, to be disposed to use this thought as a premise or assumption in reasoning and in deciding what to do. Then, once a belief has become established, considerable effort might be needed to get rid of it, even if one should come to see one ought to get rid of it, just as it is hard to get rid of other bad habits. One can't simply decide to get rid of a bad habit; one must take active steps to ensure that the habit does not reassert itself. Perhaps it is just as difficult to get rid of a bad belief.

Alvin Goldman (1978) mentions a related possibility, observing that Anderson and Bower (1973) treat coming to believe something as the establishing of connections, or "associative links," between relevant conceptual representations in the brain. Now, it may be that such connections or links, once set up, cannot easily be broken unless competing connections are set up that overwhelm the original ones. The easiest case might be that in which one starts by believing P and then comes to believe not-P by setting up stronger connections involving not-P than those involved in believing P. It might be much harder simply to give up one's belief in P without substituting a contrary belief. According to this model of belief, then, in order to stop believing P, it would not be enough simply to notice passively that one's evidence for P had been discredited. One would have to take positive steps to counteract the associations that constitute one's belief in P. The difficulties in giving up a discredited belief would then be similar in this view to the difficulties envisioned in the habit theory of belief.

Here then is one possible reason why beliefs might survive after the evidence for them has been discredited: it may be hard to get rid of a belief once one has stored that belief. If so, foundationalism could be normatively correct as an ideal, even though the ideal is one it takes considerable effort to live up to.

But this cannot be the explanation. Of course, there are cases in which one has to struggle in order to abandon a belief one takes to be discredited. One finds oneself coming back to thoughts one realizes one should no longer accept. There are such habits of thought. But this is not what is happening in the debriefing studies. Subjects in these studies are not struggling to abandon beliefs they see are discredited. On the contrary, the problem is that subjects do not see that the beliefs they have acquired have been discredited. They see all sorts of reasons for the beliefs, where the reasons consists in connections with other beliefs of a sort that the coherence theory might approve, but not the foundations theory. So the correct explanation of belief perseverance in these studies is not that beliefs that have lost their evidential grounding are like bad habits.

Positive versus Negative Undermining

So I now want to consider another and I think more plausible hypothesis as to why beliefs might survive after the evidence for them has been discredited, namely the hypotheses that people simply do not keep track of the justification relations among their beliefs. They continue to believe things after the evidence for them has been discredited because they do not realize what they are doing. They do not understand that the discredited evidence was the sole reason why they believe as they do. They do not see they would not have been justified in forming those beliefs in the absence of the now discredited evidence. They do not realize these beliefs have been undermined. My suggestion is that it is this, rather than the difficulty of giving up bad habits, which is responsible for belief perseverance.

This is to suppose people do not in fact proceed in accordance with the advice of the foundations theory. The foundations theory says people should keep track of their reasons for believing as they do and should stop believing anything that is not associated with adequate evidence. So the foundations theory implies that, if Karen has not kept track of her reason for believing her history course to have been an easy one, she should have abandoned her belief even before she was told about the mix up with her aptitude test scores.

This implication of the foundations theory is not obviously right. Indeed, if, as I suggest, people rarely keep track of their reasons, the implication would be that people are unjustified in almost all their beliefs, which seems to me an absurd result. In this case, foundationalism seems wrong even as a normative theory. So let us see whether we cannot defend the coherence theory as a normative theory.

Now, although justification in a coherence theory is always "holistic" in the sense that whether one is justified in coming to adopt a new belief depends on how that belief would fit in with everything else one believes, we have already seen how appeal might be made to a nonholisthc *causal* notion of "local justification" by means of a limited number of one's prior beliefs, namely those prior beliefs that are most crucial to one's justification for adding the new belief. To be sure, the coherence theory must not suppose there are *continuing* links of justification dependency among beliefs once these beliefs are accepted, links that can be consulted when revising one's beliefs. But the theory can admit that Karen's coming to believe certain things depended on certain of her prior beliefs in a way that it did not depend on others, where this dependence represents a kind of local justification, even though in another respect whether Karen was justified in coming to believe those things depended on everything she then believed.

Given this point, I suggest that the coherence theory might incorporate the principle that it is incoherent to believe both *P* and also that one would not be justified in believing *P* if one had relied only on true beliefs. Within the coherence theory, this implies, roughly speaking

Principle of Positive Undermining: One should stop believing *P* whenever one positively believes one's reasons for believing *P* are no good.

I want to compare this with the analogous principle within a foundations theory:

Principle of Negative Undermining: One should stop believing P whenever one does not associate one's belief in P with an adequate justification (either intrinsic or extrinsic).

The principle of positive undermining is much more plausible than the principle of negative undermining. The principle of negative undermining implies that, as one loses track of the justifications of one's beliefs, one should give up those beliefs. But one does not seem to keep track of one's justifications for most of one's beliefs. If so, the principle of negative undermining would say one should stop believing almost everything one believes, which is absurd. On the other hand, the principle of positive undermining does not have this absurd implication. The principle of positive undermining does not suppose the absence of a justification is a reason to stop believing something. It only supposes one's belief in P is undermined by the *positive* belief that one's reasons for P are no good.

In this connection it is relevant that subjects *can* be successfully debriefed after experiments involving deception, if the subjects are made vividly aware of this very phenomenon, that is, if they are made vividly aware of this very tendency for people to retain false beliefs after the evidence for them has been undercut and are also made vividly aware of how this phenomenon has acted in their own case [Nisbett and Ross 1980]. Now, someone might suggest this shows that under ideal conditions people really do act in accordance with the foundations theory after all, so that the foundations theory *is* normatively correct as an account of how one ought ideally to revise one's beliefs. But in fact this further phenomenon seems clearly to support the coherence theory, with its principle of positive undermining, and not the foundations theory, with its principle of negative undermining. The so-called "full debriefing" cannot merely undermine the evidence for the conclusions subjects have reached but must also directly attack each of these conclusions themselves. It seems clear, then, that the full debriefing works, not just by getting subjects to give up the beliefs that originally served as evidence for the conclusions they have reached, but by getting them to accept certain further positive beliefs about their lack of good reasons for each of these conclusions.

What about Our Intuitions?

This may seem counterintuitive. It may seem to fly in the face of common sense to suppose that the coherence theory is normatively correct in cases like this.

After carefully considering Karen's situation, almost everyone agrees she should give up all beliefs of hers she inferred from the original false report, excepting only those beliefs which would have been justified apart from any appeal to evidence tainted by that false information. Almost everyone's judgment about what Karen ought to do coincides with what the foundations theory says she ought to do. Indeed, psychologists who have studied the phenomenon of "belief perseverance" in the face of debriefing consider it to be a paradigm of irrationality. How *could* these very strong normative intuitions possibly be taken to be mistaken here, as they must be if the coherence theory is to be accepted as normatively correct?

The answer is that, when people think about Karen's situation, they ignore the possibility that she may have failed to keep track of the justifications of her beliefs. They imagine Karen is or ought to be aware she no longer has any good reasons for the beliefs she inferred from the false report. And, of course, this is to imagine Karen is violating the principle of positive undermining. It is very hard to allow for the possibility that she may be violating not that principle but only the foundationalist's principle of negative undermining.

Keeping Track of Justification

I have said several times that people do not seem to keep track of the justifications of their beliefs. Indeed, it seems obvious that they do not. If we tried to suppose people did keep track of their justifications, we would have to suppose either that they fail to notice when their justifications are undermined or that they do notice this but have great difficulty in abandoning the unjustified beliefs in the way a person has difficulty in abandoning a bad habit. Neither of these possibilities offers a plausible account of the sort of belief persistance I have been discussing.

It stretches credulity to suppose people always keep track of the sources of their beliefs but fail to notice when these sources are undermined. That is like supposing people always remember everything that has ever happened to them but cannot always retrieve the stored information from where they placed it in memory. To say one remembers something is to say one has stored it in a way that normally allows it to be retrieved on the appropriate occasion. Similarly, to say people keep track of the sources of their beliefs must be to say they can normally use this information when it is appropriate to do so.

I have already remarked that the other possibility seems equally incredible, namely, that people have trouble abandoning the undermined beliefs in the way they have trouble getting rid of bad habits. To repeat, participants in belief perseverance studies show no signs of knowing their beliefs are ungrounded. They do not act like people struggling with their beliefs as with bad habits. Again, I agree it sometimes happens that one keeps returning to thoughts after one has seen there can be no reason to accept those thoughts. There are habits of thought that can be hard to get rid of. But that is not what is going on in the cases psychologists study under the name of "belief perseverance".

This leaves the issue whether one should *try* always to keep track of the local justifications of one's beliefs, even if, in fact, people do not seem to do this. I want to conclude my discussion by considering the possibility that there is a good reason for not keeping track of these justifications.

On Not Reasoning Probabilistically

Consider an analogous case. It can seem that one ought not to accept beliefs in a yes-no fashion, but should believe things to various degrees, having more confidence in some things than others, where one's degree of belief represents the "subjective probability" one assigns to the truth of that belief. It can seem, furthermore, that one should also assign degrees of desirability or "utility" to various outcomes of action and decide what to do by considering how likely the person thinks one or another act will make this or that outcome. In other words, it can seem one should determine the "expected utility" of each act by adding together the utilities of the possible outcomes of the act, each multiplied by the probability that the act will lead to that outcome; and then one should do that act which has the greatest expected utility. It can also seem clear that one should assign degrees of belief, or subjective probabilities, in accordance with the principles of probability theory and, as new evidence comes in, one should "update" one's subjective probabilities by "conditionalization" on the new evidence or by using some generalization of conditionalization (Jeffrey 1983).

However, there is considerable empirical evidence that people do not do very well by these standards (Kahneman, Slovic, and Tversky 1982; Nisbett and Ross 1980). People have great difficulty with probability and make the most elementary mistakes from this point of view. Probabilistic reasoning is not something that comes naturally to people. Indeed, even experts in probability make all sorts of mistakes if they are not consciously thinking of a problem as one that should be analyzed statistically.

Now, I believe that there is a deep reason for this inability to deal with probabilities. It would be impossible to design finite creatures to operate purely probabilistically. The impossibility arises from a combinatorial explosion that occurs in probabilistic thinking [Harman forthcoming]. In order to have useful degrees of belief concerning N different matters it is not enough to assign probabilities to N propositions. One has to assign various conditional probabilities as well, or (equivalently) one has to assign probabilities to various conjunctions consisting in some of the original propositions and of negations of some of these propositions, and in the general case, $2^N - 1$ independent assignments must be recorded. This means that to have useful degrees of belief concerning ten matters, one needs to record a thousand probabilities; to have useful degrees of belief concerning twenty matters, one needs a million probability assignments; for thirty matters, one needs a billion probability assignments; and so forth.

The problem cannot be avoided by using general principles to assign probabilities. One idea along these lines would be to specify a general principle determining an initial probability distribution and to otherwise record only new evidence taken to be certain, where one's other degrees of belief are then determined by conditionalization on that evidence. The problem is that, since such evidence would have to be certain, most of it would have to be evidence about one's immediate perceptual experience, about how exactly things look, sound, smell, and so forth. This is a problem because this idea would work only if one remembered all such perceptual evidence, or at least all such evidence that affected one's degrees of belief; and that is something one simply does not do. One normally does not recall one's immediate perceptual experiences of an hour ago, to say nothing of the experiences of the past week, year, or decade. One is more apt to remember the position of the furniture and whether something was moved than how things looked from where one was standing, even though one's beliefs about the position of the furniture were based on how things looked. Of course, there are exceptions to this. Sometimes one does remember one's immediate experiences. But only in exceptional cases.

The evidence one remembers tends not to be the absolutely certain evidence of one's immediate experience but rather the somewhat less certain evidence concerning the placement of objects in the environment. But then one's current degrees of belief cannot be specified by simple conditionalization on this evidence. One must instead use something like Jeffrey's (1983) generalization of conditionalization. But that requires keeping track of the probabilities of various conjunctions of evidence statements and /or their denials, which brings back the combinatorial explosion.

So the problem cannot be avoided by specifying a general principle determining an initial probability distribution together with the evidence that has accumulated since the beginning. An alternative idea would be *always* to specify a new general principle determining one's current probability distribution. But, this won't be any improvement, either. For one thing, the problem of discovering such a general principle each time is intractable. Furthermore, if one's degrees of belief arise from Jeffrey's generalized conditionalization from one's prior degrees of belief, there will normally be no very much simpler way to specify them than that just mentioned in the previous paragraph. So the complexity of one's current principle for assigning probabilities will be affected by the same combinatorial explosion.

Clearly, this severely limits the amount of probabilistic reasoning a finite creature can do. It is therefore no wonder people are not very good at such reasoning. We cannot operate purely probabilistically. We have to reason in a different and more manageable way.

The problem does not arise with yes/no all-or-nothing belief within the framework of a coherence theory of belief revision. One's beliefs in N topics can be represented by the acceptance of N representations rather than the $2^N - 1$ representations required by a probabilistic approach. The calculations needed for updating one's views in the face of new evidence similarly do not involve the sort of combinatorial explosion that occurs in the probabilistic framework.

Clutter Avoidance

Now, the issue before us is not whether people should reason in a purely probabilistic fashion but rather whether within the sort of nonprobabilistic framework in which people must operate they should keep track of the justifications of their beliefs. I want to suggest that there are practical considerations that tell against keeping track of justifications.

In particular, there is a practical reason to avoid too much clutter in one's beliefs. There is a limit to what one can remember, a limit to the number of things one can put into long term storage, and a limit to what one can retrieve. It is important to save room for important things and not clutter one's mind with a lot of unimportant matters. This is one very important reason why one does not try to believe all sorts of logical consequences of one's beliefs. One should not try to infer all one can from one's beliefs. One should try not to retain too much trivial information. Furthermore, one should try to store in long-term memory only the key matters that one will later need to recall. When one reaches a significant conclusion from one's other beliefs, one needs to remember the conclusion but does not normally need to remember all the intermediate steps involved in reaching that conclusion. Indeed, one should not try to remember those intermediate steps; one should try to avoid too much clutter in one's mind.

Similarly, even if much of one's knowledge of the world is inferred ultimately from what one believes oneself to be immediately perceiving at one or another time, one does not normally need to remember these original perceptual beliefs or many of the various intermediate conclusions drawn from them. It is enough to recall the more important of one's conclusions about the location of the furniture, etc.

This means one should not be disposed to try to keep track of the local justifications of one's beliefs. One could keep track of these justifications only by remembering an incredible number of mostly perceptual original premises, along with many, many intermediate steps which one does not want and has little need to remember. One will not want to link one's beliefs to such justifications because one will not in general want to try to retain the prior beliefs from which one reached one's current beliefs.

The practical reason for not keeping track of the justifications of one's beliefs is not as severe as the reason that prevents one from operating purely probabilistically. The problem is not that there would be a combinatorial explosion. Still, there are important practical constraints. It is more efficient not to try to retain these justifications and the accompanying justifying beliefs. This leaves more room in memory for important matters.

Summary And Final Conclusions

To sum up: I have discussed two theories of belief revision, the foundations theory and the coherence theory. The foundations theory says one's beliefs are to be linked by relations of justification that one is to make use of in deciding whether to stop believing something. The coherence theory denies that there should be this sort of justificational structure to one's beliefs. The coherence theory takes conservatism to be an important principle—one's beliefs are justified in the absence of a special reason to doubt them. The foundations theory rejects any such conservatism.

When we consider a case like Karen's, our intuitive judgments may seem to support foundationalism. But it is important to distinguish two different principles, the coherence theory's principle of positive undermining and the foundations theory's much stronger principle of negative undermining. Once we distinguish these principles we see it is really the foundations theory that is counterintuitive, since that theory would have one give up almost everything one believes, if, as I have argued, one does not keep track of one's justifications. Furthermore, there is a very good practical reason not to keep track of justifications, namely that in the interests of clutter avoidance one should not normally even try to retain the beliefs from which one's more important beliefs were inferred.

Note

I am indebted to Jens Kulenkampff and John Pollack for helpful comments on an earlier draft of this paper.

13

Could Man Be an Irrational Animal? Some Notes on the Epistemology of Rationality

Stephen P. Stich

I

Aristotle thought man was a rational animal. From his time to ours, however, there has been a steady stream of writers who have dissented from this sanguine assessment. For Bacon or Hume or Freud or D. H. Lawrence, rationality is at best a sometimes thing. On their view, episodes of rational inference and action are scattered beacons on the irrational coastline of human history. During the last decade or so, these impressionistic chroniclers of man's cognitive foibles have been joined by a growing group of experimental psychologists who are subjecting human reasoning to careful empirical scrutiny. Much of what they have found would appall Aristotle. Human subjects, it would appear, regularly and systematically invoke inferential and judgmental strategies ranging from the merely invalid to the genuinely bizarre.

Recently, however, there have been rumblings of a reaction brewing—a resurgence of Aristotelian optimism. Those defending the sullied name of human reason have been philosophers, and their weapons have been conceptual analysis and epistemological argument. The central thrust of their defense is the claim that empirical evidence could not possibly support the conclusion that people are systematically irrational. And thus the experiments which allegedly show that they are must be either flawed or misinterpreted.

In this paper I propose to take a critical look at these philosophical defenses of rationality. My sympathies, I should note straightaway, are squarely with the psychologists. My central thesis is that the philosophical arguments aimed at showing irrationality cannot be experimentally demonstrated are mistaken. Before considering these arguments, however, we would do well to set out a few illustrations of the sort of empirical studies which allegedly show that

Reprinted from *Synthese* by permission of the author. Copyright © 1984, Stephen P. Stich.

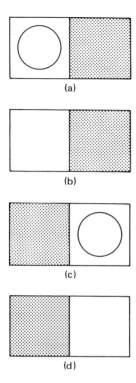

Figure 1

people depart from normative standards of rationality in systematic ways. This is the chore that will occupy us in the following section.

II

One of the most extensively investigated examples of inferential failure is the so-called "selection task" studied by P. C. Wason, P. N. Johnson-Laird and their colleagues.[1] A typical selection task experiment presents subjects with four cards like those in figure 1. Half of each card is masked. Subjects are then given the following instructions:

Which of the hidden parts of these cards do you need to see in order to answer the following question decisively?

FOR THESE CARDS IS IT TRUE THAT IF THERE IS A CIRCLE ON THE LEFT THERE IS A CIRCLE ON THE RIGHT?

You have only one opportunity to make this decision; you must not assume that you can inspect cards one at a time. Name those cards which it is absolutely essential to see.

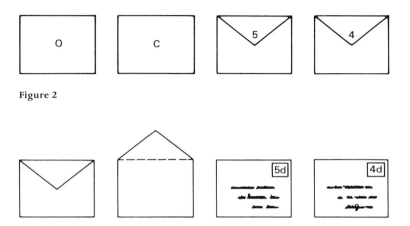

Figure 2

Figure 3

Wason and Johnson-Laird discovered that subjects, including very intelligent subjects, find the problem remarkably difficult. In one group of 128 university students, only *five* got the right answer. Moreover, the mistakes that subjects make are not randomly distributed. The two most common wrong answers are that one must see both (a) and (c), and that one need only see (a). The phenomenon turns out to be a remarkably robust one, producing essentially the same results despite significant variation in the experimental design, the wording of the question and the details of the problem. For example, subjects presented with the four envelopes in figure 2 and asked which must be turned over to determine the truth of the rule:

IF IT HAS A VOWEL ON ONE SIDE IT HAS AN EVEN NUMBER ON THE OTHER

do just as badly as subjects given the cards in figure 1. However, there are variations in the experimental design which substantially improve inferential performance. One of these is making the relation between the antecedent and the consequent of the conditional rule in the instructions more "realistic." So, for example, subjects presented with the envelopes in figure 3, and asked which must be turned over to determine the truth of the rule:

IF IT IS SEALED THEN IT HAS A 5d STAMP ON IT

do vastly better than subjects presented with the envelopes in figure 2. In one experiment using the "realistic" material, 22 out of 24 subjects got the right answer.[2]

Wason and Johnson-Laird have also explored the ways in which subjects react when they are shown that their initial inferences are mistaken. In figure 1, for example, a subject who said he must see only the hidden side of (a) might be asked to remove the masks on both (a) and (d), discovering a circle under each mask. Many subjects have a startling reaction. They note that the rule is false for these cards—in virtue of card (d)—and they continue to insist that it was only necessary to see card (a)! In further work Wason, Johnson-Laird and their colleagues have looked at the ways in which subjects react when the apparent contradiction in their claims is pointed out. The intriguing details of these studies need not detain us here.

My second example of research revealing prima facie deviation from normative standards of inference focuses on the way people assess the probability of logically compound events or states of affairs. It is a truism of probability theory that the likelihood of a compound event or state of affairs must be less than or equal to the likelihood of the component events or states of affairs. If the components are probabilistically independent, the probability of the compound is equal to the product of the probabilities of the components. If the components are not probabilistically independent, matters are more complicated. But in no case will the probability of the compound be *greater* than the probability of the components. There are, however, a number of experiments which demonstrate that people regularly violate this basic tenet of probabilistic reasoning. In one such experiment Kahneman and Tversky gave subjects personality profiles of various target persons. Subjects were then asked to assess the likelihood that the persons described in the profiles belonged to various groups. One group of subjects was asked to estimate the likelihood that profiled persons were member of noncompound groups like *lawyers* or *Republicans*. Another group of subjects was asked to estimate the probability that the profiled persons were members of compound groups like *Republican lawyers*. What Kahneman and Tversky found is that if a profiled person is judged rather unlikely to be, say, a lawyer, and rather likely to be a Republican, he will be judged moderately likely to be a Republican lawyer. That is, the likelihood of the target being a Republican lawyer is judged significantly higher than the likelihood of his being a lawyer! The explanation that Kahneman and Tversky offer for these peculiar judgments turns on what they call the representativeness heuristic. Subjects, they hypothesize, assess the likelihood that a target person is a Republican lawyer by assessing the similarity between the profile and the stereotypical Republican, assessing the similarity between the profile and the stereotypical lawyer, and then *averaging* these two likelihoods.[3]

In a similar study with alarming implications for public policy judgments, Slovic, Fischoff and Lichtenstein showed that subjects estimate the probability of a compound sequence of events to be greater than the least likely of the events in the sequence.[4] It is disquieting to speculate on how large an impact this inferential failing may have on people's assessments of the chance of such catastrophes as nuclear reactor failures which require a number of distinct events to occur in sequence.[5]

My final example of an experimental program exploring human irrationality is the work on belief perseverance by Ross, Lepper and their colleagues.[6] One of the experimental strategies used in this work is the so-called "debriefing" paradigm. In these experiments subjects are given evidence which is later completely discredited. But despite being "debriefed" and told exactly how they had been duped, subjects tend to retain to a substantial degree the beliefs they formed on the basis of the discredited evidence. In one such experiment subjects were presented with the task of distinguishing between authentic and inauthentic suicide notes. As they worked they were provided with false feedback indicating that overall they were performing at close to the average level or (for other subjects) much above the average level, or (for a third group of subjects) much below the average level. Following this, each subject was debriefed, and the predetermined nature of the feedback was explained to him. They were not only told that their feedback had been false but were also shown the experimenter's instruction sheet assigning them to the success, failure or average group, and specifying the feedback to be presented. Subsequent to this, and allegedly for quite a different reason, subjects were asked to fill out a questionnaire on which they were asked to estimate their actual performance at the suicide note task, to predict their probable success on related future tasks and to rate their ability at suicide note discrimination and other related tasks. The results revealed that even after debriefing subjects who had initially been assigned to the success group continued to rate their performance and abilities far more favorably than did subjects in the average group. Subjects initially assigned to the failure group showed the opposite pattern of results. Once again, these results appear to reflect a robust phenomenon which manifests itself in many variations on the experimental theme, including some conducted outside the laboratory setting.

The three examples I have sketched could easily be supplemented by dozens more, all apparently demonstrating that human reasoning often deviates substantially from the standard provided by normative canons of inference. Let us now turn our attention to the arguments aimed at showing that these experiments are being misinterpreted.

III

Of the three arguments I shall consider, two are due to D. C. Dennett. Both arguments are embedded in Dennett's much more elaborate theory about the nature of intentional attributions, though neither argument is developed in much detail. In a pair of previous papers I have tried to give a systematic critique of Dennett's views with due attention to problems of interpretation and the possibilities of alternative construals.[7] In the present paper I will sidestep most of these niceties. What I wish to show is that a pair of arguments are mistaken. I think it is clear that Dennett has at least flirted with each of these arguments. But for the purposes at hand, pinning the tail on the donkey is of little importance.

The first of the arguments I am attributing to Dennett might be called *the argument from the inevitable rationality of believers*. On Dennett's view, when we attribute beliefs, desires and other states of commonsense psychology to a person—or for that matter to an animal or an artifact—we are assuming or presupposing that the person or object can be treated as what Dennett calls an *intentional system*. An intentional system is one which is rational through and through; its beliefs are "those it ought to have, given its perceptual capacities, its epistemic needs, and its biography . . . . [Its desires] are those it ought to have, given its biological needs and the most practicable means of satisfying them . . . . [And its] behavior will consist of those acts that it *would be rational* for an agent with those beliefs and desires to perform."[8] According to Dennett it is in the context of this set of assumptions about rationality that our ordinary talk about beliefs, desires and other intentional states gains its meaning. If this is right, then we should expect that when a person's behavior is less than fully rational the intentional scheme would no longer apply. We could not rest content with a description of a person as holding an incoherent or irrational set of beliefs, for absent rationality we cannot coherently ascribe beliefs at all. Dennett puts the matter as follows:

Conflict arises . . . when a person falls short of perfect rationality, and avows beliefs that either are strongly disconfirmed by the available empirical evidence or are self-contradictory or contradict other avowals he has made. If we lean on the myth that a man is perfectly rational, we must find his avowals less than authorative: "You can't mean—understand—what you're saying!"; if we lean on his right as a speaking intentional system to have his word accepted, we grant him an irrational set of beliefs. Neither position provides a stable resting place; for, as we saw earlier, intentional explanation and prediction cannot be accommodated either to breakdown or to less than optimal design, so there is no coherent intentional description of such an impasse.[9]

Given this much of Dennett's view, it follows straightforwardly that no experiment could demonstrate that people systematically invoke invalid or irrational inferential strategies. The point is not that people *must* be rational. No such conclusion follows from Dennett's view. What does follow from

Dennett's view is that people must be rational *if they can usefully be viewed as having any beliefs at all*. We have no guarantee that people will behave in a way that makes it profitable for us to assume the intentional stance toward them. But intentional descriptions and rationality come in the same package; there is no getting one without the other. Thus if people infer at all, that is, if they generate new beliefs from old ones, from perceptual experience, or what have you, then they must do so rationally. Dennett is, in effect, offering us a *reductio* on the claim that people infer irrationally. If a system infers irrationally, it cannot be an intentional system; thus we cannot ascribe beliefs and desires to it. But since inference is a belief generating process, the system does not infer at all.

Now as I see it, the problem with Dennett's argument comes right at the beginning. He is simply wrong about the relationship between our ordinary notions of belief and desire and his notion of an idealized fully rational intentional system. *Pace* Dennett, it is simply not the case that our ordinary belief and desire ascriptions presuppose full rationality. There is nothing in the least incoherent or unstable about a description, cast in intentional terms, of a person who has inconsistent beliefs. The subjects in Wason and Johnson-Laird's experiments provide a clear example, one among endlessly many. Some of these subjects clearly believe that cards (a) and (c) must be removed, and defend their view with considerable vigor. Yet these subjects clearly understand the conditions of the problem and have no false beliefs about what they are being asked to do.[10]

In defending his contention that ordinary intentional ascriptions gain their meaning against the background of a theory of intentional systems, Dennett offers a pair of arguments, one long and one short. The short one is the observation, attributed to Quine, that blatant or obvious inconsistency is the best evidence we can have that we are misdescribing a subject's beliefs. This fact is readily explained if belief ascription presupposes full rationality. The longer argument has much the same structure. In effect, Dennett maintains that his intentional system explication of ordinary belief and desire talk explains many of the facts about the way we use these locutions in describing and explaining the behavior of persons, animals and artifacts. All of this I cheerfully grant. I also grant that, until recently at least, Dennett's explication of ordinary intentional locutions was the best—indeed pretty near the only— game in town. None of this, however, persuades me to accept Dennett's explication. The reason is that I think there is a better explication of the way we use our workaday belief and desire locutions, an explication that handles all the facts Dennett's can handle without the paradoxical consequence that intentional descriptions of irrational beliefs are unstable or incoherent. The basic idea of this alternative explication is that, in using intentional locutions we are presupposing that the person or system to which they are applied is, in relevant ways, similar to ourselves. Thus inferential errors that we can imagine ourselves making—errors like those recounted in my previous section—can be described comfortably in intentional terms. It is only the sort of error or incoherence that we cannot imagine falling into ourselves that undermines intentional description. This is the reason that blatant inconsistency of the sort Quine has in mind is evidence that something has gone wrong in our intentional attributions. Plainly the alternative "similar-to-us" account of intentional locutions needs a much more detailed elaboration. I have made a beginning at this in Stich (1981b).[11]

IV

The second argument Dennett offers is one which he concedes he has left uncomfortably vague. So a fair bit of interpretation will be in order. By way of a label I will call this one *the argument from natural selection*. The closest Dennett comes to setting out the argument is in a passage where he is reflecting on whether we could adopt the intentional stance toward thoroughly exotic creatures encountered on another planet. His answer is that we could provided "we have reason to suppose that a process of natural selection has been in effect." But why would the mere existence of natural selection suffice to insure that the creatures would be good approximations to the thoroughly rational ideal embodied in the notion of an intentional system? Dennett offers no detailed answer, though he does provide us with a few hints, as have other writers who have sounded similar themes. On the most charitable interpretation I can come up with, these hints may be elaborated into the following argument.

1. Natural selection will favor (i.e., select for) inferential strategies which generally yield true beliefs. This is because, in general, true beliefs are more adaptive than false ones; they enable the organism to cope better with its environment. There are exceptions, of course. But on the whole and in the long run organisms will outcompete their conspecifics if their ratio of true beliefs to false ones is higher. So after an extended period of natural selection we can expect that the inferential strategies an organism uses will be ones which generally yield true beliefs.

2. An inferential strategy which generally yields true beliefs is a rational inferential strategy. Therefore,

3. Natural selection will favor rational inferential strategies.

Now since Dennett's Martians are, ex hypothesis, the product of an extended process of natural selection we can conclude that they use rational inferential strategies. And, closer to home, since human beings are the result of millions of years of natural selection we know that they too must use rational inferential strategies. Thus any research program which claims to have evidence for widespread and systematic irrationality among humans must be misinterpreting its results. It is my suspicion that a good number of the writers who have recently been urging a naturalized or evolutionary reinterpretation of epistemology have had something very like this argument hovering in penumbral consciousness. If so, then it is all the more important to focus critical scrutiny on the argument, for such scrutiny shows the argument to be very seriously flawed.

Consider the first step. Is it true that natural selection favors inferential strategies which generally yield true beliefs? The answer, I think, is clearly no. Perhaps the most vivid way to make the point is with a brief description of some intriguing experiments by John Garcia and his co-workers.[12] In one series of experiments Garcia's group fed rats distinctively flavored water or food, and then subjected them to substantial doses of radiation, enough to induce radiation sickness. After a single episode, the rats developed a strong aversion to the distinctively flavored food or water that had been used. Workers in other laboratories have demonstrated that the same phenomenon occurs even when the rat is exposed to radiation as much as twelve hours after eating or drinking. It has also been shown that the taste of the food is the object of the rats' aversion. The rats acquire no aversion to the cage in which the distinctive food was eaten, nor do they acquire an aversion to food pellets of a distinctive size. But if two substances are eaten in sequence prior to illness, novelty is a much more potent factor than recency in determination of the aversion. In short, the rat behaves as though it believes that anything which tastes like the distinctive tasting stuff it had eaten will cause it to become deathly ill. Moreover, it is clear that this belief, if that is what it is, is the result of an innate belief (or aversion) forming strategy which is surely the result of natural selection.

Consider now how often the inferential strategy which leads to the rat's belief will lead to a true belief. In the laboratory, of course, the inferential strategy is thoroughly unreliable. It is the radiation, not the food, which causes the rat's illness. But what about rats in their natural environment? I know of no studies of rat epidemiology which indicate the most common causes of acute illness among rats. I would suspect, however, that rats, like people, fall victim to all manner of acute afflictions caused by viruses and bacteria which are not transmitted through food—still less through distinctively flavored food. If this is right, if, to be more specific, more than half of the illnesses rats endure in the wild which lead to the development of Garcia aversions are not transmitted by distinctively flavored food, it follows that *most* of the beliefs produced by the innate inferential strategy Garcia discovered are *false* beliefs. So it is just not true that natural selection favors inferential strategies which generally yield true beliefs. It is important to note that this argument does not turn essentially on my conjecture about the percentage of rat illnesses caused by distinctive tasting food. The real point of my argument is that *if* my conjecture is correct, it would pose no puzzle for the student of natural selection. Natural selection might perfectly well opt for an inferential strategy which produces false beliefs more often than true ones. The sole concern of natural selection is with reproductive success and those features that foster it. When it comes to food poisoning, natural selection may well prefer an extremely cautious inferential strategy which is very often wrong, to a less cautious one which more often gets the right answer. It might be protested that the Garcia phenomenon does not really join the issue of irrational inference since the rats acquire an aversion, and aversions are not plausibly treated as beliefs. But this reply misses the essential point. Natural selection *could* perfectly well lead to inferential strategies which generally get the wrong answer, but are right when it counts most, just as it leads to aversions to foods most of which are harmless and nourishing. Often it is more adaptive to be safe than sorry.

Thus far my critique of the argument from natural selection has been aimed at the first step, the one which claims that natural selection favors inferential strategies that generally yield true beliefs. But even if we were to grant this dubious claim, the argument from natural selection would still be defective. For its second premise is false as well. That premise, recall, is that inferential strategies which generally yield the right answer are rational inferential strategies. In many cases this simply is not so. Perhaps the clearest examples of generally truth generating inferential strategies which are not rational are the cases in which a strategy is being invoked in a domain or setting significantly different from the one in which it presumably evolved. Once again an example from the study of animal behavior provides a striking illustration. Alcock recounts that a certain species of toad is capable of learning on a single trial to avoid eating a noxious species of millipede. However, the very same toad will continue to consume BBs that are rolled past it until it quite literally becomes a living beanbag![13] With only a bit of anthropomorphism, we might describe the case as follows. On seeing a millipede of a species previously found to be noxious, the toad comes to believe (i.e., infers) that it is no good to eat. But BBs, with their bland flavor, produce no such belief. Each time a new BB is rolled by, the toad infers that it is good to eat. This belief, of course, is quite false, a fact which will become obvious the first time the BB-filled toad attempts to leap out of harm's way. But of course the inferential strategy which led to the belief *generally* yields true beliefs. Does this show that the strategy is normatively appropriate for the toad to use on the BBs? I am inclined to think that the answer is no.

For all its vividness, the toad example may not be the best one to make my point. For some would protest that they just don't know what counts as a rational inferential strategy for a toad, a protest with which I have considerable sympathy. But the moral I want to draw from the toad example is one which can be drawn also from many cases involving human inference. A common theme in the research on human inference is that people are inclined to overextend the domain of an inferential strategy, applying it to cases where it is normatively inappropriate. Nisbett and Wilson,[14] for example, suggest that many causal inferences are influenced by a primitive version of the representativeness heuristic.

People have strong a priori notions of the types of causes that ought to be linked to particular types of effects, and the simple "resemblance criterion" often figures heavily in such notions. Thus, people believe that great events ought to have great causes, complex events ought to have complex causes, and emotionally relevant events ought to have emotionally relevant causes. . . . The resemblance criterion is transparently operative in the magical thinking of prescientific cultures. [For example] Evans-Prichard . . . reported such Azande beliefs as the theory that fowl excrement was a cure for ringworm and the theory that burnt skull of red bush-monkey was an effective treatment for epilepsy. Westerners unacquainted with Azande ecology might be tempted to guess that such treatments were the product of trial and error or laborously accumulated folk wisdom. Unfortunately the truth is probably less flattering to Azande medical science. Fowl excrement resembles ringworm infection; the jerky, frenetic movements of the bush-monkey resemble the convulsive movements that occur during an epileptic seizure.[15]

Now it may well be that in a sufficiently primitive setting the primitive representativeness heuristic generally does get the right answer; it may have served our hunter-gatherer forebears in good stead. But it seems clear that the Azande are invoking the strategy in a domain where its applicability is, to say the least, normatively dubious. Nisbett and Ross go on to argue that the primitive representativeness heuristic plays a central role in psychoanalytic inference and in contemporary lay inference about the causes of disease, crime, success, etc. The normative inappropriateness of the heuristic in these settings is, I should think, beyond dispute.

The primitive representativeness heuristic is an extreme example of the overextension of an inferential strategy. For we have to go a long way back into our hunter-gatherer ancestry before coming upon life situations in which the heuristic is generally reliable and adaptive. But many of the other inferential failings recounted in the recent literature would seem to arise in a similar way. An inference pattern which generally gets the right answer in a limited domain is applied outside that domain, often to problems without precedent during the vast stretches of human and prehuman history when our cognitive apparatus evolved. Indeed, it is disquieting to reflect on how vast a gap there likely is between the inferences that are important to modern science and society and those that were important to our prehistoric forebears. As Einstein noted, "the most incomprehensible thing about the universe is that it is comprehensible." [16]

I have been arguing that inferential strategies which generally get the right answer may nonetheless be irrational or normatively inappropriate when applied outside the problem domain for which they were shaped by natural selection. If this is right, then the second premise of the argument from natural selection must be rejected. Before leaving this topic I want to digress briefly to raise a thornier issue about normatively appropriate inference. It seems beyond dispute that an inferential strategy like the primitive representativeness heuristic is out of place in modern inquiries about the causes of cancer or of reactor failures. But what about the use of these heuristics in their natural settings? Are they normatively appropriate in those domains to which natural selection has molded them and in which (let us assume) they generally do produce the right answer? If I understand Prof. Goldman's view correctly, he would answer with an unqualified affirmative. But I am less confident. At issue here is the deep and difficult question of just what we are saying of an inferential strategy when we judge that it is or is not normatively appropriate. This issue will loom large in the remaining pages of this paper.

Before leaving the argument from natural selection, we would do well to note one account of what it is for an inference strategy to be rational or normatively appropriate which had best be avoided. This is the reading which turns the conclusion of the argument from natural selection into a tautology by the simple expedient of defining *rational inferential strategy* as *inferential strategy favored by natural selection*. Quite apart from its prima facie implausibility, this curious account of rationality surely misses the point of psychological studies of reasoning. These studies are aimed at showing that people regularly violate the normative canons of deductive and inductive logic, probability theory, decision theory, etc. They do not aim at showing that people use inferential strategies which have not evolved by natural selection!

V

The final argument I want to consider is one proposed by L. Jonathan Cohen.[17] Cohen's argument grows out of an account of how we establish or validate normative theses about cognitive procedures—how we justify claims about rational or irrational inference. On Cohen's view normative theses about cognitive procedures are justified by what in ethics has come to be known as the method of *reflective equilibrium*. The basic input to the method, the data if you will, are intuitions, which Cohen characterizes as "immediate and untutored inclination[s] . . . to judge that" something is the case (I, 1). In ethics the relevant intuitions are judgements about how people ought or ought not to behave. In the normative theory of reasoning they are judgements about how people ought or ought not to reason.

According to Cohen, a normative theory of reasoning is simply an idealized theory built on the data of people's individualised intuitions about reasoning. As in science, we build our theory so as to capture the bulk of the data in the simplest way possible. Our theory, in the case at hand, will be an interlocking set of normative principles of reasoning which should entail most individualized intuitions about how we should reason in the domain in question. An idealized theory need not aim at capturing all the relevant intuitions of all normal adults. Scattered exceptions—intuitions that are not entailed by the theory—can be tolerated in the same spirit that we tolerate exceptions to the predictions of the ideal gas laws.

Cohen stresses that normative theories of reasoning are not theories about the data (that is, about intuitions) any more than physics is a theory about observed meter readings, or ethics a theory about intuitions of rightness and wrongness. Just what normative theories *are* about is a question Cohen sidesteps. "Fortunately," he writes,

it is not necessary for present purposes to determine what exactly the study of moral value, probability or deducibility has as its proper subject matter. For example, an applied logician's proper aim may be to limn the formal consequences of linguistic definitions . . . , the most general features of reality . . . or the structure of ideally rational beliefs systems. . . . But, whatever the ontological concerns of applied logicians, they have to draw their evidential data from intuitions in concrete, individual cases; and the same is true for investigations into the norms of everyday probabilistic reasoning. (I, 4)

But although a normative theory of reasoning is not a theory about reasoning intuitions, it is perfectly possible, on Cohen's view, to construct an empirical theory which is concerned to describe or predict the intuitive judgments which provide the data for the corresponding normative theory. This second theory will be a psychological theory, not a logical ... one. It will describe a competence that human beings have—an ability, uniformly operative under ideal conditions and often under others, to form intuitive judgements about particular instances of ... right or wrong, deducibility or non-deducibility, probability or improbability. This theory will be just as idealized as the normative theory. (I, 4)

Having said this much, Cohen can now neatly complete his argument for the inevitable rationality of normal people. The essential point is that the empirical theory of human reasoning, that is, the psychological theory that aims to describe and predict intuitive judgments, exploits the same data as the normative theory of reasoning, and exploits them in the same way. In both cases, the goal is to construct the simplest and most powerful set of principles that accounts for the bulk of the data. Thus, once a normative theory is at hand, the empirical theory of reasoning competence will be free for the asking, since it will be *identical* with the normative theory of reasoning! Though the empirical theory of reasoning competence "is a contribution to the psychology of cognition," Cohen writes,

it is a by-product of the logical or philosophical analysis of norms rather than something that experimentally oriented psychologists need to devote effort to constructing. It is not only all the theory of competence that is needed in its area. It is also all that is possible, since a different competence, if it actually existed, would just generate evidence that called for a revision of the corresponding normative theory.
In other words, where you accept that a normative theory has to be based ultimately on the data of human intuition, you are committed to the acceptance of human rationality as a matter of fact in that area, in the sense that it must be correct to ascribe to normal human beings a cognitive competence—however often faulted in performance—that corresponds point by point with the normative theory. (I, 4)

It is important to see that Cohen's view does not entail that people never reason badly. He can and does happily acknowledge that people make inferential errors of many sorts and under many circumstances. But he insists that these errors are performance errors, reflecting nothing about the underlying, normatively unimpeachable competence. The account Cohen would give of inferential errors is analogous to the account a Chomskian would give about the errors a person might make in speaking or understanding his own language. We often utter sentences which are ungrammatical in our own dialect, but this is no reflection on our underlying linguistic competence. On the Chomskian view, our competence consists in a tacitly internalized set of rules which determines the strings of words that are grammatical in our language, and these rules generate no ungrammatical strings. Our utilization of these rules is subject to a whole host of potential misadventures which may lead us to utter ungrammatical sentences: there are slips of the tongue, failures of memory, lapses of attention, and no doubt many more. It is certainly possible to study these failures and thereby to learn something about the way the mind exploits its underlying competence. But while such studies might reveal interesting defects in performance, they could not reveal defects in competence. Analogously, we may expect all sorts of defects in inferential performance, due to inattention, memory limitations, or what have you. And a study of these failings may indicate something interesting about the way we exploit our underlying cognitive competence. But such a study could no more reveal an irrational or defective cognitive competence than a study of grammatical errors could reveal that the speaker's linguistic competence was defective.

This is all I shall have to say by way of setting out Cohen's clever argument. As I see it, the argument comes to grief in the account it offers of the justification of normative theses about cognitive procedures. Perhaps the clearest way to underscore the problem with Cohen's epistemological account is to pursue the analogy between grammar and the empirical or descriptive theory of reasoning competence. Both theories are based on the data of intuition and both are idealized. But on Cohen's account there is one striking and paradoxical dis-analogy. In grammar we expect different people to have different underlying competences which manifest themselves in significantly different linguistic intuitions. The linguistic competence of a Frenchman differs radically from the linguistic competence of an Englishman, and both differ radically from the linguistic competence of a Korean. Less radical, but still significant, are the differences between the competence of an Alabama sharecropper, an Oxford don, and a Shetland Island crofter. Yet on Cohen's account of the empirical theory of reasoning there is no mention of different people having different idealized competences. Rather, he seems to assume that in the domain of reasoning all people have exactly the same competence. But why should we not expect that cognitive competence will vary just as much as linguistic competence? The only answer I can find in Cohen's writing is a brief suggestion that cognitive competence may be *innate*. Yet surely this suggestion is entirely gratuitous. Whether or not individuals, social groups, or cultures differ in their cognitive competence is an *empirical* question, on all fours with the parallel question about linguistic competence. It is a question to be settled by the facts about intuitions and practice, not by a priori philosophical argument. And while the facts are certainly far from all being in, I am inclined to think that studies like those reviewed at the beginning of this paper, along with hundreds of others that might have been mentioned, make it extremely plausible that there are substantial individual differences in cognitive competence.

Now if this is right, if different people have quite different cognitive competences, then Cohen's account of the justification of a *normative* theory of reasoning faces some embarrassment. For recall that on his account a normative theory of reasoning is identical with a descriptive theory of cognitive competence; they are built on the same data and idealized in the same way. So if there are *many* cognitive competences abroad in our society and others, then there are *many* normative theories of cognition. But if there are many normative theories of cognition, which is the right one? Note that just here the analogy between linguistic competence and cognitive competence breaks down in an illuminating way. For although there are obviously great variations in linguistic competence, there is no such thing as a normative theory of linguistics (or at least none that deserves to be taken seriously). Thus there is no problem about which of the many linguistic competences abroad in the world corresponds to the normatively correct one.

The problem I have been posing for Cohen is analogous to a familiar problem in ethics. For there too there is good reason to suspect that the method of reflective equilibrium would yield different normative theories for different people, and we are left with the problem of saying which normative theory is the right one. One response to the problem in ethics, though to my mind an utterly unsatisfactory one, is a thoroughgoing relativism: my normative theory is the right one *for me*, yours is the right one *for you*. One way for Cohen to deal with the problem of the multiplicity of normative theories of cognition might be to adopt an analogous relativism. My inferential competence is right for me, yours is right for you. But this move is even more unpalatable for the normative theory of cognition than it is for ethics. We are not in the least inclined to say that any old inference is normatively acceptable for a subject merely because it accords with the rules which constitute his cognitive competence. If the inference is stupid or irrational, and if it accords with the subject's cognitive competence, then his competence is stupid or irrational too, in this quarter at least.

A second strategy for dealing with the multiplicity of normative theories might be to adopt a majoritarian view according to which it is the cognitive competence of the majority that is normatively correct. This is no more plausible than the relativist alternative, however. First, it is not at all clear that there is a majority cognitive competence, any more than there is a majority linguistic competence. It may well be that many significantly different competences coexist in the world, with the most common having no more than a meagre plurality. Moreover, even if there is a majority cognitive competence, there is little inclination to insist that it must be the normatively correct one. If, as seems very likely, most people disregard the impact of regression in estimating the likelihood of events, then most people infer badly![18]

The upshot of these reflections is that Cohen has simply told the wrong story about the justification of normative theories of cognition. Given the possibility of alternative cognitive competences, he has failed to tell us which one is normatively correct. Should he supplement his story along either relativist or majoritarian lines he would be stuck with the unhappy conclusion that a patently irrational inferential strategy might turn out to be the normatively correct one.[19]

By way of conclusion, let me note that there is a variation on Cohen's reflective equilibrium story which does a much better job at making sense of our normative judgments about reasoning, both in everyday life and in the psychology laboratory. It seems clear that we do criticize the reasoning of others, and we are not in the least swayed by the fact that the principles underlying a subject's faulty reasoning are a part of his—or most people's— cognitive competence. We are, however, swayed to find that the inference at hand is sanctioned or rejected by the cognitive competence of experts in the field of reasoning in question. Many well-educated people find statistical inferences involving regression to the mean to be highly counterintuitive, at least initially. But sensible people come to distrust their own intuition on the matter when they learn that principles requiring regressive inference are sanctioned by the reflective equilibrium of experts in statistical reasoning. In an earlier paper, Nisbett and I tried to parlay this observation into a general account of what it is for a normative principle of reasoning to be justified.[20] On our view, when we judge someone's inference to be normatively inappropriate, we are comparing it to (what we take to be) the applicable principles of inference sanctioned by expert reflective equilibrium. On this account, there is no puzzle or paradox implicit in the practice of psychologists who probe human irrationality. They are evaluating the inferential practice of their subjects by the sophisticated and evolving standard of expert competence. From this perspective, it is not at all that surprising that lay practice has been found to be markedly defective in many areas. We would expect the same, and for the same reason, if we examined lay competence in physics or in economics.

There is a hopeful moral embedded in this last observation. If, as Cohen suggests, cognitive competence is innate, then normatively inappropriate competence is ominous and inalterable. But if, as I have been urging, there is every reason to think that cognitive competence, like linguistic competence, is to a significant extent acquired and variable, then there is reason to hope that competence can be improved through education and practice, much as a child from Liverpool can acquire the crisp linguistic competence of an Oxford don. There is an important disanalogy, of course. Liverpudlean cadances are harmless and charming; normatively defective inference is neither. I am inclined to think, it a singular virtue of recent studies of reasoning that they point to the areas where remedial education is most needed.

Notes

1. Wason and Johnson-Laird 1972, Chs. 13–15; Wason 1977; Johnson-Laird and Wason 1970.

2. Johnson-Laird, Legrenzi and Sonino-Legrenzi 1972. However, see also Griggs and Cox, forthcoming.

3. Kahneman and Tversky in press.

4. Slovic, Fischoff and Lichtenstein 1977.

5. Slovic and Fischoff 1978.

6. Ross, Lepper and Hubbard 1975.

7. Stich 1980 and Stich 1981a.

8. Dennett forthcoming. MS pp. 8–9.

9. Dennett 1978, p. 20.

10. For Dennett's attempt to blunt this point, cf. Dennett 1981.

11. Dennett's view is often described as of a piece with Davidson's. But this is clearly mistaken. Davidson makes no use of the notion of an ideally rational system. Like me, he insists that a person must be cognitively *similar* to ourselves if we are to succeed in understanding his speech and ascribing beliefs to him. In particular, he maintains that "if I am right in attributing [a particular] belief to you, then you must have a pattern of beliefs much like mine." (Davidson 1979, p. 295). Davidson goes on to argue that most of these beliefs must be *true*. This is a view that Dennett holds as well. But as we shall see in the next section, Dennett's defense of this doctrine turns on evolutionary considerations, while Davidson's does not. The least obscure argument Davidson offers for this conclusion goes like this: "There is nothing absurd in the idea of an omniscient interpreter" (ibid.). To interpret us, this omniscient interpreter must share the bulk of our beliefs. And since *ex hypothesis* all of his beliefs are true, it follows that the bulk of ours must be true as well. End of argument. It should be pretty clear, however, that this argument simply begs the question. Granting the point about belief similarity being necessary for interpretation, it is an open question whether an omniscient interpreter could interpret our utterances as meaning something in his language. He could do so only if the bulk of our beliefs are true. And that is just what the argument was supposed to establish.

12. Garcia, McGowan and Green 1972.

13. Alcock 1975.

14. Nisbett and Wilson 1977.

15. Nisbett and Ross 1980, pp. 115–116.

16. Quoted in Sinsheimer 1971.

17. Cohen 1981. In the pages that follow, quotes from this paper will be identified by section numbers in parentheses in the text.

18. Cf. Nisbett and Ross 1980, pp. 150ff.

19. We should note in passing that Cohen was not the first to introduce the competence-performance distinction into the debate about human rationality. Fodor 1981 has an extended and illuminating discussion of the possibility that "the postulates of . . . logic are mentally represented by the organism, and this mental representation contributes (in appropriate ways) to the causation of its beliefs" (p. 120). Since the internally represented logic would be only one among many interacting causes of belief and behavior, "the eviocnce for attributing a logic to an organism would not be that the organism believes whatever the logic entails. Rather, the appropriate form of argument is to show that the assumption that the organism internally represents the logic, when taken together with independently motivated theories of the character of the other interacting variables, yields the best explanation of the data about the organism's mental states and processes and/or the behaviors in which such processes eventuate." But if the facts turn out right, it would seem that the same sort of evidentiary considerations might also lead to the conclusion that the organism had internally represented a peculiar or normatively inappropriate "logic." This is not a possibility Fodor pursues, however, since he has been seduced by Dennett's argument from natural selection. Darwinian selection, he claims, "guarantees that organisms either know the elements of logic or become posthumous" p. 121.

20. Stich and Nisbett 1980.

Bibliography

Frederick F. Schmitt

This bibliography lists recent discussions, developments, and criticisms of naturalistic epistemology. I have included some work by psychologists that might be taken to bear on epistemological issues. The choice of articles from psychology reflects the current interest in bias in deductive and statistical inference. Limitations of space have made it necessary to omit much relevant material on attention, perception, memory, and concepts, as well as developmental and social psychology. I have also had to omit relevant material on most of the traditional epistemological topics, such as foundationalism and coherentism. (For a complete bibliography of recent epistemology as of 1979, see Nancy Kelsik, in Pappas 1979.) Finally I have omitted the relevant literature on mathematical knowledge, linguistic knowledge, social knowledge, metaphysics, the history of epistemology, philosophy of psychology, philosophy of science, confirmation theory, informal logic, artificial intelligence, intelligence theory and other aspects of educational psychology, educational theory, rhetoric ("rhetoric as epistemic"), ergonomics, information and communication theory, decision and game theory, management science, library science, evolutionary theory, and the sociology, economics, and history of knowledge.

References cited in the chapters in this book are also listed here. The chapters in which they are cited are indicated by their chapter numbers in brackets following the listing. I have separated off those works that do not directly develop or criticize naturalistic epistemology and grouped them under the heading "Other References."

Books

Armstrong, David M. 1973. *Belief, Truth and Knowledge*. London: Cambridge University Press. [7, 9]

Berkowitz, L. 1977. *Advances in Experimental Social Psychology*, vol. 10. New York: Academic Press. [10, 11]

Bieri, Peter; Horstmann, R.-P.; and Kruger, L., eds. 1979. *Transcendental Arguments and Science*. Dordrecht: Reidel. [4]

Bloor, David. 1976. *Knowledge and Social Imagery*. London: Routledge and Kegan Paul.

Bogdan, Radu, ed. 1984. *Profile: D. M. Armstrong*. Dordrecht: Reidel.

Bogdan, Radu, ed. 1985. *Belief*. Oxford: Oxford University Press. [9]

Buchler, Justus, ed. 1955. *Philosophical Writings of Peirce*. New York: Dover. [12]

Carroll, J. S., and Payne, J. W., eds. 1976. *Cognition and Social Behavior*. Hillsdale, N.J.: Lawrence Erlbaum Associates. [10, 11]

Chisholm, Roderick M., and Swartz, Robert, eds. 1973. *Empirical Knowledge*. Englewood Cliffs, N.J.: Prentice-Hall. [6]

Churchland, Paul M. 1979. *Scientific Realism and the Plasticity of Mind*. Cambridge: Cambridge University Press.

Dretske, Fred I. 1969. *Seeing and Knowing*. Chicago: University of Chicago Press, and London: Routledge and Kegan Paul.

Dretske, Fred I. 1981. *Knowledge and the Flow of Information*. Cambridge, Mass.: The MIT Press. [9]

Evans, Jonathan St. B. T. 1983. *Thinking and Reasoning*. London: Routledge & Kegan Paul.

Fishbein, M., ed. 1977. *Progress in Social Psychology*. Hillsdale, N.J.: Lawrence Erlbaum Associates. [11]

Fodor, Jerry. 1981. *Representations: Philosophical Essays on the Foundations of Cognitive Science*. Cambridge, Mass.: The MIT Press. [13]

French, Peter A.; Uehling, Theodore E., Jr.; and Wettstein, Howard K., eds. 1979. *Contemporary Perspectives in the Philosophy of Language*. Midwest Studies in Philosophy, vol. 4. Minneapolis: University of Minnesota Press. [13]

French, Peter A.; Uehling, Theodore E., Jr.; and Wettstein, Howard K., eds., and Feleppa, Robert, assoc. ed. 1980. *Studies in Epistemology*. Midwest Studies in Philosophy, vol. 5. Minneapolis: University of Minnesota Press.

French, Peter A.; Uehling, Theodore E., Jr.; and Wettstein, Howard K. 1981. *Analytic Philosophy*. Midwest Studies in Philosophy, vol. 6. Minneapolis: University of Minnesota Press.

Goldman, Alvin I., and Kim, Jaegwon, eds. 1978. *Values and Morals: Essays in Honor of William Frankena, Charles Stevenson, and Richard Brandt*. Dordrecht: Reidel. [5]

Goodman, Nelson. 1965. *Fact, Fiction and Forecast*. 2d ed. Indianapolis: Bobbs-Merrill. [2, 8]

Gulber, H. et al., eds. 1957. *Contemporary Approaches to Cognition*. Cambridge, Mass.: Harvard University Press. [10]

Guttenplan, Samuel, ed. 1975. *Mind and Language*. Oxford: Clarendon Press.

Hanson, Norwood Russell. 1958. *Patterns of Discovery*. London: Cambridge University Press. [3]

Harman, Gilbert. 1973. *Thought*. Princeton: Princeton University Press. [6, 7]

Harman, Gilbert. Forthcoming. *Change in View: Principles of Reasoned Revision*. [12]

Johnson-Laird, Philip N. 1984. *Mental Models*. Cambridge: Cambridge University Press, and Cambridge, Mass.: Harvard University Press.

Kahneman, Daniel; Slovic, Paul; and Tversky, Amos. 1982. *Judgment under Uncertainty: Heuristics and Biases*. Cambridge: Cambridge University Press. [12]

Kleinmuntz, B., ed. 1968. *Formal Representation of Human Judgment*. New York: Wiley. [10]

Kuhn, Thomas. 1962. *The Structure of Scientific Revolutions*. Chicago: University of Chicago Press. [3, 10]

Lehrer, Keith. 1974. *Knowledge*. Oxford: Oxford University Press. [5, 6, 7]

Mellor, D. H., ed. 1980. *Prospects for Pragmatism*. New York: Cambridge University Press.

Mischel, Theodore. 1971. *Cognitive Development and Epistemology*. New York: Academic Press.

Morton, Adam. 1977. *A Guide through the Theory of Knowledge*. Encino, Calif.: Dickenson.

Nisbett, Richard, and Ross, Lee. 1980. *Human Inference: Strategies and Shortcomings of Social Judgment*. Englewood Cliffs, N.J.: Prentice-Hall. [Introduction, 12, 13]

Nozick, Robert. 1981. *Philosophical Explanations*. Cambridge, Mass.: Harvard University Press.

O'Connor, D. J., and Carr, Brian. 1982. *Introduction to the Theory of Knowledge*. Minneapolis: University of Minnesota Press.

Pappas, George S., ed. 1979a. *Justification and Knowledge: New Studies in Epistemology*. Dordrecht: Reidel.

Pappas, George S., and Swain, Marshall, eds. 1978. *Essays on Knowledge and Justification*. Ithaca: Cornell University Press. [6]

Piaget, Jean. 1970. *Genetic Epistemology*. Translated by Eleanor Duckworth. New York: Columbia University Press.

Piaget, Jean. 1972. *The Principles of Genetic Epistemology*. Translated by Wolfe Mays. New York: Basic Books.

Pólya, George. 1954. *Mathematics and Plausible Reasoning*. I: Induction and Analogy in Mathematics. II: Patterns of Plausible Inference. Princeton: Princeton University Press. [3]

Quine, W. V. 1953. *From a Logical Point of View*. Cambridge, Mass.: Harvard University Press. [3]

Quine, W. V. 1960. *Word and Object*. Cambridge, Mass.: The MIT Press. [Introduction, 1, 2, 4]

Quine, W. V. 1969. *Ontological Relativity and Other Essays*. New York: Columbia University Press.

Quine, W. V. 1973. *The Roots of Reference*. LaSalle, Ill.: Open Court. [4, 8]

Quine, W. V. 1976. *The Ways of Paradox and Other Essays*. Cambridge, Mass.: Harvard University Press.

Quine, W. V., and Ullian, J. S. 1978. *The Web of Belief*. 2d ed. New York: Random House. [5]

Rescher, Nicholas. 1977. *Methodological Pragmatism*. New York: New York University Press.

Ringle, Martin. 1979. *Philosophical Perspectives in Artificial Intelligence*. New York: Humanities Press.

Rorty, Richard. 1979. *Philosophy and the Mirror of Nature*. Princeton: Princeton University Press.

Savage, C. Wade, ed. 1978. *Perception and Cognition: Issues in the Foundations of Psychology*. Minnesota Studies in the Philosophy of Science, vol. 9. Minneapolis: University of Minnesota.

Sayre, Kenneth. 1976. *Cybernetics and the Philosophy of Mind*. New York: Humanities Press.

Schilpp, Paul, ed. 1974. *The Philosophy of Karl Popper*. LaSalle, Ill.: Open Court.

Sellars, Wilfrid. 1963. *Science, Perception and Reality*. New York: Humanities [6]

Shimony, A.; Nails, D.; and Cohen, R. S. Forthcoming. *Naturalistic Epistemology: A Symposium of Two Decades*. Dordrecht: Reidel.

Shope, Robert K. 1983. *The Analysis of Knowing: A Decade of Research*. Princeton: Princeton University Press.

Stemmer, Nathan. 1984. *The Roots of Knowledge*. New York: St. Martin's Press.

Stich, Stephen P. 1975. *Innate Ideas*. Berkeley: University of California Press.

Stich, Stephen P. Forthcoming a. *The Fragmentation of Reason*. Cambridge, Mass.: The MIT Press.

Stroud, Barry. 1984. *The Significance of Philosophical Scepticism*. Oxford: Oxford University Press.

Swain, Marshall. 1981. *Reasons and Knowledge*. Ithaca: Cornell University Press.

Swartz, Robert, ed. 1965. *Perceiving, Sensing and Knowing*. Berkeley: University of California Press. [6]

Wason, P. C., and Johnson-Laird, P. N. 1972. *The Psychology of Reasoning: Structure and Content*. London: Batsford. [13]

Wickelgren, Wayne. 1974. *How to Solve Problems*. San Francisco: W. H. Freeman. [11]

Will, Frederick L. 1974. *Induction and Justification*. Ithaca: Cornell University Press.

Williams, Michael. 1977. *Groundless Belief*. New Haven: Yale University Press. [6]

Articles

Epistemology and Psychology

Replacing Epistemology with Psychology

Bogen, James. Forthcoming. "Traditional Epistemology and Naturalistic Replies to its Skeptical Critics." *Synthese*.

Churchland, Paul M. 1982. "Is *Thinker* a Natural Kind?" *Dialogue* 21, 223–238.

Peirce, C. S. 1955. "The Fixation of Belief." In Justus Buchler 1955. [12]

Putnam, Hilary. 1982. "Why Reason Cannot Be Naturalized." *Synthese* 52, 3–23.

Quine, W. V. 1969a. "Epistemology Naturalized." Chapter 1 in this book. [4]

Quine, W. V. 1969b. "Natural Kinds." Chapter 2 in this book.

Quine, W. V. 1973. *The Roots of Reference*. LaSalle, Ill.: Open Court. [4, 8]

Quine, W. V. 1975. "The Nature of Natural Knowledge." In Guttenplan 1975. [4]

Quine, W. V. 1976. "The Limits of Knowledge." In Quine 1976.

Quine, W. V. 1981. "Reply to Stroud." In French et al. 1981, 474.

Ricketts, Thomas G. 1982. "Rationality, Translation, and Epistemology Naturalized." *Journal of Philosophy* 79, 117–136.

Rorty, Richard. 1979. *Philosophy and the Mirror of Nature*. Princeton: Princeton University Press. Chap's. 3, 4, 7.

Roth, Paul. 1983. "Siegel on Naturalized Epistemology and Natural Science." *Philosophy of Science* 50, 482–493.

Sheehan, P. 1973. "Quine on Revision: A Critique." *Australasian Journal of Philosophy* 51, 95–104.

Siegel, Harvey. 1980. "Justification, Discovery, and the Naturalizing of Epistemology." *Philosophy of Science* 47, 297–321.

Siegel, Harvey. Forthcoming. "Empirical Psychology, Naturalized Epistemology, and First Philosophy." *Philosophy of Science*.

Sosa, Ernest. 1983. "Nature Unmirrored, Epistemology Naturalized." *Synthese* 55, 49–72.

Stich, Stephen P. Forthcoming a. *The Fragmentation of Reason*. Cambridge, Mass.: The MIT Press.

Stroud, Barry. 1981. "The Significance of Naturalistic Epistemology." Chapter 4 in this book.

Stroud, Barry. 1979. "The Significance of Scepticism." In Bieri et al. 1979. [4]

Woods, Michael. 1980. "Scepticism and Natural Knowledge." *Proceedings of the Aristotelian Society* 54, 231–248.

Relevance of Psychology to Epistemology

Campbell, Donald T. 1959. "Methodological Suggestions from a Comparative Psychology of Knowledge Processes." *Inquiry* 2, 152–182. [1, 3]

Cherniak, Christopher. 1981a. "Feasible Inferences." *Philosophy of Science* 48, 248–268.

Cherniak, Christopher. 1981b. "Minimal Rationality." *Mind* 90, 161–183.

Cherniak, Christopher. 1983. "Rationality and the Structure of Human Memory." *Synthese* 57, 163–186.

Cherniak, Christopher. Forthcoming a. "Computational Complexity and the Universal Acceptance of Logic." *Journal of Philosophy*.

Cherniak, Christopher. Forthcoming b. "Prototypicality and Deductive Reasoning." *Journal of Verbal Learning and Verbal Behavior*.

Churchland, Paul M. 1979. *Scientific Realism and the Plasticity of Mind*. Cambridge: Cambridge University Press.

Churchland, Paul M., and Churchland, Patricia. 1983. "Stalking the Wild Epistemic Engine" *Nous* 17, 5–18.

Cohen, L. J. 1981. "Can Human Irrationality Be Experimentally Demonstrated?" *Behavioral and Brain Sciences* 4, 317–331. Open Peer Commentary, 4, 331–359. Author's Response: "Are There Any A Priori Constraints on the Study of Rationality?" 4, 359–367. Continuing Commentary, 6, 487–510. Author's Response: "The Controversy about Rationality," 6, 510–515.

Goldman, Alan H. 1981. "Epistemology and the Psychology of Perception." *American Philosophical Quarterly* 18, 43–51.

Goldman, Alan H. 1982. "Epistemic Foundationalism and the Replaceability of Ordinary Language." *Journal of Philosophy* 79, 136–154.

Goldman, Alvin I. Forthcoming. "The Relation between Epistemology and Psychology." *Synthese*.

Goodman, Nelson. 1965. *Fact, Fiction, and Forecast*. 2d ed. Indianapolis: Bobbs-Merrill. [2, 8]

Haack, Susan. 1975. "The Relevance of Psychology to Epistemology." *Metaphilosophy* 6, 161–176.

Halstead, Robert. 1979. "The Relevance of Psychology to Educational Epistemology." *Philosophy of Education* 1979, 65–76.

Kitchener, Richard F. 1980. "Genetic Epistemology, Normative Epistemology, and Psychologism." *Synthese* 45, 257–280.

Kornblith, Hilary. 1982. "The Psychological Turn." *Australasian Journal of Philosophy* 60, 238–253.

Page, Ralph C. 1979. "Epistemology, Psychology, and Two Views of Indoctrination." *Philosophy of Education* 1979, 77–86.

Piaget, Jean. 1972. *The Principles of Genetic Epistemology.* Translated by Wolfe Mays. New York: Basic Books.

Rorty, Richard. 1979. *Philosophy and the Mirror of Nature.* Princeton: Princeton University Press. Chapter 5.

Roth, Paul. 1983. "Siegel on Naturalized Epistemology and Natural Science." *Philosophy of Science* 50, 482–493.

Siegel, Harvey. 1979. "Can Psychology Be Relevant to Epistemology?" *Philosophy of Education* 1979, 55–64.

Siegel, Harvey. 1980. "Justification, Discovery, and the Naturalizing of Epistemology." *Philosophy of Science* 47, 297–321.

Siegel, Harvey. Forthcoming. "Empirical Psychology, Naturalized Epistemology, and First Philosophy." *Philosophy of Science.*

Sober, Elliott. 1978. "Psychologism." *Journal for the Theory of Social Behavior* 8, 165–191.

Stich, Stephen P. Forthcoming a. *The Fragmentation of Reason.* Cambridge, Mass.: The MIT Press.

Stich, Stephen P., and Nisbett, Richard E. 1980. "Justification and the Psychology of Human Reasoning." *Philosophy of Science* 47, 188–202.

Epistemics

Goldman, Alvin I. 1978a. "Epistemics: The Regulative Theory of Cognition." Chapter II in this book.

Goldman, Alvin I. 1978b. "Epistemology and the Psychology of Belief." *Monist* 61, 525–535.

Goldman, Alvin I. 1979. "Varieties of Cognitive Appraisal." *Nous* 13, 23–38.

Goldman, Alvin I. 1983. "Epistemology and the Theory of Problem Solving." *Synthese* 55, 21–48.

Grandy, Richard. 1978. "On Revisiting Psychology and Reorienting Epistemology." *Journal of Philosophy* 75, 525–526.

Swain, Marshall. 1978. "Epistemics and Epistemology." *Journal of Philosophy* 75, 523–525.

Relevance of Epistemology to Psychology

Harman, Gilbert. 1973. *Thought.* Princeton: Princeton University Press. [6, 7]

Harman, Gilbert. 1976. "Inferential Justification." *Journal of Philosophy* 73, 570–571.

Harman, Gilbert. 1978. "Using Intuitions about Reasoning to Study Reasoning: A Reply to Williams." *Journal of Philosophy* 75, 433–438.

Harman, Gilbert. 1980. "Reasoning and Evidence One Does Not Possess." In French et al. 1980.

Lycan, William G. 1977. "Evidence One Does Not Possess." *Australasian Journal of Philosophy* 55, 114–126.

Sosa, Ernest. 1977. "Thought, Inference and Knowledge: Gilbert Harman's *Thought.*" *Nous* 11, 421–430.

Williams, Michael. 1978. "Inference, Justification and the Analysis of Knowledge." *Journal of Philosophy* 75, 249–263.

Knowledge

Causal Theories

Barker, John. 1972. "Knowledge and Causation." *Southern Journal of Philosophy* 10, 313–321.

Carrier, L. S. 1976. "The Causal Theory of Knowledge." *Philosophia* 6, 237–258.

Coder, David. 1974. "Naturalizing the Gettier Argument." *Philosophical Studies* 26, 111–118.

Collier, K. 1974. "Contra the Causal Theory of Knowing." *Philosophical Studies* 24, 350–351.

Dretske, Fred I., and Enc, Berent. Forthcoming. "Causal Theories of Knowledge." In *Midwest Studies in Philosophy.*

Goldman, Alvin I. 1967. "A Causal Theory of Knowing." *Journal of Philosophy* 64, 357–372. Reprinted in Pappas and Swain 1978. [4, 5, 7]

Goldstick, Daniel. 1972. "A Contribution towards the Development of the Causal Theory of Knowledge." *Australasian Journal of Philosophy* 50, 238–248.

Hanson, P. 1978. "Prospects for a Causal Theory of Knowledge." *Canadian Journal of Philosophy* 8, 457–474.

Harman, Gilbert. 1970. "Knowledge, Reasons, and Causes." *Journal of Philosophy* 67, 841–855.

Holland, A. 1977. "Can Mannison Avoid a Causal Theory of Knowledge?" *Philosophical Quarterly* 27, 158–161.

Klein, Peter D. 1976. "Knowledge, Causality and Defeasibility." *Journal of Philosophy* 73, 792–812.

Lehrer, Keith. 1971. "How Reasons Give Us Knowledge, or the Case of the Gypsy Lawyer." *Journal of Philosophy* 68, 311–313.

Loeb, Louis. 1974. "On a Heady Attempt to Befiend Causal Theories of Knowledge." *Philosophical Studies* 29, 331–336.

Mannison, D. S. 1976. " 'Inexplicable Knowledge' Does Not Require Belief." *Philosophical Quarterly* 26, 139–148.

Morawetz, Thomas. 1974. "Causal Accounts of Knowledge." *Southern Journal of Philosophy* 12, 365–369.

Paxson, Thomas D., Jr. 1974. "Professor Swain's Account of Knowledge." *Philosophical Studies* 25, 57–61. Reprinted in Pappas and Swain 1978.

Scott, R. 1976. "Swain on Knowledge." *Philosophical Studies* 29, 419–424.

Sharpe, R. 1975. "On the Causal Theory of Knowledge." *Ratio* 17, 206–216.

Skyrms, Brian. 1967. "The Explication of 'X Knows That p.'" *Journal of Philosophy* 64, 373–389.

Swain, Marshall. 1972. "Knowledge, Causality and Justification." *Journal of Philosophy* 69, 291–300.

Swain, Marshall. 1978a. "Reasons, Causes, and Knowledge." *Journal of Philosophy* 75, 229–248.

Swain, Marshall. 1978b. "Some Revisions of Knowledge, Causality and Justification." In Pappas and Swain 1978.

Swain, Marshall. 1981. *Reasons and Knowledge*. Ithaca: Cornell University Press. Chapter 6.

Tolliver, Joseph. 1978. "Note on Swain's Causal Theory of Knowledge." In Pappas and Swain 1978.

Nonaccidentality Theories

Ravitch, Harold. 1976. "Knowledge and the Principle of Luck." *Philosophical Studies* 30, 347–349.

Unger, Peter. 1968. "An Analysis of Factual Knowledge." *Journal of Philosophy* 65, 157–170. [4]

Nomic Regularity Theories

Armstrong, David M. 1973. *Belief, Truth and Knowledge*. Cambridge: Cambridge University Press. Pt. 3.

Lycan, William G. 1984. "Armstrong's Theory of Knowing." In Bogdan 1984.

Olen, Jeffrey. 1977. "Knowledge, Probability and Nomic Connections." *Southern Journal of Philosophy* 15, 521–526.

Pastin, Mark. 1978. "Knowledge and Reliability: A Critical Study of D. M. Armstrong's *Belief, Truth and Knowledge*." *Metaphilosophy* 9, 150–162.

Counterfactual Dependency Theories

Dretske, Fred I. 1970. "Epistemic Operators." *Journal of Philosophy* 67, 1007–1023. [9]

Dretske, Fred I. 1971. "Conclusive Reasons." *Australasian Journal of Philosophy* 49, 1–22. Reprinted in Pappas and Swain 1978. [4]

Dretske, Fred I. 1981. "The Pragmatic Dimension of Knowledge." *Philosophical Studies* 40, 363–378.

Goldman, Alvin I. 1976. "Discrimination and Perceptual Knowledge." *Journal of Philosophy* 73, 771–791. Reprinted in Pappas and Swain 1978. [5, 6, 7, 9]

Luper-Foy, Steven. 1984. "The Epistemic Predicament: Knowledge, Nozickian Tracking, and Scepticism." *Australasian Journal of Philosophy* 62, 26–49.

Lycan, William G. 1984. "Armstrong's Theory of Knowing." In Bogdan 1984.

Nozick, Robert. 1981. *Philosophical Explanations*. Cambridge, Mass.: Harvard University Press. Chapter 3.

Pappas, George, and Swain, Marshall. 1973. "Some Conclusive Reasons against 'Conclusive Reasons.'" *Australasian Journal of Philosophy* 51, 72–76. Reprinted in Pappas and Swain 1978.

Sanford, David H. 1981. "Knowledge and Relevant Alternatives: Comments on Dretske." *Philosophical Studies* 40, 379–388.

Schmitt, Frederick F. 1983. "Knowledge, Justification, and Reliability." *Synthese* 55, 209–229.

Schmitt, Frederick F. Forthcoming a. "Knowledge as Tracking?" *Topoi*.

Shatz, David. 1981. "Reliability and Relevant Alternatives." *Philosophical Studies* 39, 393–408.

Shope, Robert K. 1984. "Cognitive Abilities, Conditionals, and Knowledge: A Response to Nozick." *Journal of Philosophy* 81, 29–47.

Yurgrau, Palle. 1983. "Knowledge and Relevant Alternatives." *Synthese* 55, 175–190.

Reliability Theories

Audi, Robert. 1980. "Defeated Knowledge, Reliability, and Justification." In French et al. 1980.

Grandy, Richard E. 1980. "Ramsey, Reliability, and Knowledge." In Mellor 1980.

Lycan, William G. 1984. "Armstrong's Theory of Knowing." In Bogdan 1984.

Pastin, Mark. 1980. "The Multiperspectival Theory of Knowledge." In French et al. 1980.

Schmitt, Frederick F. 1983. "Knowledge, Justification, and Reliability." *Synthese* 55, 209–229.

Schmitt, Frederick F. Forthcoming a. "Knowledge as Tracking?" *Topoi*.

Informational Theories

Dretske, Fred I. 1980. "The Intentionality of Cognitive States." In French et al. 1980.

Dretske, Fred I. 1981. *Knowledge and the Flow of Information*. Cambridge, Mass.: The MIT Press. Chapter 4.

Dretske, Fred I. 1983a. "The Epistemology of Belief." *Synthese* 55, 3–19.

Dretske, Fred I. 1983b. "Précis of *Knowledge and the Flow of Information*." Chapter 9 in this book. Open Peer Commentary, *Behavioral and Brain Sciences* 6, 63–82. Author's Response: "Why Information?" 6, 82–89.

Dretske, Fred I. 1985. "Misrepresentation." In Bogdan 1985.

Sayre, Kennth. 1976. *Cybernetics and the Philosophy of Mind*. New York: Humanities Press.

Sayre, Kenneth. 1979. "The Simulation of Epistemic Acts." In Ringle 1979.

Skepticism and Naturalistic Theories of Knowledge

Dretske, Fred I. 1970. "Epistemic Operators." *Journal of Philosophy* 67, 1007–1023. [9]

Goldman, Alvin I. 1976. "Discrimination and Perceptual Knowledge." *Journal of Philosophy* 73, 771–791. Reprinted in Pappas and Swain 1978. [5, 6, 7, 9]

Luper-Foy, Steven. 1984. "The Epistemic Predicament: Knowledge, Nozickian Tracking, and Scepticism." *Australasian Journal of Philosophy* 62, 26–49.

Nozick, Robert. 1981. *Philosophical Explanations*. Cambridge, Mass.: Harvard University Press. Chapter 3.

Stine, Gail. 1976. "Skepticism, Relevant Alternatives and Deductive Closure." *Philosophical Studies* 29, 249–260.

Perceptual Knowledge

Doppelt, Gerald. 1973. "Dretske's Conception of Perception and Knowledge." *Philosophy of Science* 40, 433–446.

Dretske, Fred I. 1978. "The Role of the Percept in Visual Cognition." In Savage 1978.

Goldman, Alvin I. 1976. "Discrimination and Perceptual Knowledge." *Journal of Philosophy* 73, 771–791. Reprinted in Pappas and Swain 1978. [5, 6, 7, 9]

Goldman, Alvin I. 1977. "Perceptual Objects." *Synthese* 35, 257–284.

Grice, H. P. 1965. "The Causal Theory of Perception." In Swartz 1965.

Harman, Gilbert. 1973. *Thought*. Princeton: Princeton University Press. Chapter 11.

Kim, Jaegwon. 1977. "Perception and Reference without Causality." *Journal of Philosophy* 74, 606–620.

Nelson, Jack. Forthcoming. "The Diversity of Perception." *Synthese*.

Pears, D. F. 1976. "The Causal Conditions of Perception." *Synthese* 33, 25–40.

Introspective Knowledge

Alston, William P. 1971. "Varieties of Privileged Access." *American Philosophical Quarterly* 8, 223–241. [5]

Byrne, Richard. 1983. "Protocol Analysis in Problem Solving." In Evans 1983.

Ericson, K. A., and Simon, H. A. 1980. "Verbal Reports as Data." *Psychological Review* 87, 215–251.

Johnson-Laird, P. N., and Wason, P. C. 1970. "A Theoretical Analysis of Insight into a Reasoning Task" and "Protscript—1977." In Johnson-Laird and Wason 1977. [13]

Lundh, L. G. 1979. "Introspection, Consciousness and Human Information Processing." *Scandinavian Journal of Psychology* 20, 223–238.

Nisbett, Richard E., and Wilson, Timothy D. 1977. "Telling More Than We Can Know: Verbal Reports on Mental Processes." *Psychological Review* 84, 231–259. [13]

Redford, J. 1974. "Reflections on Introspection." *American Psychologist* 29, 245–250.

Smith, E. R., and Miller, E. R. 1978. "Limits on Perception of Cognitive Processes: A Reply to Nisbett and Wilson." *Psychological Review* 85, 355–362.

Wilson, Timothy D., and Nisbett, Richard E. 1978. "The Accuracy of Verbal Reports about the Effects of Stimuli on Evaluations and Behavior." *Social Psychology* 41, 118–131.

Inferential Knowledge

Goldman, Alvin I. 1973. "Discrimination and Inferential Knowledge." Unpublished manuscript.

Memory Knowledge

Cherniak, Christopher. 1983. "Rationality and the Structure of Human Memory." *Synthese* 57, 163–186.

Dretske, Fred I., and Yourgrau, Palle. 1983. "Lost Knowledge," *Journal of Philosophy* 80, 356–367.

Martin, C. B., and Deutscher, Max. 1966. "Remembering." *Philosophical Review* 75, 161–196.

Innate Knowledge

Goldman, Alvin I. 1975. "Innate Knowledge." In Stich 1975. [5, 6, 7]

A Priori Knowledge

Harman, Gilbert. 1967. "Unger on Knowledge." *Journal of Philosophy* 64, 390–395.

Kitcher, Philip. 1980. "A Priori Knowledge." Chapter 7 in this book.

Quine, W. V. 1953. "Two Dogmas of Empiricism." In Quine 1953. [4]

Sober, Elliott. 1981. "Revisability, A Priori Truth, and Evolution." *Australasian Journal of Philosophy*, 59, 68–85.

Thompson, Manley. 1981. "Epistemic Priority, Analytic Truth, and Naturalized Epistemology." *American Philosophical Quarterly* 18, 1–12.

Thompson, Manley. 1983. "On A Priori Truth." *Journal of Philosophy* 78, 458–482.

Unger, Peter. 1967. "Experience and Factual Knowledge." *Journal of Philosophy* 64, 152–173. [4]

Justified Belief

Justification and Causation

Audi, Robert. 1983. "The Causal Structure of Indirect Justification." *Journal of Philosophy* 80, 398–415.

Boyd, Richard. 1973. "Realism, Underdetermination, and a Causal Theory of Evidence." *Nous* 7, 1–12.

Firth, Roderick. 1978. "Are Epistemic Concepts Reducible to Ethical Concepts?" In Goldman and Kim 1978. [5]

Foley, Richard. 1984. "Epistemic Luck and the Purely Epistemic." *American Philosphical Quarterly* 21, 113–124.

Kordig, Carl R. 1978. "Discovery and Justification." *Philosophy of Science* 45, 110–117.

Kornblith, Hilary. 1980. "Beyond Foundationalism and the Coherence Theory." Chapter 6 in this book.

Kornblith, Hilary. 1982. "The Psychological Turn." *Australasian Journal of Philosophy* 60, 238–253.

Pappas, George S. 1979b. "Basing Relations." In Pappas 1979a.

Smith, Michael P., and McLean, John. 1978. "Toward a Causal Theory of Evidence." *Journal of Philosophy* 75, 424–433.

Stroud, Barry. 1979. "Inference, Belief, and Understanding." *Mind* 88, 179–196. [6]

Swain, Marshall. 1979. "Justification and the Basis of Belief." In Pappas 1979a.

Swain, Marshall. 1981. *Reasons and Knowledge.* Ithaca: Cornell University Press. Chapter 3.

Reliability Theories

Annis, David B. 1977. "Epistemic Foundationalism." *Philosophical Studies* 31, 345–352.

Bon Jour, Lawrence. 1976. "The Coherence Theory of Empirical Knowledge." *Philosophical Studies* 30, 281–312.

Bon Jour, Lawrence. 1978. "Can Empirical Knowledge Have a Foundation?" *American Philosophical Quarterly* 15, 1–13.

Boyd, Richard. 1980. "Scientific Realism and Naturalistic Epistemology." Philosophy of Science Association, *PSA* 1980, 2.

Feldman, Richard. Forthcoming. "Reliability and Justification." Unpublished manuscript.

Firth, Roderick. 1981. "Epistemic Merit, Intrinsic and Instrumental." *Proceedings and Addresses of the American Philosophical Association* 55, 5–23.

Friedman, Michael. 1979. "Truth and Confirmation." Chapter 8 in this book.

Heil, John. 1982. "Foundationalism and Epistemic Rationality." *Philosophical Studies* 42, 179–188.

Kornblith, Hilary. 1980. "Beyond Foundationalism and the Coherence Theory." *Journal of Philosophy* 77, 597–612. Chapter 6 in this book.

Nozick, Robert. 1981. *Philosophical Explanations*. Cambridge, Mass.: Harvand University Press. Chapter 3.

Pappas, George S. 1983. "Ongoing Knowledge." *Synthese* 55, 253–267.

Pollock, John. 1984. "Reliability and Justified Belief." *Canadian Journal of Philosophy* 14, 103–114.

Schmitt, Frederick F. 1981. "Justification as Reliable Indication or Reliable Process?" *Philosophical Studies* 40, 409–417.

Schmitt, Frederick F. 1983. "Knowledge, Justification, and Reliability." *Synthese* 55, 209–229.

Schmitt, Frederick F. 1984. "Reliability, Objectivity and the Background of Justification." *Australasian Journal of Philosophy*, 62, 1–15.

Shatz, David. 1983. "Foundationalism, Coherentism, and the Levels Gambit." *Synthese* 55, 97–118.

Sosa, Ernest. 1980. "The Raft and the Pyramid: Coherence versus Foundations in the Theory of Knowledge." In French et al. 1980. [12]

Sosa, Ernest. Forthcoming. "Facts and Faces of Epistemology." *Synthese*.

Swain, Marshall. 1981. "Justification and Reliable Belief." *Philosophical Studies* 40, 389–407.

Watling, John. 1955. "Inference from the Known to the Unknown." *Proceedings of the Aristotelian Society* 55, 83–108.

Psychologism

Sober, Elliott. 1978. "Psychologism." *Journal for the Theory of Social Behavior* 8, 165–191.

Stich, Stephen P., and Nisbett, Richard E. 1980. "Justification and the Psychology of Human Reasoning." *Philosophy of Science* 47, 188–202.

Epistemic Conservatism

Foley, Richard 1983. "Epistemic Conservatism." *Philosophical Studies* 41, 165–182.

Goldstick, Daniel. 1971. "Methodological Conservatism." *American Philosophical Quarterly* 8, 186–191.

Goldstick, Daniel. 1976. "More on Methodological Conservatism." *Philosophical Studies* 30, 193–195.

Kaplan, Mark, and Sklar, Lawrence. 1976. "Rationality and Truth." *Philosophical Studies* 30, 197–201.

Lycan, William G. Forthcoming a. "Conservatism and the Data Base." Unpublished manuscript.

Sklar, Lawrence. 1975. "Methodological Conservatism." *Philosophical Studies* 84, 374–400.

Sklar, Lawrence. 1981. "Do Unborn Hypotheses have Rights?" *Pacific Philosophical Quarterly* 62, 17–29.

Slote, Michael. 1981. "Confirmation and Conservatism." *American Philosophical Quarterly* 18, 79–84.

Justification and Epistemic Responsibility

Bon Jour, Lawrence. 1980. "Externalist Theories of Empirical Knowledge." In French et al. 1980.

Kornblith, Hilary. 1982. "The Psychological Turn." *Australasian Journal of Philosophy* 60, 238–253.

Kornblith, Hilary. 1983. "Justified Belief and Epistemically Responsible Action." *Philosophical Review* 92, 33–48.

Myrna, Frances. 1983. "*Father and Son*: A Case Study in Epistemic Responsibility." *Monist* 66, 283–297.

Internalism and Externalism, Subjectivism and Objectivism

Alston, William P. 1980. "Level-Confusions in Epistemology." In French et al. 1980.

Bon Jour, Lawrence. 1980. "Externalist Theories of Empirical Knowledge." In French et al. 1980.

Goldman, Alvin I. 1980. "The Internalist Conception of Justification." In French et al. 1980.

Kornblith, Hilary. 1983. "Justified Belief and Epistemically Responsible Action." *Philosophical Review* 92, 33–48.

Kornblith, Hilary. Forthcoming. "Ever Since Descartes." *Monist*.

Kvanvig, Jonathan L. 1984. "Subjective Justification." *Mind* 93, 71–84.

Lehrer, Keith, and Cohen, Stewart. 1983. "Justification, Truth, and Coherence." *Synthese* 55, 191–207.

Pollock, John. 1979. "A Plethora of Epistemological Theories." In Pappas 1979a. [12]

Pollock, John. Forthcoming. "Epistemic Norms." Unpublished manuscript.

Schmitt, Frederick F. 1984. "Reliability, Objectivity and the Background of Justification." *Australasian Journal of Philosophy* 62, 1–15.

Sosa, Ernest. Forthcoming. "Facts and Faces of Epistemology" *Synthese*.

Rational Judgment

Belief Revision

Bruner, J. S. 1957. "On Going Beyond the Information Given." In Gulber et al. 1957. [10]

Harman, Gilbert. 1984. "Positive vs. Negative Undermining in Belief Revision." Chapter 12 in this book.

Harman, Gilbert. Forthcoming. *Change in View: Principles of Reasoned Revision.* [12]

Nisbett, Richard, and Ross, Lee. 1980. *Human Inference: Strategies and Shortcomings of Social Judgment.* Englewood Cliffs: Prentice-Hall. Chapter 2.

Stich, Stephen P. 1985. "Could Man Be an Irrational Animal?" Chapter 13 in this book.

Stich, Stephen P. Forthcoming a. *The Fragmentation of Reason.* Cambridge, Mass.: The MIT Press.

Stich, Stephen P. Forthcoming b. "Rationality, Relativism and the Limits of Intentional Description." *Pacific Philosophical Quarterly.*

Problem Solving

Goldman, Alvin I. 1983. "Epistemology and the Theory of Problem Solving." *Synthese* 55, 21–48.

Richardson, John T. E. 1983. "Mental Imagery in Thinking and Problem Solving." In Evans 1983.

Deductive Inference

Cherniak, Christopher. Forthcoming b. "Prototypicality and Deductive Reasoning." *Journal of Verbal Learning and Verbal Behavior.*

Griggs, Richard A. 1983. "The Role of Problem Content in the Selection task and in the THOG Problem." In Evans 1983.

Griggs, R. A., and Cox, J. R. 1982. "The Elusive Thematic-Materials Effect in Wason's Selection Task." *British Journal of Psychology* 73, 407–420. [13]

Johnson-Laird, Philip N. 1983. "Thinking as a Skill." In Evans 1983.

Johnson-Laird, Philip N. 1984. *Mental Models.* Cambridge, Mass.: Harvard University Press.

Johnson-Laird, P. N., Legrenzi, P., and Sonino Legrenzi, M. 1972. "Reasoning and a Sense of Reality." *British Journal of Psychology* 63, 395–400. [13]

Newstead, Stephen E., and Griggs, Richard A. 1983. "The Language and Thought of Disjunction." In Evans 1983.

Wason, Peter C. 1977. "Self-Contradictions." In Johnson-Laird and Wason 1977. [13]

Wason, Peter C. 1983. "Realism and Rationality in the Selection Task." In Evans 1983.

Statistical Inference

Heuristics for probability judgments

Cohen, L. J. 1979. "On the Psychology of Prediction: Whose Is the Fallacy?" *Cognition* 7, 385–407.

Cohen, L. J. 1980. "Whose Is the Fallacy? A Rejoinder to Daniel Kahneman and Amos Tversky." *Cognition* 8, 89–92.

Cohen, L. J. 1981. "Can Human Irrationality Be Experimentally Demonstrated?" *Behavioral and Brain Sciences* 4, 317–331.

Edwards, Ward. 1968. "Conservatism in Human Information Processing." In Kleinmuntz 1968. Reprinted in Kahneman et al. 1982.

Kahneman, Daniel, and Tversky, Amos. 1979. "On the Interpretation of Intuitive Probability: A Reply to Jonathan Cohen." *Cognition* 7, 409–411.

Kahneman, Daniel, and Tversky, Amos. 1982. "On the Study of Statistical Intuitions." *Cognition* 11, 123–141. Reprinted in Kahneman et al. 1982.

Tversky, Amos, and Kahneman, Daniel. 1974. "Judgment under Uncertainty: Heuristics and Biases." *Science* 185, 1124–1131. Reprinted in Kahneman et al. 1982. [10, 11]

Representativeness

Bar-Hillel, Maya. 1982. "Studies of Representativeness." In Kahneman et al. 1982.

Evans, Jonathan St. B. T. 1983. "Selective Processes in Reasoning." In Evans 1983.

Kahneman, Daniel, and Tversky, Amos. 1972. "Subjective Probability: A Judgment of Representativeness." *Cognitive Psychology* 3, 430–454. Reprinted in Kahneman et al. 1982. [10]

Kahneman, Daniel, and Tversky, Amos. 1973. "On the Psychology of Prediction." *Psychological Review* 80, 237–251. Reprinted in Kahneman et al. 1982. [10]

Pollard, Paul, and Evans, Jonathan St. B. T. 1983. "The Role of 'Representativeness' in Statistical Inference: A Critical Appraisal." In Evans 1982.

Tversky, Amos, and Kahneman, Daniel. 1971. "Belief in the Law of Small Numbers." *Psychological Bulletin* 2, 105–110. Reprinted in Kahneman et al. 1982. [10]

Tversky, Amos, and Kahneman, Daniel. 1982. "Judgments of and by Representativeness." In Kahneman et al. 1982.

Availability

Kahneman, Daniel, and Tversky, Amos. 1982. "The Simulation Heuristic." In Kahneman et al. 1982.

Taylor, Shelley E. 1982. "The Availability Bias in Social Perception and Interaction." In Kahneman et al. 1980.

Tversky, Amos, and Kahneman, Daniel. 1973. "Availability: A Heuristic for Judging Frequency and Probability." *Cognitive Psychology* 4, 207–232. Reprinted in Kahneman et al. 1982. [10]

Reasoning about control and covariation
Einhorn, Hillel J. 1982. "Learning from Experience and Suboptimal Rules in Decision Making." In Kahneman et al. 1982.

Jennings, Dennis L.; Amabile, Teresa M.; and Ross, Lee. 1982. "Informal Covariation Assessment: Data-based versus Theory-based Judgments." In Kahneman et al. 1982.

Causal reasoning
Nisbett, Richard E.; Borgida, Eugene; Crandell, Rick; and Reed, Harvey. 1976. "Popular Induction: Information Is Not Necessarily Informative." In Carroll and Payne 1978. Reprinted in Kahneman et al. 1982.

Ross, Lee. 1977. "The Intuitive Psychologist and His Shortcomings: Distortions in the Attribution Process." In Berkowitz 1977. [10, 11]

Tversky, Amos, and Kahneman, Daniel. 1977. "Causal Schemata in Judgments under Uncertainty." In Fishbein 1977. [11]

Tversky, Amos, and Kahneman, Daniel. 1982. "Evidential Impact of Base Rates." In Kahneman et al. 1982.

Corrective procedures
Dawes, Robyn M. 1979. "The Robust Beauty of Improper Linear Models in Decision Making." *American Psychologist* 34, 571–582. Reprinted in Kahneman et al. 1982.

Fischhoff, Baruch. 1982. "Debiasing." In Kahneman et al. 1982.

Kahneman, Daniel, and Tversky, Amos. 1982. "Intuitive Predictions: Biases and Corrective Procedures." In Kahneman et al. 1982. [10, 13]

Nisbett, Richard E.; Krantz, David H.; Jepson, Christopher; and Fong, Geoffrey H. 1982. "Improving Inductive Inference." In Kahneman et al. 1982.

Ross, Lee; Lepper, M. R.; and Hubbard, M. 1975. "Perserverance in Self Perception and Social Perception: Biased Attributional Processes in the Debriefing Paradigm." *Journal of Personality and Social Psychology* 32, 880–892. [13]

Singer, Max. 1971. "The Vitality of Mythical Numbers." *Public Interest* 23, 3–9. Reprinted in Kahneman et al. 1982.

Biological Epistemology

Biological Analogies in Epistemology
Campbell, Donald T. 1974. "Evolutionary Epistemology." In Schilpp 1974.

Campbell, Donald T. 1960b. "Blind Variation and Selective Retention in Creative Thought as in Other Knowledge Processes." *Psychological Review* 67, 380–400. [3]

Pringle, J. W. S. 1951. "On the Parallel between Learning and Evolution." *Behaviour* 3, 175–215. [3]

Biological Possibility of Rationality
Sober, Elliott. 1981. "The Evolution of Rationality." *Synthese* 46, 95–120.

Epistemic Norms as Biological
Lycan, William. Forthcoming b. "Epistemic Value." *Synthese*.

Developmental Epistemology

Hamlym, D. W. 1971. "Epistemology and Conceptual Development." In Mischel 1971.

Kaplan, Bernard. 1971. "Genetic Psychology, Genetic Epistemology, and Theory of Knowledge." In Mischel 1971.

Kitchener, Richard F. 1980. "Genetic Epistemology, Normative Epistemology, and Psychologism." *Synthese* 45, 257–280.

Kitchener, Richard F. 1981. "The Nature and Scope of Genetic Epistemology." *Philosophy of Science* 48, 400–415.

Piaget, Jean. 1972. *The Principles of Genetic Epistemology*. Translated by Wolfe Mays. New York: Basic Books.

Siegel, Harvey. 1978. "Piaget's Conception of Epistemology." *Educational Theory* 28, 16–22.

Toulmin, Stephen. 1977. "Epistemology and Developmental Psychology." *Nous* 11, 51–53.

Social Epistemology

Annis, David B. 1978. "A Contextualist Theory of Justification." *American Philosophical Quarterly* 15, 213–219.

Bloor, David. 1976. *Knowledge and Social Imagery*. London: Routledge and Kegan Paul.

Campbell, Donald T. 1979. "A Tribal Model of the Social System Vehicle Carrying Scientific Knowledge." *Knowledge: Creation, Diffusion, Utilization* 1, 181–201.

Coady, C. A. J. 1973. "Testimony and Observation." *American Philosophical Quarterly* 10, 149–155.

Dretske, Fred I. 1982. "A Cognitive Cul-de-Sac." *Mind* 91, 109–111.

Kantorovich, A. 1983. "The Collective A Priori in Science." *Nature and System* 5, 77–96.

Schmitt, Frederick F. Forthcoming b. "Justification and Sociality." *Synthese*.

Welbourne, Michael. 1979. "The Transmission of Knowledge." *Philosophical Quarterly* 29, 1–9.

Welbourne, Michael. 1981. "The Community of Knowledge." *Philosophical Quarterly* 31, 302–314.

Welbourne, Michael. 1983. "A Cognitive Thoroughfare." *Mind* 92, 410–412.

Other References

The following are additional works cited in the chapters in this book.

Books

Abelson, R. P. et al., eds. 1968. *Theories of Cognitive Consistency.* Chicago: Rand McNally. [10]

Alcock, J. 1979. *Animal Behavior: An Evolutionary Approach.* Sunderland: Sinauer Associates. [13]

Anderson, J. R., and Bower, G. H. 1973. *Human Associative Memory.* Washington, D.C.: Winston. [12]

Anderson, R. C.; Spiro, R. J.; and Montague, W. E., eds. 1976. *Schooling and the Acquisition of Knowledge.* Hillsdale, N.J.: Lawrence Erlbaum Associates. [10]

Ayer, A. J. 1936. *Language, Truth and Logic.* London: Gollancz. [7]

Ayer, A. J. 1974. *The Central Questions of Philosophy.* New York: William Morrow. [6]

Ayer, A. J., ed. 1959. *Logical Positivism.* New York: Free Press. [4, 7]

Bartlett, F. C. 1932. *Remembering.* Cambridge: Cambridge University Press. [10]

Bergmann, G. 1957. *Philosophy of Science.* Madison: University of Wisconsin Press. [3]

Berkowitz, L., ed. 1978a. *Advances in Experimental Social Psychology*, vol. 11. New York: Academic Press. [10]

Berkowitz, L., ed. 1978b. *Cognitive Theories in Social Psychology.* New York: Academic Press. [10]

Bernard, E. E., and Kare, M. R., eds. 1962. *Biological Prototypes and Synthetic Systems.* New York: Plenum. [1]

Berne, E. 1964. *Games People Play.* New York: Grove Press. [10]

Black, A. H., and Prokasy, W. F., eds. 1972. *Classical Conditioning*, vol. 2: *Current Research and Theory.* New York: Appleton-Century Crofts. [13]

Bobrow, D., and Collins, A. 1976. *Representation and Understanding: Studies in Cognitive Science.* New York: Academic Press. [10]

Bridgman, P. W. 1927. *The Logic of Modern Physics.* New York: Macmillan. [3]

Brunswik, E. 1956. *Perception and the Representative Design of Psychological Experiments.* Berkeley: University of California Press. [3]

Brunswik, E. 1934. *Wahrnehmung und Gegenstandsweht*. Vienna: Deuticke. [3]

Burnyeat, M., ed. Forthcoming. *The Sceptical Tradition*. Berkeley: University of California Press. [4]

Carnap, R. 1950. *Logical Foundations of Probability*. Chicago: University of Chicago Press. [11]

Carnap, R. 1967. *The Logical Structure of the World and Pseudo-problems in Philosophy*. London: Macmillan. [4]

Chase, W. G., ed. 1973. *Visual Information Processing*. New York: Academic Press. [11]

Chisholm, R. M. 1957. *Perceiving: A Philosophical Study*. Ithaca: Cornell University Press. [6]

Chisholm, R. M. 1976. *Person and Object*. LaSalle, Ill.: Open Court. [6]

Chisholm, R. M. 1977. *Theory of Knowledge*. 2d ed. Englewood Cliffs, N.J.: Prentice-Hall. [5, 6]

Christie, R., and Geis, F. L., eds. 1970. *Studies in Machiavellianism*. New York: Academic Press. [10]

Craik, K. W. J. 1943. *The Nature of Explanation*. London: Cambridge University Press. [3]

Davidson, D., and Harman, G., eds. 1972. *Semantics of Natural Language*. Dordrecht: Reidel. [7]

Dennett, D. 1969. *Content and Consciousness*. London: Routledge and Kegan Paul. [9]

Dennett, D. 1978. *Brainstorms*. Cambridge, Mass.: Bradford Books/MIT Press. [Introduction, 13]

Dockx, S., and Bernays, P., eds. 1965. *Information and Prediction in Science*. New York: Academy Press. [2]

Doyle, J. 1980. *A Model for Deliberation, Action, and Introspection*. MIT Artificial Intelligence Laboratory Technical Report 561. Cambridge, Mass. [12, 13]

Duval, S., and Wicklund, R. A. 1972. *A Theory of Objective Self-Awareness*. New York: Academic Press. [10]

Feigl, H.; Scriven, M.; and Maxwell, G., eds. 1958. *Concepts, Theories, and the Mind-Body Problem*. Minnesota Studies in the Philosophy of Science, vol. 2. Minneapolis: University of Minnesota Press. [3]

Flavell, J. H. 1963. *The Developmental Psychology of Jean Piaget*. Princeton: Van Nostrand. [3]

Foster L., and Swanson, J. W., eds. 1970. *Experience and Theory*. Amherst: University of Massachusetts Press. [5]

French, P. A.; Uehling, T. E., Jr.; and Wettstein, H. K. 1977. *Studies in the Philosophy of Language*. Midwest Studies in Philosophy, vol. 2. Minneapolis: University of Minnesota Press. [7]

Gibson, J. J. 1950. *The Perception of the Visual World*. New York: Houghton Mifflin. [9]

Gibson, J. J. 1966. *The Senses Considered as a Perceptual System*. Boston: Houghton Mifflin. [6, 9]

Gibson, J. J. 1979. *The Ecogological Approach to Visual Perception*. Boston: Houghton Mifflin. [9]

Ginet, C. 1975. *Knowledge, Perception and Memory*. Boston: Reidel. [6]

Goffman, E. 1959. *The Presentation of Self in Everyday Life*. New York: Doubleday. [10]

Goodman, N. 1966. *The Structure of Appearance*. 2d ed. New York: Bobbs-Merrill. [2]

Gould, L., and Walker, C. A., eds. 1978. *The Management of Nuclear Wastes*. New Haven: Yale University Press. [13]

Gregory, R. L. 1970. *The Intelligent Eye*. New York: McGraw-Hill. [6]

Haber, R. N. 1969. *Information-Processing Approaches to Visual Perception*. New York: Holt, Rinehart and Winston. [9]

Hacking, Ian. 1975. *The Emergence of Probability*. Cambridge: Cambridge University Press. [Introduction]

Hartshorne, H., and May, M. 1928. *Studies in the Nature of Character*. Vol. 1: *Studies in Deceit*. New York: Macmillan. [10]

Head, H. 1920. *Studies in Neurology*. London: Oxford University Press. [3]

Healy, R., ed. 1981. *Reduction, Time and Reality*. Cambridge: Cambridge University Press.

Heider, F. 1958. *The Psychology of Impersonal Relations*. New York: Wiley. [10]

Hempel, C. G. 1952. *Fundamentals of Concept Formation in Empirical Science*. Chicago: University of Chicago Press. [3]

Hempel, C. G. 1965. *Aspects of Scientific Explanation*. New York: Free Press. [2, 11]

Higgins, E. T.; Herman, P.; and Zanna, M. P., eds. 1980. *The Ontario Symposium on Personality and Social Psychology*, vol. 1. Hillsdale, N.J.: Lawrence Erlbaum Associates. [10]

Howes, H. E., and Dienstbier, R. A., eds. 1979. *Nebraska Symposium on Motivation*, vol. 26. Lincoln: University of Nebraska Press. [10]

Jeffrey, R. C. 1983. *The Logic of Decision*. 2d ed. Chicago: University of Chicago Press. [12]

Johnson, A. B. 1947. *A Treatise on Language*. Berkeley: University of California Press. [1]

Jones, E. E., et al., eds. 1972. *Attribution: Perceiving the Causes of Behavior*. Morristown, N.J.: General Learning Press. [10]

Kelly, G. 1955. *The Psychology of Personal Constructs*. 2 vols. New York: Norton. [10]

Klatzky, R. L. 1975. *Human Memory: Structures and Processes*. San Francisco: Freeman. [11]

Koch, S., ed. 1963. *Psychology: A Study of a Science*. Vol. 6: Investigations of Man as Socius. New York: McGraw-Hill. [3]

Kyburg, H. 1961. *Probability and the Logic of Rational Belief*. Middletown, Conn.: Wesleyan University Press. [9]

LaBerge, D., and Samuels, S. J., eds. 1976. *Basic Processes in Reading Perception and Comprehension*. Hillsdale, N.J.: Lawrence Erlbaum Associates. [10]

Lewin, K. 1935. *A Dynamic Theory of Personality*. New York: McGraw-Hill. [10]

Lewis, C. I. 1946. *An Analysis of Knowledge and Valuation*. LaSalle, Ill.: Open Court. [6]

Lindzey, G., ed. 1958. *Assessment of Human Motives*. New York: Holt, Rinehart and Winston. [10]

Loeb, J. 1918. *Forced Movements, Tropisms, and Animal Conduct*. Philadelphia: Lippincott. [3]

MacKay, D. M. 1969. *Information, Mechanism and Meaning*. Cambridge: The MIT Press. [9]

Maher, B. A., ed. 1972. *Progress in Experimental Personality Research*, vol. 6. New York: Academic Press. [10]

Margenau, H. 1950. *The Nature of Physical Reality*. New York: McGraw-Hill. [3]

May, E. R. 1973. *"Lessons" of the Past*. New York: Oxford University Press. [10]

Miller, G., ed. 1957. *Reglungstechnik: Moderne Theorien und ihre Verwendbarkeit*. Munich: R. Oldenbourg. [3]

Miller, G. A.; Galanter, E.; and Pribram, K. H. 1960. *Plans and the Structure of Behavior*. New York: Holt, Rinehart, and Winston. [3]

Minsky, M. 1975. "A Framework for Representing Knowledge." In Winston 1975. [10]

Mischel, W. 1968. *Personality and Assessment*. New York: Wiley. [10]

Morgenbesser, S., ed. 1966. *Philosophy of Science Today*. New York: Basic Books. [1]

Mowrer, O. H. 1960. *Learning Theory and the Symbolic Processes*. New York: Wiley. [3]

Munitz, M. K., ed. 1971. *Identity and Individuation*. New York: New York University Press. [7]

Neisser, U. 1967. *Cognitive Psychology*. New York: Appleton-Century-Crofts. [9]

Neisser, U. 1976. *Cognition and Reality: Principles and Implications of Cognitive Psychology*. San Francisco: Freeman. [10]

Newcombe, T. M. 1929. *Consistency of Certain Extravert-Introvert Behavior Patterns in 51 Problem Boys*. New York: Columbia University, Teachers College, Bureau of Publications. [10]

Northrop, F. S. C., and Livingston, H. H., eds. 1964. *Cross-cultural Understanding: Epistemology in Anthropology*. New York: Harper & Row. [3]

Piaget, J. 1936. *La naissance de l'intelligence chez l'enfant*. Paris: Delachau et Niestle. [10]

Pollock, J. 1974. *Knowledge and Justification*. Princeton: Princeton University Press. [6, 7, 12]

Popper, K. 1959. *The Logic of Scientific Discovery*. New York: Basic Books. [3]

Popper, K. 1979. *Objective Knowledge*. New York: Oxford University Press. [6]

Posner, M. I. 1973. *Cognition: An Introduction*. Glenview, Ill.: Scott, Foresman. [11]

Putnam, H. 1975a. *Mathematics, Matter and Method*. New York: Cambridge University Press. [7]

Putnam, Hilary. 1975b. *Mind, Language and Reality*. New York: Cambridge University Press. [8]

Reichenbach, H. 1938. *Experience and Prediction*. Chicago: Chicago University Press. [8]

Rock, I. 1975. *An Introduction to Perception*. New York: Macmillan. [9]

Rosch, E., and Lloyd, B. 1978. *Cognition and Categorization*. Hillsdale, N.J.: Lawrence Erlbaum Associates. [10]

Ross, L.; Turiel, E.; Josephson, J.; and Lepper, M. R. 1978. *"Developmental Perspectives on the Fundamental Error Attribution."* Stanford University, unpublished manuscript. [10]

Russell, B. 1912. *Problems of Philosophy*. New York: Oxford University Press. [6]

Russell, B. 1948. *Human Knowledge: Its Scope and Limits*. New York: Simon and Schuster. [3, 6]

Russell, B. 1965. *An Inquiry into Meaning and Truth*. Baltimore: Penguin. [8]

Schank, R. C. 1975. *Conceptual Information Processing*. Amsterdam: North-Holland. [10]

Schank, R. C., and Abelson, R. P. 1977. *Scripts, Plans, Goals and Understanding*. Hillsdale, N.J.: Lawrence Erlbaum Associates. [10, 11]

Seligman, M. E. P. 1975. *Helplessness: On Depression, Development, and Death*. San Francisco: W. H. Freeman. [10]

Shannon, C., and Weaver, W. 1949. *The Mathematical Theory of Communication*. Urbana: University of Illinois Press. [9]

Smart, J. J. C. 1963. *Philosophy and Scientific Realism*. New York: Humanities Press. [2]

Sorabji, R. 1972. *Aristotle on Memory*. Providence: Brown University Press. [11]

Spencer, H. 1896. *Principles of Psychology*. New York: Appleton. [3]

Stroud, Barry. 1977. *Hume*. London: Routledge and Kegan Paul. [4]

Uexküll, J. von. 1934. *Streifzüge durch die Umwelten von Tieren und Menschen*. Berlin: Springer. [3]

Uhr, L. 1973. *Pattern Recognition, Learning, and Thought*. Englewood Cliffs, N.J.: Prentice-Hall. [9]

Weber, M. 1930. *The Protestant Ethic and the Spirit of Capitalism*. Translated by T. Parsons. New York: Scribners. [10]

Wilson, E. G. 1952. *An Introduction to Scientific Research.* New York: McGraw-Hill. [3]

Winston, P. H. 1975. *The Psychology of Computer Vision.* New York: McGraw-Hill. [10]

Wittgenstein, L. 1953. *Philosophical Investigations.* New York: Macmillan. [10]

Woodfield, A. 1981. *Thought and Object.* Oxford: Oxford University Press. [13].

Yovits, M. C., and Cameron, S., eds. 1960. *Self-organizing Systems.* New York: Pergamon. [3]

Articles

Abelson, R. P. 1968. "Psychological Implication." In Abelson et al. 1968. [10]

Abelson, R. P. 1976. "Script Processing in Attitude Formation and Decision Making." In Carroll and Payne 1976. [10]

Abelson, R. P. 1978. "Scripts." Invited Address to the Midwestern Psychological Association, Chicago. [10]

Arkin, R., and Duval, S. 1975. "Focus of Attention and Causal Attributions of Actors and Observers." *Journal of Experimental Social Psychology* 11, 427–438. [10]

Averbach, E., and Coriell, A. S. 1961. "Short-Term Memory in Vision." *Bell System Technical Journal* 40, 309–328. [9]

Bachem, A. 1951. "Brain Astigmatism: A Discussion of Space and Time." *American Scientist* 40, 497–498. [3]

Bartlett, F. C. 1932. *Remembering.* London: Cambridge. [3]

Bem, D. J., and Allen, A. 1974. "On Predicting Some of the People Some of the Time: The Search for Cross-situational Consistencies in Behavior." *Psychological Review* 81, 506–520. [10]

Bem, D. J., and Funder, D. C. 1978. "Predicting More of the People More of the Time: Assessing the Personality of Situations." *Psychological Review* 85, 485–501. [10]

Bergmann, G. 1943. "Outline of an Empiricist Philosophy of Physics." *American Journal of Physics* 11, 248–258, 335–342. [3]

Borgida, E., and Nisbett, R. E. 1977. "The Differential Impact of Abstract vs. Concrete Information on Decisions." *Journal of Applied Social Psychology* 7, 258–271. [11]

Bower, G.; Black, J.; and Turner, T. Forthcoming. "Scripts in Text Comprehension and Memory." *Cognitive Psychology.* [10]

Bransford, J. D., and Franks, J. J. 1971. "Abstraction of Linguistic Ideas." *Cognitive Psychology* 2, 331–350. [11]

Brunswik, E. 1928. "Zur Entwicklung der Albedowahrnehmung." *Z. Psychol.* 109, 40–115. [3]

Brunswik, E. 1937. "Psychology as a Science of Objective Relations." *Philosophy of Science* 4, 227–260. [3]

Brunswik, E. 1952. "The Conceptual Framework of Psychology." *International Encyclopedia of Unified Science* 1. [3]

Campbell, D. T. 1956. "Perception as Substitute Trial and Error." *Psychological Review* 63, 330–342. [3]

Campbell, D. T. 1958. "Common Fate, Similarity, and Other Indices of the Status of Aggregates of Persons as Social Entities." *Behavioral Science* 3, 14–25. [3]

Campbell, D. T. 1960a. "Recommendations for APA Test Standards Regarding Construct, Trait, or Discriminant Validity." *American Psychologist* 15, 546–553. [3]

Campbell, D. T. 1963. "Social Attitudes and Other Acquired Behavioral Dispositions." In Koch 1963, 94–172. [3]

Campbell, D. T. 1964a. "Operational Delineation of 'What Is Learned' via the Transposition Experiment." *Psychological Review* 61, 167–174. [3]

Campbell, D. T. 1964b. "Distinguishing Differences in Perception from Failures of Communication in Cross-cultural Studies." In Northrop and Livingston 1964. [3]

Campbell, D. T., and Fiske, D. W. 1959. "Convergent and Discriminant Validation by the Multitrait-Multimethod Matrix." *Psychological Bulletin* 56, 81–105. [3]

Cantor, N., and Mischel, W. 1977. "Traits as Prototypes: Effects on Recognition Memory." *Journal of Personality and Social Psychology* 35, 38–49. [10]

Cantor, N., and Mischel, W. 1979. "Prototypicality and Personality: Effects on Free Recall and Personality Impressions." *Journal of Research in personality* 13, 187–205. [10]

Carnap, R. 1932. "Protokollsätze." *Erkenntnis* 3, 215–228. [1]

Carnap, R. 1936. "Testability and Meaning." *Philosophy of Science* 3, 419–471; 4, 1–40. [1, 2, 8]

Castaneda, H.-N. 1967. "Indicators and Quasi-Indicators." *American Philosophical Quarterly* 4, 85–100. [7]

Castaneda, H.-N. 1968. "On the Logic of Attributions of Self-Knowledge to Others." *Journal of Philosophy* 64, 439–456. [7]

Cherry, E. C. 1951. "A History of the Theory of Information." *Proceedings of the Institute of Electrical Engineers* 98, 383–393. [9]

Clark, W. A., and Farley, B. G. 1955. "Generalization of Pattern Recognition in a Self-Organizing System." *Proceedings of the Western Joint Computer Conference I. R. E.*, 86–91. [3]

Clarke, T. 1972. "The Legacy of Skepticism." *Journal of Philosophy* 69, 754–769. [4]

Collins, B. E. 1974. "Four Components of the Rotter Internal-External Scale: Belief in a Difficult World, a Just World, a Predictable World, and a Politically Responsive World." *Journal of Personality and Social Psychology* 29, 381–391. [10]

Cooper, L. A., and Shepard, R. N. 1973. "Chronometric Studies of the Rotation of Mental Images." In Chase 1973. [11]

Cornman, J. 1978. "Foundational vs. Non-Foundational Theories of Empirical Knowledge." In Pappas and Swain 1978. [6]

Crandall, V. C.; Katovsky, W.; and Crandall, V. G. 1965. "Children's Beliefs in Their Own Control of Reinforcements in Intellectual-Academic Achievement Situations." *Child Development* 36, 91–109. [10]

Davidson, D. 1966. "Emeroses by Other Names." *Journal of Philosophy* 63, 778–780. [2]

Davidson, D. 1970. "The Anomalism of the Mental." In Foster and Swanson 1970. [5]

Davidson, D. 1973a. "On the Very Idea of a Conceptual Scheme." *Proceedings of the American Philosophical Association* 47, 5–20. [Introduction]

Davidson, D. 1973b. "Radical Interpretation." *Dialectica* 27, 313–328. [8]

Davidson, D. 1979. "The Method of Truth in Metaphysics." In French et al. 1979. [13]

Dennett, D. 1981a. "Making Sense of Ourselves." *Philosophical Topics* 12, 63–81. [13]

Dennett, D. 1981b. "Three Kinds of Intentional Psychology." In Healy 1981. [13]

De Soto, C. B. 1961. "The Predilection for Single Orderings." *Journal of Abnormal and Social Psychology* 62, 16–23. [10]

Dineen, G. P. 1955. "Programming Pattern Recognition." *Proceedings of the Western Joint Computer Conference I. R. E.*, 94–100. [3]

Donnellan, K. 1977. "The Contingent A Priori and Rigid Designators." In French et al. 1977. [7]

Doyle, J. 1979. "A Truth Maintenance System." *Artificial Intelligence* 12, 231–272. [12]

Dretske, F. I. 1977. "The Laws of Nature." *Philosophy of Science* 44, 248–268. [9]

Dummett, M. 1973. "The Justification of Deduction." *Proceedings of the British Academy* 59, 9–10. [8]

Duncker, K. 1945. "On Problem Solving." *Psychological Monographs* 58. [11]

Erwin, E. 1974. "Are the Notions 'A Priori Truth' and 'Necessary Truth' Extensionally Equivalent?" *Canadian Journal of Philosophy* 3, 591–602. [7]

Feigl, H. 1950. "Existential Hypotheses: Realistic versus Phenomenalistic Interpretations." *Philosophy of Science* 17, 35–62. [3]

Feigl, H. 1958. "The 'Mental' and the 'Physical'." In Feigl et al. 1958. [3]

Field, H. 1972. "Tarski's Theory of Truth." *Journal of Philosophy* 69, 347–375. [8]

Firth, R. 1965. "Ultimate Evidence." In Swartz 1965. [6]

Firth, R. 1969. "Coherence, Certainty and Epistemic Priority." In Chisholm and Swartz 1969. [6]

Fischhoff, B. 1975. "Hindsight $\neq$ Foresight: The Effect of Outcome Knowledge on Judgment under Uncertainty." *Journal of Experimental Psychology: Human Perception and Performance* 1, 288–299. [10]

Fischhoff, B., and Beythe, R. 1975. " 'I Knew It Would Happen'—Remembered Probabilities of Once-Future Things." *Organizational Behavior and Human Performance* 3, 552–564. [10]

Fodor, J. 1980. "Methodological Solipsism Considered as a Research Strategy in Cognitive Psychology." *Behavioral and Brain Sciences* 3, 63–110. [9]

Fodor, J. 1981. "Three Cheers for Propositional Attitudes." In Fodor 1981. [13]

Franks, J. J., and Bransford, J. D. 1971. "Abstraction of Visual Patterns." *Journal of Experimental Psychology* 90, 65–74. [11]

Garcia, J.; McGowan, B. K.; and Green, K. F. 1972. "Biological Constraints on Conditioning." In Black and Prokasy 1972. [13]

Gettier, E. 1963. "Is Justified True Belief Knowledge?" *Analysis* 23, 121–123. [9]

Glymour, C. 1975. "Relevant Evidence." *Journal of Philosophy* 72, 403–426. [8]

Hanson, N. R. 1966. "Observation and Interpretation." In Morgenbesser 1966. [1]

Harman, G. 1982. "Metaphysical Realism and Moral Relativism." *Journal of Philosophy* 79, 568–575. [Introduction]

Heider, F. 1959. "On Perception and Event Structure and the Psychological Environment." *Psychological Issues* 1, 1–123. [3]

Hempel, C. G. 1945. "Studies in the Logic of Confirmation." *Mind* 54, 1–49, 97–121. [8]

Higgins, E. T.; Rholes, W. S.; and Jones, C. R. 1977. "Category Accessibility and Impression Formation." *Journal of Personality and Social Psychology* 13, 141–154. [10]

Holst, E. von. 1954. "Relations between the Central Nervous System and the Periphery." *British Journal of Animal Behavior* 2, 89–94. [3]

Hornstein, H. A.; LaKind, E.; Frankel, G.; and Manne, S. 1975. "Effects of Knowledge about Remote Social Events on Prosocial Behavior, Social Conception, and Mood." *Journal of Personality and Social Psychology* 32, 1038–1046. [10]

Jones, E. E., and Nisbett, R. E. 1972. "The Actor and the Observer: Divergent Perceptions of the Causes of Behavior." In Jones et al. 1972. [10]

Jones, R. W. 1957. "Models, Analogues and Homologues." In Miller 1957. [3]

Kelley, H. H. 1972. "Causal Schemata and the Attribution Process." In Jones et al. 1972. [10]

Kelly, G. 1958. "Man's Construction of His Alternatives." In Lindzey 1958. [10]

Kitcher, P. 1975. "Kant and the Foundations of Mathematics." *Philosophical Review* 84, 23–50. [7]

Kitcher, P. 1978. "The Nativist's Dilemma." *Philosophical Quarterly* 28, 1–16. [7]

Kitcher, P. 1979. "Frege's Epistemology." *Philosophical Review* 88, 235–262. [7]

Kripke, S. 1971. "Indentity and Necessity." In Munitz 1971. [7]

Kripke, S. 1972. "Naming and Necessity." In Davidson and Harman 1972. [7]

Kruskal, W. H. 1960. "Some Remarks on Wild Observations." *Technometrics* 2, 1–3. [3]

Kyburg, H. 1965. "Probability, Rationality, and the Rule of Detachment." *Proceedings of the 1964 International Congress for Logic, Methodology, and Philosophy of Science.* Amsterdam: North-Holland. [9]

Lefcourt, H. M. 1972. "Internal vs. External Control of Reinforcement Revisited: Recent Developments." In Maher 1972. [10]

Levine, M. 1971. "Hypothesis Theory and Nonlearning Despite Ideal S-R Reinforcement Contingencies." *Psychological Review* 78, 130–140. [11]

Lewis, C. I. 1973. "The Bases of Empirical Knowledge." In Chisholm and Swartz 1973. [6]

Lewis, D. 1970. "Anselm and Actuality." *Nous* 4, 175–188. [7]

Lewis, D. 1976. "The Paradoxes of Time Travel." *American Philosophical Quarterly* 13, 145–152. [7]

Lorenz, K. 1941. "Kants Lehre vom Apriorishen im Lichte gegenwartigen biologie." *Blätter für Deutshe Philosophie* 15, 94–125. [3]

Lorenz, K. 1959. "Gestaltwahrnehmung als Quelle wissenschaftliche Erkenntnis." *Z. exp. angewandte Psychologie* 6, 118–165. [3]

Luchins, A. S. 1942. "Mechanization in Problem Solving." *Psychological Monographs* 54. [11]

McArthur, L. Z., and Post, D. 1977. "Figural Emphasis and Person Perception." *Journal of Experimental Social Psychology* 13, 520–535. [10]

McArthur, L. Z., and Solomon, L. K. 1978. "Perceptions of an Aggressive Encounter as a Function of the Victim's Salience and the Perceiver's Arousal." *Journal of Personality and Social Psychology* 36, 1278–1290. [10]

McCulloch, W. S., and Pitts, W. 1947. "How We Know Universals: The Perception of Auditory and Visual Forms." *Bulletin of Mathematical Biophysics* 9, 127–147. [3]

Markus, H. 1977. "Self-Schemata and Processing Information about the Self." *Journal of Personality and Social Psychology* 35, 63–78. [10]

Miller, G. A. 1956. "The Magical Number Seven, Plus or Minus Two: Some Limits on Our Capacity for Processing Information." *Psychological Review* 63, 81–97. [9]

Minsky, M. 1975. "A Framework for Representing Knowledge." In Winston 1975. [10]

Mittelstaedt, H. 1962. "Control Systems of Orientation in Insects." *Annual Review of Entomology* 7, 177–198. [3]

Moore, G. E. 1959. "Proof of an External World." In Moore 1959. [4]

Neurath, Otto. 1932–1933. "Protokollsätze." *Erkenntnis* 3, 204–214. [3] [6]

Oppenheimer, R. 1956. "Analogy in Science." *American Psychologist* 11, 127–135. [3]

Pastin, M. 1976a. "Meaning and Perception." *Journal of Philosophy* 73, 570–571 [6]

Pastin, M. 1976b. "Modest Foundationalism and Self-Warrant." In Pappas and Swain 1978. [6]

Perry, J. 1977. "Frege on Demonstratives." *Philosophical Review* 86, 474–97. [7]

Perry, J. 1979. "The Problem of the Essential Indexical." *Nous* 13, 3–21. [7]

Piaget, J. 1957. "The Child and Modern Physics." *Scientific American* 196, 46–51. [3]

Pollock, J. 1979. "A Plethora of Epistemological Theories." In Pappas 1979a. [12]

Price, R.; Green, P. E.; Goblick, T. J.; Kingston. R. H.; Kraft, L. G.; Pettengill, G. H.; Silver, R.; and Smith, W. B. 1959. "Radar Echoes from Venus." *Science* 129, 751–753. [3]

Regan, D. T., and Totten, J. 1975. "Empathy and Attribution: Turning Observers into Actors." *Journal of Personality and Social Psychology* 35, 49–55. [10]

Rosch, E. 1973. "Natural Categories." *Cognitive Psychology* 4, 328–350. [11]

Rosch, E. 1978. "Principles of Categorization." In Rosch and Lloyd 1978. [10]

Rosenblatt, F. 1960. "Perceptual Generalization over Transformation Groups." In Yovits and Cameron 1960. [3]

Ross, L. 1978. "Afterthoughts on the Intuitive Psychologist." In Berkowitz 1978. [10]

Ross, L., and Anderson, C. 1982. "Shortcomings in the Attribution Process: On the Origins and Maintenance of Erroneous Social Assessments." In Tversky et al. 1982. [10] [12]

Ross, L., Lepper, M. R.; Strack. F.; and Steinmetz, J. L. 1977 "Social Explanation and Social Expectation: The Effects of Real and Hypothetical Explanations upon Subjective Likelihood." *Journal of Personality and Social Psychology* 35, 817–829. [10]

Rotter, J. B. 1966. "Generalized Expectancies for Internal versus External Control of Reinforcement." *Psychological Monographs* 80. [10]

Rumelhart, D. E. 1976. "Understanding and Summarizing Brief stories." In Lagerge and Samuels 1976. [10]

Rumelhart, D. E., and Ortony, A. 1976. "The Representation of Knowledge in Memory." In Anderson et al. 1976. [10]

Schlick, M. 1959a. "The Foundation of Knowledge." In Ayer 1959. [7]

Schlick, M. 1959b. "Positivism and Realism." In Ayer 1959. [4]

Selfridge, O. G. 1955. "Pattern Recognition and Modern Computers." *Proceedings of the Western Joint Computer Conference* I. R. E., 91–93. [3]

Shepard, R. N., and Metzler, J. 1971. "Mental Rotation of Three-Dimensional Objects." *Science* 171, 701–703. [11]

Sinsheimer, R. L. 1971. "The Brain of Pooh: An Essay on the Limits of Mind." *American Scientist* 59, 20–28. [13]

Slovic, P., and Fischhoff, B. 1978. In Gould and Walker 1978. [13]

Slovic, P.; Fischoff, B.; and Lichtenstein, S. (1977). "Behavioral Decision Theory." *Annual Review of Psychology* 28, 1–39. [13]

Smedslund, J. 1953. "The Problem of "What is Learned?" *Psychological Review* 60, 157–158. [3]

Sosa, E. 1978. "How Do You Know?" In Pappas and Swain 1978. [6]

Sperling, G. 1960. "The Information Available in Brief Visual Presentations." *Psychological Monographs* 74, 1–29. [9]

Stich, S. P. 1980. "Headaches." *Philosophical Books* 21, 65–73. [13]

Stich, S. P. 1981a. "Dennett on Intentional Systems." *Philosophical Topics* 12, 39–62. [13]

Stich, S. P. 1981b. "On the Ascription of Content." In Woodfield 1981. [13]

Storms, M. D. 1973. "Videotape and the Attribution Process: Reversing Actors' and Observers' Point of View." *Journal of Personality and Social Psychology* 27, 165–175. [10]

Stroud, B. Forthcoming. "Kant and Scepticism." In Burnyeat forthcoming. [4]

Swinburn, R. G. 1975. "Analyticity, Necessity and Apriority." *Mind* 84, 225–243. [7]

Taylor, S. E. and Crocker, J. C. 1980. "Schematic Bases of Social Information Processing." In Higgins et al. 1980. [10]

Taylor, S. E., and Fiske, S. T. 1975. "Point of View and Perceptions of Causality." *Journal of Personality and Social Psychology* 32, 439–445. [10]

Taylor, S. E., and Fiske, S. T. 1978. "Salience, Attention and Attribution: Top of the Head Phenomena." In Berkowitz 1978. [10]

Tolman, E. C. 1948. "Cognitive Maps in Rats and Men." *Psychological Review 55, 189–208. [3]*

Tolman, E. C., and Brunswik, E. 1935. "The Organism and the Causal Texture of the Environment." *Psychological Review* 42, 43–77. [3]

Tomkins, A. 1979. "Script Theory: Differential Magnification of Affects." In Howes and Dienstbier 1979. [10]

Tversky, Amos. 1977. "Features of Similarity." *Psychological Review* 84, 327–352. [10]

Uhr, L. 1963. "Pattern Recognition: Computers as Models of Form Perception." *Psychological Bulletin* 60, 40–73. [3]

Unger, S. H. 1959. "Pattern Detection and Recognition," *Proc. I.R.E.*, 1737–1752. [3]

van Fraassen, B. 1977. "The Only Necessity Is Verbal Necessity." *Journal of Philosophy* 74, 71–85. [7]

Watanabe, S. 1965. "Une explication mathematique du classement d'objets." In Dockx and Bernays 1965. [2]

Yilmaz. H. 1962. "On Color Vision and a New Approach to General Perception." In Bernard and Kare 1962.

Yilmaz, H. 1967. "Perceptual Invariance and the Psychophysical Law." *Perception and Psychophysics* 2, 533–538. [1]

Index

Analyticity, 68, 130, 142
Anchoring effect, 225
Animals, cognition in, 36, 37, 39, 43, 52, 55, 177
A priori, 10–12, 129–143, 155
Arguments-on-paper thesis, 117
Astronomy, 55, 61–63, 68
Attention, 222
Attribution of mental states to others, 193, 201–204
 dispositional factors in, 193, 201, 203
 fundamental attribution error, 202
 situational factors in, 193, 201, 203, 204
Availability heuristic. See Heuristics

Belief dependence, 119, 121, 240
Belief perseverance, 236–239, 241, 243, 244, 253
Bentham, Jeremy, 17, 20
Binocular vision, 57, 58
Bizarre possibilities, 73, 106–107, 141, 180
Borgida, Eugene, 224
Brunswik, Egon, 49, 51, 52, 54, 56, 70, 180

Campbell, Donald T., 6, 28
Carnap, Rudolf, 18, 20, 23, 35, 41, 76, 83
Categorization, 195, 204, 210. See also Natural kinds; Similarity
Chisholm, Roderick, 95, 104, 220
Circular justification, 19, 24, 39, 74, 75, 155–157, 162, 164, 233
Clutter avoidance, 246–247
Cognition, goals of, 227–228
Cognitive capacities, modification of, 39,
40, 43, 213–214, 218
Cohen, L. Jonathan, 261–265
Coherence theory of justification, 2, 12, 104, 115, 117, 118, 122, 231–247
Combinatorial explosion, 244
Communication, mathematical theory of, 170–173
Competence and performance, 262–265
Computing time, 210
Confirmation, 69, 147–165
Conservatism, 234, 235, 237
Constancy, 54, 56
Contextual definition, 17, 20
Current time-slice theories of justification, 104

Davidson, Donald, 5
Debriefing, 238–239, 253
Deduction, justification of, 156–157
Dennett, Daniel, 5, 253–257
Descartes, René, 39, 71, 73, 91, 138, 222, 228
Dewey, John, 104, 228
Digitalization, 183
Dispositions, 41, 43, 45–46
Dretske, Fred, 12
Duhem, Pierre, 22
Dummett, Michael, 157

Entrenchment, 31, 40
Epistemological priority, 24–25, 72, 122–124
Epistemology and psychology, relation between, 1–12, 19, 21, 24, 28, 39, 71, 77, 83, 86, 115, 154–155, 160–161, 217–228
Evidence gathering, 219, 227
Executability, 221–222

Feigl, Herbert, 65, 70
Foundationalism, 3, 4, 12, 15, 104, 115,
    117, 118, 122–124, 231–247
Frege, Gottlob, 17, 68
Friedman, Michael, 12
Fundamental attribution error. *See*
    Attribution of mental states to others

Gambler's fallacy, 196
Garcia, John, 257–258
Genetic theories of justification. *See*
    Historical theories of justification
Gestalt psychology, 25, 50, 56
Gibson, J. J., 120
Gödel, Kurt, 16
Goldman, Alvin I., 8, 9, 11, 12, 115, 124,
    260
Goodman, Nelson, 31, 35, 39, 40, 163,
    164
Gregory, R. L., 120
Grue, 31, 163

Habit, 36, 37, 40, 52, 218, 239–241, 243,
    244
Hanson, Norwood Russell, 27, 65, 66,
    69, 70
Harman, Gilbert, 5–6, 12, 142
Hegel, G. W. F., 104
Hempel, Carl Gustav, 31, 32, 39, 65, 70,
    226
Heuristics, 189–215, 255
  availability, 189–195, 207, 208, 214,
    225
  representativeness, 189, 195–200, 201,
    207, 214, 225, 259
Hindsight, 194
Historical theories of justification, 104–
    105, 131
Holism, 21–23
Hume, David, 17, 18, 19, 42, 49, 68, 74,
    86, 228

Incorrigibility, 66, 96–97, 122, 234
Induction, 11, 12, 29, 31, 38, 40, 66,
    154–156, 165
Informational content, 173–176
Information and knowledge, 169, 176–
    181
Innate capacities, 36, 37, 39, 40, 43, 46,
    130, 136, 263
Intentionality, 184–186, 254
Intersubjective agreement, 26, 27

Jeffrey, Richard C., 245
Johnson, Alexander Bryan, 16–18
Johnson-Laird, Philip N., 250–252
Justification, keeping track of, 243–244,
    246–247
Justified belief, 91–111, 115–127, 132,
    133, 155, 156, 227

Kahneman, Daniel, 189, 190, 193, 195,
    196, 197, 208, 224, 225, 244, 252
Kant, Immanuel, 76, 115, 129, 130, 132,
    133, 137
Klein, Felix, 46
Knowledge, causal theory of, 79, 116
Knowledge structures, 200–213
Kuhn, Thomas, 27, 65, 66, 69, 70

Language learning, 22, 23, 28, 32, 35,
    37, 38, 40, 82, 185
Lawlikeness, 32
Lens model, 51, 56
Lorenz, Konrad, 56, 63
Lottery paradox, 179

Margenau, Henry, 65, 70
Mathematical knowledge, 68, 97–98,
    132, 133, 134, 142
Memory, 105, 108, 219, 223, 246
Moore, George Edward, 75, 76, 77, 83

Natural kinds, 31–35, 39–43
Natural selection, 4, 5, 28, 29, 38, 39,
    40, 43, 49, 53, 54, 256–260
  and false beliefs, 258–260
Neurath, Otto, 24, 39, 68
Nisbett, Richard, 12, 223, 224, 242, 244,
    259, 265
Nozick, Robert, 104

Observational evidence, 22, 25–28
Operationalism, 50, 64, 65, 67, 69
Ostension, 35, 37, 38

Pattern matching, 49, 56, 58–64, 66, 67,
    69
Pavlov, Ivan, 50
Peirce, Charles Sanders, 21, 22, 148, 149,
    151, 155, 158, 235
Personae, 204, 206–207, 211
Phi phenomenon, 58
Polányi, Michael, 27
Popper, Karl, 66, 69, 70, 104, 228

Prisoner's dilemma, 208
Privileged access, 104
Probabilistic reasoning, 10–11, 196–198, 224, 244–246, 252
Problem solving, 227–228
Processes of belief acquisition, 8, 9, 99–111, 121, 131, 133, 134, 135, 141, 155, 177, 178
  availability of, 109–110, 133
  individuation of, 101–103, 134, 135
Projectibility, 31, 32, 40, 164
Protokollsätze, 25
Psychologism, 8–9, 12
  ballpark, 9–12
Psychology and epistemology, relation between. *See* Epistemology and psychology, relation between
Pure intuition, 132, 133
Putnam, Hilary, 161

Quality space, 36–40, 43
Quine, Willard Van Orman, 3, 4, 5, 65, 66, 68, 70, 71–87, 104, 115, 156, 228, 255, 256

Rationality, 249–266
Rational reconstruction, 19, 20, 24, 25
Reduction forms, 20
Reference, theories of, 158–159
  causal, 147, 161, 162, 163, 165
  charity-based, 162, 164, 165
  disquotational, 161, 162
Reflective equilibrium, 261, 264–265
Regress argument, 119
Reichenbach, Hans, 149, 150, 151, 152, 155
Relevant alternatives, 125–127, 174, 180
Reliability, 8, 11, 12, 100, 103, 105–109, 124–127, 153–156, 158, 160, 165, 180, 256, 258, 260
Replacement thesis, 3–8
Representativeness heuristic. *See* Heuristics
Resemblance, 32–38, 40, 43–45, 196–198, 259
Ross, Lee, 12, 202, 238, 242, 244, 252, 259
Russell, Bertrand, 17, 18, 56, 57, 156

Schemas, 59, 200, 204, 205, 223
Schlick, Moritz, 76, 83
Scripts, 200, 204–206

Selection task, 250–252
Selective retention, 61
Self-knowledge, 95, 138–139
Self-presenting states, 95–96
Sense data, 18, 50, 66, 72
Sense experience, 16–19, 21, 130, 137. *See also* Sense data
Similarity. *See* Resemblance
Skepticism, 4, 9–12, 73, 75, 84–86, 141
S-R laws, 50, 51
Stich, Stephen P., 7
Stroud, Barry, 5

Template, 59
Translation, 19–23
  indeterminacy of, 22, 23, 28
Trial and error, 40, 59, 60, 61, 63
Truth, theories of, 157–161
  purely disquotational, 160
  Tarskian, 158, 160–161
Tversky, Amos, 189, 190, 193, 195, 196, 197, 199, 208, 224, 225, 244, 252

Undermining, positive and negative, 231–248

Venus, 62–63, 68
Verificationism, 21, 22, 28, 76
Vividness, 39, 224

Wason, Peter C., 250–252
Watson, John, 50
Wilson, Timothy E., 259
Wittgenstein, Ludwig, 23

Xerox principle, 175